Dante Alighieri, Arthur John Butler

The Hell of Dante Alighieri

Dante Alighieri, Arthur John Butler

The Hell of Dante Alighieri

ISBN/EAN: 9783743306660

Manufactured in Europe, USA, Canada, Australia, Japa

Cover: Foto ©ninafisch / pixelio.de

Manufactured and distributed by brebook publishing software (www.brebook.com)

Dante Alighieri, Arthur John Butler

The Hell of Dante Alighieri

PREFACE

THE editor who has begun elsewhere than at the beginning of the work which he undertakes to edit, however good his motives for taking that course may at the time have appeared, has reason to regret it when in the progress of events he is carried back to the beginning. Unless he wishes to have his book incomplete, the moment must ultimately come when he has to do for the whole work what he has done for its parts, viz. write a preface. Then he finds that he has already used up on the parts a great deal of material which would have been equally useful as an introduction to the whole, and perhaps more in place; while in some cases it is pretty sure to happen that he has appended to the later portions remarks which are out of date when what should be the earlier portion appears. On the other hand, it is to be said that the preface to the complete work is likely to involve the most labour; and of this he may, by a judicious postponement, very possibly succeed in getting a good deal taken off his hands by other people.

On the whole, the present editor may congratulate himself (and his readers) that by dealing last with the first portion of Dante's great poem he has gained more under the latter head than he has lost under the former. Since his *Purgatory* was published full eleven years have passed: and in the course of those years an immense quantity of most valuable work has been done. Indeed, it is hardly too much to say that the study of Dante has been placed on quite a different footing. Nearly all the usually-accepted statements with regard to Dante's own history, passed on without criticism from one commentator to another, have been sifted and tested, with the result that much which has long passed muster as solid fact has had to fall back into the class of amiable conjecture. Readings and interpretations, unquestioned perhaps for four hundred years, have been shown to be devoid of authority. In some cases, it may be, the process has been carried a little too far. Scepticism is all very well; but it must confine itself to its proper domain, and not extend its borders till it includes negative dogmatism. Nevertheless, the study of such works as Professor Bartoli's volume on Dante in his *History of Italian Literature*, or Dr. Scartazzini's *Prolegomeni*, can but have a bracing effect on the mind of the student.

When we pass to matters more immediately concerning the interpretation of the poem, we are still more struck with the activity of the last decade. It would be hard to say how many translations have appeared, either of the whole or of portions. Those by the late Dean of Wells and Mr. F. K. H. Haselfoot will be familiar to all who care to keep abreast of the subject. Dr. Plumptre belonged perhaps rather to the school which is just now out of favour: that which was inclined to allow its 'affection to bind its understanding' and believe with regard to Dante all that seemed pleasant to believe so long as it was not demonstrably untrue. But he was an indefatigable student, with a wide knowledge of other literature, which has not always been possessed by interpreters of Dante.

Dr. Moore's *Textual Criticism*, unfortunately as yet incomplete for the second and third Cantiche, is a piece of work of which it is hard to overrate the importance. Those who differ from Dr. Moore on a matter of reading or interpretation had better (as Hermann said of Lachmann) think twice whether he and not they be in fault; and even if they finally decide to agree with themselves and not with him, they will pretty certainly have learnt more from him than they ever knew before. Nor must his two smaller works, 'chips from the workshop,' *The Time References of the Divina Commedia* and *Dante and his Biographers*, be overlooked by any one who wishes his ideas on those points cleared.

Mention too must be made of some books which show that the importance of Dante's other works, not only to the proper understanding of the *Commedia*, but as specimens of medieval thought in literature, politics, morals, science, is beginning to be recognised. Ten years ago the *de Monarchia* and the *Vita Nuova* alone of his prose writings had been rendered into English. Now we have two translations (neither, it must be said, ideal, but showing at least a proper spirit) of the *Convito*, and one, very creditable, of the *de Vulgari Eloquentia*.

The truth is that Dante fills the stream of human history from side to side. There have been greater poets, one or two; there have been greater thinkers, greater men of affairs; but of no other poet can it be said that he was the greatest political thinker of his age; of no other philosopher or theologian that he was its greatest poet. Nor have poets as a rule taken a very high place in science or philosophers in scholarship; yet in these subjects Dante was among the first men of his age. His acquaintance with all accessible literature and his grasp of all attainable scientific knowledge were equally complete. Herein lie at once the attraction which he exercises over his would-be students and the despair to which he reduces them. You never know into what branch of investigation he may lead you; but you are sure that in a very large proportion of cases you will be (if the word may be pardoned) 'pounded' before you reach the end of it. In fact, no really adequate edition of Dante will ever be put forth until a number of students will bind themselves to read (among them) everything that Dante can have read, and to have made themselves as familiar as he with the events, small and great, of his age. All commentators save the earliest—all, at any rate, who wrote between 1400 and 1800—they may safely eschew. From the days of Benvenuto Rambaldi of Imola[1] till those of Carl Witte of Halle,[2] it is hard to point to any editor or commentator (with perhaps the exception of our own Cary) who has thrown any really fresh light on the difficulties of the *Commedia*. Landino, undoubtedly a man of much learning, and in his way an admirer of Dante, was not really capable of understanding him: as a Humanist and a Platonist his literary and intellectual sympathies were not in the direction of thirteenth-century Aristotelianism.[3] Nor could it be expected that a Medicean and Borgian age would be capable of estimating Dante, though he would have estimated it:

---

[1] Among the helps to students which the last ten years have brought forth, and of which some have been enumerated, none can compare with the edition of Benvenuto's complete commentary, due to Mr. Vernon and Sir James Lacaita. The most genial, intelligent, and shrewd of all the fourteenth-century commentators on Dante is now accessible to every one; and for those who do not feel the 'call' to read him, as he well deserves, from end to end, there are Mr. Vernon's 'Readings,' of which the *Purgatory* (Macmillan 1889) is published, while the *Hell*, it is hoped, will shortly appear. These give the more valuable parts of Benvenuto.

[2] Dr. Witte died March 1883.

[3] See Cary's remarks in the *Life of Dante* prefixed to his translation, 3rd ed. p. xlviii.

and one almost regrets that he did not come into the world
late enough to do so. In that case, however, the sentence
'igne comburatur sic quod moriatur' would probably not
have remained a mere caution. The worthy Cruscan
Academicians did their best. They gave the *Commedia* the
rank of a 'Testo di lingua,' and endeavoured, with moderate
success, to establish an accurate text. Then came the age
which admired Marino; it could hardly be expected to read
Dante. Three editions (or possibly four), and those mere
texts, and bad texts, are all that Italy produced during the 120
years ending with 1716. Occasionally some eccentric person
betrays a knowledge of the poem. Tommaso Campanella
was no doubt full of it; but he, again, belonged to a school
of philosophy as wide as the poles from that which inspired
Dante. Our own Milton, a kindred genius so far as was
possible when the Renaissance and the Reformation lay
between the two, had, it is pretty clear, saturated himself
with Dante. Beside the passages, and they are not many,
which he avowedly quotes, we find at every turn touches and
phrases in which we can hardly fail to recognise the Florentine's influence. But these are exceptions. For a hundred
and fifty years Dante practically passed out of European
literature; and even when the praiseworthy, if inadequate,
efforts of such men as Volpi, Venturi, and Lombardi had
done something to recall the attention of Italians to their
greatest man, it was still many years before his fame spread
much further. Then, however, a great stride was made.
Cary's translation, with notes, of which portions were published in 1805 and the following year, and the whole in
1814, attracted the attention of Coleridge and doubtless of
others, and brought Dante for the first time within the field
of view of educated English people. It has been frequently
reprinted, and remains, in text and commentary, unques-

tionably the best book to which the study of Dante in England has ever given birth. It is astonishing how constantly it occurs that when one has hunted up, or fortuitously come across, some passage to illustrate Dante rather out of the ordinary run of literature, one finds that Cary has got it already. He had read the Schoolmen, Brunetto, Villani, and the like; and came to the task with a better equipment than any commentator for many centuries. Then came various cultivated Italians, Foscolo and others, driven from their own country for reasons not unlike those for which Dante had to leave Florence and 'ogni cosa diletta più caramente,' who wrote and talked about him; and the average Englishman learned at least that Dante was a 'world poet,' and not merely a foreign celebrity. We need not despair of seeing him one day take his place beside (but not instead of) Homer and Virgil in the curriculum of our schools and universities.

It will perhaps not be out of place here to say a word with regard to the importance of the *Divine Comedy* as a subject of study at all, over and above its purely æsthetic merits. It is not too much to say that there is no one work of human genius which can equal it as an instrument of education, intellectual and moral. As to the former, it is only needful to realise that it is the summary of all the thought and speculation, the record of all the action of the thirteenth century: the age which of all whose memory remains to us produced the greatest number of great men. This was the age of Frederick II., Lewis IX., Simon of Montfort, Thomas Aquinas, Roger Bacon; the age which saw the revival of painting in Cimabue and Giotto, of sculpture in Nicholas; while Amiens and Westminster, the Old Palace of Florence and the Holy Field of Pisa are living evidence of what it could do in the noblest of all the arts.

It was to such an age as this that Dante's poem first gave a voice; and he who would appreciate the poem, must first have made himself in some degree familiar with the age.

In estimating the moral value of the *Divine Comedy*, I cannot do better than quote the eloquent words of the late Dean of St. Paul's, whose admirable essay ought to be in the hands of every reader of Dante:—"Those who know it best will best know how hard it is to be the interpreter of such a mind, but they will sympathise with the wish to call attention to it. They know and would wish others to know, not by hearsay, but by experience, the power of that wonderful poem. They know its austere yet subduing beauty; they know what force there is in its free and earnest yet solemn verse, to strengthen, to tranquillise, to console. It is a small thing that it has the secret of Nature and Man; that a few keen words have opened their eyes to new sights in earth and sea and sky; have taught them new mysteries of sound; have made them recognise, in distinct image or thought, fugitive feelings, or their unheeded expression by look or gesture or motion; that it has enriched the public and collective memory of society with new instances, never to be lost, of human feelings and fortune; has charmed ear and mind by the music of its stately march, and the variety and completeness of its plan. But, besides this, they know how often its seriousness has put to shame their trifling, its magnanimity their fainthearted ness, its living energy their indolence, its stern and sad grandeur rebuked low thoughts, its thrilling tenderness overcome sullenness and assuaged distress, its strong faith quelled despair and soothed perplexity, its vast grasp imparted harmony to the view of clashing truths."

To go back for a moment to our starting-point, it may be observed that the recent increase in the aids to the study of Dante has coincided with a gratifying development in the study itself. We hear on all hands of lectures and classes, where it is to be hoped that solid work is done. There is therefore the less necessity to give here advice which students will get elsewhere from more competent advisers. I may perhaps be allowed to point out that before entering on the study of the first Cantica, the sixth book of Virgil's *Aeneid* should be carefully read, in the original if possible; but good 'cribs' are available in prose and verse. The *Tesoretto* of Brunetto Latini, at any rate its opening, is also worth looking at. Aquinas is of less importance here than he becomes later; but the *Ethics* of Aristotle were constantly in Dante's mind as he wrote. Dr. Carlyle's of course remains the standard prose translation; nor should I have thought it necessary to produce another had not the law of copyright prevented me from using his. His few slips could easily have been corrected without interfering with his admirable language. Mr. Eliot Norton's recent version I have not seen; his reputation as a scholar, however, is a sufficient guarantee of its quality.

Besides the friends mentioned in my other prefaces, I may be allowed here to thank the Lu. Professor of Levtura for looking over and correcting my statement of the doctrine of colour in the note to Canto ... and in justice to t... ... not always appreciated according to its merits. Messrs. ... reader, for saving me from a great many small blunders and one or two large.

A few words of explanation as to abbreviations, etc., will suffice. The numerals 1, 2, 3, 4, 5 denote respectively the editions of Foligno, Jesi, Mantua, Naples, Florence, of Torri, and Naples 1477. The readings of the last are

indicate a MS. belonging to the University of Cambridge, Dr. Moore's 'Q.' This I collated myself for *Purgatory* and *Paradise*: in the present volume I have taken its readings on Dr. Moore's authority. Diez's *Grammar of the Romance Languages* is quoted by volume and page from the French translation of MM. Brachet, Morel-Fatio, and Gaston Paris. (Paris: Franck. 1874-76.) References to Villani are according to the chapters as they are numbered in the edition in two volumes published at Milan, without date, edited by Dr. A. Racheli. Besides these, there are, I believe, no references or abbreviations which will not explain themselves.

November 1891.

CONTENTS

CANTO I
CANTO II
CANTO III
CANTO IV
CANTO V
CANTO VI
CANTO VII
CANTO VIII
CANTO IX
CANTO X
CANTO XI
CANTO XII
CANTO XIII
CANTO XIV
CANTO XV
CANTO XVI
CANTO XVII
CANTO XVIII
CANTO XIX
CANTO XX
CANTO XXI

	PAGE
CANTO XXII .	258
CANTO XXIII	270
CANTO XXIV	282
CANTO XXV .	295
CANTO XXVI	308
CANTO XXVII	320
CANTO XXVIII .	333
CANTO XXIX	346
CANTO XXX .	358
CANTO XXXI	370
CANTO XXXII	382
CANTO XXXIII	395
CANTO XXXIV	409
GLOSSARY	421

PRELIMINARY NOTE

In the year 1300 after Christ the city of Florence was at the height of her power and fortune.[1] At that time one of her citizens, Dante Alighieri, being then thirty-five years of age, was shown as in a vision the state of those who had left this world, being led through the three regions of Hell, Purgatory, and Paradise.

Hell is represented as a conical hollow reaching to the centre of the earth, its axis being exactly beneath Jerusalem. It is divided into three main parts: that outside the river of Acheron, where are the souls of those who through weakness did neither good nor evil; that between Acheron and the walls of the City of Dis, where those are punished who have sinned by all kinds of fleshly lust: and lastly the City of Dis itself, within which are those who have done despite to God or their neighbours, these being divided into sinners by violence and sinners by fraud. There is also, just within Acheron, a *limbus* or border, where those are who have died without knowledge of God, and these are not punished, but abide without hope. At the lowest point of Hell, and at the centre of the earth, is Lucifer. The journey begins on the evening of Maundy Thursday, and ends (in the other hemisphere) on Easter morning.

[1] See Villani viii. 39.

ERRATA

Canto IV. line 42, *for* 'posci' *read* 'poscia.'
Canto V. line 24, *for* 'dontate' *read* 'dotate.'
Canto VI. line 23, *for* 'ci' *read* 'd'.'
Canto VII. line 100, *for* 'quando' *read* 'quanto.'
Canto VIII. line 28, *for* 'dietro' *read* 'dentro.'
Canto XXII. line 47, *for* 'fuo' *read* 'furo.'
Page 335, line 2. *for* 'proved' *read* 'moved.'

HELL

CANTO I

ARGUMENT

The author finds himself in a wood. On issuing from it he is met by three beasts and is rescued from them by one who declares himself to be Virgil, and prophesies of the future of Italy; afterwards undertaking to guide the author through the world of spirits.

HALFWAY upon the road of our life,[1] I came to myself amid a dark wood where the straight path was confused. And as it is a hard thing to tell of what sort was this wood, savage

NEL mezzo del cammin di nostra vita
  Mi ritrovai[2] per una selva oscura,
  Che[3] la diritta via era smarrita.
E quanto a dir qual era è cosa dura [4]
  Questa selva selvaggia ed aspra e forte

^a *Ha* G5.: *Ah* 3; *O* 5; *Eh* W.

[1] I.e. at the age of thirty-five (cf. Conv. iv. 23). This fixes the date of the action of the poem to 1300. In the same year, a few months later, Dante served the office of Prior, and as such formed for two months a part of the governing body of Florence; being at that time a member of the Guelf party.

[2] **ritrovai.** The prefix appears to be emphatic. See l. 10. **selva**: worldly cares, as the thorns in the parable of the Sower.

[3] **Che**, as frequently in Dante, is a kind of general relative. See Diez iii. 311, and note to Purg. i. 3.

[4] *see* It will be seen that I have ventured to adopt a new rendering

and rough and strong, which in the thought renews my fear, even so is it bitter; so that death is not much more; but to treat of the good which I there found, I will tell of the other things which there I marked.

I cannot well relate how I there entered; so full was I of drowsiness at that moment when I left the way of truth.

>   Che nel pensier rinnuova la paura,
> Tanto è amara, che poco è più morte :
>   Ma per trattar del ben ch' i' vi trovai,
>   Dirò dell' altre cose, ch' io v' ho scorte.
>   I' non so ben ridir com' io v' entrai ;   10
>   Tant' era pien di sonno in su quel punto,
>   Che la verace via abbandonai.

of this passage. Usually ll. 4-6 are taken as interjectional, 'ornamento rethorico el quale chiamano exclamatione,' as Landino has it; and **tanto** in l. 7 as the direct antecedent to **che**. This involves the alteration of *e* or *et*, which is the reading of nearly all the MSS. and early edd., into *ch*, *ah*, or *ahi*. (Gg. has *Ha*, which, if I am not much mistaken, has been altered from an earlier *Ma*—ſſℳ into ħ. I know of no other instance of this reading.) Benv. boldly calls *e* corrupt, and says, 'nullo modo stare potest, quia . . . illud E non haberet quid copularet.' But this difficulty is obviated by shifting the stop from the end of l. 6 to that of l. 7; and with it all perplexity as to the agreement of **amara**, which Benv., followed by others, refers to **selva**. Some, in order to sustain this construction, have even gone so far as to change *è* into *era*. By avoiding the interjection and treating **quanto tanto** as relative and antecedent, it seems to me that the passage gains in dignity, and the allusion to Jer. ii. 19, 'vide quia malum et amarum est reliquisse te Dominum Deum tuum,' is better brought out. **che**—**più** will then refer to both **dura** and **amara**. It may be added that while the words *ahi quanto* occur five times elsewhere in the poem, there is in no other case a suggestion of a v. l. *et*.

5, 9, 10 Note the threefold repetition of **io vi**.

11 Scart. refers to Rom. xiii. 11. Cf. also Eph. v. 14.

12 **la verace via**. Not merely 'the right way.' Cf. Par. vii. 30.

But after I was come to the foot of a hill at the place where that vale came to an end which had pierced my heart with fear, I looked on high, and beheld its shoulders clad already with the rays of the planet which leads any man straight through every pathway. Then was my fear a little quieted, which had endured in the pool of my heart for the night which I passed with so great pitifulness. And as the man who with panting breath having issued forth from the deep

> Ma poi che fui al piè d' un colle giunto,
>   Là dove terminava quella valle,
>   Che m' avea di paura il cor compunto,
> Guardai in alto, e vidi le sue spalle
>   Vestite già dei raggi del pianeta,
>   Che mena dritto altrui per ogni calle.
> Allor fu la paura un poco queta,
>   Che nel lago del cor m' era durata   20
>   La notte, ch' i' passai con tanta pieta.
> E come quei, che con lena affannata
>   Uscito fuor del pelago alla riva,

13, 14 It should be unnecessary to remind English readers of the hill Difficulty and the valley of Humiliation. We can scarcely suppose that Bunyan had ever heard of Dante; but several striking coincidences may be found between the opening of the Commedia and the earlier parts of the Pilgrim's Progress. Here the hill would seem more immediately to denote, as Benvenuto says, 'virtutem, quae alta ducit hominem ad caelum'; with special reference to Ps. xxxv. 7 (Vulg.): Justitia tua sicut montes Dei; and cxx. 1: Levavi oculos meos in montes, unde venit auxilium mihi. Bocc. understands rather the teaching of the Apostles (cf. Par. xxv. 38), but this seems to narrow the meaning too much at this stage of the allegory.

17 **pianeta**: the sun. In connexion with the next line, it may be noted that throughout his journey Dante's course follows that of the sun. Through Hell, which is in the northern hemisphere, he goes with, through Purgatory, in the southern, against, the 'hands of the watch'; while through Paradise he proceeds over the earth from east to west.

upon the shore turns him round to the perilous water and gazes, so my mind, which still was fleeing, turned back to look at the pass which never yet let a person go alive.

After that my weary body being a little rested I took again my way over the desert slope, so that the halted foot

> Si volge all' acqua perigliosa, e guata;
> Così l' animo mio, che ancor fuggiva,
> Si volse indietro a rimirar lo passo,
> Che non lasciò giammai persona viva.
> Poiche, posato un poco il corpo lasso,[b]
> Ripresi via per la piaggia diserta,
> Sì che il piè fermo sempre era il più basso, 30

[b] *ebbi riposato un p. Gg.* (alt.); *ei possato Cass.*: *Como io posato* 2: *ebbi riposato il c.* 3; *ei posato Ald. W.*; *E riposato un p.* 14.

[27] The words may also mean 'which no living person ever yet left'; but the rendering I have adopted seems to give better the force of **lasciò**, *laxavit*. In either case the meaning is obscure. Even if we take it as referring to the road to Hell, Dante would seem to forget St. Paul and Aeneas whom he afterwards specifies as having passed that way. On the whole, it seems best to understand it of the soul 'dead in trespasses and sins.' He would say that no man who had been so far entangled in the deceits of the world as he had ever been brought back to true life. Cf. Purg. xxx. 136, Par. xx. 106. But the symbolism of this Canto alone would need a volume to investigate it thoroughly.

[28] As to the various readings, see Moore, Text. Crit. p. 257. I do not follow him in reading *ci* = *ebbi*, as that form, though no doubt used by Dante's contemporaries, seems to have been avoided by him; and it is not required here for the construction. The use of *e* as a kind of demonstrative adverb of time (almost = Germ. *ce*) is quite recognised (see Diez iii. 317) and not unknown in Dante. Cf. xxv. 34, 50.

[30] There is some difference of opinion as to the meaning of this line. Benvenuto's explanation, 'quando homo ascendit montem, pes inferior est ille super quo funditur et firmatur totum corpus salientis,' has been accepted by most commentators; but more recent critics, observing, no doubt quite correctly, that in strict accuracy the moving foot during an ascent is as often below as above the stationary one, have thought it

was ever the lower, behold, almost at the beginning of the steep, an ounce, light and very nimble, which was covered with spotted hair. And it would not depart from before my face; nay, it so blocked my road that I had more than once

> Ed ecco, quasi al cominciar dell' erta,
> Una lonza leggiera e presta molto,
> Che di pel maculato era coperta.
> E non mi si partia dinanzi al volto;
> Anzi impediva tanto il mio cammino,
> Ch' io fui per ritornar più volte volto.

necessary to seek a new interpretation. Thus Bianchi points out that the required conditions are strictly fulfilled only in walking on level ground, and understands Dante to mean that he still had some of the plain to cross. (**Piaggia**, it may be noted, does not absolutely exclude this rendering, though it usually implies a slope.) But there seems no need for this rather pedantic accuracy, and the older interpretation agrees much better with one's ordinary impression. The motion of the moving foot is not perceived till it has passed the other, and become the higher.

These three allegorical beasts, as Witte and Scartazzini point out, are evidently suggested by Jer. v. 6: Idcirco percussit eos leo de silva, lupus ad vesperam vastavit eos, pardus vigilans super civitates eorum. Symbolically they have been from the earliest times understood as denoting: the panther, lust: the lion, pride; the wolf, avarice —the sins affecting youth, maturity, and old age. We know by his own admissions (see notes to Purg. xiii. 136, and xxvii. 49) that Dante was conscious of having yielded to the two former; and we may suppose that he deemed it possible that in time the third also might beset him. Later interpreters have found also a political meaning. According to this, the spotted pard ('pantera è una bestia tacciata di piccole tacche bianche e nere,' says the old Italian version of Brunetto's Trésor) indicates Florence with her 'Black' and 'White' parties, the object of his early love, and afterwards his enemy; the lion is the power of France (Par. vi. 108); and the wolf is the Guelf party (see note to Purg. xx. 10). That some meaning of this kind is hidden in the allegory can hardly be doubted; see xvi. 106. It should be added that some commentators, e.g. Bianchi, prefer to take the **lonza** as symbolising envy; in which case the three vices indicated are those which Brunetto in Canto xv. 68 specially attributes to Florence.

Observe the *bisticcio* or jingle of **volte volto**.

turned to go back. The time was at the first of the morn; and the Sun was mounting aloft with those stars which were with him when the Love divine first set in motion those fair things; so that to hope well of that beast with the gay hide, the hour of the clock and the sweet season were an occasion to me; but not so much that the sight of a lion which appeared to me did not give me fear. This seemed to come against me with its head high and with a raging hunger, so that it seemed as the air were in fear of it; and a she-wolf, that with all ravenings looked fraught

> Tempo era dal principio del mattino;
>   E il sol montava su con quelle stelle
>   Ch' eran con lui, quando l' amor divino
> Mosse da prima quelle cose belle;   40
>   Sì che a bene sperar m' era cagione
>   Di quella fera alla gaietta pelle,^c
> L' ora del tempo, e la dolce stagione:
>   Ma non sì, che paura non mi desse
>   La vista, che mi apparve, d' un leone.
> Questi parea, che contra me venesse
>   Con la test' alta e con rabbiosa fame,
>   Sì che parea che l' aer ne temesse:^d
> Ed una lupa, che di tutte brame
>   Sembiava carca nella sua magrezza,   50

^c *la gaietta* Gg. Cass. 12345 *All.*
^d *tremisse* Gg.; *tremasse* alias *ne temesse* Cass. 1; *tremesse* 4.

[38-40] In early times it was held that the creation of the world took place at the beginning of spring, or when the sun was entering the Ram; and Dante thus indicates the time of year at which his vision befell him.—**amor**; S. T. i. Q. 37. A. 3: Amor est proprium nomen Spiritus sancti. See note to Par. x. 1.

[42] Dr. Moore's reasons for preferring **alla** seem conclusive.

in its leanness, and has already made much people to live wretched. (This one furnished me so much of heaviness with the terror that issued from her aspect, that I lost my hope of the height. And as is he who willingly acquires, and the time comes which makes him lose, that in all his thoughts he laments and is made sad; such did the implacable beast make me, which coming against me, by little and little pushed me back to the place where the Sun is dumb.

/ Whilst I was rushing to the low ground, before my eyes was brought one who by long silence appeared faint. When

> E molte genti fe già viver grame.
> Questa mi porse tanto di gravezza
>   Con la paura, che uscia di sua vista,
>   Ch' io perdei la speranza dell' altezza.
> E quale è quei, che volontieri acquista,
>   E giugne il tempo, che perder lo face,
>   Che in tutt' i suoi pensier piange e s' attrista :
> Tal mi fece la bestia senza pace,
>   Che venendomi incontro, a poco a poco
>   Mi ripingeva là, dove il Sol tace.   60
> / Mentre ch' io rovinava in basso loco,^{c}
>   Dinanzi agli occhi mi si fu offerto
>   Chi per lungo silenzio parea fioco.

^{c} *rimirava* 4.

The simile is no doubt intended to recall the symbolical meaning of the wolf, viz. avarice.

tace: Witte observes that Dante frequently interchanges terms applying to sight and hearing, comparing v. 28. Similar idioms are common in Greek, and not unknown in English.

The objection to the ordinary rendering, 'who appeared to have become hoarse through long disuse of his voice,' seems to have occurred first to Blanc, who asks how Dante could know that the other was hoarse before he had spoken. He takes the line to mean, 'I thought,

I beheld him in the great desert, 'Have mercy on me,' I cried to him, 'whoever thou be, whether a shade, or of a certainty a man.' He answered me: 'Not a man: I was a man once, and my parents were Lombards, and both Mantuans by their country. I was born *sub Julio*, albeit it

> Quand' io vidi costui nel gran diserto,
>   Miserere di me, gridai a lui,
>   Qual che tu sii, od ombra, od uomo certo.
> Rispose mi: Non uomo, uomo già fui,
>   E li parenti miei furon Lombardi,
>   Mantovani per patria ambo e dui.
> Nacqui *sub Julio*, ancorchè fosse tardi, 70

by his saying no word to help me, that he must be weak.' In favour of this is also the fact that **fioco** appears to mean rather 'faint' than 'hoarse'; indeed, in no other passage where it occurs is the latter meaning required (see Gloss. Par. s. v.) On the whole, therefore, I have preferred to follow Blanc, though supported only, so far as I know, by Scartazzini. The symbolism will then be, 'it was so long since I had heard the voice of my reason, that it seemed to me to be grown feeble.' The old view that there is an allusion to the neglect of classical study, and particularly that of Virgil, in the previous ages, is in any case very jejune.

70 As Benvenuto saw, this line contains two apparent errors of fact. Virgil was born B.C. 69, in the consulate of Pompey and Crassus, at which time Julius Caesar was very far from being the chief man in the state, and had lived little more than half his life. The commentator's loyalty to his author will not allow him to admit the simplest explanation, which, as he says, some gave, 'quod autor pro certo erravit.' He thinks that Dante must have known what all boys know. But it must be remembered that the knowledge of antiquity had made a great advance in the fifty years since Dante's death, and that his historical attainments were probably more on a level with Villani than with Benvenuto. How confused Villani's notions about the times of Caesar were, may be seen from his first book. To Dante Caesar was merely the first of the divinely ordained emperors of Rome. **Tardi** may perhaps mean that Virgil was born too late to distinguish himself under Caesar.

was late, and I lived at Rome under the good Augustus, at the time of the false and lying gods. A poet I was, and I sang of that just son of Anchises, who came from Troy, after that the proud Ilion was burned. But thou, why returnest thou to so great bane? Why ascendest not the mount of delight, which is the beginning and cause of all joy?' 'Oh, art thou that Virgil, and that fount which spreads forth so broad a stream of speech?' I answered him with shamefast brow. 'O honour and light of all poets, let the long study and the great love avail me, which have made me search thy volume. Thou art my master and my authority; thou only art he from whom I took the fair style which has done me honour. Behold the beast,

  E vissi a Roma, sotto il buono Augusto,
   Al tempo degli Dei falsi e bugiardi.
  Poeta fui, e cantai di quel giusto
   Figliuol d' Anchise, che venne da Troia,
   Poichè il superbo Ilion fu combusto.
  Ma tu perchè ritorni a tanta noia?
   Perchè non sali il dilettoso monte,
   Ch' è principio e cagion di tutta gioia?
  Or sei tu quel Virgilio, e quella fonte,
   Che spande di parlar sì largo fiume? 80
   Risposi lui con vergognosa fronte.
  O degli altri poeti onore e lume,
   Vagliami il lungo studio e il grande amore,
   Che m' ha fatto cercar lo tuo volume.
  Tu sei lo mio maestro e il mio autore:
   Tu sei solo colui, da cui io tolsi
   Lo bello stile, che m' ha fatto onore.

Cf. Par. viii. 1 sqq.

This can hardly refer, as Witte supposes, to the De Monarchia; for even if it were certain, instead of highly improbable, that that

by reason of which I turned round; help me from her,
renowned sage, for she makes my veins and my pulses to
tremble.' 'Thee it behoves to keep another road,' he
answered, since he saw me weep, 'if thou wouldst escape
from this savage place; because this beast, for the which
thou criest out, lets not any pass by her way, but hinders
him in such wise that she slays him. And she has a nature
so evil and guilty that she never fulfils her greedy will, and
after her repast has more hunger than before. Many are
the animals with which she pairs; and more will be yet,

> Vedi la bestia, per cui io mi volsi:
>   Aiutami da lei, famoso saggio,
>   Ch' ella mi fa tremar le vene e i polsi.   90
> A te convien tenere altro viaggio,
>   Rispose, poi che lagrimar mi vide,
>   Se vuoi campar d' esto loco selvaggio:
> Chè questa bestia, per la qual tu gride,
>   Non lascia altrui passar per la sua via,
>   Ma tanto lo impedisce, che l' uccide:
> Ed ha natura sì malvagia e ria,
>   Che mai non empie la bramosa voglia,
>   E dopo il pasto ha più fame che pria.
> Molti son gli animali, a cui s' ammoglia,   100
>   E più saranno ancora, infin che il veltro

treatise had been written before 1300, Dante would surely not compli-
ment Virgil by attributing his *prose* style to the influence of the poet.
No doubt, like other scholars, he had written plenty of Latin verses in
his time, and had gained a reputation thereby. We know, indeed, that
he wrote them after this, and had even purposed so to write the Commedia.

   [99] Cf. Purg. xx. 12.

   [100] Alluding to the many intrigues of the Papal party, both with
Italian and with foreign powers.

   [101 sqq.] The question as to the identity of the 'Veltro' has from the

until the Hound shall come, who will make her die of woe. This one shall not feed on land or dross, but on wisdom

> Verrà, che la farà morir con doglia.
> Questi non ciberà terra nè peltro,

first been more debated, and with less result, than any other in the whole poem. Volumes have been written on the subject, the usual effect of which on the reader's mind is to convince him that whatever is intended, it is not what the writer supposes. The main difficulty is to find a solution which will fit both l. 105, which seems to indicate a human champion, and l. 110, which ascribes to him divine powers. The diction is obviously taken from the Messianic prophecies, so that it is no wonder if many of the older commentators, P. di Dante, Benvenuto, the later Cassinese, and Landino understand it as a prophecy of Christ's second coming, fixing their attention more on l. 110; and take **feltro** as meaning *cielo*; the first named, by a wild piece of metaphor, suggesting as an alternative 'erit naturalis et de vili natione.' Boccaccio, who says, 'I confess that I do not understand it,' rejects this view, and on the whole inclines to that which holds some leader of humble origin to be foretold. The Cassinese 'Chiose sincrone' leave it alone. The interpretation which sees a prophecy of Can Grande does not seem to have arisen before the middle of the 15th century, when Bargigi appears to hint at it. Vellutello is the first who distinctly formulates it. Then the Feltros are taken to be the modern Feltre, in the Trevisan, and Montefeltro in Romagna. This has been the favourite interpretation in modern times, adopted by Witte, Philalethes, Bianchi, etc. Villani's account (v. 29) of the election of Genghis Khan as sovereign of the Tartars, contains two or three expressions which form a curious coincidence, worthy of consideration by those who hold this view : feciono . . . signore uno fabbro di povero stato, il quale avea nome Cangius, il quale in su un povero feltro fu levato imperadore, e come fu fatto signore, fu chiamato il soprannome Cane. Boccaccio, not referring to this passage, says that some, by an explanation 'assai pellegrina,' saw a prophecy of a reform to begin in Tartary ; telling a curious story of a Tartar custom, whereby, when a king is dying, a piece of felt, to be afterwards used as his shroud, is carried round the country on a spear. Probably Dante meant us to see here, as in the DXV of Purg. xxxiii. 43, a general prophecy of a reformed and united Italy, under such a ruler as he has drawn in the De Monarchia ; and while not having any particular person definitely in his mind, may have been not unwilling to hint indirectly at Can Grande.

and love and valour, and his birthplace shall be between Feltro and Feltro. Of that lowland of Italy shall he be the salvation, for which died Camilla the maiden, Euryalus, and Turnus and Nisus of their wounds. This one shall chase her through every town, until he shall have put her back into Hell, the place whence envy first sent her forth.

'Wherefore I for thy bettering think and decide that thou follow me; and I will be thy guide, and will draw thee from here through an eternal place, where thou shalt hear

> Ma sapienza e amore e virtute,
> E sua nazion sarà tra Feltro e Feltro.
> Di quell' umile Italia fia salute,
> Per cui morì la vergine Cammilla,
> Eurialo, e Turno, e Niso di ferute:
> Questi la caccerà per ogni villa,
> Fin che l' avrà rimessa nello inferno, 110
> Là onde invidia prima dipartilla.
> Ond' io per lo tuo me' penso e discerno,
> Che tu mi segui, ed io sarò tua guida,
> E trarrotti di qui per loco eterno,

---

[104] Cf. Par. xvii. 105.

[105] **umile**: probably an *epitheton ornans*, borrowed from Aeneid iii. 522.

[107, 108] See Aen. ix. xi. xii.

[111] Here the wolf becomes clearly the sin of covetousness in its widest sense, which Dante, as will often appear, regarded as the root of all the evils of the time. He would include under it public ambition, no less than private avarice; and it is of course in the former aspect that it can be said to be caused by envy. Benvenuto thinks that the allusion is to the murder of Abel: 'Chaim motus invidia, stimulante avaritia divitiarum, mactavit Abel.' Witte, following P. di Dante, sees a reference to Wisdom ii. 24. More to the purpose is the remark of Aquinas: Amatores honoris sunt magis invidi. S. T. ii. 2. Q. 36. A. 1.

the shrieks of despair, shalt see the ancient spirits in woe,
who each cry upon the second death; and thou shalt see
those who are content in the fire, because they have hope of
coming whensoever it may be to the blessed folk; to whom
afterward if thou wouldst rise there will be a soul more meet
for this than I; with her I will leave thee in my departure.

> Ove udirai le disperate strida,
>   Vedrai gli antichi spiriti dolenti,[f]
>   Che la seconda morte ciascun grida:[g]
> E poi vedrai color, che son contenti
>   Nel fuoco, perchè speran di venire,
>   Quando che sia, alle beate genti: 120
> Alle quai poi se tu vorrai salire,
>   Anima fia a ciò di me più degna;
>   Con lei ti lascerò nel mio partire:

[f] *Di quelli ant.* edd. 1484, 1491.
[g] *Ch' alla* Cass. 2 *Ald.*

[117] It seems impossible to take **la seconda morte** in any other sense than that which it has in Rev. ii. 11, xx. 14, etc., and in which it was understood by St. Augustine, e.g. Civ. Dei xiii. 8, viz. as meaning the state of the damned after the final end of temporal things. Nevertheless almost all the commentators, ancient and modern, perhaps thinking of xiii. 118, understand by it total annihilation. Benvenuto specially charges us against understanding the day of judgement, 'nam damnati talem mortem non vocant nec optant sibi.' But where in Dante does he find *gridare* in this sense of 'to call for'? In the few places where it is transitive, as here, it always means 'to proclaim,' 'shout forth.' Further, if this interpretation were correct, we should surely not have **la** but *una*; or no article at all, but *per* or some such word. The true meaning can only be that which P. di Dante (whom Benv. in his remark quoted above is clearly glancing at) gives—though he is very undecided—when he says (after quoting Aug. de Civ. D. xxi. 3, 'secunda mors animam nolentem tenet in corpore'): idest conqueruntur de secunda morte quam habent aeternam et spiritualem.

Lubin's idea of taking **che** as = *di che*, and **ciascun** as 'everyone on earth,' can hardly be accepted.

For that Emperor who reigns there on high, seeing that I was in rebellion to His law, wills not that through me entry should be had into His city. He governs in all parts, and reigns there; there is His city and His high seat; O happy the man whom He chooses for that place!' And I to him: 'Poet, I beseech thee by that God whom thou knewest not, in order that I may escape this ill and worse, that thou lead me there where thou hast just said, so that I may see the gate of Saint Peter, and those whom thou makest out so sad.'
 Then he started, and I held after him.

> Chè quello imperador, che lassù regna,
> Perch' io fui ribellante alla sua legge,
> Non vuol che in sua città per me si vegna.
> In tutte parti impera, e quivi regge,
> Quivi è la sua città e l' alto seggio:
> O felice colui, cu' ivi elegge!
> Ed io a lui: Poeta, io ti richieggio   130
> Per quello Dio, che tu non conoscesti,
> Acciocch' io fugga questo male e peggio,
> Che tu mi meni là dov' or dicesti,
> Sì ch' io vegga la porta di san Pietro,
> E color, cui tu fai cotanto mesti.
> Allor si mosse, ed io li tenni retro.

CANTO II

ARGUMENT

Dante is in fear lest his strength should not be sufficient for the journey. Virgil bids him take courage, for that three Ladies from heaven have a care of him.

The day was departing, and the dun air was taking the living creatures that are upon the earth from their labours; and I, one only, was making me ready to endure the strife alike of the journey and of the pity, which my mind that errs not will portray. O Muses, O lofty wit, here aid me;

> Lo giorno se n' andava, e l' aer bruno
>   Toglieva gli animai che sono in terra,
>   Dalle fatiche loro; ed io sol uno
> M' apparecchiava a sostener la guerra
>   Sì del cammino e sì della pietate,
>   Che ritrarrà la mente, che non erra.
> O Muse, o alto ingegno, or m' aiutate:

---

[1] Scart. compares Aen. viii. 26, 27. The day has been occupied in the flight from the beasts, and the subsequent discourse with Virgil. It may be here noted that Dante enters Hell at sunset, Purgatory at sunrise, Paradise at noon. **sol uno**: i.e. the one living being.

[7] **Muse.** Cf. Purg. i. 8, and see note Par. i. 16. Benv. takes occasion from this line to give an account of Dante's mental and physical characteristics.

O mind that wrotest what I saw, here shall appear thy nobleness.

I began: 'Poet who guidest me, consider my virtue, if it is potent, before that thou entrust me to the high passage. Thou sayest that the father of Silvius, being yet corruptible, went to an immortal world, and was there with his senses. Wherefore, if the adversary of every evil was gracious to him, thinking on the mighty result that was to issue from him, and the who, and the what—it appears not to a man of understanding unmeet; for he was in the empyrean heaven chosen for father of Rome our parent and of her empire, both which (if one would say the truth) were estab-

> O mente, che scrivesti ciò ch' io vidi,
> Qui si parrà la tua nobilitate.
> Io cominciai: Poeta che mi guidi,   10
> Guarda la mia virtù, s' ella è possente,
> Prima che all' alto passo tu mi fidi.
> Tu dici, che di Silvio lo parente,
> Corruttibile ancora, ad immortale
> Secolo andò, e fu sensibilmente.
> Però se l' avversario d' ogni male
> Cortese i fu, pensando l' alto effetto,
> Che uscir dovea di lui, e il chi, e il quale.
> Non pare indegno ad uomo d' intelletto:
> Ch' ei fu dell' alma Roma e di suo impero   20
> Nell' empireo ciel per padre eletto:
> La quale, e il quale (a voler dir lo vero)

---

[9] Note **si** pleonastic. Diez iii. 176.
[12] **alto passo**: cf. Par. xxii. 123.
[13] I.e. Aeneas, whose youngest son was named Silvius. Aen. vi. 760.
[17] **i** for *gli*. So xxii. 73. **effetto**: the Empire.
[18] **chi – quale**: the Emperor, considered in himself and in his quality.

lished for the holy place where sits the successor of the sovereign Peter. Throughout this journey, whereof thou givest him glory, he heard things which were the cause of his victory, and of the papal robe. Afterward went there the chosen vessel, to get thence a confirmation for that faith, which is the outset to the way of salvation. But I— why come thither? or who grants it? Not Aeneas, not Paul am I; nor I nor other deems me worthy for this. Wherefore, if I resign myself in respect of coming, I fear lest the coming should be mad: thou art wise, and understandest better than I speak.'

  Fur stabiliti per lo loco santo,
   U' siede il successor del maggior Piero.
  Per questa andata, onde gli dai tu vanto,
   Intese cose, che furon cagione
   Di sua vittoria e del papale ammanto.
  Andovvi poi lo Vas d' elezione,
   Per recarne conforto a quella fede,
   Ch' è principio alla via di salvazione.   30
  Ma io perchè venirvi? o chi 'l concede?
   Io non Enea, io non Paolo sono:
   Me degno a ciò nè io nè altri 'l crede.
  Perchè se del venire io m' abbandono,
   Temo che la venuta non sia folle:
   Sei savio, intendi me' ch' io non ragiono.

---

[20] I.e. the prophecies of the Roman Empire (of which, in Dante's political scheme, the Papacy was only another aspect) in the Sixth Aeneid. See De Mon. ii. 7, and elsewhere.

[25] 2 Cor. xii. 2 sqq.

[31] **io venirvi.** For this 'independent infinitive' see Diez iii. 203.

[32-3] Contrast this with the confidence of Aeneas. Aen. vi. 122:

   Quid Theseu, magnum
 Quid memorem Alciden? et mi genus ab Jove summo.

[34] **del venire.** The use of the genitive is curious. See Diez iii. 151.

And as is he who ceases to will that he willed, and by reason of new thoughts changes purpose, so that he withdraws himself wholly from his beginning, so became I on that dark hillside; so that in my thought I made an end of the enterprise which in its commencement had been so hasty.

'If I have well understood thy word,' replied that shade of the high-souled one, 'thy soul is hindered by cowardice, which oftentimes so encumbers the man that it turns him back from honourable enterprise, as wrong-seeing does a beast when it shies. To the end that thou mayest loose thyself from this fear I will tell thee wherefore I came, and

> E quale è quei, che disvuol ciò che volle,
>   E per nuovi pensier cangia proposta,
>   Sì che dal cominciar tutto si tolle;
> Tal mi fec' io in quella oscura costa: 40
>   Perchè, pensando, consumai la impresa,
>   Che fu nel cominciar cotanto tosta.
> Se io ho ben la tua parola intesa,
>   Rispose del magnanimo quell' ombra,
>   L' anima tua è da viltate offesa:
> La qual molte fiate l' uomo ingombra,
>   Sì che d' onrata impresa lo rivolve,
>   Come falso veder bestia, quand' ombra.
> Da questa tema acciocchè tu ti solve,
>   Dirotti, perch' io venni, e quel che intesi 50

---

[45] **offesa.** Here, as frequently in Dante, *offendere* has its primitive sense of 'cause to stumble.' See note Purg. xxxi. 12.

[48] **ombra.** From the idea of 'shadow' comes easily that of anything suspicious; though the transfer of the verb from the meaning 'cast a shadow' or 'be in shadow,' to that of 'see shadows' is curious. Benv. 'sicut equus juvenis umbrosus.' Cf. our term 'to take umbrage.' The converse change is seen in *adugghiare*. (See Gloss. Purg. s. v.)

what I heard at the first moment when it grieved me for thee. I was among those who are in suspense, and a lady, blessed and fair, called me—one such that I besought her to give command. Her eyes beamed more than star; and she began to say to me sweet and clear, with voice of an angel, in her speech: O courteous Mantuan soul, whose fame yet lasteth in the world, and shall last long as the world goes onward, my friend, and not the friend of fortune, in the desert tract is so hampered on his road that he has

  Nel primo punto che di te mi dolve.
Io era tra color che son sospesi,
 E donna mi chiamò beata e bella,
 Tal che di comandare io la richiesi.
Lucevan gli occhi suoi più che la stella:
 E cominciommi a dir soave e piana,
 Con angelica voce, in sua favella:
O anima cortese Mantovana
 Di cui la fama ancor nel mondo dura,
 E durerà quanto il mondo lontana: [a]   60
L' amico mio, e non della ventura,
Nella diserta piaggia è impedito

[a] *moto lont. Gg.* (?) 1 *Ald. W.*

[52] **sospesi**: cf. iv. 45.

[55] **la stella**, as in V. N. § 23 (Canzone), Conv. iii. 9, and elsewhere, must be understood of the abstract star, not any one in particular. The locution is easier to parallel in English than in Italian; 'ruddier than the cherry' will suggest itself. It seems to have puzzled copyists and editors, who have occasionally substituted *una* for **la**.

[60] As to the readings, see Moore, Text. Crit. I have followed the weight of authority, including (which I think more important than ordinary MS. authority) that of the earliest commentators. With all respect to Foscolo, I cannot see that Virgil's 'mobilitate viget' is at all to the point here. *That* fame is not one which Virgil is likely to hear attributed to himself with any satisfaction.

[62] **diserta piaggia**: cf. i. 29.

turned back for fear; and I fear lest he be already so perplexed that I have risen to his succour too late, by what I have heard of him in heaven. Now set out, and with thy well-graced word, and with that which needs for his deliverance, aid him in such wise that I may be consoled thereof. I am Beatrice who make thee to go: I come from a place whither I am fain to return; love moved me, which causes me to speak. When I shall be before my Lord I will oftentimes speak good of thee to Him.—Then she held her peace, and afterward I began: O lady of virtue, through whom alone

> Sì nel cammin, che volto è per paura:
> E temo che non sia già sì smarrito,
>   Ch' io mi sia tardi al soccorso levata,
>   Per quel ch' io ho di lui nel Cielo udito.
> Or muovi, e con la tua parola ornata,
>   E con ciò ch' è mestieri al suo campare,
>   L' aiuta sì, ch' io ne sia consolata.
> Io son Beatrice, che ti faccio andare: 70
>   Vegno di loco, ove tornar disio:
>   Amor mi mosse, che mi fa parlare.
> Quando sarò dinanzi al Signor mio,
>   Di te mi loderò sovente a lui.
> Tacette allora, e poi comincia' io:
>   O donna di virtù, sola per cui

---

[67] **muovi**: intrans. See Diez iii. 177.

[74] **mi loderò**: so Fr. *se louer de* 'to express oneself as pleased with.' The formation is somewhat curious; but all the Romance languages show a tendency to these quasi-reflexive forms. Diez iii. 175.

[76] **virtù.** It may be as well to say here that I have usually rendered this word simply by *virtue*. Of course it must be understood that it is often used in the same sense as that which it has retained in the phrase 'by virtue of,' but which has otherwise pretty much disappeared from

the human species exceeds all content of that heaven which has its circles least, so much does thy commandment do me pleasure that to obey, if it had already come to pass, is late to me : no further needest thou to open to me thy will. But tell me the reason why thou dost not reck of descending hither into this centre from the wide space whither thou burnest to return.—Since thou wouldest know so far into the matter,

> L' umana spezie eccede ogni contento
> Da quel ciel, che ha minor li cerchi sui :
> Tanto m' aggrada il tuo comandamento,
>   Che l' ubbidir, se già fosse, m' è tardi ;   80
>   Più non t' è uopo aprirmi il tuo talento.[b]
> Ma dimmi la cagion, che non ti guardi
>   Dello scender quaggiuso in questo centro
>   Dall' ampio loco, ove tornar tu ardi.
> Da che tu vuoi saper cotanto addentro,

[b] *uopo che apr. Gg.*

modern English. For a further discussion of its meaning, see note at end of Purg. iv.

In order to understand the full force of these lines, it is necessary to bear in mind that as the Purgatory and the Paradise respectively embody the teaching of the De Anima and Metaphysics of Aristotle, so this Cantica is based on the Ethics. The terms in which Virgil is made to address Beatrice contain an obvious allusion to the tenth book of that treatise. Beatrice, as must never be forgotten, denotes allegorically the contemplative life, the θεωρία which Aristotle identifies with happiness, informed by the Christian revelation. Τῶν δ' ἄλλων ζώων, says the philosopher (Eth. Nic. x. 8. 1178 b) οὐδὲν εὐδαιμονεῖ, ἐπεὶ οὐδαμῇ κοινωνεῖ θεωρίας. In this sense then it may be said that through Beatrice the human race is superior to all else within the circle of the moon (cf. vii. 64) that is, upon the earth. Further, εὐδαιμονία being ἐνέργεια κατ' ἀρετήν, she is rightly called **donna di virtù**.

I.e. if I had already fulfilled your commands, I should seem to be late in doing so. The construction is somewhat mixed ; but the present è where we should expect *era* gives vividness. Perhaps more simply : If I was ever in haste to obey, I am now.

I will tell thee briefly, she answered me, why I fear not to come in hither. There need be fear only of those things which have power to do one harm: of the others none, for they are not fearful. I am made by God, of His grace, such that your misery touches me not, nor does a flame of this burning assail me. There is a noble dame in Heaven who has such compassion of this hindrance whereto I send thee, that she breaks down stern judgement there on high. She bade Lucy to her behest, and said: Now has thy faithful one need of thee, and I recommend him to thee.

> Dirotti brevemente, mi rispose,
> Perch' io non temo di venir qua entro.
> Temer si dee di sole quelle cose
>   Ch' hanno potenza di fare altrui male:
>   Dell' altre no, che non son paurose.
> Io son fatta da Dio, sua mercè, tale,
>   Che la vostra miseria non mi tange,
>   Nè fiamma d' esto incendio non m' assale.
> Donna è gentil nel ciel, che si compiange
>   Di questo impedimento, ov' io ti mando,
>   Sì che duro giudizio lassù frange.
> Questa chiese Lucia in suo dimando,
>   E disse: Or ha bisogno il tuo fedele
>   Di te, ed io a te lo raccomando.

[80] **altrui** as in i. 18, Purg. iv. 54.

[84] **sua mercè**. Corticelli regards this as an instance of a dropped preposition, and Littré s. v. *merci* takes the same view; in which case we must render 'through His grace.' But is it not rather that the verb is omitted, 'thanks be His'? Cf. Purg. vi. 129, Par. xv. 53, where the (derived) meaning of 'thanks' can hardly be mistaken. But the ideas of 'by favour of' and 'thanks to' are closely connected.

[94] **Donna gentil**: the Virgin Mary. For the symbolism of this passage see note at end of the Canto.

Lucy, enemy of every cruel wight, set forth and came to the place at which I was, where I was sitting with the ancient Rachel. She said: Beatrice, very praise of God, why succourest thou not him who loved thee so greatly that for thee he issued forth from the common multitude? Hearest thou not the pity of his weeping? Seest thou not the death that is battling with him upon the river wherein the sea has

> Lucia, nimica di ciascun crudele,   100
>   Si mosse, e venne al loco dov' io era,
>   Che mi sedea con l' antica Rachele.
> Disse : Beatrice, loda di Dio vera,
>   Chè non soccorri quei che t' amò tanto,
>   Che uscìo per te della volgare schiera ?
> Non odi tu la pieta del suo pianto,
>   Non vedi tu la morte che il combatte
>   Su la fiumana, ove il mar non ha vanto ?

[102] Cf. Par. xxxii. 9.

[104] The commentators seem agreed that the 'river' intended is that which flows through Hell; of which we shall hear much more. As to the reason why the sea cannot boast of (or over) it, they are less decided ; some thinking that it is because it does not flow into the sea ; others, that it is more dangerous than any sea. Neither of these explanations is wholly satisfactory; and it seems better to take **ove il mar non ha vanto** as meaning merely 'not belonging to this earth'; all the waters of which, as Dante holds, depend for their origin ultimately on the sea. De Aq. et Ter. § 6: cum mare sit principium omnium aquarum, ut patet per philosophum in Meteoris suis. The passage referred to is no doubt Meteor. ii. 2 ; but Aristotle, though at the beginning of the chapter he seems inclined to this view, and gives a correct statement of the processes of evaporation and condensation, sums up with τελευτὴ μᾶλλον ὕδατος ἢ ἀρχή ἐστιν ἡ θάλαττα. It may be noticed that in this chapter Ar. criticises Plato's theory (Phaedo lx. lxi. 111 C-113 C) according to which the rivers of the earth have their origin in the nether world. In Dante's scheme, on the contrary, the rivers of Hell have their source on the earth's surface ; but not as other rivers. See xiv. 94 sqq.

no boast?—Never were persons in the world quick to work their own good and to fly their own hurt, as did I, after such words spoken, come down here from my seat in bliss, putting my trust in thy honourable speech, which does honour to thee and to those that have heard it.—After that she had made this discourse to me, she turned her beaming eyes tearfully, so that she made me more brisk of coming. And I came to thee in such wise as she would; I raised thee up before the face of that beast which had taken from thee the short road to the fair mount. Now then, what is it? why, why dost thou stay? why makest for such cowardice a bed in thy heart? Why hast not daring and a free spirit, since ladies three so blessed have a care of thee in the court of heaven, and my speech makes promise to thee of so great good?'

> Al mondo non fur mai persone ratte
>   A far lor pro, nè a fuggir lor danno,   110
>   Com' io, dopo cotai parole fatte,
> Venni quaggiù dal mio beato scanno,
>   Fidandomi del tuo parlare onesto,
>   Che onora te e quei che udito l' hanno.
> Poscia che m' ebbe ragionato questo,
>   Gli occhi lucenti lagrimando volse;
>   Perchè mi fece del venir più presto:
> E venni a te così, com' ella volse;
>   Dinanzi a quella fiera ti levai,
>   Che del bel monte il corto andar ti tolse.   120
> Dunque che è? perchè, perchè ristai?
>   Perchè tanta viltà nel core allette?
>   Perchè ardire e franchezza non hai?
> Poscia che tai tre donne benedette
>   Curan di te nella corte del cielo,
>   E il mio parlar tanto ben t' impromette?

As the flowers, bent down and closed by the frost of night, after that the Sun dawns upon them erect themselves all open on their stalks, so became I with my flagging power; and so good a daring sped to my heart that I began, as a person set free: 'O pitiful she who succoured me! and courteous thou who obeyedst in haste the words of truth which she set forth to thee! Thou hast with desire so disposed my heart toward coming, with thy words, that I am returned again to my first purpose. Now on, for one sole will is in both of us; thou leader, thou lord, and thou master.'

So spake I to him, and when he had started, I entered by the deep forest path.

    Quali i fioretti dal notturno gelo
        Chinati e chiusi, poi che il Sol gl' imbianca,
        Si drizzan tutti aperti in loro stelo ;
    Tal mi fec' io, di mia virtute stanca :   130
        E tanto buono ardire al cor mi corse,
        Ch' io cominciai come persona franca :
    O pietosa colei che mi soccorse,
        E tu cortese, che ubbidisti tosto
        Alle vere parole che ti porse !
    Tu m' hai con desiderio il cor disposto
        Si al venir, con le parole tue,
        Ch' io son tornato nel primo proposto.
    Or va, che un sol volere è d' ambo e due ;
        Tu duca, tu signore e tu maestro :   140
        Cosi gli dissi ; e poichè mosso fue,
    Entrai per lo cammino alto e silvestro.

NOTE TO LINES 94 SQQ.

The symbolism of all this part is extremely involved and obscure, and more especially that embodied in the three heavenly ladies, the

'Donna gentil,' St. Lucy, and Beatrice, who interest themselves in Dante's salvation. The first of these is not expressly named, but it is clear that she cannot be a mere abstraction; and as a 'Donna' in Heaven with authority to command other saints to do her bidding can only be 'Our Lady,' she must be intended. This is also probable from other considerations; see Purg. Appendix A. The regular interpretation, from P. di Dante downwards, is that the two first denote respectively the two main aspects which belong to each of the several modes of division of grace that may be adopted. These modes of division are represented in the following table :—

	a	b	c	
Gratia { 1	gratum faciens	operans	preveniens	} S.T.ii.1. Q.111.
2	gratis data	cooperans	subsequens	

a (1) relates to the good pleasure of God, owing to which, from pure love, He justifies man; *a* (2) to grace imparted to and manifested in man; *b* (1) and (2) good thought or good action, according as they refer to the mind or the will, *operans* being where God moves either of these, *cooperans* where it also moves the man; *preveniens* and *subsequens* are correlative, as cause and effect, though even the effects of grace (healing of the soul, a right will, right action, perseverance, attainment of glory) follow a certain order, so that the grace which is prevenient in regard to any one is subsequent in regard to its predecessor. (See also note to Par. xiv. 37.) In each division it will be seen that (1) regards solely the Divine source, and is thus fitly typified by the Virgin, whose goodness 'liberamente al dimandar precorre' (Par. xxxiii. 18), while (2) involves also the free will of man. Beatrice of course is *beatitudo*, the ultimate end of man, Aristotle's εὐδαιμονία, the special attribute of God (in the *lode di Dio vera* of line 103 we can hardly fail to see an allusion to the φορτικὸς ἔπαινος, *onerosa laus*, of Eth. x. 1178 b), which is coextensive with θεωρία—which, again, must have been, if not by Aristotle himself, certainly by his Christian followers, derived from θεὸν ὁρᾶν. Here then we may perhaps look for what P. di Dante, following his father, calls the 'anagogic' or spiritual interpretation. But this clearly does not exhaust the symbolism. For one thing, it gives no account of the term applied to Lucia, '*nimica di ciascun crudele.*' P. di Dante's 'idest crudi et grossi intellectus' will hardly do. At the same time we may feel sure (in spite of Boccaccio's warning not to look too minutely for allegory) that a phrase so marked as this must have a meaning. Now according to Aquinas (S. T. ii. 2. QQ. 157, 159) 'crudelitas excedit modum in puniendo,' whence, by a comparison of Eth. iv. 11 (1126 a), we find that it is equivalent to Aristotle's χαλεπότης, the contrary to which is πραότης, *mansuetudo*. Again, in commenting on this passage of the Ethics, he says: 'Cum dicitur aliquis mansuetus, signatur quod non sit punitivus, sed magis remittat et condonet poenas.' While he makes *clementia* the direct opposite of *crudelitas*, and refines between this and *mansuetudo*, he allows (Q. 157. A. 1.) that though not 'penitus idem,' yet 'concurrunt in eundem effectum'; *mansuetudo* being that virtue which restrains the passion resulting in the action which *clementia* moderates. Then from Art. 4 we learn that 'mansuetudo praeparat hominem ad Dei cognitionem, removendo impedimentum.' Now this is exactly the function fulfilled here by Lucia. (Cf. also Ps. xxiv. 9: Diriget mansuetos in judicio. The whole Psalm bears on these two Cantos.) Boccaccio suggests that Lucia is 'la clemenza divina'; but grotesquely enough makes the *Donna gentil* denote Dante's prayer for help! Why St. Lucy should be selected to typify meekness is not quite clear; but it may be noted that in the service for her festival not only is Ps. xliv. (Eructavit cor meum) recited, as forming part of the office common to all virgin saints, but (as for St. Agatha, with whom she is connected) the verse 'propter veritatem, mansuetudinem, et justitiam' is specially repeated. Further, a homily of St. Gregory is read, in which occur the words 'maligni autem spiritus iter nostrum quasi quidam latrunculi obsident.' —As the old commentators are fond of saying 'Alia per te vide.'

CANTO III

ARGUMENT

They enter through a door, over which are certain words inscribed, and pass a crowd of the souls of such as were unworthy to enter Hell. Then they come to the river Acheron, and Charon the ferryman.

Through me is the way into the woeful city; through me is the way to the eternal woe; through me is the way among the lost folk. Justice moved my high Maker; my Maker was the power of God, the supreme wisdom, and the primal love. Before me were no

> 'Per me si va nella città dolente,
> Per me si va nell' eterno dolore,
> Per me si va tra la perduta gente.
> Giustizia mosse il mio alto fattore:
> Fecemi la divina potestate,
> La somma sapienza e il primo amore.
> Dinanzi a me non fur cose create,

5. " By **potestate, sapienza, amore** are indicated the Persons of the Trinity. See note Par. x. 1.

7. " Looking to Par. xxix. 22 sqq. it would appear that the **cose eterne** are form and matter.—A theory as to the means by which Hell was brought into existence is suggested in xxxiv. 121 sqq.

THINGS CREATED SAVE THINGS ETERNAL, AND ETERNAL I ABIDE; LEAVE EVERY HOPE, O YE THAT ENTER.

These words, of a gloomy colour, did I see written above a gate; wherefore I: 'Master, their sense is hard to me.' And he to me, as a person who takes heed: 'Here it behoves to lay aside every suspicion; every cowardice behoves that it here be dead. We are come to the place where I have told thee that thou shalt see the woeful folk, who have lost the good of the understanding.' And after he had laid his hand

> Se non eterne, ed io eterno duro:[a]
> Lasciate ogni speranza, voi ch' entrate!'
> Queste parole di colore oscuro   10
> Vid' io scritte al sommo d' una porta:
> Perch' io: Maestro, il senso lor m' è duro.
> Ed egli a me, come persona accorta:
> Qui si convien lasciare ogni sospetto;
> Ogni viltà convien che qui sia morta.
> Noi siam venuti al loco ov' io t' ho detto,
> Che tu vedrai le genti dolorose,
> Ch' hanno perduto il ben dello intelletto.
> E poichè la sua mano alla mia pose,

[a] *eterna* 23 W.

* **eterno** should be taken as in 'aeternumque sedebit infelix Theseus,' i.e. almost as an adv., though there is no need, even were it an adj., for the fem.

* **il ben dello intelletto**: explained by Conv. ii. 14: la Verità... ch' è ultima perfezione nostra, siccome dice il Filosofo nel sesto dell' Etica, quando dice che il vero è il bene dello intelletto. Per queste, con altre similitudini molte, si può la Scienza Cielo chiamare. The passage referred to is Eth. vi. 2 (1139 a): τῆς θεωρητικῆς διανοίας ... τὸ εὖ ... τἀληθές ἐστι. (See also S. T. ii. 2. Q. 20. A. 1.) Remembering that Beatrice is θεωρία, we may compare such passages as Par. x. 37 sqq.

upon mine, with cheerful mien, whereof I took courage, he brought me within, to the hidden things.

There sighs, lamentations, and loud wailings were resounding through the starless air; wherefore I at the beginning wept for them. Divers languages, horrible speech, words of woe, accents of rage, voices loud and faint, and sounds of hands with them, made a tumult, which ever in that air eternally tinted circles as the sand when it is blowing up for a whirlwind. And I, who had my head girt about with a shudder, said: 'Master, what is that which I hear? And what folk is it that seems so overcome

> Con lieto volto, ond' io mi confortai, 20
> Mi mise dentro alle segrete cose.
> Quivi sospiri, pianti ed alti guai
> Risonavan per l' aer senza stelle,
> Perch' io al cominciar ne lagrimai.
> Diverse lingue, orribili favelle,
> Parole di dolore, accenti d' ira,
> Voci alte e fioche, e suon di man con elle,
> Facevano un tumulto, il qual s' aggira
> Sempre in quell' aria senza tempo tinta,
> Come la rena quando a turbo spira.[b] 30
> Ed io, ch' avea d' orror la testa cinta,[c]
> Dissi: Maestro, che è quel ch' i' odo?
> E che gent' è, che par nel duol si vinta?

[b] *il turbo* Gg. Cass.: *quando t.* 3.
[c] *la t. dorror* Gg.: *error* al. *dorror* Cass.: *error* 14. *I.T.*

[25] **Diverse**: perhaps better 'uncouth,' as in vi. 13, xxii. 10.

[30] **spira.** If, with some, we take **arena** as the subject, it would seem as if Dante connected *spirare* with *spira*, 'a coil,' 'eddy.'

[31] There is little doubt but that **orror** is the correct reading here; *error* having been introduced by some early scribe who did not recognise the use of *orror* in its original Latin sense of 'shuddering.' Scart. points out that there is obviously a reminiscence of Aen. ii. 559.

in its woe?' And he to me: 'This wretched fashion keep the sorry souls of those who lived without infamy and without praise. They are mingled with that caitiff band of the angels who were not rebel, nor were faithful to God, but were for themselves. Heaven chased them, that it should not be less fair, nor does the deep hell receive them, since the damned would have some boasting

> Ed egli a me : Questo misero modo
> Tengon l' anime triste di coloro,
> Che visser senza infamia e senza lodo.^d
> Mischiate sono a quel cattivo coro
> Degli angeli, che non furon ribelli,
> Nè fur fedeli a Dio, ma per sè foro.
> Cacciànli i Ciel per non esser men belli :   40
> Nè lo profondo inferno gli riceve,
> Chè alcuna gloria i rei avrebber d' elli.

^d *senza fama* Gg. Cass. 12345 Ald.

³⁶ Here again is a famous v. l. arising from the mistaken criticism of early editors, who could not see why people who had lived **senza infamia** should be damned. Even Benvenuto here and in l. 31 adopts the less probable reading.

³⁸ **angeli.** This notion of a class of neutral angels seems to be Dante's own. It may have been suggested by a phrase in De Civ. Dei xi. 11, where St. Augustine is discussing whether the angels who fell ever had perfect beatitude. They must, he argues, have either foreseen or not foreseen what was going to befall them. 'Si autem,' he continues, 'utrum sempiternum, an quandoque finem habiturum esset bonum suum, *in neutram partem firma assensione ferantur,*' this in itself was inconsistent with perfection. Is it possible that Dante misunderstood the words in italics?

⁴² Bianchi understands this as referring to the angels only : 'those who had fought would have occasion to boast when they saw that those who were neutral had no better fate than themselves.' But this is hardly consistent with the scorn which is expressed all through this passage for the character which avoids sin only through pusillanimity. It clearly means that their presence in the lower Hell would provide

of them.' And I: 'Master, what grief have they so great as to make them so mightily lament?' He answered, 'I will tell it thee very briefly. These have no hope of death, and their blind life is so base that they are envious of every other lot. Fame of them the world suffers not to exist; mercy and justice disdain them: let us not talk of them, but look thou and pass on.'

And I, who looked, beheld an ensign which was running in circles so quickly that it seemed to me indignant of any halt; and behind it came so long a trail of folk that I had never deemed that death had undone so many. After that I

> Ed io: Maestro, che è tanto greve
> > A lor, che lamentar gli fa sì forte?
> > Rispose: Dicerolti molto breve.
> Questi non hanno speranza di morte,
> > E la lor cieca vita è tanto bassa,
> > Che invidiosi son d' ogni altra sorte.
> Fama di loro il mondo esser non lassa,
> > Misericordia e giustizia gli sdegna: 50
> > Non ragioniam di lor, ma guarda e passa.
> Ed io, che riguardai, vidi una insegna,
> > Che girando correva tanto ratta,
> > Che d' ogni posa mi pareva indegna:
> E dietro le venia sì lunga tratta
> > Di gente, ch' i' non avrei mai creduto,
> > Che morte tanta n' avesse disfatta.

the greater sinners with a kind of foil. It may be as well to point out here that neither in Hell nor in Purgatory are the sufferings arranged in any gradation of severity. See Purg. xix. 117.

54 **indegna**: so 'disdained' is used actively, 1 Hen. IV. A. i. Sc. 3. l. 183.

had recognised some there, I beheld and knew the shade of him who through cowardice made the great renunciation. Forthwith I understood and was aware that this was the sect of the caitiffs displeasing to God and to His enemies. These wretches, who never were alive, were naked, and sore stung of gadflies and of wasps that were there. These were

> Poscia ch' io v' ebbi alcun riconosciuto,
>   Vidi e conobbi l' ombra di colui ^c
>   Che fece per viltate il gran rifiuto.   60
> Incontanente intesi, e certo fui,
>   Che quest' era la setta dei cattivi,
>   A Dio spiacenti ed ai nemici sui.
> Questi sciaurati, che mai non fur vivi,
>   Erano ignudi e stimolati molto
>   Da mosconi e da vespe ch' erano ivi.

^c *Guardai e vidi* Ald. (and all subsequent edd. of sixteenth century except *Vellutello* 1544).

59, 60 From very early times the most common opinion has been that the allusion here is to Pietro Morrone, who was taken from his hermitage at the age of 80 and elected Pope 1294. He took the name of Celestine V., reigned for five months only, and abdicated. Boniface VIII., to whom Dante ascribes much of the evil of his time, succeeded, which may account for the severe judgement passed here upon the poor old hermit. The incident produced a good deal of astonishment at the time. Villani tells the story at length (viii. 5), and it is mentioned even in the almost contemporary Icelandic saga of Bishop Laurence. It should be said that Benv. rejects this interpretation, though admitting it was common in his time, and prefers to see an allusion to Esau. P. di Dante, however, seems to have little doubt, and Boccaccio in his commentary on Canto ix. mentions that in his time 600 persons had been burnt as heretics for holding that since Celestine there had never been a legal pope. Fazio degli Uberti, writing before 1360, alluding to the passage, names Celestine (Ditt. iv. 21).

bathing their visages with blood, which mingled with tears at their feet was gathered by loathsome worms.

And when I had set myself to look beyond, I saw folk on the bank of a great river; wherefore I said: 'Master, now grant me to know who they are, and what fashion makes them seem so fain of crossing, as I perceive through the dim light.' And he to me: 'Things will be clear to thee when we stay our steps on the sad shore of Acheron.' Then with eyes shamefast and cast down, fearing lest my speech had been irksome to him, as far as the river I withdrew myself from talking.

And behold came towards us in a boat an old man

> Elle rigavan lor di sangue il volto,
>   Che, mischiato di lagrime, ai lor piedi
>   Da fastidiosi vermi era ricolto.
> E poi che a riguardare oltre mi diedi,   70
>   Vidi gente alla riva d' un gran fiume:
>   Perch' io dissi: Maestro, or mi concedi
> Ch' io sappia quali sono, e qual costume
>   Le fa di trapassar parer sì pronte,
>   Com' io discerno per lo fioco lume.
> Ed egli a me: Le cose ti fien conte,
>   Quando noi fermerem li nostri passi
>   Sulla trista riviera d' Acheronte.
> Allor con gli occhi vergognosi e bassi,
>   Temendo no 'l mio dir gli fusse grave.   80
>   Infino al fiume di parlar mi trassi.
> Ed ecco verso noi venir per nave

---

72 One of the few instances in which the sentence continues without any stop whatever from one terect to the next.

82 The introduction of Charon is of course suggested directly by Aen. vi. 298 sqq. But it will be found throughout that Dante makes

white by reason of ancient hair, crying, 'Woe to you, perverse souls! Hope not again to see the sky; I come to bring you to the other bank, among the eternal gloom, to heat and to cold. And thou who art there, a living soul, depart thee from these who are dead.' But when he saw that I did not depart, he said: 'By other ways, by other ferries shalt thou come to the shore, not here: in order to pass, it behoves that a bark more buoyant carry thee.' And the Leader to him: 'Charon, vex not thyself; thus is it willed in that place where what is willed can be; and ask no more.' Then were at rest the shaggy jaws of the pilot

> Un vecchio bianco per antico pelo,
>   Gridando: Guai a voi anime prave:
> Non isperate mai veder lo cielo!
>   I' vegno per menarvi all' altra riva,
>   Nelle tenebre eterne, in caldo e in gelo.
> E tu che sei costi, anima viva,
>   Partiti da cotesti che son morti.
>   Ma poi ch' ei vide, ch' io non mi partiva,   90
> Disse: Per altra via, per altri porti
>   Verrai a piaggia, non qui; per passare
>   Più lieve legno convien che ti porti.
> E il duca a lui: Caron non ti crucciare;
>   Vuolsi così colà, dove si puote
>   Ciò che si vuole, e più non dimandare.
> Quinci fur quete le lanose gote
>   Al nocchier della livida palude,

use of many personages of classical mythology to serve as officials of the Christian plan of punishment; some of them being, so far as appears, entirely of his own selection.

lanose gote ... occhi di fiamme: the *canities incalta* and *stant lumina flamma* of Aen. vi. 300. — **livida palude**: the *vada livida* of l. 320.

of the livid swamp, who had wheels of flame around his eyes. But those souls, who were weary and naked, changed colour and gnashed their teeth, so soon as they heard the cruel words. They fell to blaspheming God and their parents, the human kind, the place, the time, and the seed of their begetting and of their birth. Then they dragged them all together, wailing loud, to the baleful bank, which awaits every man that fears not God. Fiend Charon, with eyes red-hot, beckoning to them assembles them all; he beats with his oar whoso delays. As in autumn the leaves come off one after the other until the branch sees on the earth

> Che intorno agli occhi avea di fiamme rote.
> Ma quell' anime ch' eran lasse e nude, 100
> Cangiar colore e dibattero i denti,
> Ratto che inteser le parole crude.
> Bestemmiavano Iddio e lor parenti,
> L' umana specie, il luogo, il tempo e il seme
> Di lor semenza e di lor nascimenti.
> Poi si ritrasser tutte quante insieme,
> Forte piangendo, alla riva malvagia
> Che attende ciascun uom che Dio non teme.
> Caron dimonio con occhi di bragia
> Loro accennando tutte le raccoglie; 110
> Batte col remo qualunque s' adagia.
> Come d' autunno si levan le foglie
> L' una appresso dell' altra, infin che il ramo
> Vede alla terra tutte le sue spoglie,[f]

[f] *Rond.* 145.

[f3] Contrast this with the blessed praying for their parents in Par. xiv. 64.
[112] See Aen. vi. 309:
> Quam multa in silvis auctumni frigore primo
> Lapsa cadunt folia.

all its spoils, in like manner the evil seed of Adam throw themselves from that shore one by one by reason of his signs, as does a bird for its recall. Thus they go their way over the brown wave, and before they are disembarked on that side, yet a new troop is assembled on this.

'My son,' said the courteous Master, 'those who die in the wrath of God all come together here from every land; and they are fain to pass the stream, for the justice of God so spurs them that their fears turn to desire. Here never passes a good soul; and therefore if Charon frets him because of thee, well mayest thou now know what his tale means.'

This ended, the gloomy champaign trembled so mightily

> Similemente il mal seme d' Adamo
>   Gittansi di quel lito ad una ad una,
>   Per cenni, come augel per suo richiamo.
> Così sen vanno su per l'onda bruna,
>   Ed avanti che sian di là discese,
>   Anche di qua nuova schiera s' aduna.   120
> Figliuol mio, disse il Maestro cortese,
>   Quelli che muoion nell' ira di Dio
>   Tutti convegnon qui d' ogni paese:
> E pronti sono a trapassar lo rio,
>   Chè la divina giustizia gli sprona
>   Sì che la tema si volge in disio.
> Quinci non passa mai anima buona;
>   E però se Caron di te si lagna,
>   Ben puoi saper omai che il suo dir suona.
> Finito questo, la buia campagna   130

---

117 The first of the many similes from falconry which will be found in the D. C.

125 Cf. Purg. xxi. 64.

130 sqq. Compare with this the manner in which, at the end of Plato's

that the remembrance of the terror yet bathes me with sweat. The tear-soaked earth gave forth a wind which flashed a ruddy lightning, the which overcame in me every feeling; and I fell, as the man whom slumber seizes.

> Tremò sì forte, che dello spavento
> La mente di sudore ancor mi bagna.
> La terra lagrimosa diede vento,
> Che balenò una luce vermiglia,
> La qual mi vinse ciascun sentimento:
> E caddi, come l' uom cui sonno piglia.

Republic, the souls waiting to be reborn are brought to the upper world with thunder and earthquake. Why Dante should employ a similar artifice here is not apparent; but it will be observed that his actual entry into each of the divisions of the future world is made unconsciously. Cf. Purg. ix. 49-60; Par. i. 70-75.

CANTO IV

ARGUMENT

They reach the Limbo or border of Hell, where they find the spirits of those who have died unbaptized not having committed grievous sin. Among them are Homer and other poets, who receive the author into their number. He sees Aristotle and other great scholars of old time.

THE deep sleep within my head a heavy thunder broke, so that I roused myself like a person who is waked perforce, and moved my rested eye around, having risen upright, and gazed fixedly to have knowledge of the place where I was. True it is that I found myself on the brink of the woeful valley of the pit, which collects a thunder of endless wails. Gloomy, deep it was, and so murky that for all fastening

  RUPPEMI l' alto sonno nella testa
   Un greve tuono, sì ch' io mi riscossi,
   Come persona che per forza è desta:
  E l' occhio riposato intorno mossi,
   Dritto levato, e fiso riguardai
   Per conoscer lo loco dov' io fossi.
  Vero è che in su la proda mi trovai
   Della valle d' abisso dolorosa,
   Che tuono accoglie d' infiniti guai.
  Oscura, profond' era e nebulosa,   10

my gaze on the depth, I there discerned no thing soever.

'Now descend we down into the sightless world,' began the Poet, all amort; 'I will be first, and thou shalt be second.' And I, who took note of his hue, said: 'How shall I come if thou art afraid, who art wont to be a support to my doubting?' And he to me: ''The anguish of those folk who are below there paints on my face that pity which thou dost hold for fear. Let us go, for the long road urges us on.' Thus he set himself and thus he caused me to enter upon the first circle that rings the pit. Here, so far as

> Tanto che, per ficcar lo viso al fondo,
>   Io non vi discerneva alcuna cosa.
> Or discendiam quaggiù nel cieco mondo,
>   Cominciò il poeta tutto smorto:
>   Io sarò primo, e tu sarai secondo.
> Ed io, che del color mi fui accorto,
>   Dissi: Come verrò, se tu paventi,
>   Che suoli al mio dubbiare esser conforto?
> Ed egli a me: L' angoscia delle genti
>   Che son quaggiù, nel viso mi dipigne   20
>   Quella pietà che tu per tema senti.
> Andiam, chè la via lunga ne sospigne:
>   Così si mise, e così me fe entrare
>   Nel primo cerchio che l' abisso cigne.
> Quivi, secondo che per ascoltare,

[11] **per ficcar**: so *per parlar* xvi. 93, *per narrar* xxviii. 3. This use of *per* explains the 'concessive' use of *perchè*, as in Purg. v. 58, where see note. It is of course *per* 'pro,' not *per* 'per.'

[16] **color**: cf. ix. 1.

[25] **secondo che** without a finite verb is an unusual construction, and two or three variants exist; probably invented in order to avoid it. There may be a confusion between 'secondo l' ascoltare' and 'secondo che era per asc.'; but the construction is not without analogies.

listening went, lamentation was not, save of sighs which
made the everlasting mist tremble. And this befel of woe
without torments which the crowds had, that were many and
great, both of infants and of women and of men. The good
Master to me: 'Thou demandest not what spirits these are
whom thou seest? Now will I that thou know ere thou go
further, that they did not sin; and if they have deserts, it
suffices not; because they had not baptism, which is a
part of the faith which thou believest. And if they were

>   Non avea pianto, ma che di sospiri,
>   Che l' aura eterna facevan tremare:
>   Ciò avvenia di duol senza martiri,
>   Ch' avean le turbe, ch' eran molte e grandi,
>   D' infanti e di femmine e di viri.   30
>   Lo buon Maestro a me: Tu non dimandi
>   Che spiriti son questi che tu vedi?
>   Or vo' che sappi, innanzi che più andi,
>   Ch' ei non peccaro: e s' elli hanno mercedi
>   Non basta, perchè non ebber battesmo,
>   Ch' è parte della fede che tu credi:
>   E se furon dinanzi al Cristianesmo,

[26] **ma** has here, as elsewhere, in the combination *ma che*, its original meaning of *magis*.

[27] **aura.** See note Purg. i. 15.

[32] The doctrine of a region on the confines of Hell, set apart for the souls of those who, from whatever cause, have died without baptism seems to have been first formulated by the Schoolmen, by inference from such passages as Job xvii. 16, the parable of Dives and Lazarus, etc. It was divided into *limbus patrum* ('supremus et minus tenebrosus locus,' S. T. Suppl. Q. 69. A. 5), where the souls of the patriarchs awaited Christ's coming, which, of course, ceased to exist after their liberation; and *limbus puerorum*, occupied primarily by unbaptized children, but assigned in Dante's scheme (though not apparently in that of strict theology) to the virtuous heathen also.

before Christianity, they adored not God duly; and of this sort am I myself. For such defects, not for other crime, we are lost; and we are harmed only in so far as we live without hope in longing.'

Great woe seized me in my heart when I heard it, because I was aware that folk of much worth were in suspense within that border. 'Tell me, my Master, tell me, Sir,' I began, through a will to be assured with that faith which overcomes every error, 'has any ever issued thence, either through his own merit, or through that of another, so that thereafter he was in bliss?' And he, who understood my shrouded speech, answered: 'I was new in this state when I saw come here a Mighty one, crowned with a sign

  Non adorar debitamente Dio:
   E di questi cotai son io medesmo.
  Per tai difetti, non per altro rio,
   Semo perduti, e sol di tanto offesi,
   Che senza speme vivemo in disio.
  Gran duol mi prese al cor quando lo intesi,
   Perocchè gente di molto valore
   Conobbi che in quel limbo eran sospesi.
  Dimmi, Maestro mio, dimmi, Signore,
   Comincia' io, per voler esser certo
   Di quella fede che vince ogni errore:
  Uscicci mai alcuno, o per suo merto,
   O per altrui, che poi fosse beato?
   E quei, che intese il mio parlar coperto,
  Rispose: Io era nuovo in questo stato,
   Quando ci vidi venire un possente
   Con segno di vittoria coronato.

    40-42 Cf. ix. 18, Purg. iii. 41.

of victory. He drew from us the shade of the first parent,
of Abel his son, that of Noah, of Moses the lawgiver, the
obedient; patriarch Abraham and King David; Israel with
his father and with his sons, and with Rachel for whom he
wrought so much, and many others, and made them blessed;
and I would have thee to know that before these no human
spirits were saved.'

We left not our going, for that he talked, but were passing the forest all the time, the forest I mean of crowded
spirits. Not far was yet our way on the hither side of my

> Trasseci l' ombra del primo parente,
>> D' Abel suo figlio, e quella di Noè,
>> Di Moisè legista e ubbidiente;
> Abraam patriarca, e David re,
>> Israel con lo padre, e coi suoi nati,
>> E con Rachele, per cui tanto fe, 60
> Ed altri molti; e fecegli beati:
>> E vo' che sappi che, dinanzi ad essi,
>> Spiriti umani non eran salvati.
> Non lasciavam l' andar, perch' ei dicessi,
>> Ma passavam la selva tuttavia,
>> La selva dico di spiriti spessi.
> Non era lunga ancor la nostra via
>> Di qua dal sonno; quando vidi un foco,^a

^a *sommo* 134.

⁵⁹ **di qua dal sonno.** This seems to be undoubtedly the right read-
ing, though Benv. prefers *sono*; with reference to the 'thundering' of
l. 2. *Sommo*, which Bianchi and some other modern edd. adopt, on
the authority of a few MSS., is clearly wrong. Dante is very careful to
use *di qua* and *di là* with reference to the place or time in which he is
speaking. Here he is addressing the reader, and consequently is speaking in this world, and after his return. He is therefore on the 'opposite
side of the summit,' i.e. the mouth of Hell: though in regard to his

slumber when I saw a fire which overcame a hemisphere of
darkness. We were still distant from it a little, but not so
that I failed to discern in part how honourable a folk possessed that place. 'O thou, who dost honour to knowledge and art, who are these that have so great honouring
that it divides them from the fashion of the others?' And

> Ch' emisperio di tenebre vincia.
> Di lungi v' eravamo ancora un poco, 70
> Ma non sì ch' io non discernessi in parte
> Che orrevol gente possedea quel loco.
> O tu, che onori scienzia ed arte,[b]
> Questi chi son, ch' hanno cotanta onranza,
> Che dal modo degli altri li diparte?

[b] *Onde io con ogni scientia* Gg.; *on. ogni sc.* ed. 1484; *Ald. etc.*

slumber, he is of course on the same side of it as when the events
described were happening.

[69] This is taken to refer merely to the fact that a fire burning on the
ground can naturally send its light through a hemisphere only. It is
seldom, however, that Dante introduces an image of this kind without
intending his readers to look further; and there is evidently a symbolism
here. The people whom he is approaching are the wise and good
of pre-Christian times, who, as Virgil elsewhere says (Purg. vii. 35), followed blamelessly the moral virtues which they knew. In Conv. iii. 15
moral goodness is the outward manifestation of the beauty of 'philosophy,' and the righteous will, which is the offspring of a delight in the
teachings of morality, is compared to 'flames of fire' which proceed
therefrom. But as the moral virtues only compose one-half of man's
duty, so their light illuminates a hemisphere only.

[72] *sqq.* Notice the constant repetition, in one form or another, of
onore.

[73] The ordinary reading *ogni scienza* has little or no support from
MSS. or edd. before 1480. On the other hand, Witte's *onori e scienza*
will not scan. There is plenty of analogy for treating *scienzia* as four
syllables.

[74, 75] I.e. who are allowed to be in the light while the rest are in
darkness.

he to me : 'The honoured reputation which of them is heard above in thy life gains grace in Heaven which thus promotes them.' Therewithal a voice was heard by me : 'Honour the most high poet; his shade returns which had departed.' After that the voice was at rest and was quiet, I saw four mighty shades come to us : a mien they had neither sad nor joyous. The good Master began to say to me : 'Look at him with that sword in hand, who comes in front of the three in manner as a lord. He is Homer, poet supreme,

> E quegli a me : L' onrata nominanza,
>   Che di lor suona su nella tua vita,
>   Grazia acquista nel ciel che sì gli avanza.
> Intanto voce fu per me udita :
>   Onorate l' altissimo poeta ;   80
>   L' ombra sua torna, ch' era dipartita.
> Poichè la voce fu restata e queta,
>   Vidi quattro grand' ombre a noi venire ;
>   Sembianza avevan nè trista nè lieta.
> Lo buon Maestro cominciò a dire :
>   Mira colui con quella spada in mano,
>   Che vien dinanzi ai tre sì come sire.
> Quegli è Omero poeta sovrano,

77 **nella tua vita** : i.e. in the world where you live. For **vita** cf. Purg. xxiii. 118.

80 There is nothing here, as in the somewhat similar passages, Purg. xxx. 19, Par. xxiii. 103, to indicate who the speaker is. The commentators do not speculate : only Benv. surmises that it was either Ovid or Horace. Bianchi can hardly be right in supposing that all four spoke : taking **sola** in l. 92 as equivalent to 'unita.'

83 Benvenuto has one of his dry sarcasms on other expounders here. 'Some,' he says, 'go about to expl. in this too subtly, saying that by the four poets are denoted the four cardinal virtues,' and so forth : 'verumtamen, licet ista expositio videatur pulcra, tamen judicio meo nihil facit ad propositum.' It is pleasant to meet with so much common sense.

the next is Horace the satirist who comes, Ovid is the third, and the last is Lucan. Because that each shares with me in the name which the solitary voice sounded, they do me honour, and therein they do well.'

Thus saw I unite the fair school of those lords of the most lofty strain which soars like an eagle above the others.

After they had conversed together awhile they turned toward me with a sign of salutation; and my Master smiled thereat. And yet far more of honour did they do me, for

<pre>
       L' altro è Orazio satiro, che viene,
       Ovidio è il terzo, e l' ultimo Lucano.   90
    Perocchè ciascun meco si conviene
       Nel nome, che sonò la voce sola,
       Fannomi onore, e di ciò fanno bene.
    Cosi vidi adunar la bella scuola
       Di quei signor dell' altissimo canto,^c
       Che sopra gli altri com' aquila vola.
    Da ch' ebber ragionato insieme alquanto,
       Volsersi a me con salutevol cenno:
       Perchè il Maestro sorrise di tanto:
    E più d' onore ancora assai mi fenno,   100
</pre>

^c *di quel signor* 124 *Add.*: *signori* G. 3.

95 **quei** with either **signor** or **signori** is the reading of more than three-fourths of the MSS. If so, we must (as the forms *quegli*, *altri*, etc., do not appear to be used in the singular except when they stand alone) understand the words as referring to the whole five, not as often taken, e.g. by Philalethes and Bianchi, to Homer alone. In that case **che** in l. 96 will refer to **canto**. Thus Boccaccio: Come l' aquila vola sopra ogni altro uccello, così il canto poetico, e massimamente quello di questi poeti, vola sopra ogni altro canto. The same view is adopted by Witte and Scartazzini.

they made me of their band, so that I was the sixth among so great wisdom.

Thus we went even to the light, talking of things whereof it is seemly to say nought, as it was to talk of them in that place where I was.

We came to the foot of a noble castle, seven times circled with lofty walls, fenced round with a fair moat.

> Ch' esser mi fecer della loro schiera,
>   Sì ch' io fui sesto tra cotanto senno.
> Così n' andammo infino alla lumiera,
>   Parlando cose, che il tacere è bello,
>   Sì com' era il parlar colà dov' era.
> Venimmo al piè d' un nobile castello,
>   Sette volte cerchiato d' alte mura,
>   Difeso intorno d' un bel fiumicello.

104, 105 The commentators have troubled themselves over these lines less than might have been expected. Bocc. indeed says that there were some who laboured to divine the subjects of this conversation; adding judiciously 'il che mi par fatica superflua.' In this opinion most seem to have acquiesced. Benv. thinks that there might be many subjects which could properly be discussed with pagan philosophers and poets, but were not for a Christian public; even as a doctor of divinity may discuss with philosophers and masters of arts metaphysical questions of which he would keep clear in the pulpit.

106 sqq. The 'noble castle' is generally understood as symbolising philosophy. About its sevenfold walls there is more diversity of opinion. Benv. and Comm. Cass. take these to denote the seven 'Liberal Arts,' Grammar, Logic, Rhetoric, Music, Arithmetic, Geometry, Astronomy. Landino prefers to see in them the 'virtù liberali,' i.e. apparently the four cardinal virtues, with the addition of wisdom, knowledge, and understanding. These do not, however, seem to have much significance here. On the other hand, he seems to be undoubtedly right in interpreting the stream as *eloquence*, which is a defence and aid to learning, but in which the wise man does not allow himself to be submerged.

This we passed as it had been hard land; through seven
gates I entered with these sages; we came into a meadow
of fresh greenery. Folk were there with slow and serious
eyes, of great authority in their visages; they talked seldom,
with gentle voices. With that we drew ourselves from one
of the corners into an open place, well-lit and lofty, so that
they could be seen every one. Right there, upon the green
enamel, were shown to me the mighty spirits, whom for
having seen I inwardly magnify myself. I saw Electra

> Questo passammo, come terra dura;
> > Per sette porte intrai con questi savi; 110
> > Giugnemmo in prato di fresca verdura.
> Genti v' eran con occhi tardi e gravi,
> > Di grande autorità nei lor sembianti;
> > Parlavan rado, con voci soavi.
> Traemmoci così dall' un dei canti
> > In loco aperto luminoso ed alto,
> > Sì che veder poteansi tutti e quanti.
> Colà diritto, sopra il verde smalto,
> > Mi fur mostrati gli spiriti magni,
> > Che del vederli in me stesso n' esalto. 120
> Io vidi Elettra con molti compagni,

[111] Cf. Aen. vi. 638: Devenere locos laetos et amoena vireta; which again is perhaps suggested by the 'asphodel meadow' of Odyssey xi. Dante, with whom all is symbolical, no doubt intends us to see in the green the emblem of ever-flourishing fame; cf. Purg. xi. 92.

[118] **smalto.** Mr. Ruskin in a well-known passage (M. P. Part iv. ch. 14) enlarges upon Dante's use of this word to characterise the grass of Hell: 'that it is not any more fresh or living grass, but a smooth silent lifeless bed of eternal green.' He has apparently overlooked the **fresca verdura** of l. 111, and also the fact that in Purg. viii. 114 the same word is used of the Earthly Paradise.

[121] Looking to the fact that she is accompanied by heroes and heroines of Troy and Rome, and to the mention of her in De Mon. ii. 3,

with many companions, among whom I was aware of Hector
and Aeneas; Caesar in arms with eyes as of a hawk. I saw
Camilla and Penthesilea on the other side; and I saw the
king Latinus, who was sitting with Lavinia his daughter. I
saw that Brutus who chased Tarquin; Lucretia, Julia,
Marcia and Cornelia; and alone, aside, I saw Saladin.
After I had raised my eyes a little more, I saw the Master of
them that know sitting among a philosophic household. All

> Tra' quai conobbi Ettore ed Enea,
>   Cesare armato con gli occhi grifagni.
> Vidi Cammilla e la Pentesilea
>   Dall' altra parte, e vidi il re Latino,
>   Che con Lavinia sua figlia sedea.
> Vidi quel Bruto che cacciò Tarquino,
>   Lucrezia, Julia, Marzia e Corniglia,
>   E solo in parte vidi il Saladino.
> Poi che innalzai un poco più le ciglia,   130
>   Vidi il Maestro di color che sanno,
>   Seder tra filosofica famiglia.

the commentators are probably right in taking this Electra to be the
daughter of Atlas and mother of Dardanus (Aen. viii. 134 sqq.) Villani
(i. 7) makes her to be the wife of Atlas, who was himself the founder of
Fiesole. It is curious that while Dante gives a place among the great
ones of old time to Camilla, the opponent of Aeneas in Italy, he allows
none of the Greek heroes who fought before Troy to appear here. It
will of course be remembered that he regards Aeneas as the virtual
founder of the Empire. See De Mon. loc. cit.

[124] The introduction of Penthesilea is probably due to the mention of
her in connexion with Camilla, Aen. xi. 662.

[128] **Marzia**; the wife of Cato. See Purg. i. 79.

[129] Saladin, like Henry III. in Purg. vii. 131, is apart from the rest
of this group, as being unconnected with the Empire.

[131] Aristotle; called in Conv. iv. 6, 'dignissimo di fede e d' obbe-
dienza,' 'Il maestro e duca della umana ragione.' Of him and the
others named an account will be found in any history of Greek philosophy.

gaze on him, all do him honour; there saw I both Socrates and Plato, who in front of the others stand nearer him. Democritus, who reposed the world on chance, Diogenes, Anaxagoras, and Thales, Empedocles, Heraclitus and Zeno; and the good assembler of qualities I saw, I mean Dioscorides; and I saw Orpheus, Tully, and Linus, and Seneca the moralist; Euclid the geometer and Ptolemy, Hippo-

> Tutti lo miran, tutti onor gli fanno.
>   Quivi vid' io Socrate e Platone,
>   Che innanzi agli altri più presso gli stanno.
> Democrito, che il mondo a caso pone,
>   Diogenes, Anassagora e Tale,
>   Empedocles, Eraclito e Zenone:
> E vidi il buono accoglitor del quale,
>   Dioscoride dico: e vidi Orfeo,   140
>   Tullio e Lino e Seneca morale:
> Euclide geometra e Tolommeo,

[139, 140] **Dioscorides.** There were several more or less eminent physicians of this name towards the end of the first century. The one referred to here was of Anazarba in Cilicia, and wrote a great treatise, περὶ ὕλης ἰατρικῆς (de materia medica), treating of plants and their medicinal qualities. This enjoyed a great reputation, and was translated into Arabic.

[141] **Lino.** The great majority of the MSS. read *Alino*; but there can be little doubt that Linus is meant. He is frequently coupled with Orpheus, e.g. Ecl. iv. 55-57.

[142] **Tolommeo**: Claudius Ptolemy, astronomer, geographer, and mathematician of Alexandria, lived in the second century of our era. His great work on Astronomy, known from the Arabic corruption of its Greek name as 'Almagest,' was the established authority on the science for nearly 1500 years. In Geography he was the first to indicate with any approach to accuracy the conformation of the earth's surface as known to the ancients, and to fix the latitudes and longitudes. The 47th proposition of the first book of Euclid is also due to him. Benvenuto gives a minute description of his personal appearance and habits, the authority for which does not appear.

crates, Avicenna, and Galen; Averroes, who made the great comment. I cannot make record of all in full, seeing that my long theme drives me on, so that oftentimes speech comes short of the fact. The sixfold company dwindles to two: through another way my wise Guide leads me, forth from the quiet into the mist which trembles; and I come into a region where there is nought to give light.

> Ippocrate, Avicenna e Galieno,
> Averrois, che il gran comento feo.
> Io non posso ritrar di tutti appieno;
> Perocchè sì mi caccia il lungo tema,
> Che molte volte al fatto il dir vien meno.
> La sesta compagnia in due si scema:
> Per altra via mi mena il savio duca,
> Fuor della queta, nell' aura che trema;   150
> E vengo in parte, ove non è che luca.

[143] **Hippocrates**, the greatest of early physicians, was born at Cos, B.C. 460. Plato speaks of him more than once; see Phaedr. 270 C, Protagoras 311 B. He is again alluded to Purg. xxix. 137; and see Par. xi. 4.

Avicenna (Ibn Sina), physician and philosopher, of Ispahan, was born in Bokhara, A.D. 980. Like Averroes, he was one of the great Mussulman thinkers who carried on the succession of the Aristotelian philosophy and prepared the way for the Schoolmen.

Galieno: Claudius Galenus, of Pergamus, was born A.D. 130. He studied at Alexandria, and was body-physician to several emperors. His writings were most voluminous; and he is still to some extent an authority.

[144] **Averroes** (Ibn Roschd), of Cordova (A.D. 1126-1198), was the last and greatest of the Arab philosophers of the West. He also was a physician; and a lawyer as well. He followed Aristotle very closely, and commented on nearly the whole of his works, which he knew through Arabic translations. The place which Dante assigns him shows that he was not yet regarded as the typical opponent of Christian doctrine; the character in which later Italian art recognised him. Boccaccio, indeed, thinks that but for him Aristotle might have remained unknown.

[148] The use of **sesta** in this sense is curious. Perhaps it is due to the fact that Latin possessed no word for 'sixfold,' so that the ordinal has to supply its place.   [151] Cf. l. 27.

CANTO V

ARGUMENT

They enter the second circle of Hell, where they find the souls of carnal sinners driven about in a great tempest. Dante speaks with Francesca of Rimini.

Thus I descended from the first circle down into the second, which girds a less space, and so much the more woe, which stings to groaning. There stands Minos in horrible wise, and snarls; he examines their sins at their

> Così discesi del cerchio primaio
> Giù nel secondo, che men loco cinghia,
> E tanto più dolor che pugne a guaio.
> Stavvi Minos orribilmente e ringhia:
> Esamina le colpe nell' entrata,

---

² The second circle, being the first of Hell properly so called, in which the unchaste are punished. It is worthy of note that while this sin is treated, when mortal, with most leniency, it requires the most severe purgatorial discipline; and further, that the regions assigned to its punishment and purgation are so situated, that every soul is compelled to pass through one or the other. Aquinas quotes Augustine, 'quod inter omnia Christianorum certamina, duriora sunt praelia castitatis, ubi est quotidiana pugna et rara victoria'; and Isidore, 'quod magis per carnis luxuriam genus humanum subditur diabolo, quam per aliquod aliud.'

⁴ Minos is of course borrowed from Aen. vi. 432.

incoming, judges and makes order according as he wraps himself. I mean that when the soul born to ill comes before him, it confesses itself wholly; and that appraiser of the sins sees what place of hell is meet for it; he girds himself with his tail so many times as the degrees he will that it be sent down. Ever before him are standing many of them; they come in turn each to the judgement; they say, and hear, and then are turned downward.

'O thou, who comest to the woeful hostelry,' cried Minos to me, when he beheld me, leaving the discharge of so great an office, 'look how thou enterest, and in whom thou trustest; let not the width of the entry deceive thee.'

    Giudica e manda, secondo che avvinghia.
Dico, che quando l' anima mal nata
    Li vien dinanzi, tutta si confessa;
    E quel conoscitor delle peccata
Vede qual loco d' inferno è da essa: 10
    Cignesi colla coda tante volte,
    Quantunque gradi vuol che giù sia messa.
Sempre dinanzi a lui ne stanno molte:
    Vanno a vicenda ciascuna al giudizio;
    Dicono e odono, e poi son giù volte.
O tu, che vieni al doloroso ospizio,
    Disse Minos a me, quando mi vide,
    Lasciando l' atto di cotanto ufizio,
Guarda com' entri, e di cui tu ti fide:
    Non t' inganni l' ampiezza dell' entrare!   20

" *avvinghia.* This use of a transitive verb without a pronoun in a reflexive sense is common to all modern languages, but especially frequent in Italian. Diez (iii. 177. S) gives several examples.

" For an instance of this operation see xxvii. 124 sqq.

And my Leader to him: 'Wherefore criest thou? Hinder not his destined going: thus is it willed in that place where that which is willed is possible; and ask no more.'

Now begin the notes of woe to make themselves heard by me; now am I come there where much wailing strikes me. I came into a place of every light mute, which roars as does the sea in time of tempest, if it is beaten about by contrary winds. The whirlwind of hell, which never rests, draws the spirits with its clutch, vexes them with whirling and beating. When they come in front of its rush, there

> E il duca mio a lui: Perchè pur gride?
> Non impedir lo suo fatale andare:
>   Vuolsi così colà, dove si puote
>   Ciò che si vuole, e più non dimandare.
> Ora incomincian le dolenti note
>   A farmisi sentire: or son venuto
>   Là dove molto pianto mi percote.
> Io venni in loco d' ogni luce muto,
>   Che mugghia, come fa mar per tempesta,
>   Se da contrari venti è combattuto.   30
> La bufera infernal, che mai non resta,
>   Mena gli spirti con la sua rapina,
>   Voltando e percotendo li molesta.
> Quando giungon davanti alla ruina,

23, 24 Repeated from iii. 95, 96, after the fashion of Homer or Virgil, rather than of Dante himself.

25 Witte observes that the punishments of Hell begin at this point: the *sciagurati* of Canto iii., though punished enough, not being strictly in Hell.

28 **di luce muto.** Cf. i. 60.

34 **ruina.** This is variously explained. Some take the word as in xii. 4, or Purg. iii. 50 (if it be the right reading there); some (e.g. Dan., Witte, Bianchi, Philal.) understanding it to be the precipice leading

are the cries, the complaining and the lamentation; they
blaspheme there the power of God. I was aware that to a
torment thus fashioned are condemned the carnal sinners
who made their reason subject to their inclination. And as
their wings bear away the starlings in the cold season, in a
broad and thick flock, so did that blast the evil spirits. On
this side, on that, up and down it sways them; no hope
ever comforts them, I say not of rest, but of a lesser penalty.

> Quivi le strida, il compianto e il lamento,
> Bestemmian quivi la virtù divina.
> Intesi, che a così fatto tormento
> Enno dannati i peccator carnali,
> Che la ragion sommettono al talento.
> E come gli stornei ne portan l' ali, 40
> Nel freddo tempo, a schiera larga e piena,
> Così quel fiato gli spiriti mali.
> Di qua, di là, di giù, di su gli mena:
> Nulla speranza gli conforta mai,
> Non che di posa, ma di minor pena.

down to the next circle, over which the souls are afraid of being blown;
Blanc thinks it is the rocky entrance to the circle. Benv. and Land.
speak merely of what they suppose it to symbolise. Boccaccio, whom
Vellutello follows, seems right in taking it to be the blast of the storm
(cf. Aen. i. 85). The spirits would naturally break out into lamentations on first becoming aware of the nature of their punishment.

 Cf. Rev. xvi. 9, 11. It may be noted that *odium Dei* is specified
by St. Thomas as one of the effects (*filiae*) of *luxuria*.

 Cf. Eth. vii. 6 (1149 b) ὁ τοῦ θυμοῦ ἀκρατὴς τοῦ λόγου πως
ἡττᾶται, ὁ δὲ τῆς ἐπιθυμίας καὶ οὐ τοῦ λόγου. Many other similar
passages will occur to readers of this book. St. Thomas, S. T. ii. 2.
Q. 53. A. 6, renders: Incontinens irae audit quidem rationem sed non
perfecte; incontinens autem concupiscentiae totaliter eam non audit.
talento: see note Purg. xxi. 64.

And as the cranes go chanting their lays, making a long row of themselves in air, so saw I come with long-drawn wails shades carried by the aforesaid tumult; wherefore I said: 'Master, who are these folk, whom the black air so chastises?' 'The first of those of whom thou wouldst know news,' he said to me then, 'was empress of many tongues. With vice of luxury was she so corrupt, that lustful she made lawful in her decree, to take away the ill-fame into which she had been brought. She is Semiramis, of whom we read that she succeeded to Ninus and was his wife. She

> E come i gru van cantando lor lai,
>   Facendo in aer di sè lunga riga;
>   Così vid' io venir, traendo guai,
> Ombre portate dalla detta briga:
>   Perch' io dissi: Maestro, chi son quelle   50
>   Genti, che l' aura nera sì gastiga?
> La prima di color, di cui novelle
>   Tu vuoi saper, mi disse quegli allotta,
>   Fu imperatrice di molte favelle.
> A vizio di lussuria fu sì rotta,
>   Che libito fe licito in sua legge,
>   Per torre il biasmo, in che era condotta.
> Ell' è Semiramis, di cui si legge,
>   Che succedette a Nino, e fu sua sposa:

---

[46] The simile of the cranes is again introduced Purg. xxvi. 43, and with reference to the same class of sinners.

[56] 'His lustes were all lawe in his decree,' Chaucer, Monk's Tale, 3667. 'Abusive dicit . . . cum dicat Philosophus: voluntas legislatoris est ut faciat homines bonos.'—P. di D.

[58] The reading *sugger dette*, which seems to have been first brought into notice in a sermon of the fifteenth century, in spite of its having practically no MS. authority (it is found as an *original* reading in two only), has of late years met with some defenders. Bianchi first, I

held the land which the Sultan rules. The other is she who slew herself, full of love, and broke faith with the ashes of Sichaeus; next is luxurious Cleopatra. See Helen for whose sake so long a time of guilt rolled on, and see the great Achilles who on love's side fought to the end. See

> Tenne la terra che il Soldan corregge. 60
> L' altra è colei, che s' ancise amorosa,
> E ruppe fede al cener di Sicheo;
> Poi è Cleopatras lussuriosa.
> Elena vedi, per cui tanto reo [a]
> Tempo si volse, e vedi il grande Achille,
> Che con amore al fine combatteo.

[a] *vidi Gg.* 23 *Ald. W.*

believe, among editors admitted it, though with hesitation, into the text of his fourth ed. of 1854, and Lubin has followed his example; while Prof. Scarabelli and the late Dr. Barlow have supported it warmly. Witte (Dante Forschungen, i. 190 sqq.) spent almost more pains than it was worth in demonstrating its futility. It is quite sufficient to observe that nothing of the kind is to be 'read' in Orosius, whose version of the story (Hist. bk. i. chap. 4) Dante here follows almost word for word. The *seno dette* of some French edd. has no value whatever, and is said to be not Italian.

[61] Dido. See Aen. iii. iv.

[64] The reading *vedi* is so unquestionably superior in dramatic force to *vidi* that I have adopted it; though the latter appears to have rather more authority. See Moore ad loc., and Scart., who while retaining *vidi* treats it as the imperative. But in such a case as this MS. authority is not of much weight; the difference between *e* and *i* being often hardly perceptible.

[65] The account of the death of Achilles as Dante had it was that he was inveigled into the temple of Apollo Thymbraeus in Troy by the promise of a meeting with Polyxena. Paris was there lying in wait for him, and stabbed him with a dagger or slew him with an arrow aimed at his vulnerable heel. This version of the story seems to have been unknown to Ovid, who describes the death of Achilles in Metam. xii., but it appears in the works ascribed to Dictys Cretensis and Dares Phrygius, which were the great authority in medieval times for

Paris, Tristan——' and more than a thousand shades he showed me, and in pointing named to me how love departed them from our life.

After that I had heard my Teacher name the dames of yore and the cavaliers, pity overcame me, and I was as it were at my wits' end. I began: 'O poet, willingly would I speak to those two who go together, and seem to be so light on the wind.' And he to me: 'Thou shalt see when they are nearer to us, and then do thou pray them by

> Vedi Paris, Tristano; e più di mille
> > Ombre mostrommi e nominommi a dito,
> > Che amor di nostra vita dipartille.
> Poscia ch' io ebbi il mio dottore udito 70
> > Nomar le donne antiche e i cavalieri,
> > Pietà mi giunse, e fui quasi smarrito.
> Io cominciai: Poeta, volentieri
> > Parlerei a quei due, che insieme vanno,
> > E paion sì al vento esser leggieri.
> Ed egli a me: Vedrai, quando saranno
> > Più presso a noi; e tu allor li prega

the Trojan history. 'Dolo me atque insidiis,' says Achilles, 'Deiphobus atque Alexander Polyxenae gratia circumvenere.'—Dict. Cret. iv. The popular work on the subject, written by Guido dalle Colonne of Messina, was finished in 1287, but Dante seems to have gone to the original authorities, as they were then held, for himself. The story of Tristan and Isolde is well known to readers of modern poetry. Dante probably knew it from the Fr. version by Christian of Troyes (W.)

68 **nominommi** appears to have the preponderating authority, while *nominolle* is very likely to be due to supposed needs of euphony, or to the influence of the *-lle* in the neighbouring lines.

121 **Che**–**dipartille**. Diez (iii. 58) gives this as an instance of the pleonastic use of the pronoun, such as is pretty common in Italian (cf. vii. 64, 65, 'di queste anime ... farne') and universal in relative clauses in Spanish; but it seems simpler to take **che** as the general 'link-word' between two sentences—in this case implying narration.

that love which sways them, and they will come.' So soon as the wind swings them toward us I raised my voice: 'O toilworn souls, come to speak to us, if Another denies it not.' As doves summoned by their longing, with their wings upraised and steady, fly to their sweet nest, borne through the air by their own will, so they issued from the troop where Dido is, coming to us through the air malign; so strong was the cry of my affection. 'O living creature,

> Per quell' amor che i mena; e quei verranno.
> Sì tosto come il vento a noi li piega,
> > Mossi la voce: O anime affannate,   80
> > Venite a noi parlar, s' altri nol niega.
> Quali colombe dal disio chiamate,
> > Con l' ali alzate e ferme, al dolce nido
> > Volan per l' aer dal voler portate:
> Cotali uscir della schiera ov' è Dido,
> > A noi venendo per l' aer maligno,
> > Sì forte fu l' affettuoso grido.
> O animal grazioso e benigno,

⁸¹ **altri.** It is to be noted that God is never named by the lost spirits (save once, in defiance, by the brigand Vanni Fucci, xxv. 3), nor by Dante in speaking to them. For **altri** cf. xxvi. 141, Purg. i. 133.

⁸²⁻⁴ Imitated from Aen. v. 213 sqq.:

> Qualis spelunca subito commota columba,
> Cui domus et *dulces* latebroso in pumice nidi
> . . . . mox aere lapsa quieto
> Radit iter liquidum celeres *neque commovet alas.*

⁸⁴ Scart., reading *vengon*, puts a colon after that word, and a comma at **portate**; because animals do not possess will!

⁸⁸ **animal**, of men, is frequent in Dante: e.g. Purg. xxix. 139. So Vulg. El. i. 5, 'nobilissimum animal'; 9, 'instabilissimum et variabilissimum a.' Bianchi quotes ii. 10, 'homo rationale animal est, et sensibilis anima et corpus est animal.'

gracious and kindly, who goest visiting through the dark gray air us who stained the world with blood-red, if the King of the universe were a friend we would pray Him for thy peace, since thou hast pity of our wayward ill. Of that whereof it pleases thee to hear and speak will we hear and speak to you, so long as the wind, as now, is hushed for us. The land where I was born lies on the sea-shore where the Po comes down, to have rest with his tributaries. Love, who

> Che visitando vai per l' aer perso
> Noi che tignemmo il mondo di sanguigno :   90
> Se fosse amico il re dell' universo,
> Noi pregheremmo lui per la tua pace,
> Poichè hai pietà del nostro mal perverso.
> Di quel che udire e che parlar ti piace
> Noi udiremo e parleremo a vui,
> Mentrechè il vento, come fa, ci tace.^b
> Siede la terra, dove nata fui,
> Sulla marina dove il Po discende
> Per aver pace coi seguaci sui.

^b *si tace* 2 *II*.

[89] **perso.** See note, Purg. ix. 97. Probably it is not more than a coincidence that the colours named in this and the following line should be those named in the line of Chaucer quoted in that note. At the same time there is very probably some suggestion intended by their juxtaposition.

[90] **perverso**: because they were relations, says Benvenuto ; in which case **mal** must be taken as 'sin.'

[97] **terra**: Ravenna. The speaker is Francesca, daughter of Guido da Polenta and aunt to Dante's friend and patron of that name. She was betrothed for political reasons to Giovanni, known as Gianciotto (Lame John), heir of the rival house of Malatesta at Rimini. His younger brother Paul came as his proxy for the betrothal, and being both in character and personal appearance much the more attractive, won the love of Francesca. Ultimately both were slain by the husband.

soon teaches himself to the noble heart, seized this one for the fair form which was reft from me—and the manner is still my undoing. Love, who excuses no loved one from loving, seized me for his joy in me so mightily that, as thou seest, it leaves me not yet. Love led us to one death; Cain is awaiting him who quenched our life.' These words from them were borne to us.

> Amor, che al cor gentil ratto s' apprende, 100
>   Prese costui della bella persona
>   Che mi fu tolta, e il modo ancor m' offende.
> Amor, che a nullo amato amar perdona,
>   Mi prese del costui piacer sì forte,
>   Che, come vedi, ancor non mi abbandona.
> Amor condusse noi ad una morte:
>   Cain attende chi vita ci spense.
>   Queste parole da lor ci fur porte.

The story is told at some length by Boccaccio, who must have known the facts from the report of contemporaries.

    [99] Taken from a line of Guido Guinicelli: Foco d'amore in gentil cor s'apprende.

    [102] Through failure to understand the force of **offende** some have preferred to read *mondo* for **modo** here. The two words are of course practically indistinguishable in most MSS. The reading was supported by the late Dr. Barlow in a pamphlet (*Francesca da Rimini*) of which the upshot was, that though Dante, in compliance with popular report, placed her in Hell, he believed her to be innocent of all actual guilt! It would be better, and not unlike Dante's style, to read *Che mi fu tolta al mondo, e ancor m' offende*. The commentator in V. da Spira's ed. (? Jacopo della Lana) has some suggestion of this, though he is confused. His note is: La quale persona li fu tolta al mondo, cioè che morì di gladio; e dice che ancora il mondo gli offende, cioè la nominanza e la fama. But the ordinary reading gives a perfectly good sense. 'The manner of my death,' i.e. that I was slain in the commission of sin, 'is what injures me, causes my trouble,'—of course an euphemism. For **offende**, cf. vii. 71, Par. viii. 78. Cf. Chaucer, Knight's Tale, 1536: And, as I trowe, with love offended most.

    [107] **Cain** seems better than *Caina*. See Dr. Moore's note (Textual

When I heard those storm-tossed souls, I bowed my face, and held it down so long till the Poet said to me, 'What art thou musing?' When I answered, I began: 'Alas! what number of sweet thoughts, how great desire brought these to their woeful pass!' Then turned I back to them, and spoke, and began: 'Francesca, thy torments make me ready to weep in grief and pity. But tell me, in the time of the sweet sighs, to what point and in what fashion did Love grant thee to become aware of thy unexpressed desires?' And she to me: 'No greater woe is there than to call to mind the

> Da che io intesi quelle anime offense,
>   Chinai il viso, e tanto il tenni basso,   110
>   Finchè il poeta mi disse: Che pense?
> Quando risposi, cominciai: O lasso,
>   Quanti dolci pensier, quanto disio
>   Menò costoro al doloroso passo!
> Poi mi rivolsi a loro, e parla' io
>   E cominciai: Francesca, i tuoi martiri
>   A lagrimar mi fanno tristo e pio.
> Ma dimmi: al tempo dei dolci sospiri,
>   A che e come concedette amore,
>   Che conoscesti i dubbiosi desiri?   120
> Ed ella a me: Nessun maggior dolore,
>   Che ricordarsi del tempo felice

Criticism, pp. 38, 39), where there is an apt reference to Isaiah xiv. 9 sqq. In either case the allusion is explained by Canto xxxii.

[109] **offense**: see note Purg. xxxi. 12.

[117] **fanno a lagrimar** seems to be the causal form corresponding to such a phrase as *sto a lagr*. Diez iii. 218.

[120] **dubbiosi**: 'perciocchè quantunque per molti appaia che l'uno ami l'altro, e l'altro l'uno, tuttavia suspicano non sia così come a lor pare, insino a tanto che del tutto discoperti e conosciuti sono,' Bocc.

happy time in your misery, and that thy Teacher knows. But if thou hast so great desire to know the first root of our love, I will tell as one who weeps and tells. We were reading one day, for delight, of Lancelot, how Love constrained him; alone were we, and without any suspicion. Many times did that reading impel our eyes, and change the hue of our visages; but one point only was it that overcame us. When we read that the wished-for smile was kissed by such

> Nella miseria; e ciò sa il tuo dottore.
> Ma se a conoscer la prima radice
>   Del nostro amor tu hai cotanto affetto,
>   Dirò come colui che piange e dice.^c
> Noi leggevamo un giorno per diletto
>   Di Lancilotto, come amor lo strinse:
>   Soli eravamo e senza alcun sospetto.
> Per più fiate gli occhi ci sospinse   130
>   Quella lettura, e scolorocci il viso:
>   Ma solo un punto fu quel che ci vinse.
> Quando leggemmo il disiato riso
>   Esser baciato da cotanto amante,

^c *Parò* 12 *Ald. II*.

[125] **tuo dottore.** Bocc. and Benv. both understand this to be Virgil, though the former quotes the passage from Boethius. Blanc is convinced that the words allude to no saying, but to some real experience of the person intended. (How then are they appropriate to Virgil? Still, in spite of the objection raised by Blanc that Dante elsewhere calls no one but Virgil his *dottore*, it can hardly be doubted that the allusion is to Boethius, Bk. ii. Pr. 4: In omni adversitate fortunae infelicissimum genus est infortunii, fuisse felicem. It is probably only a coincidence that Peter Damian (see Par. xxi. 106) has in his poem on the joys of Paradise the line, 'Praesens malum auget boni perditi memoriam.' Trench, Sacr. Lat. Poetry, p. 296.

[127] The passage from the romance of Lancelot which is here referred to is given in full by Scartazzini.

a lover, this one who never from me shall be parted kissed me on the mouth all trembling. A Gallehault was the book, and he who wrote it. That day we read no further in it.'

While the one spirit said this, the other was wailing so, that for pity I fainted, as a man who were dead; and I fell as a dead body falls.

> Questi, che mai da me non fia diviso,
> La bocca mi baciò tutto tremante:
> Galeotto fu il libro e chi lo scrisse:
> Quel giorno più non vi leggemmo avante.
> Mentre che l' uno spirto questo disse,
> L' altro piangeva sì, che di pietade 140
> Io venni meno sì com' io morisse;
> E caddi, come corpo morto cade.

[137] Sir Gallehault (by no means to be confused with Sir Galahad) was the knight by whose pleading, according to the story, Guinivere was persuaded to give the first kiss to Lancelot. In the middle ages his reputation was on a level with that of 'Sir Pandarus of Troy.' See note Par. xvi. 15.

[141] **Io venni meno.** Curiously enough the very same phrase occurs in the story: hebbe si grande angoscia che mancò poco che non si venisse meno.

CANTO VI

ARGUMENT

They enter the third circle, passing Cerberus who guards it, and find the souls of gluttons lying in the mire under perpetual rain. Dante talks with one of Florence, who foretells the future to him.

At the returning of my mind, which had closed itself in presence of the piteous case of the two kinsfolk, which wholly confounded me with grief, new torments and new sufferers I see around me, whereas I move, and turn, and whereas I set my gaze. I am at the third circle, of the rain eternal, accursed, chill and heavy; measure and quality never has it new. Coarse hail, and sleet, and snow are poured out

> Al tornar della mente, che si chiuse
>   Dinanzi alla pietà dei due cognati,
>   Che di tristizia tutto mi confuse,
> Nuovi tormenti e nuovi tormentati
>   Mi veggio intorno, come ch' io mi mova,
>   E ch' io mi volga, e come ch' io mi guati.
> Io sono al terzo cerchio della piova
>   Eterna, maledetta, fredda e greve:
>   Regola e qualità mai non l' è nuova.
> Grandine grossa, e acqua tinta, e neve   10

I.e. it is always heavy and cold, not like rain on earth, which varies in these respects.

Benv. in a curious and somewhat disgusting passage explains

through the gloomy air; the earth stinks which receives it. Cerberus, beast cruel and uncouth, with three throats barks in dog-wise over the folk that there is submerged. Scarlet eyes has he, and his beard greasy and black, and his belly large, and his paws armed with nails. He claws the spirits, mouths them and tears them up. The rain makes

> Per l' aer tenebroso si riversa:
> Pute la terra che questo riceve.
> Cerbero, fiera crudele e diversa,
>   Con tre gole caninamente latra
> Sopra la gente che quivi è sommersa.
> Gli occhi ha vermigli, la barba unta ed atra,
>   E il ventre largo, e unghiate le mani;
> Graffia gli spiriti, ingoia, ed isquatra.[a]

[a] *e in guglia* 2: *ingola* 4; *scuoia* W.

these various forms of downfall as symbolical of the ailments incurred on earth by gluttons.—**acqua tinta**, says Bianchi, is a local name in Tuscany for 'a cold rain, almost frozen.' Bocc. seems to support this, his words being: queste tre cose causate da' vapori caldi ed umidi, e da aere freddo, nell' aere si generano; which he would hardly have said if he had with later commentators, e.g. Landino, taken the meaning to be 'dirty water.'

[13] Cerberus, of course, is here in virtue of the place he holds in Aen. vi. 417 sqq. It will be observed that he is treated with much less consideration by Virgil than by the Sibyl.—**diversa**, as in xxii. 10. The idea is, no doubt, 'different from what we know,' and so exactly equivalent to 'uncouth.'

[15] **ingoia.** So, in one form or another, the great majority of MSS., and apparently every edition and commentary till the Cruscan of 1595. Modern edd. with one accord have *scuoia*; why, it is not easy to see, for Scartazzini's objection that Dante does not explain how, if Cerberus swallowed them, they reappeared, applies with equal force to **isquatra**: since we are not told how after 'quartering' they came together again. Moreover, there is no need to suppose an actual swallowing. Cerberus *mumbles* them, as a dog a bone; but *flaying* is not an operation for which a dog's blunt claws would naturally be suited.

them howl like dogs; with one of their sides they make a shelter for the other; often the wretched outcasts turn themselves over.

When Cerberus, the great worm, was aware of us, he opened his mouths and showed us his tusks; he had no limb which remained still. And my Leader, both his hands spread wide, took the soil, and with his fists full threw it within the greedy pipes. As is that dog who baying yearns for his food, and is quiet again after he bites it, for only to devour it he strains and fights, such grew those foul faces of the demon Cerberus, who thunders so at the souls that they would fain be deaf.

> Urlar gli fa la pioggia come cani:
>> Dell' un dei lati fanno all' altro schermo;   20
>> Volgonsi spesso i miseri profani.
>
> Quando ci scorse Cerbero, il gran vermo,
>> Le bocche aperse, e mostrocci le sanne:
>> Non avea membro che tenesse fermo.
>
> E il duca mio distese le sue spanne;
>> Prese la terra, e con piene le pugna
>> La gittò dentro alle bramose canne.
>
> Qual è quel cane che abbaiando agugna,
>> E si racqueta poi che il pasto morde,
>> Che solo a divorarlo intende e pugna;   30
>
> Cotai si fecer quelle facce lorde
>> Dello demonio Cerbero che introna
>> L' anime sì, ch' esser vorrebber sorde.

21 **profani.** 'Profano,' says Boccaccio, 'propriamente si chiama quello luogo il quale alcuna volta fu sacro, poi è ridotto ad uso comune d' ogni uomo ... così si può dire degli spiriti dannati ... partita da loro la grazia dello Spirito Santo, sono rimasi profani.' Scart. refers appositely to Heb. xii. 16.

22 **vermo**: so of Lucifer, xxxiv. 108.

We passed over the shades whom the heavy rain quells, and kept putting our feet on their emptiness which seems a form. They were lying on the ground, all of them, save one which raised itself to sit, soon as it saw us pass in front. 'O thou, who art brought through this Hell,' it said to me, 'remember me, if thou canst; thou wast made ere I was unmade.' And I to it: 'The anguish that thou hast, perchance, takes thee out of my mind so that it seems not that I ever saw thee. But tell me who thou art, that art set

> Noi passavam su per l' ombre che adona
>   La greve pioggia, e ponevam le piante
>   Sopra lor vanità che par persona.
> Elle giacean per terra tutte e quante,
>   Fuor ch' una che a seder si levò, ratto
>   Ch' ella ci vide passarsi davante.
> O tu, che sei per questo inferno tratto,   40
>   Mi disse, riconoscimi, se sai:
>   Tu fosti, prima ch' io disfatto, fatto.
> Ed Io a lei: L' angoscia che tu hai¹
>   Forse ti tira fuor della mia mente,
>   Sì che non par, ch' io ti vedessi mai.
> Ma dimmi chi tu sei, che in sì dolente

¹ *a lui* 4.

³⁶ **vanità**: cf. Purg. xxi. 135. Does Dante mean to imply that they felt no resistance to their feet from the bodies of the spirits? If so, how did he get any hold of Bocca degli Abati's hair, in Canto xxxii.? See note Purg. xxi. 132.

³⁷ **elle**: fem. in agreement with **ombre**. So lei in l. 43. **messa**, l. 47.

⁴² **disfatto, fatto**: as in Purg. v. 134.

⁴⁵⁻⁴⁶ Notice that here, as in Purgatory (Purg. xxiii. 43), the only acquaintance whom Dante fails to recognise at once is one who is suffering for the sin of gluttony. 'Nota quod autor ideo hoc fingit quia istud vicium gulae saepe ita transformat hominem in brevi, quod non videtur ille qui prius erat.' Benv.

in so woeful a place, and to a penalty so fashioned that if any other is greater, none is so displeasing.' And he to me: 'Thy city which is so full of envy that already the sack is running over, held me with it in the life of light. You citizens called me Ciacco: for the ruinous fault of

> Loco sei messa, ed a sì fatta pena,
> Che s' altra è maggio, nulla è sì spiacente.
> Ed egli a me: La tua città, ch' è piena
> D' invidia sì, che già trabocca il sacco,   50
> Seco mi tenne in la vita serena.
> Voi cittadini mi chiamaste Ciacco:
> Per la dannosa colpa della gola,

50 **invidia.** From this, the first mention of Florence in the poem, to the last (Par. xxxi. 39), it will be seen that *envy*, by which he means want of due subordination, or as we now should say 'the principle of equality' (Conv. i. 4), is regarded by Dante as the special sin of his own countrymen. '.Avvenne che per le invidie si cominciarono trai cittadini le sette.' Villani viii. 39. In Dante's scheme this sin is closely akin to 'cupidigia,' and with it forms the direct antithesis to 'giustizia,' the allowing willingly to every man his own, whether in honours, power, or wealth. See note, Purg. xx. 10; and cf. Par. ix. 129.

52 **Ciacco** seems to have been the name, or nickname, of a celebrated 'diner out' in Dante's younger days. He died in 1286, i.e. when Dante was 21, so they would doubtless have met. In the Decameron, Day ix. Nov. 8, will be found a story of a practical joke (somewhat elementary in its humour) played off by him on another personage of the same kind. Longfellow gives a translation of the story. From this it would seem that Ciacco, though open to an invitation anywhere, was more especially a parasite of Corso Donati. Boccaccio says he was 'dato del tutto al vizio della gola ... senzachè fuor di questo egli era costumato uomo ... ed eloquente ed affabile e di buon sentimento.' Ciacco ('Jimmy') seems, according to Buti (who, writing about 1385, states it with 'alquanti dicono') and subsequent commentators, to have been a pet name for a pig in Tuscany; though, as the earlier writers make no allusion to this, it is quite as likely that the animal got the name from the man as the converse. It must be remembered that mediæval Florence was a small and quick-witted community, where all men and their ways were known.

gluttony, as thou seest, I flag under the rain. And I, sorry soul, am not alone, for all these stand in a like penalty for a like fault:' and further he said no word. I answered him: 'Ciacco, thy distress weighs on me so that it summons me to weep; but tell me if thou knowest, to what will come the citizens of the divided city; if any there is righteous; and tell me the cause wherefore so great discord has assailed it.' And he to me: '.After long strain they will come to

> Come tu vedi, alla pioggia mi fiacco;
> Ed io anima trista non son sola,
> Chè tutte queste a simil pena stanno
> Per simil colpa: e più non fe parola.
> Io gli risposi: Ciacco, il tuo affanno
> Mi pesa sì, che a lagrimar m' invita:
> Ma dimmi, se tu sai, a che verranno   60
> Li cittadin della città partita;
> S' alcun v' è giusto; e dimmi la cagione,
> Perchè l' ha tanta discordia assalita.
> Ed egli a me: Dopo lunga tenzone
> Verranno al sangue, e la parte selvaggia

[54] **fiacco**: so vii. 14: and see Gloss. Purg.

[58, 59] It will be observed that this is almost a repetition of the terms in which he addressed Francesca, v. 116, 117, but slightly less sympathetic.

[64 sqq.] With all this passage compare Par. xvii. 46 sqq., and see notes.

[65] **al sangue.** The first blood seems to have been drawn about a month later than this, on 1st May, when a young gentleman of the Cerchi got his nose cut off. Vill. viii. 39.—**selvaggia.** This epithet seems to have been applied to the White party, and their leaders, the Cerchi, in the sense of ' rustics.' As appears from Par. xvi. 65, the Cerchi were newcomers in Florence, and from various sources we learn that their manners were not approved by the more polished citizens. Thus Villani viii. 38: uomini erano salvatichi ed ingrati, siccome genti venuti di piccolo tempo in grande stato e podere. (All this chapter, and those before and after it, should be read.)

blood, and the woodland party shall chase the other with overthrow of many. After that it is ordained that this shall fall within three years, and that the other shall arise with the might of a certain one who just now is coasting. On high shall it a long time hold its head, keeping the other

> Caccerà l' altra con molta offensione.
> Poi appresso convien, che questa caggia
> Infra tre soli, e che l' altra sormonti
> Con la forza di tal che testè piaggia.
> Alte terrà lungo tempo le fronti,   70

[56] **offensione**: so in Par. xvii. 52, the Whites, fallen in their turn, become 'la parte offensa.'

[61] There is some difference of opinion as to the person indicated in this line, depending to some extent upon the interpretation given to **piaggia**. Bocc. says: Dicesi appo i Fiorentini colui piaggiare, il quale mostra di voler quello che egli non vuole. (If this be so, our slang term 'kidding' would most nearly represent the force of the word here.) He understands the reference to be to Boniface VIII., who at this time was apparently trying to mediate, but really favouring the Black or ultra-Guelf party. Buti takes the same view. None of the succeeding commentators however, until Witte, has ventured to adopt it. Most understand **piaggia** to mean 'stays still, like a ship on shore,' and see in the words an allusion to Charles of Valois, who at this moment was warring in Flanders, quite unconscious, so far as appears, of the scheme which was to be developed a few months later. A few others, e.g. P. di Dante and the Cassinese postillator, somewhat absurdly think it is the course of the heavens which is waiting (the latter rendering **piaggia** by *ploret*); while the comm. in Vind. da Spira's ed. (? J. di Lana) says 'colla forza di Dio che ora sta cheta.' Perhaps the weakest of all is Lombardi, who thinks it is Charles, 'che tra poco verrà in qualità di paciere,' taking the present 'per enallage' for the future, and misinterpreting Buti's 'star in mezzo' as if it meant 'mediate.' The best recognised meaning of *piaggiare* seems, however, to be 'to coast,'— 'andare tra la terra e l' alto mare,' as Buti puts it, and this of course applies excellently to Boniface's conduct at the time of speaking; while against the consensus of comm. during the 15th and 16th centuries must be set the fact that people were becoming cautious in their remarks concerning Popes. Villani (vii. 69) uses the word as = 'takes sides.'

under heavy loads, howsoever it may lament for this and have shame thereof. Just men are there two, but they are not regarded there; pride, envy, and avarice are the three sparks that have set men's hearts on fire.' Here he put an end to his doleful words.

And I to him: 'Yet would I that thou inform me, and that thou make me a gift of further talking. Farinata and Tegghiaio who were so worthy, James Rusticucci, Arrigo,

> Tenendo l' altra sotto gravi pesi,
>   Come che di ciò pianga, e che ne adonti.
> Giusti son due, ma non vi sono intesi:
>   Superbia, invidia ed avarizia sono
>   Le tre faville che hanno i cori accesi.
> Qui pose fine al lagrimabil suono.
>   Ed io a lui: Ancor vo' che m' insegni,
>   E che di più parlar mi facci dono.
> Farinata e il Tegghiaio, che fur si degni,
>   Jacopo Rusticucci, Arrigo e il Mosca,   80

[73] It seems useless to inquire who the two just men were, as Bocc., with his usual good sense, sees. Benv. more boldly assumes that Dante himself and his friend Guido Cavalcanti (x. 63) are meant; the former on the ground that 'de se nullus sapiens dubitat'; and he has been followed by most succeeding commentators. Vellutello 'holds it for certain' that Dante refers to two good men, Giovanni da Vespignano and Barduccio, whose death, and the miracles wrought at their tombs, Villani (x. 179) records under the date 1331. It is hardly likely that their reputation would be so great thirty years earlier.

[74] Cf. Villani viii. 39 (where he is speaking of Donati and Cerchi): per la conversazione della loro invidia colla bizzarra salvatichezza, nacque il superbo isdegno tra loro.

[79, 80] We shall meet with Farinata in Canto x., Tegghiaio and Rusticucci in xvi., and Mosca in xxviii. Arrigo does not appear, nor is it certain who is the person meant. Some suppose him to be the Odérigo dei Fifanti, who took part in the murder of Buondelmonte (note, Par. xvi. 133); but Dante would hardly put one name for another; and Bocc.

and Mosca, and the others who set their wits on doing good, tell me where they are, and make me have knowledge of them; for a great desire urges me of knowing if heaven gives them its sweets or hell its poison.' And that one: 'They are among the blackest souls; divers sin weighs them down toward the bottom; if thou goest down so far, thou wilt be able to see them. But when thou art in the sweet world, I pray thee that thou bring me to others' mind; more I tell thee not, and more I answer thee not.' His forthright gaze he turned then to blinking; he looked at me a little, and afterward bowed his head; he dropped with it to a level with the other blind. And my Leader said to me,

> E gli altri che a ben far poser gl' ingegni,
> Dimmi ove sono, e fa ch' io li conosca;
>   Chè gran desio mi stringe di sapere,
>   Se il ciel gli addolcia o lo inferno gli attosca.
> E quegli: Ei son tra le anime più nere;
>   Diversa colpa giù li grava al fondo:^c
>   Se tanto scendi, li potrai vedere.
> Ma quando tu sarai nel dolce mondo,
>   Pregoti che alla mente altrui mi rechi:
>   Più non ti dico e più non ti rispondo.   90
> Gli diritti occhi torse allora in biechi:
>   Guardommi un poco, e poi chinò la testa:
>   Cadde con essa a par degli altri ciechi.
> E il duca disse a me: Più non si desta

^c *Diverse colpe* Gg. Cass. 12345 Add.; *qui li gr.* 2; *aggr. Add.* supplies the family name as *Giandonati*, but says no more. The Giandonati also had a feud with the Buondelmonti (Vill. viii. 1), and finally divided among themselves, the more part going with the white Guelfs.

  diversa, merely, I think, 'different from that which is punished here.' It is curious that most MSS. and early edd. read *diverse colpe*.

  biechi: the demeanour of one falling into stupor. See Gloss. Par.

'He rises up no more on this side the sound of the angelic trump. When the power that is their foe shall come, each will find again his sorry tomb, will take again his flesh and his own shape, will hear that which thunders to eternity.'

So crossed we over the foul mixture of the shades and of the rain, with slow paces, touching a little upon the future life; wherefore I said: 'Master, these torments, will they increase after the great sentence, or become less, or be as scorching?' And he to me: 'Return to thy science, which

> Di qua dal suon dell' angelica tromba:
> Quando verrà la nimica podesta,
> Ciascun ritroverà la trista tomba,
> Ripiglierà sua carne e sua figura,
> Udirà quel che in eterno rimbomba.
> Sì trapassammo per sozza mistura   100
> Dell' ombre e della pioggia, a passi lenti,
> Toccando un poco la vita futura:
> Perch' io dissi: Maestro, esti tormenti
> Cresceranno ei dopo la gran sentenza,
> O fien minori, o saran sì cocenti?
> Ed egli a me: Ritorna a tua scienza,

---

[99] I.e. the last sentence.

[106-108] He probably has in his mind such passages as Ar. Eth. x. 4 (1174 b): κατὰ πᾶσαν αἴσθησίν ἐστιν ἡδονή, ὁμοίως δὲ καὶ διάνοιαν καὶ θεωρίαν, ἡδίστη δ' ἡ τελειοτάτη; or, ib. 7 (1177 b), ἡ τελεία εὐδαιμονία αὕτη ἂν εἴη ἀνθρώπου, λαβοῦσα μῆκος βίου τέλειον· οὐδὲν γὰρ ἀτελές ἐστι τῆς εὐδαιμονίας. The idea of the bad being able to attain a kind of perfection in their own way may be derived from Met. δ 16 1021 b). It will be observed that with Aristotle τέλειος is capable of different interpretations, as indeed he shows in the passage last referred to that he is well aware. In the hands of his Christian followers these became extended, until we find the *vita perfetta* developed from the βίος τέλειος. Cf. Par. xiv. 46.

holds, in proportion as the thing is more perfect, it is more conscious of the good, and so of suffering. Albeit this accursed folk may never go on to true perfection, it expects to be more on the further than on the hither side.

We wound around that road, talking far more than I repeat; we came to the place where it passes downward: there we found Pluto, the great enemy.

> Che vuol, quanto la cosa è più perfetta,
>   Più senta il bene, e così la doglienza.
> Tuttochè questa gente maledetta
>   In vera perfezion giammai non vada, 110
>   Di là più che di qua essere aspetta.
> Noi aggirammo a tondo quella strada,
>   Parlando più assai ch' io non ridico:
>   Venimmo al punto dove si digrada:
> Quivi trovammo Pluto il gran nemico.

[115] **Pluto.** There is some doubt as to whether Pluto or Plutus is intended. Bocc., Benv., P. di Dante, and the earlier people generally take the former view—some tracing the connexion with riches through his other name of Dis,—while the moderns hold for Plutus. Probably Dante did not very clearly distinguish the two, if indeed he had ever heard of Plutus (Blanc); but it is obvious that Pluto would most fitly come in the same order with Minos, Cerberus, etc. At the same time his position as guardian of those who have sinned in the use of money shows affinities with Plutus. As to the form of the word, of course *Pluto* for *Pluton* is on a par with *Plato* (Purg. iii. 43).

CANTO VII

ARGUMENT

At the entrance of the fourth circle they find Pluto; passing whom they come to the souls of those who on earth have misused riches. These roll heavy stones to and fro, and have no features whereby they may be recognised. Virgil discourses of Fortune. They come to the shore of a marsh called Styx, in which lie the souls of the wrathful and sullen, and pass along to a tower.

'*PAPE SATAN pape Satan aleppe*,' began Pluto with his clucking voice. And that noble Sage who knew all, said, to sustain me: 'Let not thy fear do thee a mischief; for power

> Pape Satan pape Satan aleppe,
> Cominciò Pluto colla voce chioccia.
> E quel Savio gentil, che tutto seppe,
> Disse per confortarmi: Non ti noccia
> La tua paura, chè, poter ch' egli abbia,

---

[1] This piece of jargon has called forth, as might be expected, commentary enough to fill a very large volume. The earlier people inform us that *papae* is an exclamation of surprise, and *aleph* the first letter of the Hebrew alphabet, and deduce from this that Pluto is calling Satan to see what is going on. Rossetti, on the other hand, read *Paf' è Satan*, thus gaining valuable support for his theory of the Commedia. Cellini's whimsical story of the judge in the Law Courts at Paris, 'vero aspetto di Plutone,' who shouted to some disturbers of order, *Paix, paix, Satan, allez, paix*, is well known; and his notion that Dante, when he was in Paris, had heard the same, and made use of it, is no better nor worse than any of the rest.

[5] **poter ch' egli abbia.** The construction is somewhat uncommon.

though he have, he will not take from thee thy descent of this rock.' Then he turned round to that swollen lip, and said: 'Be silent, cursed wolf; consume thee inwardly with thine own rage. Our journey to the depth is not without cause; it is willed on high, there where Michael wrought the vengeance on the proud ravisher.' As in the wind the puffed sails fall in a tangled heap when the mast snaps, so fell to earth the cruel monster.

Thus we descended into the fourth hollow, taking more

> Non ti torrà lo scender questa roccia.
> Poi si rivolse a quell' enfiata labbia,
>   E disse: Taci, maledetto lupo:
>   Consuma dentro te con la tua rabbia.
> Non è senza cagion l' andare al cupo: 10
>   Vuolsi nell' alto là dove Michele
>   Fe la vendetta del superbo strupo.
> Quali dal vento le gonfiate vele
>   Caggiono avvolte, poichè l' alber fiacca:
>   Tal cadde a terra la fiera crudele.
> Così scendemmo nella quarta lacca,

We should have expected—a few MSS. even give—*per*, as in Purg. xxv. 16, 'per l' andar che fosse ratto.' It may be a compressed way of saying, 'Let him have what power he may,' **abbia** doing duty, as it were, twice over.

  7 'Labia appellatur habilitas faciei apud Florentinos.' Benv.

  maledetto lupo. Cf. Purg. xx. 10.

  12 'È chiamato strupo, quasi violatore col suo superbo pensiero della divina potenza.' Bocc. Cf. Psalm lxxiii. (lxxii. Vulg.) 27.—**vendetta** may be followed by the genitive of either the offence or the offender.

  13 The position of the words shows that **dal vento** is intended to apply to both clauses; the wind both swells the sail and snaps the mast.

  14-16 The rhymes suggest a contrast with Purg. vii. 70 sqq.

of the woeful slope, which enwraps all the ill of the universe. Ah justice of God! who crowds all the new labours and pains that I saw? and wherefore does our sin so bring us low? As does the surge there over Charybdis, which breaks itself with that against which it dashes itself, so behoves it that here the folk dance. Here saw I folk more thick than elsewhere, both on one side and on the other,

> Pigliando più della dolente ripa,[a]
> Che il mal dell' universo tutto insacca.
> Ahi giustizia di Dio, tante chi stipa
> Nuove travaglie e pene, quante io viddi? 20
> E perchè nostra colpa sì ne scipa?
> Come fa l' onda là sovra Cariddi,
> Che si frange con quella in cui s' intoppa,
> Così convien che qui la gente riddi.
> Qui vid' io gente più che altrove troppa,
> E d' una parte e d' altra, con grand' urli,

[a] *Prendendo* Ald. W.

[17] **Pigliando.** So *prendere*, not uncommonly, e.g. Purg. i. 108, xxviii. 5. But nearly all the authority is for *pigliando* here: and the form of expression is exactly similar to that of Purg. xi. 109. If the rendering there given is correct, the meaning here must be 'hastening our pace over the slope.'

[22] Benvenuto quotes the famous 'Incidit in Scillam cupiens vitare Charybdim' (from the *Alexandreis* of Gualtier de Lille): and it is very probable that the line was in Dante's mind when he selected this image to introduce the description of the sinners who have avoided one form of sin to fall into another as deadly.

[25] **più che altrove troppa.** Cf. Purg. xx. 11.

[26] Those who have misused their possessions by undue eagerness to acquire or insufficient care to retain are here, as in Purgatory (xxii. 50), punished similarly. Dante's estimate of the harm done by prodigality would seem to be more severe than that of either Aristotle (Eth. iv. 1) or Aquinas, who both consider that the man who spends too freely

with loud howls rolling weights by push of breast. They
kept striking against each other, and then on the spot
each turned round, rolling back, crying: 'Why holdest?'
and 'Why squanderest?' Thus would they turn through
the foul circle, from every quarter to the opposite joust,
crying ever in their shameful measure. Then each would
turn round when he was come through his half-circle to the
other joust. And I, who had my heart as it were pierced
through, said: 'My Master, now show me what folk this is,
and if they all were clerks, these tonsured ones on our left
hand.' And he to me: 'Each and all were so bleared in

    Voltando pesi per forza di poppa:
Percotevansi incontro, e poscia pur li
    Si rivolgea ciascun, voltando a retro,
    Gridando: Perchè tieni, e: Perchè burli?   30
Così tornavan per lo cerchio tetro,
    Da ogni mano all' opposito punto,
    Gridandosi anche loro ontoso metro:
Poi si volgea ciascun, quando era giunto
    Per lo suo mezzo cerchio all' altra giostra.
    Ed io che avea lo cor quasi compunto,
Dissi: Maestro mio, or mi dimostra
    Che gente è questa, e se tutti fur cherci
    Questi chercuti alla sinistra nostra.
Ed egli a me: Tutti e quanti fur guerci   40

is nearer to the virtuous mean of liberality than he who is greedy of gain.
Probably, however, he felt strongly the mischief which unbridled luxury
had done to the society of his own time.

  " Each division occupies half the circle. When they meet, they
turn back and meet again at the other end of the diameter.

  " **tieni—burli**. Are these technical terms of any game?

their mind in the former life, that they made no spending with moderation. Clearly enough their voice bays it forth, when they come to the two points of the circle, where a contrary fault unmates them. These were clerks, who have no covering of hair on their head, and popes and cardinals, in whom avarice uses its mastery.' And I: 'Master, among these of this kind I ought surely to recognise some, who were defiled with these evils.' And he to me: 'Thou puttest a vain thought together; the unrecognising life,

> Sì della mente in la vita primaia,
> Che con misura nullo spendio ferci.
> Assai la voce lor chiaro l' abbaia,
> Quando vengono ai due punti del cerchio,
> Ove colpa contraria li dispaia.
> Questi fur cherci, che non han coperchio
> Piloso al capo, e Papi e Cardinali,
> In cui usa avarizia il suo soperchio.
> Ed io: Maestro, tra questi cotali
> Dovre' io ben riconoscere alcuni,   50
> Che furo immondi di cotesti mali.
> Ed egli a me: Vano pensiero aduni:
> La sconoscente vita, che i fe sozzi,

[46 sqq.] The avarice of the clergy is, of course, a favourite subject of reproach with Dante, e.g. xix. 3, 4, Par. xxvii. 55, etc.; but here there seems to be some confusion of ideas. From l. 46 it would appear that those who are tonsured, or shorn, were the clerics only; but in l. 57 and in Purg. xxii. 46 it seems to be implied that this mark was common to all those who are punished for avarice. Philalethes, indeed, thinks that l. 46 refers to tonsure only, and l. 57 to total absence of hair, and doubtless the clergy would fall rather into the class 'with closed fist'; but it is curious, if so, that Dante should not have guarded against misunderstanding.

[53] **sconoscente**: quia in vita nesciverunt uti temporalibus. Benv. But none of the early commentators seems to have been struck by this

that made them filthy, now makes them dim to every recognition. For ever will they come to the two shocks; these shall arise from the tomb with the fist shut, and these with the hair cut short. Ill-giving and ill-keeping have taken from them the world of beauty, and placed them in this scuffle; of what sort that is, I here use no fine words. Now canst thou, my son, see the short game of the goods which are entrusted to Fortune, for which the human race buffet each other. For all the gold that is beneath the moon and that ever was, of these wearied souls could never make one of them rest.'

> Ad ogni conoscenza or li fa bruni;
> In eterno verranno alli due cozzi;
>   Questi risurgeranno del sepulcro
>   Col pugno chiuso, e questi coi crin mozzi.
> Mal dare e mal tener lo mondo pulcro
>   Ha tolto loro, e posti a questa zuffa:
>   Qual ella sia, parole non ci appulcro.   60
> Or puoi, figliuol, veder la corta buffa
>   Dei ben, che son commessi alla Fortuna,
>   Perchè l' umana gente si rabbuffa.
> Chè tutto l' oro, ch' è sotto la luna,
>   E che già fu, di queste anime stanche [b]
>   Non poterebbe farne posar una.

[b] *O che* 2 *Ald. W.*

tremendous conception, which appears to be entirely Dante's own: the obliteration of all outward marks of individuality by persistence in a sordid disregard of the true use of wealth.

Notice the construction of this line, in which **loro** does duty first as a dative, then as an accusative.

farne. For *ne* pleonastic see Diez iii. 58. With this line cf. Conv. iv. Ode: 'Chè, quantunque collette, non possan quietar,' and chap. 11.

'Master,' said I to him, 'now tell me also; this Fortune, on which thou dost touch to me, what is she, that has the goods of the world so within her claws?' And he to me: 'O foolish creatures, how great ignorance is that which makes you trip! Now will I that thou swallow my opinion thereof.

> Maestro, diss' io lui, or mi di' anche:
> Questa Fortuna, di che tu mi tocche,
> Che è, che i ben del mondo ha sì tra branche?
> E quegli a me: O creature sciocche, 70
> Quanta ignoranza è quella che vi offende!
> Or vo' che tu mia sentenza ne imbocche:

[70] This outburst appears, say the more recent commentators, to be due to Dante's having used the disrespectful word **branche** in referring to Fortune. But this seems rather a poor conceit; and it is better to follow Bocc., who regards it as an apostrophe to mankind in general for their folly in supposing that Fortune is anything but a minister of God in the distribution of wealth. To place her on a level with the 'intelligences' that move the heavens of the planets would seem to be an original and daring conception of Dante's own. It looks almost as if, with a view of saving the theory of heavenly influences enunciated in Par. viii. 102, Conv. ii. 5, and elsewhere, he had enrolled 'Fortune,' who is practically much the same as the ἀνάγκη or πλανωμένη αἰτία of Timaeus xvii., among the heavenly motors, and assigned to her the special charge of the region below the sphere of the moon, and, as a consequence, of the distribution of worldly wealth. (Cf. Juvenal's Nos te, nos facimus, Fortuna, deam, caeloque locamus.) There is a hint of the doctrine in Conv. ii. 5: Altri furono, siccome Plato, uomo eccellentissimo, che puosono non solamente tante Intelligenze quanti sono li movimenti del cielo, ma eziandio quante sono le spezie delle cose ... siccome una spezie tutti gli uomini, *e un altra tutto l'oro, e un' altra tutte le larghezze* (*al.* le richezze, *al.* l' argento), e così di tutto; e vollero che siccome le intelligenze dei cieli sono generatrici di quelli, ciascuna del suo, così queste fossero generatrici dell' altre cose ... e chiamate Plato idee, che è tanto a dire quanto forme e nature universali. Li Gentili le chiamavano Dei e Dee. In Conv. iv. 11 he enlarges further on the distribution of wealth by fortune, but has not yet arrived at personifying (or rather deifying) her. See further Par. viii. 97 sqq. Boethius de Cons. Phil. Book ii. may also be referred to.

He, whose knowledge transcends all, made the heavens, and gave them their guide, so that every part shines on every part, distributing equally their light. Similarly to the splendours of the world He ordained a general minister and leader, to change in due season the vain goods from people to people and from one to another race, beyond the guarding of human wisdom. Wherefore one folk has the mastery and another dwindles, following the decree of her who is hidden, as the snake in grass. Your knowledge has

> Colui, lo cui saper tutto trascende,
>   Fece li cieli, e diè lor chi conduce,
>   Sì che ogni parte ad ogni parte splende,
> Distribuendo ugualmente la luce:
>   Similemente agli splendor mondani
>   Ordinò general ministra e duce,
> Che permutasse a tempo li ben vani
>   Di gente in gente e d' uno in altro sangue,   80
>   Oltre la difension dei senni umani:
> Perchè una gente impera, e l' altra langue,
>   Seguendo lo giudizio di costei,
>   Che è occulto, come in erba l' angue.
> Vostro saper non ha contrasto a lei;

---

[80] Here again he slightly modifies the doctrine of Conv. iv. 11; where riches, etc., are held to come in some cases from fortune aided by or aiding reason. For the doctrine here expressed, Dante is severely rated by his contemporary Cecco d' Ascoli, in the curious treatise called 'L'Acerba.' He says (Book ii. st. 3):

> In ciò peccasti, Fiorentin poeta,
> Ponendo chegli ben de la fortuna
> Necessitati sieno con lor meta.
> Non è fortuna che ragion non vinca;

and a good deal more to the same effect.

no means to withstand her; she foresees, judges, and
pursues her reign, as the other gods do theirs. Her shiftings
have no respite; necessity makes her to be swift; so quickly
comes he who follows up a change. This is she who is so
crucified by the very men who ought to give her praise,
giving her blame amiss, and an ill report. But she is in
bliss, and hears not that; with the other prime created
things in joy she rolls her sphere, and enjoys her, being
blessed.

> Questa provvede, giudica e persegue [c]
> Suo regno, come il loro gli altri Dei.
> Le sue permutazion non hanno triegue:
> Necessità la fa esser veloce,
> Si spesso vien chi vicenda consegue. 90
> Quest' è colei, ch' è tanto posta in croce
> Pur da color che le dovrian dar lode,
> Dandole biasmo a torto e mala voce.
> Ma ella s' è beata, e ciò non ode:
> Con l' altre prime creature lieta
> Volve sua spera, e beata si gode.

[c] *Elia 2 Ald. W.*

[87] **Dei**. Cf. Par. xxviii. 121.

[88–9] Cf. Boeth. ii. Pr. 1: Hi semper ejus mores sunt; ista natura,
Servavit circa te propriam potius in ipsa sui mutabilitate constantiam.

[91] So Lactantius Div. Inst. iii. 28: Non dissimili errore credunt esse
fortunam quasi deam quandam res humanas variis casibus illudentem
... Jam quicunque aliquos consolati sunt ob interitum amissio-
nemque carorum fortunae nomen acerrimis accusationibus prosciderunt.

[93] διὸ καὶ ἐγκαλεῖται τῇ τύχῃ, κ.τ.λ. Eth. iv. (1120 b).

[95] **prime creature**: used of angels in Purg. xxxi. 77.

[96] **spera**. The wheel of Fortune ('Rotam volubili orbe versamus,'
she says in Cons. Phil. ii. Pr. 2) becomes, in this conception of her, the
'sphere' which she governs.

'Now let us next descend to a greater pity. By this time every star is setting, which was rising when I set forth, and too long staying is forbidden.'

We cut off the circle to the other bank, past a fount which boils, and pours out through a trench which leads from it. The water was very far darker than perse; and we in company with the dingy waves entered downward by a strange road. It makes a marsh which has to name Styx, this sorry brook, when it has descended to the foot of the

> Or discendiamo omai a maggior pieta:
>   Già ogni stella cade, che saliva
>   Quando mi mossi, e il troppo star si vieta.
> Noi ricidemmo il cerchio all' altra riva   100
>   Sopra una fonte, che bolle e riversa
>   Per un fossato che da lei deriva.
> L' acqua era buia assai vie più che persa:
>   E noi, in compagnia dell' onde bige,
>   Entrammo giù per una via diversa.
> Una palude fa, che ha nome Stige,
>   Questo tristo ruscel, quando è disceso
>   Al piè delle maligne piaggie grige.

[97] I.e. to the worse torments of the inner Hell.

[98, 99] I.e. every star which was then between the horizon and the meridian has now passed its 'southing.' Dante does not appear to take account here of 'circumpolar' stars. As Virgil had started (ii. 141) in the evening, this would make the actual time just after midnight. Cf. the Sibyl's injunction: Nox ruit, Aenea, in Aen. vi. 539.

[103] **persa**: see v. 89.

[106] **Stige**. Whether Dante knew that the name Στύξ implied hatred, or, as Boccaccio puts it, *tristitia*, sullenness, we cannot say. It will be observed, however, that those who are immersed in it are such as lived without love for their neighbours or the world around them; treating the former with ill-temper, and the latter with sullen indifference.

malign gray slopes. And I, who was standing intent to gaze, saw folk miry in that slough, all naked and with mien of one tripped up. These were beating each other, not only with hand, but with the head and with the breast and with the feet, maiming each other with their teeth piecemeal. The good Master said: 'My son, now seest thou the souls of them whom wrath overcame; and, moreover, I will that thou believe for sure that under the water are folk which sigh, and make this water to bubble at the surface, as the eye tells thee wherever it roams. Fixed in the mud they say: "Grievous were we in the sweet air which is gladdened by the sun, carrying within us a sullen smoke; now are we

> Ed io, che di mirar mi stava inteso,
>   Vidi genti fangose in quel pantano,   110
>   Ignude tutte e con sembiante offeso.
> Questi si percotean, non pur con mano,
>   Ma con la testa, col petto e coi piedi,
>   Troncandosi coi denti a brano a brano.
> Lo buon Maestro disse: Figlio, or vedi
>   L' anime di color cui vinse l' ira:
>   Ed anche vo' che tu per certo credi,
> Che sotto l' acqua ha gente che sospira,
>   E fanno pullular quest' acqua al summo,
>   Come l' occhio ti dice, u' che s' aggira.   120
> Fitti nel limo dicon: Tristi fummo
>   Nell' aer dolce che dal sol s' allegra,
>   Portando dentro accidioso fummo:

[112] **si percotean**: not, I think, 'smote themselves.' Both here and in **troncandosi**, two lines lower, **si** must have the same force as in such words as *battersi*. They could not have struck *themselves* with breast and head; though in the next canto we shall find Filippo Argenti biting himself.

[123] It is hardly necessary, with Danielllo (followed by Philalethes), to confine this to the sullen or sluggish form of anger. He argues, and

grieving in the black slush." This chant they gurgle in their throat, for they cannot say it with speech complete.'

Thus we turned round a great arc of the foul pond, between the dry bank and the swamp, with our eyes turned on whoso is swallowing of the mire. We came to the foot of a tower at the last.

> Or ci attristiam nella belletta negra.
>   Quest' inno si gorgoglian nella strozza,
>   Che dir nol posson con parola integra.
> Così girammo della lorda pozza
>   Grand' arco tra la ripa secca e il mezzo,
>   Con gli occhi volti a chi del fango ingozza:
> Venimmo appiè d' una torre al dassezzo.^d   130

^d *al piè della ripa* 1.

indeed without some weight, if rather too dogmatically, against all his predecessors (who have understood the sin of 'Accidia' to be implied in the words), that in this division of Hell only sins of incontinence are punished; and that the 'Accidiosi' are to be found, if anywhere, among the 'sciaurati che mai non far vivi' of the outer Hell. But it is hardly likely that Dante would have relegated to that region one of the recognised deadly sins, or have used here a technical theological term like **accidioso** in a general sense; and, moreover, Hugh of St. Victor, according to Scartazzini, distinctly places *accidia* in a comparative list of vices, as the opposite extreme to *rixa*. Dante's contemporary, Cecco d' Ascoli, too, in his 'Acerba,' when giving a list of sins, couples *ira* with *accidia*. This sin, which is discussed S. T. ii. 2. Q. 35, it should be remembered, is a great deal more than merely sloth. The name *accidia* (from ἀκηδία, originally equivalent to the Latin *indolentia*) denotes, in the words of St. Thomas, a *tristitia de spirituali bono* (against which he quotes Ecclus. vi. 26, where the Vulgate has 'ne accedieris vinculis ejus'); and a *taedium operandi*, which he illustrates by the words of the Psalm: 'Their soul abhorred all manner of meat.' It is a form of *tristitia*; and the *tristis* is equal to the Νεμηρός of Aristotle; in our colloquial phrase 'a nuisance to himself and his neighbours.' *Malitia* and *rancor* are its offspring; and not only these, but also *evagatio circa illicita*. The man who has ceased to take delight in spiritual and intellectual goods seeks after carnal pleasures; and thus Daniello's objection appears to be met. (See also Purgatory, Appendix A.)

CANTO VIII

ARGUMENT

They cross the marsh of Styx in a ferry-boat, and as they go Dante sees the spirit of one Philip, a Florentine. On the further side is a city with walls of iron; entrance whereinto is hindered by the demons who guard it.

I SAY continuing that long before we were at the foot of the lofty tower, our eyes went up to the summit thereof, by

> Io dico seguitando, ch' assai prima
> Che noi fussimo al piè dell' alta torre,
> Gli occhi nostri n' andar suso alla cima,

[1] **Io dico seguitando.** Boccaccio tells us that the preceding cantos were written before Dante's exile; that some five or six years later, when things had somewhat quieted down, those who had claims against any of the exiles began to bring them against those who had succeeded to the confiscated property; that Dante's wife was advised that she might thus recover her dowry; and that she asked a friend, a nephew of Dante's, to search for certain necessary documents in a chest which had at the time of the exile been got to a place of security. In the search he came upon a good deal of MS., including these seven cantos. Being struck with them, he took them to Dino Frescobaldi, a well-known man of letters, who sent them to the Marquis Malaspina, with whom Dante then was, begging him to induce the poet to proceed with the work; and so the Divine Comedy was completed. Curiously enough, this story was told to Boccaccio by two persons, each of whom claimed to have been the finder; but it is of course not impossible that both may have been present. The strongest point against the story, as Boccaccio sees, is that it requires the prophecy of Ciacco vi. 64-72 to

reason of two flamelets which we saw set out there, and another from afar send back the sign, from so far that hardly could the eye take it up. And I turned round to the ocean of all wisdom; I said: 'What says this? and what does that other fire answer? and who are they that make it?' And he to me: 'Over the slimy waves now canst thou

> Per due fiammette che i' vedemmo porre,
>   E un' altra da lungi render cenno
>   Tanto, ch' a pena il potea l' occhio torre.
> Ed io mi volsi al mar di tutto il senno;
>   Dissi: Questo che dice? e che risponde
>   Quell' altro foco? e chi son quei che il fenno?
> Ed egli a me: Su per le sucide onde   10

have been written while some of the events foretold were still really in the future. He will not allow that the passage can have been inserted later; because Dino Frescobaldi had distributed copies at once, and some of these would still be in existence. But it will be observed that this prophecy is somewhat vague, or at any rate allows a large margin. It may well have been apparent to any student of public affairs in Florence during 1301 that the supremacy of the White Guelfs would not last out the three years which Ciacco gives as its outside limit. As a matter of fact, it lasted barely two years. Benvenuto tells the story briefly, as would appear, independently, and without the slightest doubt of its truth. Landino quotes it as from Boccaccio; but thinks that as it makes no difference to the interpretation of the text, it is of no particular interest. Daniello does not refer to it. Dr. Scartazzini seems to think it is merely an 'opinion' of Boccaccio, and informs us, on the authority of his own forthcoming volume (published in 1890), that it is erroneous. Most readers will probably be inclined to stretch their faith a little in favour of it.

⁴ **due**: probably, as Witte says, to indicate the number of the newcomers.

⁵ **altra**: *fiamma* says Bocc.; *torre* says Benv. The question is not very important; but on the whole it would rather seem to be the place where the beacon is lit than the beacon itself that gives the sign.

⁶ **chi son quei?** A question to which no answer ever appears, so far as regards the beacon on the hither side.

perceive that which is awaited, if the fog from the marsh hides it not from thee.' Never did bowstring drive an arrow from it to speed away through the air so quick as I saw a little bark come through the water toward us meanwhile, under the guidance of a single boatman, who was crying: 'So! art come, caitiff soul?' 'Phlegyas, Phlegyas, thou art crying in vain,' said my Lord, 'for this time; thou wilt have us no longer than but crossing the mud.' Like him who listens to a great deceit that has been wrought for him, and then is vexed thereat, such became Phlegyas in his

  Già puoi scorgere quello che s' aspetta,
   Se il fummo del pantan nol ti nasconde.
  Corda non pinse mai da sè saetta,
   Che sì corresse via per l' aere snella,
   Com' io vidi una nave piccioletta
  Venir per l' acqua verso noi in quella,
   Sotto il governo d' un sol galeoto,
   Che gridava: Or sei giunta, anima fella?
  Flegias, Flegias, tu gridi a voto,
   Disse lo mio signore, a questa volta: 20
   Più non ci avrai, che sol passando il loto.
  Quale colui, che grande inganno ascolta
   Che gli sia fatto, e poi sè ne rammarca,
   Fecesi Flegias nell' ira accolta.

[16] **in quella**: so xii. 22. Understand probably *ora*.

[19] Phlegyas seems to owe his position here, as Rhipeus (Par. xx. 68) his in heaven, to a couple of lines in the Aeneid. He is mentioned (Aen. vi. 618) in terms which make him the type of all those who infringe the laws which should govern the dealings of man with other men, or with God: 'Discite justitiam moniti, et non temnere divos.' Hence he is appropriately put to guard the access to the inner division of Hell, where sins of these classes are punished.

[21] You will only have us in your power while the passage lasts.

gathered wrath. My Leader went down into the boat, and then made me enter after him; and only when I was in, did it seem laden.

Soon as my Leader and I were in the vessel, the ancient prow goes on its way cutting more of the water than it is wont with others.

While we were speeding over the dead channel, one covered with mire put himself in front of me and said: 'Who art thou that comest before thy time?' And I to him: 'If I come, I do not stay. But who art thou that art become thus loathly?' He answered: 'Thou seest that I am one who lament.' And I to him: 'With lamenting and

> Lo duca mio discese nella barca,
>   E poi mi fece entrare appresso lui,
>   E sol quand' io fui dentro parve carca.
> Tosto che il duca ed io nel legno fui,
>   Secando se ne va l' antica prora
>   Dell' acqua più che non suol con altrui.   30
> Mentre noi corravam la morta gora,
>   Dinanzi mi si fece un pien di fango,
>   E disse: Chi sei tu che vieni anzi ora?
> Ed io a lui: S' io vegno, non rimango:
>   Ma tu chi sei, che sei sì fatto brutto?
>   Rispose: Vedi che son un che piango.
> Ed io a lui: Con piangere e con lutto,

As we shall presently learn, this is one Filippo de' Cavicciuli, of the clan of the Adimari (see Par. xvi. 115), known from his lavish display of wealth as Filippo Argenti. He is one of the personages in Boccaccio's story (already referred to: note vi. 52) in which Ciacco plays a part. Benvenuto here recites it in full.

It is curious to observe that Dante's demeanour towards the lost spirits whom he meets changes from this point. Except to some extent in the case of Brunetto Latini, there is, even where he shows respect,

with sorrow, accursed spirit, remain; for I know thee, all filthy though thou be.' Then he stretched forth both his hands to the vessel; wherefore the Master being aware pushed him away, saying: 'Be off there, with the other dogs.' Then girt he my neck with his arms, he kissed my face, and said: 'Disdainful soul, blessed is she that bare thee. This man was in the world a person full of arrogance; there is no goodness which adorns his memory; thus is his shade here furious. How many now hold themselves great kings up there who shall stand here like swine in the slush, leaving horrible dispraise of themselves!' And I: 'Master,

> Spirito maledetto, ti rimani:
> Ch' io ti conosco, ancor sia lordo tutto.
> Allora stese al legno ambo le mani: 40
> Perchè il Maestro accorto lo sospinse,
> Dicendo: Via costà con gli altri cani.
> Lo collo poi con le braccia mi cinse,
> Baciommi il volto, e disse: Alma sdegnosa,
> Benedetta colei che in te s' incinse
> Quei fu al mondo persona orgogliosa:
> Bontà non è che sua memoria fregi:
> Così s' è l' ombra sua qui furiosa.
> Quanti si tengon or lassù gran regi,
> Che qui staranno come porci in brago,   50
> Di sè lasciando orribili dispregi!

none of the sympathy which he has hitherto expressed; and here we find him behaving towards Filippo exactly as Filippo in life had behaved towards him and others. He would doubtless justify himself by Aristotle's description of the μεγαλόψυχος (Eth. iv. 3) as φανερομισσος, and οὐ κακολόγος εἰ μὴ δι᾽ ὕβριν.

⁵ **in te s' incinse.** So Dec. iii. 9: La donna ingravidò in due figliuoli maschi. Littré's explanation of *enceinte* from *in in ct*, as though = 'ungirt,' can hardly be correct.)

I should be very fain to see him stifled in this stew, before that we have issued from the lake.' And he to me: 'Before that the bank lets itself be seen by thee thou shalt be satisfied; of such a desire it is meet that thou have enjoyment.' A little thereafter I saw the miry folk make of him that rending, that I still praise God thereof and give Him thanks. They all began to cry: 'At Philip Argenti!' And the wrathful spirit from Florence turned upon himself with his own teeth.

There we left him, for I relate no more of him; but a woe smote me in the ears; wherefore I give my eye freedom to fix on the front. The good Master said: 'Now, my son,

> Ed io: Maestro, molto sarei vago
> Di vederlo attuffare in questa broda,
> Prima che noi uscissimo del lago.
> Ed egli a me: Avanti che la proda
> Ti si lasci veder, tu sarai sazio:
> Di tal disio converrà che tu goda.
> Dopo ciò poco vidi quello strazio
> Far di costui alle fangose genti,
> Che Dio ancor ne lodo e ne ringrazio. 60
> Tutti gridavano: A Filippo Argenti:
> E il Fiorentino spirito bizzarro
> In sè medesmo si volgea coi denti.
> Quivi il lasciammo, chè più non ne narro:
> Ma negli orecchi mi percosse un duolo,
> Perch' io avanti l' occhio intento sbarro:
> Lo buon Maestro disse: Omai, figliuolo,

vidi — far — alle: see Diez iii. 122, 123, and notes Purg. viii. 106 and xxii. 96.

bizzarro: so Villani viii. 39 speaks of the 'bizzarra salvatichezza' of the Donati.

is getting near the city which has Dis to name, with its burthened citizens, with its great array.' And I: 'Master, its minarets already I clearly discern there within the valley, scarlet as though they had come out of fire.' And he said to me: 'The eternal fire, which fires them inwardly, shows them ruddy as thou seest in this nether Hell.'

We came right into the deep moats which fence that disconsolate land; it seemed to me that the walls were

> S' appressa la città che ha nome Dite,
>   Coi gravi cittadin, col grande stuolo.
> Ed io: Maestro, già le sue meschite   70
>   Là entro certo nella valle cerno
>   Vermiglie, come se di foco uscite
> Fossero. Ed ei mi disse: Il foco eterno,
>   Ch' entro l' affoca, le dimostra rosse,
>   Come tu vedi in questo basso inferno.
> Noi pur giugnemmo dentro all' alte fosse,^a
>   Che vallan quella terra sconsolata :
>   Le mura mi parean che ferro fosse.

^a *Noi sing. Gg. : Ma pur Cass.*

⁶⁹ **gravi cittadini.** I have followed the usual interpretation, according to which the 'citizens' are the lost souls, heavy with the burthen of their sins; but there is a good deal to be said in favour of Ponta's suggestion which Bianchi quotes, that the citizens of the city of Hell are the devils, in which case **gravi** will mean 'odious' or 'fearful.' Whichever way we take it, there is no doubt an irony intended in this use of the word, which may be called the regular complimentary epithet of 'citizens.'

⁷⁰ **meschite:** the same word which we have made into *mosque*. This form is nearer to the Indian *musjid*.

⁷⁵ Notice **fosse** sing., following the number of the nearer noun. Diez iii. 277.—For the description generally cf. Aen. vi. 548 sqq. :

> subito et sub rupe sinistra
> Moenia lata videt, triplici circumdata muro,

iron. Not without first making a great circuit we came to a
place where the boatman cried loud to us, 'Go forth; here
is the entry.' I saw more than a thousand above the gates,
fallen from heaven, who angrily said: 'Who is this that
without death goes through the realm of the dead folk?'
And my sage Master made sign of wishing to speak with
them secretly. Then they put a close somewhat to their
great disdain and said: 'Come thou alone, and let this one
go his way, who has come so boldly through this realm; let
him return alone over his foolish road; let him try if he

> Non senza prima far grande aggirata,
>   Venimmo in parte, dove il nocchier, forte,   80
>   Uscite, ci gridò, qui è l' entrata.
> Io vidi più di mille in sulle porte
>   Da ciel piovuti, che stizzosamente [b]
>   Dicean: Chi è costui, che senza morte
> Va per lo regno della morta gente?
>   E il savio mio Maestro fece segno
>   Di voler lor parlar segretamente.
> Allor chiusero un poco il gran disdegno,
>   E disser: Vien tu solo, e quei sen vada,
>   Che sì ardito entrò per questo regno.   90
> Sol si ritorni per la folle strada:

[b] *Dal ciel* G5. 23; *Da' ciel* W.

Quae rapidus flammis ambit torrentibus amnis.
. . . .
Porta adversa ingens . . . .
Vis ut nulla virum, non ipsi exscindere bello
Caelicolae valeant; stat ferrea turris ad auras.

[*] Devils appear here for the first time; and here, as Witte points out, for the first time we find an attempt at resistance to the Divine decree, in virtue of which Dante is passing through.

knows it; for thou shalt remain here who hast escorted him through so dark a country.' Think, reader, if I was in discomfort at the sound of their accursed words; for I deemed that I never should return hither.

'O, dear my Leader, who more than seven times hast restored security to me, and drawn me from depth of danger which stood against me, leave me not,' I said, 'thus undone; and if to go further is denied to us, let us quickly find our tracks again together.' And that Lord who had led me there said to me: 'Fear not, for none can take from us our passage; by such an One is it granted. But await me here; and thy weary spirit comfort and feed with a good

> Provi se sa; chè tu qui rimarrai,
>   Che gli hai scorta sì buia contrada.
> Pensa, Lettor, se io mi sconfortai
>   Nel suon delle parole maledette:
>   Ch' io non credetti ritornarci mai.
> O caro duca mio, che più di sette
>   Volte m' hai sicurtà renduta, e tratto
>   D' alto periglio che incontra mi stette.
> Non mi lasciar, diss' io, così disfatto: 100
>   E se il passar più oltre c' è negato,
>   Ritroviam l' orme nostre insieme ratto.
> E quel signor, che lì m' avea menato,
>   Mi disse: Non temer, che il nostro passo
>   Non ci può torre alcun: da tal n' è dato.
> Ma qui m' attendi; e lo spirito lasso
>   Conforta e ciba di speranza buona,

---

* Observe that **mi** represents the dative in the first clause 'm' hai **renduta**' and the accusative in the second 'm' hai **tratto**'. Cf. for another 'Zeugma,' if so it may be called, vii. 59.

hope, for I will not desert thee in the world below.' Thus goes his way, and abandons me there my sweet father; and I remain in doubt, for *yes* and *no* hold contention in my head.

I could not hear what he held forth to them; but he had not stayed there with them long when each one vied in running back within. Those our adversaries shut the gates in front of my Lord, who remained without, and turned back to me with slow paces. He had his eyes earthward, and his brows shorn of all boldness, and was saying with sighs: 'Who has forbidden me the abodes of woe?' And to me he said: 'Thou, because I am wroth, be not cast down; for I will win the trial, whatever be rolled up within

> Ch' io non ti lascerò nel mondo basso.
> Così sen va, e quivi m' abbandona
>   Lo dolce padre, ed io rimango in forse;   110
>   Che il sì e il no nel capo mi tenzona.
> Udir non potei quel ch' a lor si porse:
>   Ma ei non stette là con essi guari,
>   Che ciascun dentro a prova si ricorse.
> Chiuser le porte quei nostri avversari
>   Nel petto al mio signor, che fuor rimase,
>   E rivolsesi a me con passi rari.
> Gli occhi alla terra, e le ciglia avea rase
>   D' ogni baldanza, e dicea nei sospiri:
>   Chi m' ha negate le dolenti case?   120
> Ed a me disse: Tu, perch' io m' adiri,
>   Non sbigottir, ch' io vincerò la prova,
>   Qual ch' alla difension dentro s' aggiri.

[11] **forse**: cf. xvii. 95. For this use (frequent in Dante) of an adverb as a subst. see Diez iii. 289.

[12] **aggiri**: probably with a suggestion of the various engines used in those days in the defence of a fortified place.

for their defence. This their overweening is not new, for they practised it once at a less secret gate, the which is still found without bolt. Over it thou sawest the dead writing; and already on this side of it is one descending the steep, passing through the circles without escort, such that by him will the earth be opened to us.'

> Questa lor tracotanza non è nuova,
>   Chè già l' usaro a men secreta porta,⁶
>   La qual senza serrame ancor si trova.
> Sopr' essa vedestù la scritta morta:
>   E già di qua da lei discende l' erta,
>   Passando per li cerchi senza scorta,
> Tal che per lui ne fia la terra aperta. 130

⁶ *a me in sec.* 134; *in me sec.* 2.

[125] I.e. at the main gate of Hell, when Christ descended, to 'preach to the spirits in prison' and to bring away the saints of the old dispensation.

CANTO IX

ARGUMENT

While they are staying outside the gate, the Furies appear on the tower, and threaten to bring the Gorgon Medusa. Virgil covers Dante's eyes. Presently there appears a heavenly messenger moving over the marsh, at whose command the gate opens, and they enter a place full of tombs, wherein lie the heretics.

THAT colour which cowardice painted me outwardly, seeing my Leader turn to retreat, the sooner restrained within him his unwonted hue. He stopped, intent as one who listens; for the eye could not bring him far through the black air and through the packed mist. 'Nay, it will behove us to

> QUEL color che viltà di fuor mi pinse,
> Veggendo il duca mio tornare in volta,
> Più tosto dentro il suo nuovo ristrinse.
> Attento si fermò com' uom che ascolta;
> Chè l' occhio nol potea menare a lunga
> Per l' aer nero e per la nebbia folta.
> Pure a noi converrà vincer la punga,

---

[1] I.e. seeing that Dante was alarmed, Virgil allowed his own countenance to recover its natural hue.

[7] The train of thought connecting these broken exclamations seems to be: 'In spite of this check we must win, unless we are deserted by the powers of heaven; and after the aid promised us that is scarcely possible; yet the delay is long.' As will be seen, the theme of the first part of this canto is *despair*; and these words of Virgil are obviously intended to lead up to it. Benvenuto, with reason, considers the

win the fight,' began he; 'unless . . . such aid was offered us; O how long it is to me ere another come hither!'

I saw clearly how he overlaid his beginning with the other that came after, which was words diverse from the first; but none the less his speech gave me fear, because I turned the curtailed word perchance to a worse purport than he held.

'Into this depth of the shell of sorrow does any ever descend from the first level which for penalty has only hope cut off?' This question I made. And he: 'Rarely comes

>   Cominciò ei: se non . . . tal ne s' offerse.
>   Oh quanto tarda a me ch' altri qui giunga!
>   Io vidi ben, sì com' ei ricoperse   10
>   Lo cominciar con l' altro che poi venne,
>   Che fur parole alle prime diverse.
>   Ma nondimen paura il suo dir dienne,
>   Perch' io traeva la parola tronca
>   Forse a peggior sentenza ch' ei non tenne.
>   In questo fondo della trista conca
>   Discende mai alcun del primo grado,
>   Che sol per pena ha la speranza cionca?
>   Questa question fec' io: e quei: Di rado

---

passage 'difficillima et intricatissima,' and bids us take it thus: '*pro a me* (sic) *conven* (sic) *vincer la pugna*, idest istam probam. Et debet legi voce alta ad modum irati, *se non*, debet legi voce submissa et debet suppleri: et si non poterimus vincere pugnam, *tal ne s' offers*, idest talis obtulit se nobis ad succursum, quod ejus auxilio bene intrabimus, et dimittit verbum suspensum. . . . Potes etiam ponere literam magis aperte ut dicas: *tal se n' offerse*,' etc. Boccaccio appears to take **se non** as unconnected and almost random words, but offers no general explanation.

[16] **conca.** The image is of course from the spiral shells, such as Tritons in pictures blow; which fairly represent the shape of Hell as Dante imagines it.

[18] Cf. iv. 42.

it to pass,' he answered me, 'that any of us makes the journey upon which I go. It is true that another time I was conjured down here by that cruel Erichtho, who would call the shades back to their bodies. A little while had my flesh been bare of me, when she made me enter within that wall, to draw thence a spirit of the circle of Judas. That is the lowest place and the darkest, and the farthest from the heaven which turns the whole. I know the way well; therefore assure thyself. This marsh that breathes

> Incontra, mi rispose, che di nui 20
> Faccia il cammino alcun per quale io vado.
> Ver' è ch' altra fiata quaggiù fui
> Congiurato da quella Eriton cruda,
> Che richiamava l' ombre ai corpi sui.
> Di poco era di me la carne nuda,
> Ch' ella mi fece entrar dentro a quel muro,
> Per trarne un spirto del cerchio di Giuda.
> Quell' è il più basso loco e il più oscuro,
> E il più lontan dal ciel che tutto gira:
> Ben so il cammin: però ti fa sicuro. 30
> Questa palude, che il gran puzzo spira,

*Erichtho was the witch employed by Sextus Pompey on the night before the battle of Pharsalia (Luc. Phars. vi.) to resuscitate one of his soldiers, that he might learn what was to be the issue of the campaign. Of her subsequent dealings with the shade of Virgil no record appears to remain; though we can hardly suppose with Benvenuto that it is simply an invention of Dante's for the present occasion. This would be quite unlike Dante's usual method; and it is far more probable that he found the germ of the story in some of the many legends about Virgil which were current in the middle ages. In Lucan's description there is no suggestion that another spirit was sent in order to fetch the one required; and with regard to this, it is expressly stated that 'primo pallentis hiatu Haeret adhuc Orci.' Moreover, at the time of the incantation narrated by Lucan, Virgil had still many years to live.

forth the great stench girds round the city of woe, where we cannot now enter without a quarrel.' And else he said, but I have it not in mind, seeing that my eye had drawn me wholly towards the high tower with the ruddy top, where in one moment had suddenly reared up three furies of hell the hue of blood, who had limbs and fashion of

> Cinge d' intorno la città dolente,
> U' non potemo entrare omai senz' ira.
> Ed altro disse, ma non l' ho a mente;
> Perocchè l' occhio m' avea tutto tratto
> Ver l' alta torre alla cima rovente,
> Dove in un punto furon dritte ratto
> Tre furie infernal di sangue tinte,
> Che membra femminili aveano ed atto;

[38] sqq. The allegory of all this passage seems to have perplexed the commentators a good deal. Some take it as referring to sensual pleasure, others to theological doubt, and so on. This uncertainty appears due chiefly to the fact that they set to work to expound Dante without referring to the sources whence he drew his system of theology. Dante himself seems from his expression in ll. 61-63 to have anticipated that this would be so. Yet the mystery does not seem very hard to unravel. A critical point in the journey has been reached, and for the first time we are brought into contact with beings over whom the mere recital of God's command has no power. These are resolved to use any means to hinder Dante's progress; that is, the advance of the soul towards true penitence. One of the most effectual means to this end is to call up the recollection of past sins (the Furies), and cause the soul to persist in sin (Bocc.) by urging to despair of God's mercy, indicated here by the Gorgon, who turns men to stone. 'Desperatio,' says St. Thomas S.T. ii. 2. Q. 20. A. 3, 'provenit ex hoc quod homo non sperat se bonitatem Dei participare'; and he quotes Isidore: 'Perpetrare flagitium aliquod mors est; sed desperare est descendere in infernum.' Again: 'Quod damnati non sperant . . . est pars damnationis eorum.' Further, he tells us that *desperatio* springs from *luxuria* and *acedia*; and in Q. 14. A. 2 he identifies it with the sin against the Holy Ghost, a sin which is committed by every one 'qui veritatem contemnit aut circa fratres malignus est, aut circa Deum ingratus.' This, as will be

women; and with greenest water-snakes were they girt;
small serpents and horned snakes had they for hair, wherewith their savage temples were bound. And he, who well
recognised the menials of the queen of the eternal wailing,
said to me: 'Look at the fierce Erinnyes. This is Megaera
on the left side; she who wails on the right is Alecto; Tisi-
phone is in the middle.' And with that he was silent.
With her claws each was rending her breast; they were
beating themselves with their palms, and were crying so
loud that I clung close to the Poet through dread. 'Let
Medusa come, so will we make him of enamel,' they all
began to cry, looking downward; 'ill did we fail to avenge

> E con idre verdissime eran cinte: 40
> Serpentelli e ceraste avean per crine,
> Onde le fiere tempie eran avvinte.
> E quei, che ben conobbe le meschine
> Della regina dell' eterno pianto:
> Guarda, mi disse, le feroci Erine.
> Questa è Megera dal sinistro canto:
> Quella, che piange dal destro, è Aletto:
> Tesifone è nel mezzo: e tacque a tanto.
> Con l' unghie si fendea ciascuna il petto;
> Batteansi a palme e gridavan sì alto, 50
> Ch' io mi strinsi al poeta per sospetto.
> Venga Medusa: sì 'l farem di smalto,
> Dicevan tutte riguardando in giuso:

seen, exactly summarises the classes of sinners within the fortress of
Dis; and the position of the Furies and the Gorgon is thus accounted
for. See also note Purg. viii. 19. The whole picture is suggested by
Aen. vi. 554.

52 It will be remembered that the visit of Ulysses to the shades was
brought to an end by fear 'lest Persephone should send me the head of
the Gorgon, terrible monster.' Od. λ 634.

upon Theseus his assault.' 'Turn thee round backwards, and keep thy face shut in; for if the Gorgon shows herself, and thou behold her, nought would there ever be of the return upwards.' Thus said the Master; and I myself turned me round, and he did not stay at my own hands, but shut me in with his as well. O ye who have your understandings sound, look at the teaching which is hidden under the veil of my strange verses.

And by this was coming over the turbid waves a clatter

<blockquote>
Mal non vengiammo in Teseo l' assalto.[a]
Volgiti indietro, e tien lo viso chiuso;
  Chè se il Gorgon si mostra, e tu il vedessi,
  Nulla sarebbe del tornar mai suso.
Così disse il Maestro; ed egli stessi
  Mi volse, e non si tenne alle mie mani,
  Che con le sue ancor non mi chiudessi.   60
O voi, che avete gl' intelletti sani,
  Mirate la dottrina che s' asconde
  Sotto il velame degli versi strani.
E già venìa su per le torbid' onde
</blockquote>

[a] *Ma non* Cass.; *vegliamo* 23.

54 **mal**, as in xii. 66, Purg. iv. 72, Par. xix. 141. 'Istud est vulgare tuscum non lombardum,' says Benvenuto. The descent of Theseus and Pirithous with the intention of carrying off Proserpine is frequently alluded to by classical authors, and various versions of it seem to have prevailed. Virgil of course in a famous line tells us that Theseus will never be set free; but Dante seems to have followed Apollodorus, according to whom he remained in Hades till set free by Hercules.

59, 60 Lit. 'did not stay at my hands, so as not to close.' We have in this turn of phrase the origin of *non che* in the sense of 'much more,' e.g. Purg. xxxii. 114.

63 Human reason can resist for a while the temptation to despair by refusing to contemplate it.

of a sound full of affright, through which both the banks trembled; not otherwise in fashion than as of a wind impetuous by reason of the heats that it encounters; which smites the wood, and without any holding back shivers the branches, beats them down, and bears them abroad; dust-clad in front it goes proudly, and makes the beasts and the shepherds fly. He set my eyes free, and said: 'Now direct the nerve of thy sight over that ancient scum, by the direction where that smoke is most bitter.' As the frogs before

> Un fracasso d' un suon pien di spavento,
>   Per cui tremavano ambo e due le sponde;
> Non altrimenti fatto che d' un vento
>   Impetuoso per gli avversi ardori,
>   Che fier la selva, e senza alcun rattento
> Li rami schianta, abbatte, e porta fuori;[b]   70
>   Dinanzi polveroso va superbo,
>   E fa fuggir le fiere e li pastori.
> Gli occhi mi sciolse, e disse: Or drizza il nerbo
>   Del viso su per quella schiuma antica,
>   Per indi ove quel fummo è più acerbo.[c]

[b] *porta i fiori* Ald.; *p. fiori* W.
[c] *Per indi unde* Cass. 2: *Proz ide ove* 5.

avversi ardori: probably with allusion to the fact of which Aristotle, though his phraseology is obscure, seems to have been aware, that wind, being caused by the air rushing to fill up a heated space, blows from the colder to the hotter region. See Meteor. ii. 4, 5: iii. 1.

The reading **fuori** has the great preponderance of authority, and is perfectly satisfactory. No one who has watched the effect of a storm on a forest would hesitate to accept the whirling away of branches as a feature. *Flowers*, moreover, do not as a rule grow on forest-trees, in Europe at all events; and without going so far as Bianchi, who says of the supporters of the reading *fiori*, 'Dio perdoni loro il mal gusto,' we may safely set it aside. (See Moore, Textual Criticism.

their foe the snake all melt away through the water, until each is huddled on the dry ground, thus saw I more than a thousand ruined souls fly in front of one who at a foot's-pace was passing Styx with his soles dry. From his face he was removing that thick air, bringing his left hand often in

> Come le rane innanzi alla nimica
> > Biscia per l' acqua si dileguan tutte,
> > Fin che alla terra ciascuna s' abbica;
> Vid' io più di mille anime distrutte
> > Fuggir cosi dinanzi ad un, che al passo   80
> > Passava Stige colle piante asciutte.
> Dal volto rimovea quell' aer grasso,
> > Menando la sinistra innanzi spesso;

[76] The image of the frogs is appropriate to the spirits lying in the marsh.

[80] There is a good deal of difference in the opinions of commentators as to the personage here introduced. Boccaccio, indeed, takes the simple, and one would say obvious view that he is an angel; but P. di Dante and Benvenuto seem to treat it as a matter of course that Mercury is intended (and have a good deal to say about the power of eloquence!); Daniello thinks that it is an angel in the form of Mercury. Finally the late Duke of Sermoneta wrote at some length to prove that the messenger was no other than Aeneas. Any heathen, whether god or man, would seem, as Lubin points out, to be excluded by the words **del ciel messo** (though it must be said that the reading *dal ciel*, which might mean '*by* heaven,' has some authority), while the similarity of l. 87 to Purg. ii. 28, 29 allows hardly any doubt that a being of the same kind is intended in both places. At the same time, some part of the passage is evidently suggested by the opening lines of Stat. Theb. ii., where the descent of Mercury is described, which may account for Benvenuto's theory.

> > Undique pigrae
> > Ire vetant nubes, et turbidus implicat aer.
> > Nec Zephyri rapuere gradum; sed foeda silentis
> > Aura poli. Styx inde novem circumflua campis,
> > Hinc objecta vias torrentum incendia eludunt.

front; and only with that toil he seemed weary. Well perceived I that he was sent from heaven; and I turned to the Master, and he made a sign that I should stand still, and bow myself to that one. Ah, how full of disdain appeared he to me! He reached the gate, and with a wand he opened it, for no bar was there. 'O ye chased from heaven, folk despised,' he began, upon the horrible threshold, 'whence does this overweening make its abode in you? Wherefore kick ye at that will whose end can never be cut short, and which many times has increased woe upon you? What boots it to make head against the fates? Your Cerberus, if ye well call to mind, bears yet his chin and

> E sol di quell' angoscia parea lasso.
> Ben m' accors' io ch' egli era del ciel messo,
>   E volsimi al Maestro: ed ei fe segno,
>   Ch' io stessi cheto, ed inchinassi ad esso.
> Ahi quanto mi parea pien di disdegno!
>   Venne alla porta, e con una verghetta
>   L' aperse, che non ebbe alcun ritegno. 90
> O cacciati del ciel, gente dispetta,
>   Cominciò egli in su l' orribil soglia,
>   Ond' esta oltracotanza in voi s' alletta?
> Perchè ricalcitrate a quella voglia,
>   A cui non puote il fin mai esser mozzo,
>   E che più volte v' ha cresciuta doglia?
> Che giova nelle fata dar di cozzo?
>   Cerbero vostro, se ben vi ricorda,
>   Ne porta ancor pelato il mento e il gozzo.

⁹⁷ **dar di cozzo.** This curious construction, frequent in Dante, seems to have been overlooked by Diez. The force of *di* is intermediate apparently between partitive and instrumental. For other examples see note, Purg. xvi. 11.

^{98,99} Hercules descended into the infernal regions at the bidding of

his throat peeled therefrom.' Then he turned back to the filthy road, and said no word to us, but made semblance of one whom a care constrains and pricks other than of the man who is before him. And we moved our feet to the land, secure after the holy words.

We entered in there without any conflict; and I, who had a desire to behold the condition which such a fortress enlocks, so soon as I was within, send my eye around; and I see on every hand a great champaign filled with woe and with torment of sin. As at Arles, where the Rhone makes

> Poi si rivolse per la strada lorda, 100
>   E non fe motto a noi: ma fe sembiante
>   D' uomo, cui altra cura stringa e morda,
> Che quella di colui che gli è davante.
>   E noi movemmo i piedi in ver la terra,
>   Sicuri appresso le parole sante.
> Dentro v' entrammo senza alcuna guerra:
>   Ed io, ch' avea di riguardar disio
>   La condizion che tal fortezza serra,
> Com' io fui dentro, l' occhio intorno invio;
>   E veggio ad ogni man grande campagna 110
>   Piena di duolo e di tormento rio.
> Sì come ad Arli, ove Rodano stagna,

Eurystheus to bring up Cerberus, as his last 'labour' (Odyssey Λ 623). On the same occasion he released Theseus, or, according to one version, Pirithous. See l. 54. The words of Apollodorus are: κρατῶν ἐκ τοῦ τραχήλου καὶ ἄγχων τὸ θηρίον ἔπεισε. Just before this he has met Meleager and *Medusa*, and when about to draw his sword on the latter, has been told by Hermes that she is an empty shade. (Cf. Aen. vi. 290-294.)

108 I have taken **fortezza** in the generally accepted meaning, as in xviii. 14; but it will not give a bad sense if we take it, as in xxxiv. 21, to mean 'fortitude'; 'that which was so strongly defended against our entrance.'

112, 113 Every traveller on the line to Marseilles knows the ancient

a swamp, as at Pola, hard by the Quarnero which shuts Italy in and bathes its confines, the sepulchres make all the place uneven, so did they there on every side, save that there the fashion was harsher; for among the tombs flames were scattered, by the which they were so wholly heated that no craft soever demands iron more so. All their lids were ajar, and forth of them issued lamentations so grievous, that they were well seen to come from wretches and overthrown. And I: 'Master, who are these folk that, buried within these chests, make themselves perceived with their woeful sighs?' And he to me: 'Here are the heresiarchs

> Sì com' a Pola presso del Quarnaro,
> Che Italia chiude e suoi termini bagna,
> Fanno i sepolcri tutto il loco varo:
> Così facevan quivi d' ogni parte,
> Salvo che il modo v' era più amaro;
> Chè tra gli avelli fiamme erano sparte,
> Per le quali eran sì del tutto accesi,
> Che ferro più non chiede verun' arte.
> Tutti gli lor coperchi eran sospesi,
> E fuor n' uscivan sì duri lamenti,
> Che ben parean di miseri e d' offesi.
> Ed io: Maestro, quai son quelle genti,
> Che seppellite dentro da quell' arche
> Sì fan sentir con gli sospir dolenti?
> Ed egli a me: Qui son gli eresiarche

cemetery or Aliscamps (*Elysios campos*) at Arles, with its great sarcophagus tombs, close to which the railway now passes. The legend of the time, of which Boccaccio—Benvenuto following him—speaks with some scepticism, was that they contained the bodies of those who had fallen in a great battle between Christians and Saracens; but they are not improbably older. The tombs at Pola in Istria are less well known. **Quarnaro**: the gulf separating Istria from Dalmatia; no longer the frontier of Italy.

with their followers of every sect, and much more than thou deemest are the tombs charged. Like with like is here buried, and the monuments are hotter and less hot.'

And after he had turned to the right hand, we passed between the tortures and the high battlements.

> Coi lor seguaci d' ogni setta, e molto
> Più che non credi, son le tombe carche.
> Simile qui con simile è sepolto, 130
> E i monimenti son più, e men caldi.
> E poi ch' alla man destra si fu volto,
> Passammo tra i martiri e gli alti spaldi.^d

^d *altri* Gg. (orig.) Cass. 1234.

[130] Benv. holds that each sect has one tomb and no more to hold all its adherents, but this hardly agrees with the description at the beginning of the next canto, where it seems to be implied that the 'Epicureans' alone fill a considerable space.

[132] The general direction of the route throughout is always *with* the sun. This would mean in Hell, a turn towards the left whenever a new circle is reached. The reason of the exception in this case is not very clear. It is merely a digression from the regular line, as we see at the end of the next canto; and possibly may have some allusion to the heretic leaving the direct rule of faith. (See note, xvii. 32.)

CANTO X

ARGUMENT

They pass among the tombs where the souls of those lie who had denied the life to come. Dante talks with Farinata, who foretells his exile in dark words; and with Cavalcanti the elder.

Now along a hidden path between the wall of the land and the torments my Master goes his way, and I behind his shoulders. 'O highest virtue that through the sinful circles dost turn me,' I began, 'at thy will speak to me, and give me satisfaction to my desires. The folk that lies among the tombs, could they be seen? already all the covers are lifted, and none keeps guard.' And he to me: 'All will be locked,

> ORA sen va per un secreto calle
>   Tra il muro della terra e li martiri
>   Lo mio Maestro, ed io dopo le spalle.
> O virtù somma, che per gli empi giri
>   Mi volvi, cominciai, com' a te piace
>   Parlami, e satisfammi ai miei desiri.
> La gente, che per li sepolcri giace,
>   Potrebbesi veder? già son levati
>   Tutti i coperchi, e nessun guardia face.
> Ed egli a me: Tutti saran serrati,   10

---

² **terra**: the 'city of Dis,' within which they now are, is regarded as a separate territory from that outside the wall.

when from Jehoshaphat they shall return hither with the bodies which they have left above. In this part have their burial-place with Epicurus all his followers, who make the soul dead with the body. Wherefore to the demand that thou makest to me shalt thou shortly have satisfaction within this place, and also to the desire which thou speakest not to me.' And I : 'Good Leader, I do not keep concealed from

> Quando di Josaffàt qui torneranno
> Coi corpi che lassù hanno lasciati.
> Suo cimitero da questa parte hanno
> Con Epicuro tutti i suoi seguaci,
> Che l' anima col corpo morta fanno.
> Però alla dimanda che mi faci
> Quinc' entro satisfatto sarai tosto,
> Ed al disio ancor che tu mi taci.
> Ed io : Buon Duca, non tegno riposto

[11] The 'valley of Jehoshaphat' near Jerusalem is the traditional scene appointed for the last judgement, on the authority of Joel iii. 2, 12. See S. T. Suppl. Q. 84. A. 4 ; a curious and characteristic piece of argument to show that Joel's words may be and are to be taken literally of an actual spot. (Jehoshaphat = ' the Lord is judge.')

[15] 'Dico, che intra tutte le bestialitadi quella è stoltissima vilissima e dannosissima, che crede dopo questa vita altra vita non essere.' Conv. ii. 9. Since writing that passage Dante would seem to have extended his study of Epicurus, for he makes no reference to him there ; and later on (ib. iv. 22), when referring to his tenets, he makes no mention of this particular dogma. The use of the word *bestialitadi* should be noticed, as serving to justify the placing of heretics within the city of Dis. Cf. xi. 83.

[18] Dante does not indicate of what nature the desire was of which he did not speak. Possibly, as Benv. seems to think, the allusion may be to the wish which he has expressed vi. 79 to see some of the more famous men of his city. It will be found that his unspoken wishes are constantly divined by Virgil and Beatrice ; e.g. xxiii. 21.

[19-21] Dante appears to regard Virgil's last words as a reproach, and defends himself by reference to Virgil's own admonitions to be brief. No

thee my heart, save in order to say little; and thou hast not now only disposed me to this.'

'O Tuscan, that alive through the city of the fire goest thy way thus speaking in so honourable wise, may it please thee to halt in this place. Thy manner of speech makes thee manifest as a native of that renowned fatherland to which I was haply too harmful.' Suddenly this sound issued from one of the arks, wherefore I drew in fear a little more to my Leader's side. And he said to me: "Turn thee; what doest

  A te mio cor, se non per dicer poco;   20
  E tu m' hai non pur mo a ciò disposto.
O Tosco, che per la città del foco
  Vivo ten vai, così parlando onesto,
  Piacciati di restare in questo loco.
La tua loquela ti fa manifesto
  Di quella nobil patria natio,
  Alla qual forse fui troppo molesto.[a]
Subitamente questo suono uscìo
  D' una dell' arche: però m' accostai,
  Temendo, un poco più al duca mio.   30
Ed ei mi disse: Volgiti: che fai?

[a] *forse fu' io* Gg.; *forsi fui* 2; *f. io fui* W.

instance of these has yet occurred (for in iii. 79, to which Scartazzini refers, there is nothing to show that Dante's fears were warranted), but we shall find such cases: e.g. Purg. xiii. 78. It is worth noticing that what may be called the relations between Dante and Virgil are much less easy during this part of their journey than they afterwards become. Dante is constantly in fear of Virgil's reproof, which he occasionally feels; in some cases, as xxx. 131, pretty severely.

[a] Dante is several times addressed as 'Tosco,' but usually by persons belonging to other parts. In this case, some think that his use of the word **mo** (for *modo*) betrayed him here. Virgil, however, elsewhere uses the same word, so it would not seem to be specially Tuscan. It probably is merely through his general intonation that he is detected, as xxiii. 91, or Purg. xvi. 137.

thou? See there Farinata who has reared himself; all from the waist upwards wilt thou see him.' I had already fixed my gaze on his; and he was erecting himself with his breast and with his front, as though he had Hell in great despite. And the hands of my Leader bold and ready urged me between the sepulchres to him, saying: 'Let thy words be ordered.' As soon as I was at the foot of his tomb he gazed at me a little, and then as though in disdain asked me:

> Vedi là Farinata che s' è dritto:
> Dalla cintola in su tutto il vedrai.
> I' avea già il mio viso nel suo fitto;
> Ed ei s' ergea col petto e colla fronte,
> Come avesse lo inferno in gran dispitto:
> E l' animose man del duca e pronte
> Mi pinser tra le sepolture a lui,
> Dicendo: Le parole tue sien conte.
> Com' io al piè della sua tomba fui,
> Guardommi un poco, e poi quasi sdegnoso

---

[32] Farinata degli Uberti was, at the time of Dante's birth, a man of very great influence among the Florentine Ghibelines ('capo di parte in Firenze e quasi in tutta Toscana,' says Boccaccio). After the battle of Montaperti (Vill. vi. 78) in 1260, between the Guelfs and the banished Ghibelines, aided by a detachment of Manfred's Germans under Count Giordano, in which the latter gained a complete success, the victors marched upon Florence. At a council held at Empoli, Giordano suggested that the city should be completely razed, but Farinata refused to hear of this, and declared that if he was left alone, he would resist the proposal, sword in hand, as long as life remained in him (Vill. ib. 81). The other prudently gave in, and the city was saved.

[39] **conte**: 'cioè composte e ordinate,' Bocc.; 'familiariter clare,' Benv.; 'klar, deutlich,' Blanc. The meanings of the word are various, and seem to comprise nearly everything that can be expressed by either *cognitus* or *comptus*. See Glossary, and note to Purg. ii. 56. Here it would appear that Virgil is cautioning Dante to address the old Florentine hero with due heed to his words.

'Who were thy forefathers?' I, who was desirous to obey, concealed it not from him, but opened it all to him; wherefore he lifted up his brows a little; then he said: 'Fiercely were they adverse to me and to my forerunners and to my party, so that at two times I scattered them.' 'If they were driven out, they returned from every quarter,' I answered him, 'both the one and the other time; but your side have not well learned that art.'—Then arose to sight a shade, uncovered, alongside of this one, as far as the chin; I think

> Mi dimandò: Chi fur li maggior tui?
> Io, ch' era d' ubbidir desideroso,
>   Non gliel celai, ma tutti gliel' apersi:
>   Ond' ei levò le ciglia un poco in soso;
> Poi disse: Fieramente furo avversi
>   A me ed ai miei primi ed a mia parte,
>   Sì che per due fiate gli dispersi.
> S' ei fur cacciati, ei tornar d' ogni parte,
>   Rispos' io lui, l' una e l' altra fiata;   50
>   Ma i vostri non appreser ben quell' arte.
> Allor surse alla vista scoperchiata
>   Un' ombra lungo questa infino al mento:

[48] First in 1248, in the days of Frederick II.: shortly before whose death in 1250 the Guelfs regained the upper hand (Vill. vi. 33, 38). The second time was after the battle of Montaperti already mentioned. This time the Ghibelines had a longer turn of power, for they were not expelled till Martinmas in 1266; mainly as a result of Manfred's defeat by Charles of Anjou in the previous year. See the most graphic account given by Villani, vii. 14, 15.

[51] Cf. the closing words of Villani, vii. 15: e parve che fosse giudicio di Dio, che mai poi non tornarono in istato. It must not be forgotten that Dante was a Guelf by birth, and at this time (1300) an avowed member of the party, though leaning to the 'White' side, which afterwards became associated in exile with the Ghibelines.

[52] This is Cavalcante, father of Dante's friend Guido de' Cavalcanti. Guido had married Farinata's daughter, during a short effort that was

that it had lifted itself on its knees. It looked all around me, as though it had an impulse to see if any other was with me. But after that his suspicion was wholly extinguished, weeping he said: 'If through this blind prison thou goest for loftiness of wit, where is my son? why is he not with thee?' And I to him: 'I go not of my own self; he who is waiting there, brings me through here, whom haply your Guido had in disdain.' His words and the fashion of his punishment had already read me the name of this one: therefore was my answer thus full. Suddenly rearing up he cried: 'How saidst thou he *had*? lives he not still? strikes

> Credo che s' era in ginocchie levata.
> D' intorno mi guardò, come talento
>   Avesse di veder s' altri era meco;
>   Ma poi che il suspicar fu tutto spento,
> Piangendo disse: Se per questo cieco
>   Carcere vai per altezza d' ingegno,
>   Mio figlio ov' è, e perchè non è teco?   60
> Ed io a lui: Da me stesso non vegno.
>   Colui, che attende là, per qui mi mena,
>   Forse cui Guido vostro ebbe a disdegno.
> Le sue parole e il modo della pena
>   M' avevan di costui già letto il nome:
>   Però fu la risposta così piena.
> Di subito drizzato gridò: Come
>   Dicesti: egli ebbe? non viv' egli ancora?

^b *detto* Cant. 14: *ditto* 2.

---

made to reconcile the two parties by means of such domestic alliances (Vill. l. c.). Judging by the temper which Farinata displays here ll. 73-75 we can hardly be surprised that little came of it.

   ^a **per altezza d' ingegno**; cf. ii. 7.

   ^b 'Perciocchè la filosofia gli pareva, siccome ella è, da più che la poesia, ebbe a sdegno Virgilio e gli altri poeti.' Bocc.

not the sweet light upon his eyes?' When he was aware of some delay which I made before my answer, he fell backward, and appeared no more outside.—But that other high-souled one, at whose order I had halted, changed not visage, nor moved neck, nor bent his side. 'And if,' said he, continuing the former speech, 'they have ill learned that art, that torments me more than this couch. But not fifty times shall be rekindled the face of the dame who rules here, that thou shalt know how great the weight of that art is. And, so mayest thou yet return to the sweet world, tell me wherefore

  Non fiere gli occhi suoi lo dolce lome?
Quando s' accorse d' alcuna dimora   70
  Ch' io faceva dinanzi alla risposta,
  Supin ricadde, e più non parve fuora.
Ma quell' altro magnanimo, a cui posta
  Restato m' era, non mutò aspetto,
  Nè mosse collo, nè piegò sua costa.
E se, continuando al primo detto,
  S' egli han quell' arte, disse, male appresa,
  Ciò mi tormenta più che questo letto.
Ma non cinquanta volte fia raccesa
  La faccia della donna che qui regge,   80
  Che tu saprai quanto quell' arte pesa.
E se tu mai nel dolce mondo regge,

---

[79] Fifty moons from April 1300 bring us to the spring of 1304: at which time the banished White Guelfs and Ghibelines were engaged in endeavouring, with the aid of the new Pope, Benedict XI., to procure a reversal of the decrees in force against them. In June these efforts finally failed, and in July a part of the exiles attempted to return by force, but were beaten. Vill. viii. 69, 72.

[80] **la donna**: not, of course, Proserpine, but Hecate 'caeloque Ereboque potens'; identified with Luna by mythology.

[82] **regge** *vide = riedi*.

that people is so pitiless against mine in its every law?' Wherefore I to him: 'The slaughter and the great example which made the Arbia dyed in red, caused such prayer to be made in our temple.'

After he had with a sigh shaken his head, 'Thereat was I not alone,' he said, 'nor certes without cause should I have set out with the others; but I alone was, in the place where leave was given by every man to take Florence away,

> Dimmi, perchè quel popolo è sì empio
> Incontro ai miei in ciascuna sua legge?
> Ond' io a lui: Lo strazio e il grande scempio,
> Che fece l' Arbia colorata in rosso,
> Tale orazion fa far nel nostro tempio.
> Poi ch' ebbe sospirando il capo scosso,
> A ciò non fui io sol, disse, nè certo
> Senza cagion con gli altri sarei mosso: 90
> Ma fu' io sol colà, dove sofferto
> Fu per ciascun di torre via Fiorenza,

[84] The Uberti were always excepted in any decree made at Florence in favour of the banished Ghibelines.

[85] The battle of Montaperti already mentioned. Benvenuto says that 4000 men were slain there. He reads, curiously enough, *lo strazio grande e scempio*: explaining 'idest fatuum et immane facinus,' as though **scempio** had here the same meaning as in Par. xvii. 62. A good and clear account of the battle and the events which led to it may be found in Witte's note.

[86] **colorata in**: the use of *in* is curious; but the English 'painted in red' is similar. See Diez iii. 158.

[87] Benvenuto says that councils were held at Florence in a chapel adjoining the palace of the Priors, which had once belonged to the Uberti, and in which they were buried; hence the special force of **tempio**: but the Florentine commentators do not seem to know anything of this. Landino says that **tempio** is only used as a sequence to **orazione**. Bianchi, however, mentions a story that a special petition for the benefit of the Uberti was actually added to the litanies.

the one who defended her with open face.' 'Pray you, so may your seed ever have rest,' I besought him, 'loose for me that knot which here has entwined my opinion. It appears that ye see, if I hear aright, beforehand that which time is bringing with it, but in the present ye hold another fashion.' 'We see, like him who has a bad light,' said he, 'the things which are afar from us; so much yet the supreme Leader beams upon us. When they draw near, or exist, vain is all our understanding; and if another make not his way to us, nought know we of your human state. Where-

>Colui che la difesi a viso aperto.
>Deh, se riposi mai vostra semenza,
>   Prega' io lui, solvetemi quel nodo,
>   Che qui ha inviluppata mia sentenza.
>Ei par che voi veggiate, se ben odo,
>   Dinanzi quel che il tempo seco adduce,
>   E nel presente tenete altro modo.
>Noi veggiam, come quei ch' ha mala luce,   100
>   Le cose, disse, che ne son lontano;
>   Cotanto ancor ne splende il sommo Duce:
>Quando s' appressano, o son, tutto è vano
>   Nostro intelletto: e s' altri non ci apporta,
>   Nulla sapem di vostro stato umano.

nel ci ap. W.

⁹⁴ **se riposi**: so **se regge** in l. 82, and many other instances. It is the *se* with subj. of Latin.

⁹⁵ It has appeared from Cavalcante's remark, l. 68, that he is not aware of what is actually taking place on earth; while at the same time Ciacco and Farinata have been able to foretell the future.

¹⁰⁴ **apporta**: for the intrans. form (from *portus* — cf. *approdare*) see Dict. Cruse. Witte, as if it were from *portio*, with no necessity, and not much authority, reads *ci sa*.

fore thou canst understand that wholly dead will our knowledge be from that moment when the door of the future shall be shut.' Then, as though in compunction for my fault, I said: 'Now you will tell then to that one who fell that his son is yet joined to the living. And if I before was dumb at my answer, make him to know that I did it because I was already in thought, under the error from which you have set me free.'

And already my Master was calling me back; wherefore I besought the spirit in more haste that he would tell me who was stationed with him. He said to me: 'Here with more than a thousand I lie; within here is the second

> Però comprender puoi, che tutta morta
>   Fia nostra conoscenza da quel punto
>   Che del futuro fia chiusa la porta.
> Allor, come di mia colpa compunto,
>   Dissi: Or direte dunque a quel caduto   110
>   Che il suo nato è coi vivi ancor congiunto.
> E s' io fui innanzi alla risposta muto,
>   Fat' ei saper che il fei, perchè pensava
>   Già nell' error che m' avete soluto.
> E già il Maestro mio mi richiamava:
>   Perch' io pregai lo spirto più avaccio
>   Che mi dicesse chi con lui si stava.
> Dissemi: Qui con più di mille giaccio:
>   Qua entro è lo secondo Federico,

---

[108] **After the judgement**, when time will no longer exist, and there will consequently be no future. The idea that the damned, while they can to some extent foresee the future, have no knowledge of what is actually taking place on earth, appears to be an invention of Dante's own; or at any rate, not due to Aquinas.

[119] **Qua entro**: probably with an allusion to the epitaph on Frederick's tomb:—

Frederick, and the Cardinal; and of the others I say nought.'
Then he hid himself; and toward the ancient poet I turned
my steps, thinking over again on that speech which had
seemed hostile to me. He passed on, and then going thus
he said to me: 'Why art thou so perplexed?' and I gave
him satisfaction to his question. 'Let thy mind keep what
thou hast heard against thyself,' that Sage commanded me,
'and now give heed here'— and he held up his finger.
'When thou shalt be in presence of her sweet ray, whose

>   E il Cardinale, e degli altri mi taccio.   120
> Indi s' ascose: ed io in ver l' antico
>   Poeta volsi i passi, ripensando
>   A quel parlar che mi parea nimico.
> Egli si mosse; e poi così andando,
>   Mi disse: Perchè sei tu sì smarrito?
>   Ed io li satisfeci al suo dimando.
> La mente tua conservi quel ch' udito
>   Hai contra te, mi comandò quel Saggio,
>   Ed ora attendi qui: e drizzò il dito.
> Quando sarai dinanzi al dolce raggio   130
>   Di quella, il cui bell' occhio tutto vede,

Si probitas, sensus, virtutum gratia, census,
Nobilitas orti, possent resistere morti,
Non foret extinctus Fredericus qui jacet *intus*.
(Villani vi. 41.)

[120] **il Cardinale**: Ottaviano degli Ubaldini, of whom it is recorded that he said 'If I have a soul, I have lost it for the Ghibelines.' Villani (vi. 80) tells how he alone of the Sacred College rejoiced at the news of the battle of Montaperti; and how a cardinal Bianco, 'grande astrologo e maestro di nigromanzia,' foretold the speedy return of the Guelfs. Philalethes gives reasons for doubting whether the story which describes him as a strong Ghibeline is correct.

fair eye sees all, from her shalt thou know the journey of thy life.'

Next he turned his foot to the left hand: we left the wall and went toward the centre by a path which strikes down to a valley, which even up to there made its ill savour to be displeasing.

> Da lei saprai di tua vita il viaggio.
> Appresso volse a man sinistra il piede:
> Lasciammo il muro, e gimmo in ver lo mezzo
> Per un sentier ch' ad una valle fiede,
> Che infin lassù facea spiacer suo lezzo.

[132] As a matter of fact, it is from Cacciaguida rather than from Beatrice that Dante is to learn the destiny that awaits him.

[135, 136] Hitherto, it will be observed, there has been very little actual descent. From the first to the second circle (v. 1) and from the third to the fourth (vi. 114) a change of level is mentioned, but not as the important feature which it presently becomes. Now, however, they have come to the brink of the real pit of Hell, and begin to perceive the stench which arises from it.

CANTO XI

ARGUMENT

They halt on the brink of a steep descent, to inure themselves to the stench rising from it. Virgil expounds to Dante the ordering of the punishments of Hell, and the reason thereof.

Upon the far edge of a lofty bank, which great broken rocks in a circle made, we came above a more cruel stowage; and there by reason of the horrible excess of the stench which the deep abyss throws up, we took refuge behind a cover belonging to a great tomb, where I saw a writing that said: *I hold Pope Anastasius, the which*

> In su l' estremità d' un' alta ripa,
>   Che facevan gran pietre rotte in cerchio,
>   Venimmo sopra più crudele stipa:
> E quivi, per l' orribile soperchio
>   Del puzzo, che il profondo abisso gitta,
>   Ci raccostammo dietro ad un coperchio
> D' un grande avello, ov' io vidi una scritta
>   Che diceva: Anastasio papa guardo,

[3] **stipa.** Boccaccio thinks the term is used as applied to the packing of a ship's cargo; Benv. says it was used for 'cage.' The former gives the better image, and recalls ix. 129.

The history of Anastasius II. (496-498) appears to be this: In 482 the emperor Zeno had put forth his 'Henotikon,' designed to calm the dissensions which had prevailed ever since the Council of Chalcedon in 451. The Roman pontiffs did not approve this, and excommunicated

Photinus drew from the right way. 'It behoves that our descent be slow, so that our sense may first get used a little to the sorry exhalation; and then will it be of no account.' Thus the Master; and I said to him: 'Some compensation find, that the time pass not and be lost.' And he: 'See how I think on that.'

'My son, within these rocks,' he began then to say, 'are three small circles from step to step, like those which thou art leaving. All are full of spirits accursed; but in order

> Lo qual trasse Fotin della via dritta.
> Lo nostro scender conviene esser tardo,   10
>   Sì che s' ausi un poco prima il senso
>   Al tristo fiato, e poi non fia riguardo.
> Così il Maestro; ed io: Alcun compenso,
>   Dissi lui, trova, che il tempo non passi
>   Perduto; ed egli: Vedi che a ciò penso.
> Figliuol mio, dentro da cotesti sassi,
>   Cominciò poi a dir, son tre cerchietti
>   Di grado in grado, come quei che lassi.
> Tutti son pien di spirti maledetti:

the Byzantine patriarchs who supported it, including Acacius († 488). In the pontificate of Anastasius, his namesake the emperor was desirous of restoring the name of Acacius to the 'diptych' or roll of patriarchs deceased in the orthodox faith; and Photinus, a deacon of Thessalonica, was sent to treat with Pope Anastasius on the subject, and persuaded him to allow it. (It is not improbable that Photinus was in later times confused with Photius, whom the Latins held responsible for the schism of the Churches.) Ultimately the belief grew up that Anastasius had been tainted with the Nestorian heresy. Gratian (Par. x. 104) seems to have been the authority for this misrepresentation.

    [12] **poi non fia**, etc. Literally, 'then will there be no account' [of it]. 'Quia assuetis non fit passio,' says Bocc.

that hereafter the sight alone may suffice to thee, understand how and wherefore they are in bonds. Of every badness which earns hatred in heaven, injury is the end; and every such end either by force or by fraud causes grief to another. But because fraud is an ill peculiar to man, it more displeases God; and for this cause the fraudulent have their station below, and woe assails them more. To the violent belongs all the first circle; but whereas force may be

> Ma perchè poi ti basti pur la vista,   20
> Intendi come, e perchè son costretti.
> D' ogni malizia, ch' odio in cielo acquista,
> Ingiuria è il fine, ed ogni fin cotale
> O con forza o con frode altrui contrista.
> Ma perchè frode è dell' uom proprio male,
> Più spiace a Dio; e però stan di sutto
> Gli frodolenti, e più dolor gli assale.
> Dei violenti il primo cerchio è tutto:
> Ma perchè si fa forza a tre persone,

[20] Philalethes points out that henceforth Dante does not (as in v. 50 or vii. 38) inquire the general character of the sin punished in any part of Hell; but only asks for information about individuals.

[21] **costretti.** Generally taken as referring to **spirti**; and this seems quite satisfactory. Blanc, however, finds the subject of the sentence in **cerchietti**, and understands 'how and why the circles are arranged.' There seems no need for this, which, as he himself points out, would involve a somewhat unusual use of a common word on Dante's part.

[22] The following classification of the sins punished in the lower part of Hell is so clear that comment on it is hardly necessary. **ch' odio in cielo acquista**: i.e. spiritual, not physical 'badness.' So Boccaccio, evidently thinking of the distinction made in Eth. iii. 5 between αἱ τῆς ψυχῆς and αἱ τοῦ σώματος κακίαι.

[23] ἀδικία ὅλη κακία, Eth. v. i.

[24] **con forza—con frode**: βίαια—λαθραῖα, ib. 2.

[25] While violence is common to man and the beasts, and hence is a form of *bestialità*.

wrought upon three persons, it is divided and arranged in three rings. On God, on a man's self, on his neighbour can force be wrought; I mean in themselves and in the things that are theirs, as thou shalt hear with evident reasoning. By force are inflicted on one's neighbour death and painful hurts, and on his possessions destruction, fires, and ruinous levies; whence homicides and whoso smites wrongfully, pillagers and plunderers, the first ring in divers groups torments them all. A man can lay a violent hand on

>   In tre gironi è distinto e costrutto.^a   30
> A Dio, a sè, al prossimo si puone
>   Far forza, dico in loro ed in lor cose,
>   Come udirai con aperta ragione.
> Morte per forza e ferute dogliose
>   Nel prossimo si danno, e nel suo avere
>   Ruine, incendi e tollette dannose:
> Onde omicide e ciascun che mal fiere,^b
>   Guastatori e predon, tutti tormenta
>   Lo giron primo per diverse schiere.
> Puote uomo avere in sè man violenta   40

^a *tre giorni* 15; *gioni* 4.
^b *Odii homicidii* Gg. *first six edd.*; *Tutti*; *Ogni Benv.*

36 **tollette.** There seems little authority for the reading *ollette* which some adopt. It must, however, be said that *c* and *t* are very much alike in MSS. Whether the word here refers to plunder generally, or to quasi-legal extortion, as by feudal superiors, e.g. in the tax known as the *male tolte*, is not certain. Against the latter view is the fact that in the next terzina, where the classes guilty of the crimes specified are named, this is matched only by **predoni**. It will be seen, however, in the next Canto that Dante drew no distinction between public and private conduct, and put Eccelino and Alexander in the same category as highway robbers.

37 The reading *odii homicidii* has considerable support, and is perhaps even better than that in the text. Have we here a variant due to the author himself?

himself and on his goods; and therefore in the second ring it behoves that he bootlessly repent whosoever strips himself of your world, gambles and melts away his resources, and weeps where he ought to be joyous. Force can be wrought upon the Godhead, by denying with the heart and blaspheming It, and by misprising nature and her goodness; and therefore the smallest circle stamps with its seal Sodom and Cahors, and whoso speaks with his own heart, misprising God. The fraud, wherewith every conscience is pricked, man can practise towards the one who trusts

> E nei suoi beni : e però nel secondo
> Giron convien che senza pro si penta
Qualunque priva sè del vostro mondo,
> Biscazza e fonde la sua facultade,
> E piange là dove esser dee giocondo.
Puossi far forza nella Deitade,
> Col cor negando e bestemmiando quella,
> E spregiando natura e sua bontade :
E però lo minor giron suggella
> Del segno suo e Sodoma e Caorsa, 50
> E chi, spregiando Dio, col cor favella.
La frode, ond' ogni coscienza è morsa,
> Può l' uomo usare in colui che in lui fida,

---

⁴⁵ Suicides.

⁴⁶ Because he might have used his means wisely, and been happy. It cannot have any reference to the spiritual sin of *tristitia*, which has already been dealt with.

⁵⁰ Cahors, in Languedoc, seems to have been at this time the special home of money-lenders. 'Civitas in Gallia, in qua quasi omnes sunt foenerantes,' says Benvenuto. See Ashley, Economic History, i. p. 196. Boccaccio says that even the servant-maids there used to lend the money they received as wages.

¹ **col cor**: with allusion to Psalms xiii. 1 and liv. 1 : 'Dixit insipiens in corde suo.' He means, doubtless, also to draw a distinction between careless profanity and convinced unbelief.

him, and towards him who has no confidence in store. This latter mode seems to destroy only the bond of love that nature makes; whence in the second circle have their nests hypocrisy, flatteries, and whoso uses arts; forgery, robbery, and simony; pandars, jobbers, and suchlike filth. By the second mode is forgotten that love which nature makes, and that which later is added, from which special trust comes to pass; wherefore in the smallest circle, where is the centre of the Universe, upon which Dis has his seat, whosoever betrays is consumed to eternity.'

And I: 'Master, clearly enough proceeds thy argu-

>   Ed in quel che fidanza non imborsa.
>   Questo modo di retro par che uccida
>   Pur lo vinco d' amor che fa natura;
>   Onde nel cerchio secondo s' annida
>   Ipocrisia, lusinghe e chi affattura,
>   Falsità, ladroneccio e simonia,
>   Ruffian, baratti e simile lordura.   60
>   Per l' altro modo quell' amor s' obblia
>   Che fa natura, e quel ch' è poi aggiunto,
>   Di che la fede spezial si cria :
>   Onde nel cerchio minore, ov' è il punto
>   Dell' universo, in su che Dite siede,
>   Qualunque trade in eterno è consunto.
>   Ed io : Maestro, assai chiaro procede^c

^c *chiara* Gg. Cass. 1234.

⁵⁶ **che fa natura** : i.e. which exists between man and man.

⁵⁸ **affattura** : id est malefici qui affacturant et faciunt malias et incantationes. Benv. *Factura* : sortilegium, maleficium, Italis factura incantatio (Ducange). There is perhaps a confusion with *fatuarius*.

⁶³ I.e. the special bond of relationship, fellow-citizenship, or friendship.—For the distinction between *fa* and *cria* cf. Par. iii. 87.

^{64, 65} Witte contrasts this with the point (Par. xxviii. 41, 42) 'from which Heaven and all nature depend.'

ment; and well enough it distinguishes this gulf and the people that possess it. But tell me; those of the thick marsh, whom the wind carries, and whom the rain beats, and who meet each other with so rough tongues, why are not they punished within the red-hot city, if God holds them in anger? and if he holds them not so, why are they in such case?' And he said to me: 'Why does thy wit go so far astray from what it is wont? or is thy mind looking otherwhither? Hast thou no memory of those words, with which thy Ethics handle the three dispositions which

> La tua ragione, ed assai ben distingue
> Questo baratro e il popol che il possiede.
> Ma dimmi: Quei della palude pingue, 70
> Che mena il vento, e che batte la pioggia,
> E che s' incontran con sì aspre lingue,
> Perchè non dentro dalla città roggia
> Son ei puniti, se Dio gli ha in ira?
> E se non gli ha, perchè sono a tal foggia?
> Ed egli a me: Perchè tanto delira,
> Disse, lo ingegno tuo da quel che suole?
> Ovver la mente dove altrove mira?
> Non ti rimembra di quelle parole,
> Colle quai la tua Etica pertratta 80
> Le tre disposizion che il ciel non vuole:

---

81. The reference is to the opening words of Eth. vii.: Μετὰ δὲ ταῦτα λεκτέον, ἄλλην ποιησαμένοις ἀρχὴν, ὅτι τῶν περὶ τὰ ἤθη φευκτῶν τρία ἐστὶν εἴδη, κακία, ἀκρασία, θηριότης. Witte considers that Dante does not follow this threefold division, but ignores θηριότης: and that the only point of the reference here is to show why the sins of incontinence are outside the city of Dis. But it seems better to see, with Philalethes, the representatives of θηριότης in the sins of the 7th circle, some of which indeed are expressly mentioned by Aristotle (vii. 5) as illustrations of his use of the term. Besides these we have heresy, to which the word is actually applied by Dante (see note x. 15), which

Heaven brooks not, incontinence, malice, and mad beastliness? and how incontinence less offends God and earns less blame? If thou well regard this opinion, and bring to thy mind who these are, who above undergo penance outside, thou wilt clearly see why they are separated from these wretches, and why less wrathfully the vengeance of God crushes them.' 'O Sun that healest every troubled sight, so dost thou content me when thou solvest, that doubting gives me no less pleasure than knowing. Turn thee yet a

> Incontinenza, malizia e la matta
>   Bestialitade? e come incontinenza
>   Men Dio offende e men biasimo accatta?
> Se tu riguardi ben questa sentenza,
>   E rechiti alla mente, chi son quelli,
>   Che su di fuor sostengon penitenza,
> Tu vedrai ben, perchè da questi felli
>   Sien dipartiti, e perchè men crucciata
>   La divina vendetta gli martelli.[d]
> O Sol che sani ogni vista turbata,
>   Tu mi contenti sì, quando tu solvi,
>   Che, non men che saper, dubbiar m' aggrata.

[d] *giustizia* most edd. after 1480. Vell. etc. ed.

occupies as it were a middle station between it and incontinence. So we shall later on find usury forming the link between θηριότης and κακία. See notes l. 25 and xvii. 45.

** Eth. vii. 6: Ἔτι ταῖς φυσικαῖς μᾶλλον συγγνώμη ἀκολουθεῖν ὁρέξεσιν, and below: ἔτι ἀδικώτεροι οἱ ἐπιβουλότεροι. In the same chapter: ἐλάττον δὲ θηριότης κακίας, which again supports the view taken in the last note, in so far as their relative positions in Hell are concerned.

** **su di fuor**: above where they now are, and outside the city of Dis.

little backward,' I said, 'to that point where thou sayest that usury offends the divine goodness; and unloose the tangle.' 'Philosophy,' he said to me, 'to whoso looks narrowly on her, notes not in one place only, how nature takes her course from the understanding of God, and from His workmanship; and if thou well observe thy Physics, thou wilt find, after not many pages, that your workmanship, so far as it can, follows her, as the learner does the master, so that your workmanship is as it were second in descent from God. From these two, if thou bring to thy mind Genesis,

> Ancora un poco indietro ti rivolvi,
>   Diss' io, là dove di' che usura offende
>   La divina bontade, e il groppo solvi.
> Filosofia, mi disse, a chi la intende,
>   Nota non pure in una sola parte,
>   Come natura lo suo corso prende
> Dal divino intelletto e da sua arte;   100
>   E se tu ben la tua Fisica note,
>   Tu troverai non dopo molte carte,
> Che l' arte vostra quella, quanto puote,
>   Segue, come il maestro fa il discente,
>   Sì che vostr' arte a Dio quasi è nipote.
> Da queste due, se tu ti rechi a mente*

_{* queste cose Cfr. Cass. 124.}

[98-9] Dante, as the words imply, does not seem to have any particular passage in view. That God is the author of Nature is directly deducible from the language of the Timaeus, from Ar. Met. A. and many other places.

[101] The reference appears to be to Ar. Phys. ii. 2 (194 a): εἰ δὲ ἡ τέχνη μιμεῖται τὴν φύσιν.

[104] God, nature, human workmanship, is the order of descent.

[106] Genesis i. 28: Crescite et multiplicamini: and iii. 19: in sudore vultus tui vesceris pane. The first refers to the natural increase of the

towards the beginning, it behoves folk to take their life, and to prosper. And because the usurer holds another course, he despises Nature both for herself and for her follower; because he places his hope in another thing. But now follow me, for going pleases me; for the Fishes are flickering above the horizons, and all the Wain lies over Caurus; and the ledge descends a good deal further on.'

> Lo Genesi dal principio, conviene
> Prender sua vita ed avanzar la gente.
> E perchè l' usuriere altra via tiene,
> Per sè natura, e per la sua seguace   110
> Dispregia, poichè in altro pon la spene.
> Ma seguimi oramai, che il gir mi piace :
> Chè i Pesci guizzan su per l' orizzonta,
> E il Carro tutto sopra il Coro giace,
> E il balzo via là oltra si dismonta.

race; the second to the increase of wealth by labour. It is the latter law which the usurer violates. It is not therefore strictly correct to speak of him as a sinner against *nature*; rather against the divinely-appointed order of production. (Boccaccio, it may be noted, understands the clauses of l. 108 inversely: 'get their *livelihood*, and increase.' Aquinas discusses the question, S.T. ii. 2. Q. 78, and comes to the conclusion of the time, that all usury, by which he means any lending of money on interest, is sinful. At the same time it is pretty clear that his own argument did not convince him.

[113] Again we have an imitation of Aen. vi. 539. The Sun being in the Ram, the Fish are the last sign to rise before him. The meaning therefore is that it is close upon sunrise in the upper world. At this season the Great Bear would at the same hour be in the North-West, indicated by the name of the N.W. wind, *Caurus*. They have almost completed one night in Hell, and it is the morning of Good Friday.

CANTO XII

ARGUMENT

They descend a steep rocky slope, passing the Minotaur, and reach the first ring of the seventh circle, where those who have done wrong by violence to their neighbours lie in a river of seething blood. They meet a troop of Centaurs, one of whom, by name Nessus, helps them on their way, and shows them many renowned conquerors and other robbers and murderers.

THE place whither we came to descend the bank was mountainous, and by reason of that which, moreover, was there, such that every view would have been shy of it. Such as is that downfall which hitherward of Trent smote the Adige

> ERA lo loco, ove a scender la riva
> Venimmo, alpestro e, per quel ch' ivi er' anco,
> Tal, ch' ogni vista ne sarebbe schiva.
> Qual è quella ruina, che nel fianco
> Di qua da Trento l' Adice percosse

---

[4] The early commentators (except Boccaccio, who reads *di là*, and is vague as to the spot) see an allusion to a great landslip known as the Slavino di Marco, opposite Mori. This fell in the 9th century, and deflected the Adige considerably. According to Benvenuto it is mentioned by Albertus Magnus. Scartazzini has found in G. della Corte's 'Storia di Verona' a record of another great landslip which took place near Verona in 1309. But setting aside the testimony of P. di Dante ('in contrata quadam quae dicitur Marco modo') and others, it is not likely that Dante would have indicated a spot close to Verona by its position in regard to Trent.

in the side, whether through earthquake or through lack of support; for from the top of the mountain whence it started, to the plain, the rock is so shattered that it would afford some way to one that was above—such was the descent of that ravine; and just at the point where the cistern was broken the infamy of Crete was outstretched which was conceived in the counterfeit cow: and when it saw us, it bit itself, like one whom anger inwardly is bursting. My Sage cried towards it: 'Haply thou deemest that the Duke of Athens is here, who dispensed death to thee in the

> O per tremuoto o per sostegno manco:
> Chè da cima del monte, onde si mosse,
> Al piano è sì la roccia discoscesa,
> Ch' alcuna via darebbe a chi su fosse:
> Cotal di quel burrato era la scesa: 10
> E in su la punta della rotta lacca
> L' infamia di Creti era distesa,
> Che fu concetta nella falsa vacca:
> E quando vide noi, sè stesso morse
> Sì come quei, cui l' ira dentro fiacca.
> Lo savio mio inver lui gridò: Forse ^a
> Tu credi che qui sia il duca d' Atene,
> Che su nel mondo la morte ti porse?

^a *Lo s. m. Virgilio gr. Ald.*

[11] **lacca.** Used vii. 16, and (of the Valley of Princes) Purg. vii. 71. Properly the word would seem to mean a shallow well or cistern; though Bocc., Benv., and others render it by *ripa*. See Glossary.

[12] The Minotaur, offspring of her 'che s' imbestiò nell' imbestiate schegge,' is fitly put as the sentinel over those who are punished for θηριότης, 'la matta bestialitate.'

Note the form **Creti**, perhaps from Gr. Κρήτη. So (xx. 47) *Luni* for *Luna*, doubtless owing to the plural *Lunae*, which seems to have been used as well as the singular for the city of that name.

[17] The title 'Duke of Athens' would be familiar enough to Dante's readers.

world above. Off with thee, beast, for this man comes not schooled by thy sister, but is going on his way to see your punishments.' As is that bull who breaks his leash at the moment when he has already received the death-stroke, that he cannot go, but reels hither and thither, in such wise saw I the Minotaur behave. And he perceiving cried: 'Run to the passage; while he is in a fury, it is good that thou go down.' So we took the way down by the discharge of those stones, which often moved under my feet by reason of their unwonted burthen.

I was going in thought; and he said: 'Thou art thinking perchance on this ruin, which is guarded by that bestial wrath which I just quenched. Now I will thou know, that the other time when I came down here into the nether

> Partiti, bestia, chè questi non viene
>   Ammaestrato dalla tua sorella,   20
>   Ma vassi per veder le vostre pene.
> Qual è quel toro che si slaccia in quella
>   Che ha ricevuto già il colpo mortale,
>   Che gir non sa, ma qua e là saltella,
> Vid' io lo Minotauro far cotale.
>   E quegli accorto gridò: Corri al varco;
>   Mentre ch' è in furia, è buon che tu ti cale.
> Così prendemmo via giù per lo scarco
>   Di quelle pietre, che spesso moviensi
>   Sotto i miei piedi per lo nuovo carco.   30
> Io già pensando; e quei disse: Tu pensi
>   Forse a questa rovina, ch' è guardata
>   Da quell' ira bestial ch' io ora spensi.
> Or vo' che sappi, che l' altra fiata
>   Ch' io discesi quaggiù nel basso inferno,

---

sorella. Ariadne.   *l' altra fiata :* see ix. 22.

Hell, this rock had not yet tumbled. But certainly a little time, if I discern aright, before He came who carried off from Dis the great booty of the uppermost circle, on all sides the deep foul vale trembled so that I thought the Universe felt love (through the which there is who deems that the world has more than once been turned to chaos); and in that instant this old rock here and elsewhere made

> Questa roccia non era ancor cascata.
> Ma certo poco pria, se ben discerno,
> Che venisse Colui, che la gran preda
> Levò a Dite del cerchio superno,
> Da tutte parti l' alta valle feda 40
> Tremò sì, ch' io pensai che l' universo
> Sentisse amor, per lo quale è chi creda
> Più volte il mondo in Caos converso:
> Ed in quel punto questa vecchia roccia
> Qui ed altrove tal fece riverso.

[37] **poco pria** : i.e. at the moment of our Lord's death, when 'the earth did quake, and the rocks rent.' We shall find further results of this earthquake lower down. Benvenuto considers the symbolism to be that a blow was then given to violence and cruelty.

[42, 43] The allusion is to Empedocles, whose theory that the alternate supremacy of hate and love was the cause of periodic destruction and construction in the scheme of the universe is criticised by Aristotle, Metaph. β. 4 (1000 a, b). Dante, however, appears to have taken a remark made by Aristotle in controverting the theory as part of Empedocles's own doctrine: ὁμοίως δ' οὐδ' ἡ φιλότης τοῦ εἶναι [αἴτιον]· συνάγουσα γὰρ εἰς τὸ ἓν φθείρει τἆλλα. See also Phys. viii. 1 144 a. Or he may be thinking of the consequence of the theory, that at the close of a period during which love predominated, individual existences would have disappeared, and all things be merged in a homogeneous whole. But the word *chaos* hardly applies so well to this state as to the confusion which hate produces.—L. 43 seems to be a syllable short. Ought we not to read *in un caos*; or, transposing the words, *il mondo in caos p. v. c.*; or (with some MSS.) *caos c.* cf. *Nannucci*, Par. ix. 137.?

such an overturn. But fix thine eyes downwards, for there draws near the river of blood, in the which boils whoso offends by violence towards another.'

O blind covetousness! O foolish wrath! that dost so spur us in our short life, and afterward in the life eternal dost in such evil wise steep us! I saw a wide foss bent into an arc, as that which embraces the whole plain, according as my Escort had said; and between the foot of

> Ma ficca gli occhi a valle; chè s' approccia
> La riviera del sangue, in la qual bolle
> Qual che per violenza in altrui noccia.
> O cieca cupidigia, o ira folle,[b]
> Che sì ci sproni nella vita corta,
> E nell' eterna poi sì mal c' immolle! 50
> Io vidi un' ampia fossa in arco torta,
> Come quella che tutto il piano abbraccia,
> Secondo ch' avea detto la mia scorta:
> E tra il piè della ripa ed essa, in traccia

[b] *ria e folle* Gg. 1345; *e ria e f.* 2 W.

[48] The reading I have adopted has the support of Cass., Benv., and most edd. after 1480. It is certainly the more effective, and is almost required; anger being as frequent a cause as covetousness of the crimes here punished.

[51] *immollare*, to soften by steeping; doubtless contrasted with **sproni**.

[52] They reach the first ring of the seventh circle.

[53] See xi. 39.

[55] Benvenuto sees in the Centaurs a lively image of the 'stipendiarii' or mercenaries (famous in later times as *condottieri*), by whom Italy was beginning to be infested. 'In hace tempora,' he exclaims, 'infelicitas mea me deduxit, ut viderem hodie miseram Italiam plenam barbaris socialibus omnium nationum. Hic enim sunt Anglici sanguinei, Alemanni furiosi, Britones bruti, Vascones rapaces, Hungari immundi.'

the bank and it, in file were trotting Centaurs armed with
arrows, as they were wont in the world to go a-hunting.
Seeing us come down each one halted, and from the troop
three broke off with bows and darts already selected. And
one cried from afar: "To what torment are ye coming, who
descend the hillside? Tell it from where you are; if not,

   Corrcan Centauri armati di saette,
   Come solean nel mondo andare a caccia.
 Vedendoci calar ciascun ristette,
   E della schiera tre si dipartiro
   Con archi ed asticciuole prima elette: 60
 E l' un gridò da lungi: A qual martiro
   Venite voi, che scendete la costa?
   Ditel costinci, se non, l' arco tiro.

[56] For Dante the Centaurs, with their half-bestial form, typify, like the Minotaur, the sins falling under θηριότης, *bestialità*.

[59] The three, as will appear presently, are Chiron, Nessus, and Pholus. The two former were sufficiently renowned; though Chiron appears more frequently in Greek poetry than in Latin. The story of Nessus is recorded at length in Ov. Met. ix. 101; but Pholus is only named, with other Centaurs, twice by Virgil, once by Ovid, and (in close association with Nessus and Chiron) by Lucan, Phars. vi. 391. It is somewhat strange that Dante should apply the epithet **pien d' ira** to him especially. As a matter of fact, from the accounts of him that we have, he appears to have been a particularly gentle and kindly Centaur; the counterpart among the Arcadian Centaurs of Chiron among the Thessalian. The story of his hospitality to Hercules, and the trouble that befell therefrom, is told by Apollodorus (Biblioth. ii. 5); but his narrative is confused, if the text be not defective. Boccaccio knows nothing of Pholus, save that 'he was the son of Ixion and a cloud, like the other Centaurs'; an unlucky guess, since he was the son of Silenus and Melia (the ash), as Chiron of Saturn and Philyra (the linden). It is also not clear why the Centaurs, unlike the other warders of the damned, make no opposition to Dante and Virgil, but rather help them on their way.

I draw the bow.' My Master said: 'The answer will we make to Chiron there close at hand; thy will was always to its hurt so hasty.' Then he touched me, and said: 'That is Nessus, who died for the fair Deianira, and himself wreaked vengeance for himself. And that one in the middle who looks at his own breast is the great Chiron who brought up Achilles; that other is Pholus who was so full of wrath.' About the foss they go by thousands shooting at whatsoever soul plucks itself away from the blood more than its crime has allotted to it. We drew near to those swift beasts. Chiron took a shaft, and with the notch put his beard back about his jaws. When he had uncovered his great mouth, he said to his companions: 'Do ye observe that the hindmost one moves what he touches? So are not

> Lo mio Maestro disse: La risposta
>   Farem noi a Chiron costà di presso:
>   Mal fu la voglia tua sempre sì tosta.
> Poi mi tentò, e disse: Quegli è Nesso,
>   Che morì per la bella Deianira,
>   E fe di sè la vendetta egli stesso:
> E quel di mezzo, che al petto si mira,   70
>   È il gran Chirone, il qual nudrì Achille:
>   Quell' altro è Folo, che fu sì pien d' ira.
> D' intorno al fosso vanno a mille a mille,
>   Saettando quale anima si svelle
>   Del sangue più, che sua colpa sortille.
> Noi ci appressammo a quelle fiere snelle:
>   Chiron prese uno strale, e con la cocca
>   Fece la barba indietro alle mascelle.
> Quando s' ebbe scoperta la gran bocca,
>   Disse ai compagni: Siete voi accorti,   80
>   Che quel di retro move ciò ch' ei tocca?

the feet of the dead wont to do.' And my good Leader who by this was at his breast, where the two natures are in company, answered: 'He surely is alive, and to him thus alone is it meet that I show the gloomy vale; necessity leads us on, and not enjoyment. Such an one separated herself from singing *Alleluia*, that committed this new duty to me; he is no thief, and I no runagate soul. But by that virtue through which I move my steps over so savage a road, give us one of thy band, to whom we may keep near, to show us the place where the ford is, and to carry this man on his croup, for he is no spirit to go through the air.'

    Cosi non soglion fare i piè dei morti.
        E il mio buon Duca, che già gli era al petto
        Dove le duo nature son consorti,
    Rispose: Ben è vivo, e si soletto
        Mostrarli mi convien la valle buia:
        Necessità c' induce, e non diletto.
    Tal si partì da cantare alleluia,
        Che mi commise quest' uficio nuovo;
        Non è ladron, nè io anima fuia.
    Ma per quella virtù, per cui io movo
        Li passi miei per sì selvaggia strada,
        Danne un dei tuoi, a cui noi siamo a pruovo.
    Che ne dimostri là dove si guada,
        E che porti costui in su la groppa:
        Che non è spirto che per l' aer vada.

il conduce Gg. 124: *il condusse* Benv.; il c in. Cass. Ald. W.

[93] **a pruovo**: 'cioè allato,' Bocc.; 'idest prope.' Benv., and this no doubt is right; for Buti's 'a prolazione' gives no good sense. See Glossary.

Chiron turned himself over the right breast and said to Nessus: 'Go back, and guide them so; and if another troop falls in with you, make them give way.'

We set out with our trusty escort along the shore of the crimson brew, where the boiled ones were uttering loud shrieks. I saw folk beneath it up to the brow, and the great Centaur said: 'They are tyrants, who clutched at blood and possessions. Here they bewail their ruthless mischiefs; here is Alexander, and fierce Dionysius who made Sicily to have woeful years; and that forehead that

> Chiron si volse in sulla destra poppa,
>   E disse a Nesso: Torna, e sì li guida,
>   E fa cansar, s' altra schiera v' intoppa.
> Noi ci movemmo colla scorta fida   100
>   Lungo la proda del bollor vermiglio,
>   Ove i bolliti facean alte strida.
> Io vidi gente sotto infino al ciglio;
>   E il gran Centauro disse: Ei son tiranni,
>   Che dier nel sangue e nell' aver di piglio.
> Quivi si piangon li spietati danni:
>   Quivi è Alessandro, e Dionisio fero,
>   Che fè Sicilia aver dolorosi anni:

107 **Alessandro.** All the early commentators understand Alexander the Great; though Benvenuto refers, but only to flout it, to an 'opinio vulgi,' which held that some one else was intended. Bargigi appears to be the first who mentions (though he does not adopt) the suggestion that the person meant is Alexander, tyrant of Pherae (368-359 B.C.): Vellutello, the first to defend the claims of that tyrant, 'de la cui ingiustitia e tirannie scrive Giustino.' This rather lowers the value of his opinion, because, as Lombardi quite truly points out, Justin writes nothing of the kind. However, Alexander of Pherae and Dionysius are coupled by Cicero, De Off. ii. 7, and, which is more to the purpose, by Val. Max. ix. 13: in neither case, however, as examples of tyranny. Modern editors have almost invariably followed Vellutello, Lombardi

has its hair so black is Ezzelin; and that other who is fair is Obizzo of Este, who of a truth was extinguished by his

> E quella fronte ch' ha il pel così nero
> È Azzolino; e quell' altro ch' è biondo 110
> È Obizzo da Esti, il qual per vero

(whose note is extremely sensible) and Blanc alone holding with the older people. Philalethes is loath to go against their authority; Lubin and Bianchi doubt; but Biagioli, Poggiali, Volpi, Witte, Scartazzini, all support the claims of the Pheraean. One of their arguments is that in Conv. iv. 11, Dante speaks of the 'reali beneficii' of Alexander the Great. But in the same list of men renowned for munificence he includes Bertrand de Born, whom he has condemned to a yet lower depth of Hell. On the other side, it is to be observed that two of his chief authorities in this portion of the poem, Lucan and Orosius, treat Alexander the Great as one of the great spoilers of the world. The former (Phars. x. ad init.) calls him 'proles vesana Philippi, felix praedo,' 'terrarum fatale malum ... sidus iniquum gentibus'; while the latter (Hist. iii. 18) says of him: humani sanguinis insatiabilis, sive hostium sive etiam sociorum, recentem semper sitiebat cruorem.

It is probable also that the two are brought in here, not so much on the score of cruelty—for Dionysius, tyrant of Syracuse, B.C. 405-367, was not specially notorious on this account—as for lust of power and conquest. Nor, on Dante's own principle (Par. xvii. 138), is he likely to have selected the comparatively obscure tyrant of Pherae in preference to his great namesake of Macedonia.

[110] Eccelino da Romano (1194-1260), called by the Tuscans Azzolino, was one of Frederick II.'s stoutest champions in Lombardy; and by marriage with his natural daughter Selvaggia, his son-in-law. He became lord of the Trevisan March, of Padua, Vicenza, Verona, Brescia, and other towns; and was finally conquered and slain by the Cremonese Ghibelines themselves, under the Marquis Palavicino (Vill. vi. 74). He left behind him a reputation for savagery and cruelty which seems to have impressed even his contemporaries. See Kington-Oliphant, Frederick the Second, vol. ii. pp. 310-312. Cf. also Par. ix. 25 sqq.

[111] Obizzo II. of Este, lord of Ferrara, and later of Reggio and Modena (Philal.), came of a house which had stoutly withstood Frederick and Eccelino: he himself was born, according to Benvenuto, when his father Rinaldo, son of Azzo II., was in an Apulian prison as hostage.

stepson in the world above.' Then I turned to the Poet, and he said: 'Let this one for the present be first with thee, and me second.' A little further on the Centaur stopped above a folk who as far as the throat seemed to issue from that seething. He showed us a shade on one side alone, saying: 'That one clove in the lap of God the

> Fu spento dal figliastro su nel mondo.
>   Allor mi volsi al Poeta, e quei disse:
>   Questi ti sia or primo, ed io secondo.
> Poco più oltre il Centauro s' affisse
>   Sopra una gente che infino alla gola
>   Parea che di quel bulicame uscisse.
> Mostrocci un' ombra dall' un canto sola,
>   Dicendo: Colui fesse in grembo a Dio

There seems no special reason for his selection as a typical tyrant. The story of his murder by his son Azzo III. ('quel d' Esti' of Purg. v. 77), Benvenuto says, was taken by Dante from Riccobaldo, a Ferrarese chronicler of the time. He died 1293.

[112] **figliastro**: either to note the unnaturalness of the crime (Benv.), or to hint that the son's mother had been unfaithful (Bocc.).

[118] Guy of Montfort, son of Sir Simon, who, in vengeance for the death of his father, stabbed his cousin Henry, son of Richard of Cornwall, at the moment of the elevation of the Host, in the Cathedral of Viterbo, towards the end of 1270. Guy, who was at the time holding the office of Vicar in Tuscany for Charles of Anjou, appears to have been in some measure shielded by him. The outrage aroused very strong reprobation in Italy. 'Istud fuit nimis excessivum homicidium,' says Benvenuto. Villani, in narrating it (vii. 40), takes occasion to quote lines 119, 120, one of the few instances in which he actually quotes Dante by name; if indeed any of the quotations which appear in the first edition, but are omitted by modern editors, be not a later insertion. Henry's heart was brought to England in a gold casket, which, according to the early commentators, who probably misunderstood Dante's words, was placed on a pillar over London Bridge. **sola**: probably because Guy, as an Englishman, was nationally outside of the Empire. See note iv. 129.

heart which yet is honoured on the Thames.' Next I saw folk who were holding out of the stream the head and also the whole of the chest, and of these I recognised full many. Thus by more and more sank that blood, so that it cooked only the feet; and here was our passage of the foss. 'As thou on this hand seest how the seething stuff ever dwindles,' said the Centaur, 'so I would have thee believe that on this other by more and more it lowers its bed, until it comes back to where it behoves that tyranny groan. The justice of God on this side stings that Attila who was a scourge on

> Lo cor che in sul Tamigi ancor si cola. 120
> Poi vidi gente, che di fuor del rio
>   Tenea la testa ed ancor tutto il casso:
>   E di costoro assai riconobb' io.
> Così a più a più si facea basso
>   Quel sangue sì, che cocea pur li piedi:[d]
>   E quivi fu del fosso il nostro passo.
> Sì come tu da questa parte vedi
>   Lo bulicame che sempre si scema,
>   Disse il Centauro, voglio che tu credi,
> Che da quest' altra più a più giù prema 130
>   Lo fondo suo, infin ch' ei si raggiunge
>   Ove la tirannia convien che gema.
> La divina giustizia di qua punge
>   Quell' Attila che fu flagello in terra,

[d] *copria All.*

[134] Attila was a hero of legend in the Middle Ages. Among other achievements he was credited with burning Florence and attacking Rome. He is confused with Totila, as by Villani at the beginning of his second book; and perhaps with Alaric.

earth, and Pyrrhus, and Sextus; and to eternity draws out the tears which with the boiling it unlocks from Rinier of Corneto, from Rinier Pazzo, who caused upon the highway so much strife.' Then he turned round, and passed him back over the ford.

> E Pirro, e Sesto; ed in eterno munge
> Le lagrime, che col bollor disserra
>   A Rinier da Corneto, a Rinier Pazzo,
>   Che fecero alle strade tanta guerra :
> Poi si rivolse, e ripassossi il guazzo.

[135] Pyrrhus, probably the king of Epirus; though the son of Achilles has from early times had supporters. Sextus Pompey.

[137] Two robber nobles. Rinieri Pazzo, of Arezzo, is said to have specially plundered churchmen.

NOTE TO LINES 4, 5.

Otto of Freisingen (vii. 15) writing of events about 1120 says: Circa idem tempus terremotus horribilis oppida templa villas montesque plurimos, sicut usque hodie in valle Tridentina apparet, subvertit. This seems even better to suit the event to which Dante alludes.

CANTO XIII

ARGUMENT

They come into a wood, the trees of which are of strange fashion and contain the souls of such as had done violence to their own lives. Dante talks with Petrus de Vineis, and sees the punishment of certain Florentines who in life had squandered their substance.

NESSUS had not yet reached the bank on the other side when we betook ourselves through a wood, which was marked by no path.[1] Not green leafage, but of a brown hue, not smooth branches, but knotty and entangled, not apples were there, but thorns with poison. So rough stems nor so thick inhabit not those wild woodland beasts which

> Non era ancor di là Nesso arrivato,
> Quando noi ci mettemmo per un bosco,
> Che da nessun sentiero era segnato.
> Non fronda verde, ma di color fosco,*
> Non rami schietti, ma nodosi e involti,
> Non pomi v' eran, ma stecchi con tosco.
> Non han si aspri sterpi nè si folti
> Quelle fiere selvagge, che in odio hanno

* *frondi verdi* G., Ald. W.

[1] **di là**: on the side whence they had come, now the farthest which regards them.

hold in enmity the tilled ground between Cecina and Corneto. Here the foul Harpies make their nests, which chased the Trojans from the Strophades with sad presage of mischief to come. Wide wings they have, and necks and faces of men, feet with talons, and their great bellies feathered; they make upon the trees uncouth lamentations. And the good Master: 'Before thou enterest further, know that thou art in the second ring,' began he to say to me; 'and shalt be, so long as thou art coming to the horrible sand. Therefore look well, and so shalt thou see things which would take away credence from my speech.'

> Tra Cecina e Corneto i luoghi colti.
> Quivi le brutte Arpie lor nidi fanno,   10
>   Che cacciar delle Strofade i Troiani
>   Con tristo annunzio di futuro danno.
> Ale hanno late, e colli e visi umani,
>   Piè con artigli, e pennuto il gran ventre:
>   Fanno lamenti in su gli alberi strani.
> E il buon Maestro: Prima che più entre,
>   Sappi che sei nel secondo girone,
>   Mi cominciò a dire, e sarai, mentre
> Che tu verrai nell' orribil sabbione.
>   Però riguarda bene, e sì vedrai   20
>   Cose, che torrien fede al mio sermone.

⁹ The Cecina and the Marta (on which stands the town of Corneto) flow into the sea a little south of Leghorn and north of Civitavecchia respectively, and mark approximately the northern and southern limits of the wild coast-land, or Maremma, of Tuscany.

¹¹ Aen. iii. 209 sqq.

¹⁷ In the second division of the seventh circle.

²¹ I.e. if I were to mention them. Benv. in the previous line reads *guarda bene se vedrai*: which might mean, 'see if you can see anything not confirming what I have said.'

I heard on all sides wailings long-drawn, and saw no person to make them; wherefore all bewildered I stopped.

I believe that he believed that I believed that voices in such number were issuing, among those stocks, from folk who by reason of us were hiding themselves. 'Therefore,' said the Master, 'if thou break off any twig of one of these plants, the thoughts that thou hadst shall be all brought to nought.' Then I reached my hand a little forward, and plucked a small bough from a great sloe; and its trunk cried: 'Why rendest thou me?' When it had become thereafter brown with blood, it began again to cry: 'Why pluckest thou me? Hast thou no spirit of pity whatever? Men we were; and now are we turned to stems. Thy

> Io sentia da ogni parte traer guai,
>   E non vedea persona che il facesse:
>   Perch' io tutto smarrito m' arrestai.
> Io credo ch' ei credette ch' io credesse,
>   Che tante voci uscisser tra quei bronchi
>   Da gente che per noi si nascondesse.
> Però, disse il Maestro, se tu tronchi
>   Qualche fraschetta d' una d' este piante,
>   Li pensier ch' hai si faran tutti monchi. 30
> Allor porsi la mano un poco avante,
>   E colsi un ramicel da un gran pruno:
>   E il tronco suo gridò: Perchè mi schiante?
> Da che fatto fu poi di sangue bruno,
>   Ricominciò a gridar: Perchè mi scerpi?
>   Non hai tu spirto di pietate alcuno?
> Uomini fummo, ed or sem fatti sterpi:

---

31 sqq. Taken from Aen. iii. 23 sqq., where Aeneas in like manner breaks a shoot of the tree containing the spirit of Polydorus, with a like result.

hand ought surely to have been more pitiful if we had been souls of serpents.' As in a green log which is being burnt at one of its ends, that at the other it drips, and squeaks by reason of wind which is escaping, so from that splinter issued at the same time words and blood; wherefore I let the end fall, and stood like the man who is in fear. 'If he had been able to believe sooner,' replied my Sage, 'O injured soul, that which he has seen, through my verse only, he would not have stretched forth his hand upon thee; but the incredibleness of the thing made me persuade him to the act, which weighs on myself. But tell him who thou art, so that in place of some amends he may refresh thy

> Ben dovrebb' esser la tua man più pia,
>   Se state fossim' anime di serpi.
> Come d' un stizzo verde, che arso sia   40
>   Dall' un dei capi, che dall' altro geme,
>   E cigola per vento che va via;
> Così di quella scheggia usciva insieme
>   Parole e sangue: ond' io lasciai la cima
>   Cadere, e stetti come l' uom che teme.
> S' egli avesse potuto creder prima,
>   Rispose il Savio mio, anima lesa,
>   Ciò ch' ha veduto pur con la mia rima,
> Non avrebbe in te la man distesa;
>   Ma la cosa incredibile mi fece   50
>   Indurlo ad opra, che a me stesso pesa.
> Ma dilli chi tu fosti, sì che, in vece
>   D' alcuna ammenda, tua fama rinfreschi

Cf. Chaucer, Knight's Tale, ll. 1479-82:

> 'And as it quenched, it made a whistling,
> As doth a were brand in his burning,
> And at the brondes end outran anon,
> As it were bloody dropes many one.'

fame in the world above, whither it is permitted him to return.'

And the trunk: 'So dost thou entice me with thy pleasant speech, that I cannot be silent; and let it not vex you because to converse a little ensnares me. I am he that

> Nel mondo su, dove tornar gli lece.
> E il tronco: Sì con dolce dir m' adeschi,
>   Ch' io non posso tacere; e voi non gravi
>   Perch' io un poco a ragionar m' inveschi.
> Io son colui, che tenni ambo le chiavi

58 sqq. Petrus de Vineis (Pier dalle Vigne) was born at Capua of extremely poor parents, about the end of the twelfth century. He contrived to study at Bologna, living on charity; and having attracted the notice of the Archbishop of Palermo, was by him recommended to Frederick II. By 1225 he was a judge; and he rose rapidly till he became the emperor's private secretary and most intimate adviser. (Oddly enough, the title of Chancellor, which nearly all commentators give him, seems to be about the only one which he did not hold.) He was sent on many important missions; on one occasion visiting England, to arrange for Frederick's marriage with Isabella, sister of Henry III. Like his master, he was a poet, and wrote the first sonnet in the Italian language, beginning—

'Perocche amore no se po vedere.'

Suddenly, in 1249, he fell into disgrace. There is much obscurity as to the cause; but the version most widely believed is that he was charged with having intrigued with the Pope, and endeavoured at his instigation to poison Frederick. He was blinded, and paraded through Tuscany as a traitor; and committed suicide, according to the picturesque version of Boccaccio, by dashing his head against the wall of a church in Pisa. Even as to this there seems to be some doubt. Villani, who like Dante considers that the charges brought against him were only based on his rivals' envy, says 'per dolore si lasciò tosto morire in pregione, e chi disse ch' egli medesimo si tolse la vita' (vi. 22).—**ambo le chiavi**: doubtless an allusion to the frequent parallels which in the time of his prosperity his flatterers drew between his position and that of his namesake the Apostle. For examples, see Oliphant's 'Frederick the Second,' ii. p. 480.

held both the keys of Frederick's heart, and that turned them locking and unlocking so gently, that from his secrets I removed almost every man; faith I bore to my glorious office, so much that I lost therefrom my slumbers and my heartbeats. The harlot, who never from the abode of Cæsar has turned her vile eyes, deadly to all men, and a plague of courts, inflamed all minds against me; and they being

> Del cor di Federico, e che le volsi
>   Serrando e disserrando sì soavi,   60
> Che dal secreto suo quasi ogni uom tolsi:
>   Fede portai al glorioso offizio,
>   Tanto ch' io ne perdei i sonni e i polsi.[b]
> La meretrice, che mai dall' ospizio
>   Di Cesare non torse gli occhi putti,
>   Morte comune, e delle corti vizio,
> Infiammò contra me gli animi tutti,

[b] *le vene e i p.* Gg. Benv. (?) 145. *Ald. W.*: *i sensi* 3.

[a] There can be little doubt that **sonni**, which has the great preponderance of MS. authority, is the correct reading; though *vene* has considerable support, and is found very early. But, as Dr. Moore points out, while perfectly appropriate in i. 90, it is not the word here. (It seems just possible, however, that even if *vene* were the word originally selected by Dante himself, he might have meant the same as by the afterthought *sonni*. Cf. Ov. Met. xii. 316-17, where the text until emended by Heinsius had 'cunctis sine fine jacebat Sopitus venis.' Aristotle, de Somno, makes the veins play an important part in the physiology of sleep.)—**polsi**: 'i polsi son quelle parti nel corpo nostro, nelle quali si comprendono le qualità de' movimenti del cuore, e in questi più o men correnti si dimostrano le virtù morali.'—Bocc. But, looking to Arist. de Respiratione, σφύζει μᾶλλον τοῖς νεωτέροις τῶν πρεσβυτέρων, it may mean merely, I grew old.

[c] Quoted by Chaucer; Legend of Good Women (Prologue):

> 'Envy is lavander of the court alway;
> For she ne parteth neither night nor day
> Out of the house of Caesar, thus saith Dant.'

inflamed so inflamed Augustus that my glad honours turned to sorry grief. My mind, through taste of disdain, thinking to fly disdain with dying, made me unrighteous against my righteous self. By the new roots of this tree I swear to you that never did I break faith to my Lord, who was so worthy of honour. And if either of you returns to the world, let him stablish my memory, which is prostrate yet from the stroke which envy dealt it.'

He waited a little, and then: 'Seeing he is silent,' said the Poet to me, 'lose not the moment, but speak and inquire of him if it lists thee more.' Wherefore I to him: 'Ask thou further of whatsoever thou deemest will satisfy me; for I could not; so great pity pricks my heart.' Therefore he

> E gl' infiammati infiammar sì Augusto,
>   Che i lieti onor tornaro in tristi lutti.
> L' animo mio per disdegnoso gusto,
>   Credendo col morir fuggir disdegno,
>   Ingiusto fece me contra me giusto.
> Per le nuove radici d' esto legno
>   Vi giuro che giammai non ruppi fede
>   Al mio signor, che fu d' onor sì degno.
> E se di voi alcun nel mondo riede,
>   Conforti la memoria mia, che giace
>   Ancor del colpo che invidia le diede.
> Un poco attese, e poi: Da ch' ei si tace,
>   Disse il Poeta a me, non perder l' ora;
>   Ma parla, e chiedi a lui se più ti piace.
> Ond' io a lui: Domandal tu ancora
>   Di quel che credi che a me satisfaccia;
>   Ch' io non potrei; tanta pietà m' accora.

ora is here an adverb; and the construction is like *ancora a qua*, Purg. iii. 37.

began again: 'So may this man do for thee freely that wherefore thy word prays him, O spirit imprisoned, let it yet please thee to tell us how the soul is bound in these gnarls; and tell us, if thou canst, if any is ever unwrapped from such limbs?' Then blew the trunk mightily, and afterward that wind was turned into such voice as this: 'Briefly shall answer be made to you. When the fierce soul parts from the body whence it has torn itself away, Minos sends it to the seventh entry. It falls in the wood, and no part is selected for it; but in the place where fortune shoots it, there it sprouts like a grain of spelt. It rises to a sapling, and to a woodland plant; the Harpies, feeding thereafter from its leaves, cause woe, and make for

Perciò ricominciò: Se l' uom ti faccia
   Liberamente ciò che il tuo dir prega,
   Spirito incarcerato, ancor ti piaccia
Di dirne come l' anima si lega
   In questi nocchi; e dinne, se tu puoi,
   S' alcuna mai da tai membra si spiega.   90
Allor soffiò lo tronco forte, e poi
   Si convertì quel vento in cotal voce:
   Brevemente sarà risposto a voi.
Quando si parte l' anima feroce
   Dal corpo, ond' ella stessa s' è disvelta,
   Minos la manda alla settima foce.
Cade in la selva, e non l' è parte scelta;
   Ma là dove fortuna la balestra,
   Quivi germoglia come gran di spelta;
Surge in vermena, ed in pianta silvestra: 100
   L' Arpie, pascendo poi delle sue foglie,
   Fanno dolore, ed al dolor finestra.

the woe an outlet. Like the others, we shall come for our spoils, but not to the end that any may again be clad therewith; for it is not just that a man have that which he takes from himself. Here shall we drag them, and throughout the sad wood will our bodies be hung, each on the thornbush of its baneful shade.'

We were still giving heed to the trunk, deeming that it would say else to us, when we were surprised by an uproar in manner like to him, who at his post is aware of the boar and the chase coming, when he hears the beasts and the twigs crash. And lo! two on our left side, naked

> Come l' altre, verrem per nostre spoglie,
>   Ma non però ch' alcuna sen rivesta:
>   Chè non è giusto aver ciò ch' uom si toglie.
> Qui le strascineremo, e per la mesta
>   Selva saranno i nostri corpi appesi,
>   Ciascuno al prun dell' ombra sua molesta.
> Noi eravamo ancora al tronco attesi,
>   Credendo ch' altro ne volesse dire,
>   Quando noi fummo d' un romor sorpresi,
> Similemente a colui, che venire
>   Sente il porco e la caccia alla sua posta,
>   Ch' ode le bestie e la frasche stormire.
> Ed ecco duo dalla sinistra costa,

spoglie: our earthly bodies. See S. T. Suppl. Q. 79. According to Benvenuto, some people appear to have been a little scandalised by Dante's modification, in the case of suicides, of the strict orthodox doctrine respecting the connexion of soul and body after the resurrection.

molesta: because, through the fault of the soul, it has come to this pass.

These are sinners who have 'wasted their substance in riotous living.' They belong to the class of ἄσωτοι who spend εἰς ἃ μὴ δεῖ, 'prodigals' in our sense of the word; to be distinguished from the

and scratched, flying so hard that they were breaking every switch of the wood. The one in front was crying: 'Now hasten, hasten hither, death'; and the other, who appeared to be over-hurried: 'Lano, not thus were thy legs smart at the jousts of Il Topo.' And since perchance his breath failed him, of himself and of a bush he made a group.

Behind them the wood was full of black hounds eager

>   Nudi e graffiati, fuggendo sì forte,
>   Che della selva rompièno ogni rosta.
>   Quel dinanzi: Ora accorri, accorri, morte.
>   E l' altro, a cui pareva tardar troppo,
>   Gridava: Lano, sì non furo accorte   120
>   Le gambe tue alle giostre del Toppo.
>   E poichè forse gli fallia la lena,
>   Di sè e d' un cespuglio fece un groppo.
>   Diretro a loro era la selva piena
>   Di nere cagne, bramose e correnti,

'prodigals' of the fourth circle, whose sin is rather that they 'boasted themselves in the multitude of their riches,' and spent ὅσα μὴ δεῖ. Eth. Nic. iv. 2 (1120 b).

[119] Lit. 'for whom there seemed to be too great delay.' **a cui** depends on **tardar** (impersonal, as ix. 9, xxi. 25), not on **pareva**. Bocc. renders 'cioè esser troppo lento,' etc., as if he read *chi pareva*.

[120] Boccaccio tells us that Lano was a young man of Siena, a member of the so-called 'Spendthrift Brigade' (see xxix. 130). In 1288 a force of Sienese was cut to pieces by the Aretines under Buonconte of Montefeltro, at a spot near Arezzo called the ford of Pieve del Toppo (Villani vii. 120); and it appears that Lano, being ruined and desperate, chose to fight and be killed, rather than to run away when he might.—**accorte**, much like *scorta* in Purg. xix. 12. Possibly the use here of the compound, which is less usual in this sense, may be meant to suggest a kind of mocking echo of Lano's **accorri**.

[125] P. di Dante and Bargigi consider that the hounds suggest the *creditors* who pursue the spendthrift. Benvenuto, who, with a carelessness unusual in him, represents the souls as pursued by hunters as

and running, like greyhounds that have issued from the leash. In the one who was crouching they set their teeth and tore him up piece by piece; then they carried away those woeful limbs.

Then my Escort took me by the hand, and brought me to the bush which was wailing in vain through its bloody rents. 'O James,' it was saying, 'of Sant' Andrea, what has it helped thee to make a screen of me? What blame have I for thy guilty life?' When the Master had stood still over it, he said: 'Who wast thou, that through so many pricks breathest out with thy blood a woeful speech?' And

> Come veltri che uscisser di catena.
> In quel, che s' appiattò, miser li denti,
>   E quel dilaceraro a brano a brano;
>   Poi sen portar quelle membra dolenti.
> Presemi allor la mia scorta per mano, 130
>   E menommi al cespuglio che piangea
>   Per le rotture sanguinenti invano.
> O Jacomo, dicea, da sant' Andrea,
>   Che t' è giovato di me fare schermo?
>   Che colpa ho io della tua vita rea?
> Quando il Maestro fu sopr' esso fermo,
>   Disse: Chi fusti, che per tante punte
>   Soffi con sangue doloroso sermo?

---

well as dogs, sees the creditors in the former: the dogs being the various 'incommoda' to which a bankrupt is subjected.

[133] James 'of the Chapel of St. Andrew' was a young Paduan noble of the house of Monselice, whose eccentric fashions of wasting his money seem to have kept his memory alive for several generations after his own death, which, according to Witte, took place in 1239, when he was killed by order of Eccelino. His chief peculiarity would appear to have been a mania for arson, which he gratified at the cost of his own and his tenants' houses.

he to us: 'O souls that are come to see the unseemly rending which has thus detached my leaves from me, collect them again at the foot of the sorry tussock. I belonged to the city which into the Baptist changed its first patron; wherefore he for this cause will ever make it sorry through his craft. And if it were not that above the

> Ed egli a noi : O anime che giunte
>   Siete a veder lo strazio disonesto, 140
>   Ch' ha le mie fronde sì da me disgiunte,
> Raccoglietele al piè del tristo cesto :
>   Io fui della città che nel Batista
>   Mutò il primo patrono : ond' ei per questo
> Sempre con l' arte sua la farà trista :
>   E se non fosse che in sul passo d' Arno

[143] According to the current history, Florence was originally under the special patronage of Mars, to whom a great temple had been erected in the time of Augustus, soon after the first foundation of the city, to commemorate the victory of the Romans over the Fiesolans (Villani i. 42). Then when the Florentines became Christian, they converted the temple into a church dedicated to St. John the Baptist, and put the statue of Mars in a tower near the Arno (ib. 60, ii. 1). Afterwards, when Attila (who is confused with Totila) destroyed the city, all except the temple, which was built under such a combination of stars as to be indestructible, the tower and image fell into the river. The image remained there until the city was rebuilt by Charles the Great, when it was fished out in a mutilated state (Boccaccio ; Vill. iii. 1), and set up on a pillar at the head of the Ponte Vecchio (see Par. xvi. 47), where it remained till it was carried away by a flood in 1333 (Villani xi. 1).

Benvenuto, who will not allow that Dante, as a good Christian, could attribute to a heathen god the power, which this passage seems to imply, of plaguing a city in revenge for its conversion to Christianity, holds that the words have a hidden meaning, and refer to the abandonment by the Florentines of their old soldierly simplicity, and their devotion to money-making ; the Baptist being, as in Par. xviii. 134, taken to suggest the florin stamped with his effigy. This suggestion seems ingenious.

passage of Arno there remains yet some sight of him, those citizens who set it up again afterwards upon the ashes which remained from Attila would have had the work done fruitlessly. I made a gibbet for myself of my own house.'

> Rimane ancor di lui alcuna vista;
> Quei cittadin, che poi la rifondarno
>   Sopra il cener che d' Attila rimase,
>   Avrebber fatto lavorare indarno.   150
> Io fei giubbetto a me delle mie case.

[151] It is not known who the speaker is. Benv. says that many Florentines hanged themselves about this time, notably one Rocco dei Mozzi, and a jurist, Lotto degli Agli.

CANTO XIV

ARGUMENT

They issue from the wood upon a plain of sand where fire is ever falling; and pass along the margin of the river of blood. Here some are lying still, some going onwards, being those who had been violent against God and against natural laws. Virgil relates the origin of the rivers which flow through Hell.

BECAUSE the love of my birthplace constrained me, I gathered again the scattered leaves, and gave them back to him, who by this time was faint of speech. Then we came to the boundary where the second ring is divided from the third, and where is seen a gruesome device of justice.

Rightly to explain the new things I say that we arrived

> Poichè la carità del natio loco
>   Mi strinse, raunai le fronde sparte,
>   E rendei le a colui ch' era già fioco.
> Indi venimmo al fine, ove si parte
>   Lo secondo giron dal terzo, e dove
>   Si vede di giustizia orribil arte.
> A ben manifestar le cose nuove,

---

[1] Because the sinner was a fellow-citizen of his own. It is hard to say whether the words are ironical. They may be compared, or contrasted, with the opening lines of Canto xxvi.

[2] **fioco**: it would seem that the power of speech in these animate shrubs only lasted while the wound was recent, and the sap flowing. Cf. xiii. 8o.

at a land which from its bed rejects every plant. The
woeful wood is a fringe to it round about, as to that is the
foss of sorrow: here we stayed our feet upon the very edge.
The space was one sand, dry and dense, made not in other
fashion than that which once was trodden by the feet of Cato.
O vengeance of God, how oughtest thou to be feared by
each one who reads that which was manifested to my eyes!
Many troops of naked souls I saw, which all were wailing
right piteously; and divers law seemed to be laid upon
them. Some folk were lying supine on the ground, some
were sitting all gathered up, and others were continually

> Dico che arrivammo ad una landa,
> Che dal suo letto ogni pianta rimove.
> La dolorosa selva l' è ghirlanda   10
> Intorno, come il fosso tristo ad essa:
> Quivi fermammo i passi a randa a randa.
> Lo spazzo era un' arena arida e spessa,
> Non d' altra foggia fatta che colei,
> Che fu dai piè di Caton già soppressa.
> O vendetta di Dio, quanto tu dei
> Esser temuta da ciascun che legge
> Ciò che fu manifesto agli occhi miei!
> D' anime nude vidi molte gregge,
> Che piangean tutte assai miseramente,   20
> E parea posta lor diversa legge.
> Supin giaceva in terra alcuna gente;
> Alcuna si sedea tutta raccolta,
> Ed altra andava continuamente.

---

[15] With allusion to the description in Lucan Phars. ix. 411, sqq. of Cato's march through the Libyan desert (where, by the way, the famous anecdote of Sir Philip Sidney and the cup of water is anticipated).

22-24 Nota quod autor pulcerrime fingit blasphemos jacere, quia sunt fulminati et prostrati ad terram (perhaps rather, as Scart. says, to denote

going. They that were going round were more in number, and less those who were lying in the torment, but to their woe they had their tongues more loosed. All over the sand with a slow fall were showering broad flakes of fire, as of snow upon a windless alp. As Alexander, in those hot parts of India, saw falling upon his host flames

> Quella che giva intorno era più molta,
>   E quella men, che giaceva al tormento,
>   Ma più al duolo avea la lingua sciolta.
> Sopra tutto il sabbion d' un cader lento
>   Piovean di foco dilatate falde,
>   Come di neve in alpe senza vento. 30
> Quali Alessandro in quelle parti calde
>   D' India vide sopra lo suo stuolo

the impotence of man when he sets himself up against God]; sodomitas fingit currere, quia currunt quo ardor concupiscentiae trahit eos [cf. the carnal sinners of Canto v.]; usurarios vero fingit sedere, quia . . . magnam partem vitae expendunt sedendo ad bancum in calculando rationes et numerando pecunias.—Benv.

[31] This story occurs in the apocryphal letter of Alexander to Aristotle 'concerning the Marvels of India,' which was very popular in the Middle Ages. As they were going through the deserts (at the head of the Persian Gulf, as it would seem), about the time of the equinox, first snow fell heavily, which Alexander ordered his soldiers to trample down; then followed rain; and then 'visae sunt nubes ardentes de caelo tanquam faces (al. falces) descendere . . . Jussi itaque milites scissas vestes opponere ignibus.' A later version, which Dante probably never saw, since it seems doubtful whether it existed before the 14th century, but which became very popular under the title 'Historia Alexandri de preliis,' and was frequently printed before 1500, gives the same story, but in somewhat different, and varying, words. Dante, it will be seen, has confused the treatment applied to the fire and the snow. For information as to the medieval Alexander legends, see a letter by Mr. Paget Toynbee in the 'Academy' for February 2, 1889. Zacher's 'Pseudo-Callisthenes' (Halle 1867) may also be consulted; and Prof. Skeat's prefaces to Nos. i. and xxxi. Early English Text Society's 'Extra Series.'

unbroken even to the ground, wherefore he had the foresight to trample down the soil with his troops, to the end that the vapour might better be extinguished while it was isolated; so came down the eternal heat, whereby the sand was set on fire like kindling under a hearth, to double their woe. Without rest for ever was the dance of their wretched hands, now from this side, now from that beating off from themselves the fresh burning.

I began: 'Master, thou that overcomest all things save the stubborn Demons who issued out against us at the entering of the gate, who is that mighty one who seems not

>   Fiamme cadere infino a terra salde;
> Perch' ei provvide a scalpitar lo suolo
>   Con le sue schiere, acciocchè il vapore
>   Me' si stingeva mentre ch' era solo:
> Tale scendeva l' eternale ardore;
>   Onde l' arena s' accendea, com' esca
>   Sotto focile, a doppiar lo dolore.
> Senza riposo mai era la tresca
>   Delle misere mani, or quindi or quinci
>   Iscotendo da sè l' arsura fresca.
> Io cominciai: Maestro, tu che vinci
>   Tutte le cose, fuor che i Demon duri,
>   Che all' entrar della porta incontro uscinci,
> Chi è quel grande, che non par che curi

---

[40] **tresca**: Nota, ut bene videas si autor venatus fuit ubique quicquid faciebat ad suum propositum, quod tresca est quaedam dancia, sive genus tripudii, quod fit Neapoli artificialiter valde. . . . Stant enim plures sibi invicem oppositi, et unus elevabit manum ad unam partem, et subito alii intenti facient idem; deinde movebit manum ad aliam partem, ita facient ceteri; aliquando ambas manus simul . . . unde est mirabile videre tantam dimicationem manuum et omnium membrorum.—Benv. Boccaccio to the same effect, but less fully.

to care for the burning, and lies despiteful and turned so that the rain seems not to be ripening him?' And that same one, who was aware that I was asking my Leader of him, cried: 'As I was living such am I dead. If Jove were to weary out his smith from whom in his wrath he

> L' incendio, e giace dispettoso e torto
> Sì che la pioggia non par che il maturi?^a
> E quel medesmo, che si fue accorto
> Ch' io domandava il mio duca di lui, 50
> Gridò: Qual io fui vivo, tal son morto.
> Se Giove stanchi il suo fabbro, da cui

^a *marturi* Cass. 2 ; *maturi* 4.

[47] **torto**, i.e. facie ad caelum (Benv.); but more probably 'turned half round,' as the usual position was 'supine' (l. 22).

[48] **maturi** is the reading with far the most authority; and the truly Dantesque irony of it, comparing the sinners under the roasting heat to ripening fruit, makes it in every way preferable to the tamer *marturi*. Cf. xxxii. 117.

[49] This is Capaneus, one of the seven chiefs who assaulted Thebes. His position here is accounted for by his language in the description of his end in Stat. Theb. iii. 661: Primus in orbe deos fecit timor, etc. See too x. 897 sqq. He challenges the gods to come to the aid of the city, taunting Jupiter especially.

> Tu potius venias, quis enim concurrere nobis
> Dignior? en cineres Semeleaque busta tenentur.
> Nunc age, nunc totis in me connitere flammis,
> Juppiter . . .

Jupiter is at last aroused, and saying

> Quaenam spes hominum tumidae post praelia Phlegrae?
> Tune etiam feriendus?

calls for a thunderbolt, and strikes Capaneus, who refuses to fall, and dies upright, supported by the walls of the city against which he leans –

> paulum si tardius artus
> Cessissent, poterat fulmen meruisse secundum.

To this doubtless is the allusion in ll. 52 sqq.

took the keen thunderbolt wherewith on my last day I was struck; or if he were to weary out the others turn by turn in Etna at the black smithy, crying, Good Vulcan, help, help; just as he did at the fight of Phlegra, and were to shoot at me with all his might, he would not be able to have thereby a glad revenge.' Then my Leader spoke with vehemence, in so much that I had not heard him so vehement: 'O Capaneus, in that thy pride is not mortified, art thou more punished; no torment would be beside thy rage to thy madness woe complete.' Then turned he to me with a better countenance, saying: 'That was one of the seven kings who besieged Thebes; and he held, and it seems that he holds God in disdain, and little seems it

  Crucciato prese la folgore acuta,
   Onde l' ultimo dì percosso fui;
O s' egli stanchi gli altri a muta a muta
  In Mongibello alla fucina negra,
   Chiamando: Buon Vulcano, aiuta aiuta,
Sì com' ei fece alla pugna di Flegra,
  E me saetti di tutta sua forza,
   Non ne potrebbe aver vendetta allegra.   60
Allora il Duca mio parlò di forza
  Tanto, ch' io non l' avea sì forte udito:
   O Capaneo, in ciò che non s' ammorza
La tua superbia, sei tu più punito:
  Nullo martirio, fuor che la tua rabbia,
   Sarebbe al tuo furor dolor compito.
Poi si rivolse a me con miglior labbia,
  Dicendo: Quel fu l' un dei sette regi
   Ch' assiser Tebe; ed ebbe, e par ch' egli abbia
Dio in disdegno, e poco par che il pregi: 70

that he prizes Him; but as I said to him, his own despite is to his heart adornment meet enough. Now come behind me, and see that thou put not thy feet hereafter on the scorched sand but keep them ever close to the wood.'

In silence we came to the place where gushes forth of the wood a little brook, the redness whereof yet makes me shudder. As from Bulicame the streamlet issues, which the sinful women then divide among them, so did that go its way downward through the sand. Its bottom and both its banks are made of stone, and the borders at the side;

> Ma, come io dissi a lui, li suoi dispetti
> Sono al suo petto assai debiti fregi.
> Or mi vien dietro, e guarda che non metti
> Ancor li piedi nell' arena arsiccia:
> Ma sempre al bosco li ritieni stretti.
> Tacendo divenimmo là ove spiccia
> Fuor della selva un picciol fiumicello,
> Lo cui rossore ancor mi raccapriccia.
> Quale del Bulicame esce un ruscello,
> Che parton poi tra lor le peccatrici. 80
> Tal per l' arena giù sen giva quello.
> Lo fondo suo ed ambo le pendici
> Fatt' eran pietra, e i margini da lato:

[79] **Bulicame**: the 'Boiler' (as xii. 117). As a proper name it denotes a hot sulphureous spring near Viterbo, hot enough, says Fazio degli Uberti (Dittam. iii. 10), to cook a sheep while a man walked a quarter of a mile, and sovereign against the stone. Like similar establishments in all times, it was the resort of loose women; who being compelled to reside in a special quarter, had their own special supply of water from the source, distributed by pipes to their houses.

This, as appears from ll. 134, 135, is Phlegethon, the third of the rivers of Hell. It may be supposed to be an extension of it, such as we have found in the case of the two former rivers Acheron and Styx, which forms the 'foss' of Canto xii.

whereupon I took note that the passage was there. 'Among all the rest that I have shown thee since we entered by the gate, the threshold whereof is refused to none, nothing has been perceived by thine eyes of note as is this present stream, which above itself deadens all flames.' These words were my Leader's; wherefore I prayed him to impart to me the repast, the desire whereof he had imparted to me.

'In mid-sea lies a waste country,' said he then, 'which is

> Perch' io m' accorsi che il passo era lici.
> Tra tutto l' altro ch' io t' ho dimostrato,
>   Posciachè noi entrammo per la porta,
>   Lo cui sogliare a nessuno è negato.
> Cosa non fu dagli tuoi occhi scorta
>   Notabil, come lo presente rio,
>   Che sopra sè tutte fiammelle ammorta:
> Queste parole fur del Duca mio:
>   Perchè il pregai, che mi largisse il pasto
>   Di cui largito m' aveva il disio.
> In mezzo mar siede un paese guasto.

[84] I.e. the passage across the plain of burning sand.

[87] Land. refers to Aen. vi. 127. It is of course contrasted here with the inner gate, alluded to in l. 45.

[91] I.e. by the steam (xv. 2) rising from it (not, of course, with its water, which would be no protection to those on its banks). There is no doubt some reason of symbolism for the introduction of this line; but it is obscure, and the commentators mostly have nothing to say. Landino indeed interprets that the contemplation of vice under the guidance of reason is a safeguard against the assaults of passion. Not less far-fetched, though much less in accordance with the facts of human nature, is Lubin's suggestion that the career of tyrants is incompatible with indulgence in carnal sins.

[94] sqq. The general notion of a composite image as described in these lines is obviously suggested by Daniel ii.; but the symbolism is quite different. Here the image undoubtedly typifies the history of the human race. It is placed in Crete on Mount Ida no doubt in conformity with

called Crete, under whose king the world once was sinless. There is a mountain, which erst was glad with waters and with leaves, which was called Ida; now is it desert, like a decayed thing. Rhea chose it on a time for a trusty cradle to her son, and to hide him better, when he wailed, she let the cries be made there. Within the mountain stands erect

> Diss' egli allora, che s' appella Creta,
> Sotto il cui rege fu già il mondo casto.
> Una montagna v' è, che già fu lieta
> D' acqua e di fronde, che si chiamò Ida;
> Ora è diserta come cosa vieta.
> Rea la scelse già per cuna fida   100
> Del suo figliuolo, e, per celarlo meglio,[b]
> Quando piangea, vi facea far le grida.
> Dentro dal monte sta dritto un gran veglio,

[b] *D' un suo W.*

Aen. iii. 105: Mons Idaeus ubi et gentis cunabula nostrae (i.e. of the Trojans, and hence of the Romans); but that island is otherwise specially appropriate from its position at the point where the boundaries of Europe, Asia, and Africa meet. The division into metals of course follows the commonplace of all poets; Dante may have followed Ovid as much as Daniel. He varies, as will be seen, from the prophet (or at least from the version of the Vulgate) by making the brass terminate with the trunk. This, no doubt, is to indicate the dual organisation of Church and Empire on which rests his whole political theory; and Benvenuto is probably right in seeing in the leg which terminated in the foot of 'baked earth' the symbol of the ecclesiastical power, which, he says, had ever since Constantine's time been the stronger (cf. Purg. xvi. 109). Lubin's view that the two legs are the eastern and western empires can hardly be accepted; if only for the reason that, as the figure is placed, the right leg clearly ought to denote, not the Roman, but the Byzantine monarchy.

[a] Saturn.
[b] With allusion to the cries of the Corybantes.

a great elder, who holds his shoulders turned toward
Damietta, and gazes at Rome as his mirror. His head is
fashioned of fine gold; and pure silver are his arms and
breast; then is he of brass even to the fork; from thence
downward is he all choice iron, save that his right foot is
baked earth, and upon the first more than upon the other
he stands upright. Every part beside the gold is burst with
a cleft which drips tears, the which, collected, pierce this
cavern. Their course into this vale is from rock to rock;
they make Acheron, Styx, and Phlegethon, afterwards they
go their way down through this narrow conduit, even to the
place where there is no more descending: they make Cocytus; and of what sort is that pool, thou wilt see: therefore

> Che tien volte le spalle inver Damiata,
>   E Roma guata sì come suo speglio.
> La sua testa è di fin' oro formata,
>   E puro argento son le braccia e il petto,
>   Poi è di rame infino alla forcata:
> Da indi in giuso è tutto ferro eletto,
>   Salvo che il destro piede è terra cotta,   110
>   E sta in su quel, più che in sull' altro, eretto.
> Ciascuna parte, fuor che l' oro, è rotta
>   D' una fessura che lagrime goccia,
>   Le quali accolte foran quella grotta.
> Lor corso in questa valle si diroccia:
>   Fanno Acheronte, Stige e Flegetonta;
>   Poi sen va giù per questa stretta doccia
> Infin là dove più non si dismonta:
>   Fanno Cocito; e qual sia quello stagno,

104, 105 Turning his back on the old monarchies, of which Egypt is the type, and looking in the direction of the 'course of empire.'

112 All ages after the golden were subject to sin and sorrow.

it is not related here.' And I to him: 'If the watercourse before us thus flows down from our world, why does it appear to us at this rim only?' And he to me: 'Thou knowest that the place is round, and albeit thou hast come far indeed to the left in descending towards the bottom, thou hast not yet turned through the whole circle; wherefore if a new thing appears to us, it ought not to bring wonder to thy countenance.' And I again: 'Master, where are found Phlegethon and Lethe, for of the one thou speakest not, and the other thou sayest that it is formed of this fall?' 'In all thy questions thou surely pleasest me,' he answered;

    Tu il vederai: però qui non si conta.   120
Ed io a lui: Se il presente rigagno
    Si deriva così dal nostro mondo,
    Perchè ci appar pure a questo vivagno?
Ed egli a me: Tu sai che il luogo è tondo
    E tutto che tu sii venuto molto
    Pur a sinistra giù calando al fondo,[c]
Non sei ancor per tutto il cerchio volto;
    Perchè, se cosa n' apparisce nuova,
    Non dee addur maraviglia al tuo volto.
Ed io ancor: Maestro, ove si trova   130
    Flegetonta e Letè, chè dell' un taci,
    E l' altro di' che si fa d' esta piova?
In tutte tue question certo mi piaci,

[c] *Più a s. Cass.* 1234 *II*.

[126] **Pur a sinistra:** see note ix. 132. There they were *not* descending but going on a level during their temporary change of direction.

[128] It would seem that Acheron, Styx, and Phlegethon follow various courses down the sides of Hell, and that their waters combined at the bottom form Cocytus.

'but the boiling of the red water ought well to have solved one that thou makest. Lethe thou shalt see, but outside of this foss, in the place where the souls go to wash themselves when their fault has been repented and put away.' Then he said: 'Now it is time to go aside from the wood; see that thou come behind me; the borders make a way, for they are not heated, and over them all vapour is dispersed.'

> Rispose; ma il bollor dell' acqua rossa
> Dovea ben solver l' una che tu faci.
> Letè vedrai, ma fuor di questa fossa,
> Là dove vanno l' anime a lavarsi,
> Quando la colpa pentuta è rimossa.
> Poi disse: Omai è tempo da scostarsi
> Dal bosco: fa che diretro a me vegne: 140
> Li margini fan via, che non son arsi,
> E sopra loro ogni vapor si spegne.

[134] You might guess by the boiling that this is Phlegethon.

CANTO XV

ARGUMENT

Dante talks as they go with Master Brunetto Latini, and hears from him a prophecy concerning that which is to befall him. He sees the spirits of other learned men.

Now one of the hard borders bears us on our way, and the steam of the brook shadows overhead so that it saves from the fire the water and the embankment. As the Flemings between Wissant and Bruges, fearing the flood that is

> Ora cen porta l' un dei duri margini,
> E il fummo del ruscel di sopra aduggia
> Si, che dal foco salva l' acqua e gli argini.
> Quale i Fiamminghi tra Guizzante e Bruggia,

[1] **Guizzante.** Most modern commentators, German and English, understand Cadsand, at the mouth of the Scheldt, to the north-east of Bruges, relying apparently on a statement by Ludovico Guicciardini, who resided in the Low Countries, in the service of Charles V., during the latter half of the sixteenth century, and wrote a description of them. 'Questo,' he says, 'è quel medesimo luogo del quale il nostro gran Poeta Dante fa menzione nel quinto decimo capitolo dell' Inferno, chiamandolo scorrettamente Guizzante.' An objection to this is that Cadsand is not and never has been within the boundaries of Flanders. Also, where it is mentioned by Italian writers (e.g. Villani xi. 72), it is called *Gaggiante*. On the other hand, *Guizante* in contemporary writings is Wissant, between Calais and Cape Grisnez, sacked by Edward III. after Crecy (Villani xii. 68). This would do fairly well to denote the western limit of the coast of Flanders, as known to Dante; Bruges indicating the east of it. There seems to be no doubt of the reading.

blown their way, make their screen, to the end that the sea may keep back; and as the Paduans along the Brenta, to defend their villages and their castles, before that Chiarentana feels the heat; after such fashion were those made, albeit that neither so high nor so thick did the master, whoever he was, make them.

> Temendo il fiotto che ver lor s' avventa,
> Fanno lo schermo, perchè il mar si fuggia;
> E quale i Padovan lungo la Brenta,
> Per difender lor ville e lor castelli,
> Anzi che Chiarentana il caldo senta:
> A tale imagine eran fatti quelli,   10
> Tutto che nè sì alti nè sì grossi,
> Qual che si fosse, lo maestro felli.

⁵ For Dante's knowledge of the tides, see note Par. xvi. 82. It may be added that Fazio degli Uberti (v. 16) is exceedingly vague on the subject; while Boccaccio, to this passage, gives a very intelligent description, and specially remarks on the tide at Venice. This line of course indicates the effect of a flood-tide with the wind behind it.

⁹ **Chiarentana** can hardly be anything else than Carantania, Carinthia. The word has no other meaning in the language of the time, e.g. Dittamondo iii. 2: Benvenuto seems to have no doubt as to what is intended, though he makes the mistake (if it be one) of supposing that the Brenta rises in Carinthia. No doubt that is not the case according to present political divisions; but it may be observed that in the early Middle Ages the duchy of Carinthia embraced both Val Sugana, where the head-waters of the river are, and also the city of Padua. Of this last, indeed, the Dukes claimed the lordship down to 1322 and later see Villani ix. 192. But probably Dante meant no more than to name an Alpine district in the neighbourhood of north-east Italy. The idea (which Witte suggests, and Scartazzini dogmatically adopts) that an obscure mountain-group near Trent is intended does not commend itself.

¹¹ This touch has often been noticed, as showing Dante's vivid realisation of his scenes, and his freedom from any idea of impressing by vague exaggeration.

We were already remote from the wood, so far that I had not seen where it was, for all I had turned me back, when we met a troop of souls which was coming along the embankment, and each was looking at us, as one man is wont to look at the other at evening under a new moon; and they pointed their eyelashes towards us, in such wise as an old tailor does at his needle's eye. Thus eyed by such a tribe, I was recognised by one who took me by the hem, and cried: 'What a marvel!' And I, when he stretched his arm to me, fixed my eyes on his baked countenance, so

> Già eravam dalla selva rimossi
>   Tanto, ch' io non avrei visto dov' era,
>   Perch' io indietro rivolto mi fossi,
> Quando incontrammo d' anime una schiera,
>   Che venia lungo l' argine, e ciascuna
>   Ci riguardava, come suol da sera
> Guardar l' un l' altro sotto nuova luna;
>   E sì ver noi aguzzavan le ciglia,   20
>   Come il vecchio sartor fa nella cruna.
> Così adocchiato da cotal famiglia,
>   Fui conosciuto da un, che mi prese
>   Per lo lembo, e gridò: Qual maraviglia?
> Ed io, quando il suo braccio a me distese,
>   Ficcai gli occhi per lo cotto aspetto

---

[19] **Perchè.** For this use see Diez iii. 32; and cf. Purg. v. 58; vi. 38, etc. There is a good instance, Vill. vii. 14: 'perchè il popolo fosse armato . . . erano più per paura che per offendere al conte.'

[21] For the use of **fa** to avoid (like our 'does') the repetition of a foregoing verb, see Diez iii. 383, and cf. the well-known passage of Thucydides (ii. 49) πολλοὶ τοῦτο ἔδρασαν (i.e. threw themselves) ἐς φρέατα. So Purg. iv. 131; xxvi. 70, etc.

[22] **famiglia**: cf. Par. x. 49.

that the scorched visage did not keep the recognition of him from my understanding; and stooping my hand to his face I answered: 'Are you here, Master Brunetto?' And

> Sì, che il viso abbruciato non difese
> La conoscenza sua al mio intelletto;
> E chinando la mano alla sua faccia,[a]
> Risposi: Siete voi qui, ser Brunetto?   30

[a] *chin. la mia* ed. 1484; *alla mia* f. Ald.

[29] **mano** has the great preponderance of authority, and the support of the early illustrations almost without exception. The gesture implied is a very natural one, of either surprise, or deprecation, or merely reverence. Scartazzini's objection to *mia* is, however, singularly unfortunate, for Dante does presently go with his head bowed to Brunetto's. Of course **a** need not imply that he stooped till he was on a level with his interlocutor.

[30] Of Brunetto, son of Bonaccorso Latini (or Latino), we know—besides what may be gathered from this Canto, from some scattered notices in documents, and from a few lines in the Tesoretto—little more than Villani tells us (vi. 73, 79; viii. 10), viz. that he was 'dittatore' or secretary to the Republic, that he went on the mission sent by the Florentines in 1260 to Alfonso of Arragon, to bespeak his aid for the Guelf party; that with the rest of the Guelfs he was banished (probably before he had returned from his mission) in the latter part of the same year, after their defeat at Montaperti, and returned with them after the death of Manfred; that he was the first to introduce the systematic study of oratory and political science in Florence, and was generally a great philosopher, and wrote the books called Tesoro and Tesoretto, but was 'mondano uomo'; and that he died in 1294. From this, and some of Dante's expressions, a myth has grown up that he was in some special way Dante's tutor or instructor, for which there is no evidence. The relations between them were probably only such as might be expected to exist between a youth and an old man (Brunetto seems to have been about fifty when Dante was born)—possibly a family friend—with a reputation for learning and statesmanship. For his writings see below, l. 119. His portrait is said on the strength of a statement of Vasari's to be one of those associated with Dante's in the Bargello.

he: 'O my son, let it not displease thee, if Brunetto Latini turns back a little way with thee, and lets the line go.' I said to him: 'With all my power I pray you for that; and if you will that I sit me down with you, I will do so, if it pleases this man, for I am going with him.' 'O son,' said he, 'whoever of this flock halts for a moment, lies afterwards a hundred years without fanning himself when the fire strikes him. Therefore go forward: I will come at thy skirts, and then I will rejoin my company, that go weeping their eternal loss.' I dared not descend from the path to go level with him; but I held my head bowed, as a man who goes reverently.

> E quegli: O figliuol mio, non ti dispiaccia,
>   Se Brunetto Latini un poco teco [b]
>   Ritorna indietro, e lascia andar la traccia.
> Io dissi a lui: Quanto posso ven preco;
>   E se volete che con voi m' asseggia,
>   Farol, se piace a costui, chè vo seco.
> O figliuol, disse, qual di questa greggia
>   S' arresta punto, giace poi cent' anni
>   Senza arrostarsi quando il fuoco il feggia.[c]
> Però va oltre; io ti verrò ai panni,   40
>   E poi rigiugnerò la mia masnada,
>   Che va piangendo i suoi eterni danni.
> Io non osava scender della strada
>   Per andar par di lui: ma il capo chino
>   Tenea, come uom che reverente vada.

[b] *Ser Gg.* 12345: *Latino Cass.* 35.
[c] *Senza restarsi Gg.* (alt.) *Cass.* 23: *feggia* 3.

[c] **feggia**: pres. subj. from *fedire* (= *fiedere*, *ferire*). For the form, cf. *regga* from *redire* (= *riedere*), x. 82.

He began: 'What fortune or what destiny brings thee down here before thy last day? and who is this that is showing thee the road?' 'Up there, in the bright life,' I answered him, 'I went astray in a valley before my age was at the full. Only yesterday morning did I turn my back on it; this one appeared to me, as I was returning to it; and he is leading me homeward again by this pathway.' And he to me: 'If thou follow thy star, thou canst not fail of a

> Ei cominciò: Qual fortuna o destino
>   Anzi l' ultimo dì quaggiù ti mena?
>   E chi è questi che mostra il cammino?
> Là su di sopra in la vita serena,
>   Rispos' io lui, mi smarri' in una valle,   50
>   Avanti che l' età mia fosse piena.
> Pure ier mattina le volsi le spalle:
>   Questi m' apparve, tornand' io in quella,
>   E riducemi a ca per questo calle.
> Ed egli a me: Se tu segui tua stella,

[47] Cf. Purg. i. 58.

[51] Probably only 'before the measure of my days was fulfilled.' There seems no need to refer, as in the first line of the poem, to Conv. iv. 23, with its comparison of the life of man to an arch, and suppose the meaning to be 'before I had reached my thirty-fifth year.' If for no other reason, **età piena** would hardly be the appropriate word to express what Dante elsewhere calls *mezzo del cammin*.

[53] Observe that Dante makes no other reply to Brunetto's question, who his companion is; and cf. x. 62. As Scartazzini notes, Virgil comes under the rule which Dante observes, of never mentioning any sacred personage by name so long as he is in Hell.

[55-57] It is quite unnecessary to infer, as some have done, from these lines that Brunetto was a student of astrology, and had cast Dante's horoscope. From what he says in his own works, and perhaps still more from what he does not say, we may gather on the contrary that he had no faith in divination by the stars. See, e.g., Tesoretto x. 25-27. Benv., with his usual shrewdness, after mentioning this view, adds 'vel

glorious port, if I well observed in the fair life. And if I had not died so betimes, seeing the heaven thus kind to thee, I should have given thee strengthening in thy task. But that thankless and malign commons that came down from Fiesole *ab antiquo* and still partakes of the mountain

> Non puoi fallire al glorioso porto,
> Se ben m' accorsi nella vita bella:
> E s' io non fossi sì per tempo morto,
> Veggendo il cielo a te così benigno,
> Dato t' avrei all' opera conforto.   60
> Ma quell' ingrato popolo maligno,
> Che discese di Fiesole *ab antico*,

melius credo quod judicat secundum bonam physionomiam . . . quia consideravit saepe bonam indolem istius pueri.'

[60] This expression is curious, as Brunetto died at a good old age, and when Dante was of sufficiently mature years, it might be supposed, to stand in no need of 'conforto.' Is it possible that some definite plans were now on foot for forming a third party free from the vulgar partisanship of Guelfs or Ghibelines, which a man like Brunetto might have been expected to join?

[61] Note that Villani, who always adhered to the Guelf side, uses just the same language of the commons of Florence. Thus after the defeat of Montaperti, he says (vi. 78): 'Così s' adonò la rabbia dell' ingrato e superbo popolo di Firenze.' In xii. 44 again he speaks of the treatment suffered by such men as 'Messer Farinata degli Uberti che guarenti Firenze che non fosse disfatta . . . e messer Vieri de' Cerchi, e Dante Alighieri, e altri cari cittadini e guelfi, caporali e sostenitori di questo popolo.' Then he goes on, in words borrowed from Dante, to speak of 'i danni fatti loro per lo ingrato popolo maligno che discese de' Romani e de' Fiesolani *ab antiquo*.'

[62] The prevalent view seems to have been that the nobles of Florence were originally of Roman blood, the commons immigrants from Fiesole, who came to live there when their town was destroyed by the Florentines (Vill. iv. 6). These, he tells us, 'sempre si tennono co' Goti, e poi co' Lombardi e con tutti i ribelli e nemici dello 'mperio di Roma e di Santa Chiesa' (ii. 21). See also iii. 1, where he expresses the view, which he afterwards repeats more than once (e. g. iv. 7), that this mix-

and of the quarry, shall, for thy good deeds, become thy
enemy. And reason it is; for among the harsh sorbs it is
unmeet that the sweet fig should bear fruit. An old fame
in the world calls them blind; a folk it is greedy, envious, and
proud; from their habits see that thou cleanse thyself. Thy
fortune reserves such honour for thee that the one side and
the other will hunger for thee; but far will be the fodder
from the muzzle. Let the beasts from Fiesole make litter
of their own selves, and let them not touch the plant, if any

> E tiene ancor del monte e del macigno,
> Ti si farà, per tuo ben far, nimico:
> Ed è ragion; chè tra li lazzi sorbi
> Si disconvien fruttare al dolce fico.
> Vecchia fama nel mondo li chiama orbi,
> Gent' è avara, invidiosa e superba:
> Dai lor costumi fa che tu ti forbi.
> La tua fortuna tanto onor ti serba, 70
> Che l' una parte e l' altra avranno fame
> Di te: ma lungi fia dal becco l' erba.
> Faccian le bestie Fiesolane strame
> Di lor medesme, e non tocchin la pianta,

ture of races was the source of all the troubles of Florence. Cf. too Par. xvi. 67.

[61] **macigno.** Witte remarks that the town of Florence is mainly built of stone from the quarries of Fiesole.

[64] **per tuo ben far,** i.e. for the opposition to the entry of Charles of Valois, which was one of the ostensible grounds of Dante's banishment. With all this compare Cacciaguida's prophecy, Par. xvii. 46 sqq.

[67] **orbi.** Bocc. and Benv. say that the Florentines owed this nickname to a trick played on them by the Pisans in 1117, over a division of the plunder taken by the latter from Majorca. Villani, though he mentions this story (iv. 31), ascribes the name to another cause. According to him, it was the blindness of the Florentines in admitting 'Totila' within their gates which earned it (Vill. ii. 1, 68). Cf. vi. 74.

yet springs in their dungheap, in which revives the holy seed
of those Romans, who remained there when was made the
nest of such wickedness.' 'If all my desire had been fulfilled,' I answered him, 'you would not yet be put in banishment from humankind; for in my mind is fixed, and now
goes to my heart the dear and good fatherly image of you,
when in the world from time to time you taught me how the
man becomes eternal; and how much I hold it in gratitude,
while I live it is meet that in my speech it be discerned.
That which you relate of my course I write, and keep it for

  S' alcuna surge ancor nel lor letame,[d]
 In cui riviva la semente santa
  Di quei Roman, che vi rimaser, quando
  Fu fatto il nido di malizia tanta.
 Se fosse tutto pieno il mio dimando,
  Risposi lui, voi non sareste ancora
  Dell' umana natura posto in bando:
 Chè in la mente m' è fitta, ed or mi accora
  La cara e buona imagine paterna
  Di voi, quando nel mondo ad ora ad ora
 M' insegnavate come l' uom s' eterna:
  E quant' io l' abbia in grado, mentre io vivo
  Convien che nella mia lingua si scerna.
 Ciò che narrate di mio corso scrivo,

[d] *in lor* Cass. W.

---

* I.e. at the legendary rebuilding of Florence under Charles the
Great. Vill. iii. 1, 2.

* s' eterna. No doubt with allusion to the ἐφ' ὅσον ἐνδέχεται ἀθα-
νατίζειν of Eth. x. 7 (1177 b). Brunetto was a student and expounder
of the Ethics, of which he gives a paraphrase in his Trésor.

commenting with another text, for a lady who will know it, if I attain to her. Thus much would I have to be manifest to you, so only that my conscience chide me not, that I am ready for fortune, as she wills. Such earnest is not new to my ears; wherefore let fortune turn her wheel as pleases her, and the churl his mattock.'

My Master then turned back, on the side of the right cheek, and looked at me; then he said: 'Well listens he who marks it.' Nor by so much the less do I go on, talking with Master Brunetto; and I ask who are his companions best known and of highest rank. And he to me: 'To know

> E serbolo a chiosar con altro testo
> A donna che saprà, se a lei arrivo.   90
> Tanto vogl' io che vi sia manifesto,
> Pur che mia coscienza non mi garra,
> Che alla fortuna, come vuol, son presto.
> Non è nuova agli orecchi miei tale arra:
> Però giri fortuna la sua rota,
> Come le piace, e il villan la sua marra.
> Lo mio Maestro allora in sulla gota
> Destra si volse indietro, e riguardommi:
> Poi disse: Bene ascolta chi la nota.
> Nè per tanto di men parlando vommi   100
> Con ser Brunetto, e domando chi sono
> Li suoi compagni più noti e più sommi.
> Ed egli a me: Saper d' alcuno è buono:

---

[89] I.e. with what he has heard from Ciacco and Farinata, Cantos vi. and x.' as to his future; 'quorum uterque fecit textum obscurum satis,' says Benvenuto.

[96] **villan**: with allusion to the admixture of families from the country districts with the true burghers of Florence, to which the growth of party quarrels is ascribed, as in Par. xvi. 67, 135, etc.

of some is good; of the others it will be praiseworthy to be
silent, for the time would be short for so much talk. Know
in sum, that all were clerks, and great men of letters and
of great fame, by one and the same sin defiled in the world.
Priscian goes his way with that grim crowd, and Francis of
Accorso; and thou canst also see there, if thou hadst had a
desire of such scurf, him who by the servant of servants was

> Degli altri fia laudabile tacerci,
>   Chè il tempo saria corto a tanto suono.
> In somma sappi, che tutti fur cherci,
>   E letterati grandi, e di gran fama,
>   D' un peccato medesmo al mondo lerci.
> Priscian sen va con quella turba grama,
>   E Francesco d' Accorso; anco vedervi.   110
>   S' avessi avuto di tal tigna brama,
> Colui potei che dal servo dei servi

[109] Priscian is of course the famous grammarian, who lived in the sixth century. There is no evidence of his having been guilty of the sin here punished; and he is probably chosen as a representative of teachers of youth. It has been suggested that Dante confused him, as indeed Benvenuto, who says 'monachus fuit et apostatavit,' appears to do, with Priscillian, a Spanish heretic of the fourth century, for whom see Gibbon, chap. xxvii. But the reference here is evidently to a 'letterato.'

[110] Francesco, son of Accorso or Accursius, the famous jurist, and himself a lawyer of great fame, was brought from Bologna to England by Edward I., and professed at Oxford. His fellow-citizens, to mark their sense of his value, confiscated his goods, which, however, were restored on his return. He died 1294. Benvenuto gives a terrible account of the prevalence of this sin at Bologna, when he himself was lecturing on Dante there in 1375, and says that he incurred some danger for having denounced it to the papal legate.

[111] *Servus servorum Dei* is the style used by all Popes since Gregory I., says Boccaccio. In this case the Pope referred to is Boniface VIII.; and it is characteristic that the first reference to him in the poem should represent him as condoning gross vice.

[112] The commentators all agree that the person spoken of is Andrea

translated from Arno to Bacchiglione, where he left his nerves
stretched to sin. More would I say; but my going and my
discourse cannot be longer, because I see there a new smoke
arise from the sand. A folk is coming with whom I must not
be. Let my Treasure be recommended to thee, wherein I still

> Fu trasmutato d' Arno in Bacchiglione,
> Dove lasciò li mal protesi nervi.
> Di più direi; ma il venir e il sermone
> Più lungo esser non può, però ch' io veggio
> Là surger nuovo fummo del sabbione.
> Gente vien con la quale esser non deggio;
> Siati raccomandato il mio Tesoro

de' Mozzi, who was translated about 1295 from the see of Florence to that of Vicenza; Bocc. says, at the request of his brother, who wished to free Florence from the scandal of his conduct. Benv. adds that he was 'vir simplex et fatuus,' and gives several instances of his grotesque *naïveté* in preaching. The family of the Mozzi were White Guelfs. See Philalethes for a fuller account.

114 Those who care to dwell on the subject may consult the old commentators as to the savage satire implied in this line.

115 Vellutello is doubtless right in his explanation: Perciocchè essendo della schiera de' contemplativi, non dovea andar con quella degli attivi.

119 Brunetto's great work 'Li Tresors' was written during his stay in France at the time of the Ghibeline predominance in Florence. (There is not much evidence for the statement that he was banished on a charge, true or false, of forgery. We know that he left Florence on an honourable service, and that he must have returned thither, for Dante to have known him.) It is written in French, as being 'more delightful and more generally known than other languages'; but was soon translated into Italian. Of the Italian version early editions exist; but the original was not printed till our own time. It is a concise Encyclopedia of history, natural science, ethics, rhetoric, and politics. His smaller work, Il Tesoretto, is a kind of popular version of the other. It is written in heptasyllabic couplets, and in Italian. The favourite machinery of an allegorical journey is employed; and it cannot be doubted

live; and more I ask not.' Then he turned round, and seemed of these who at Verona run the green cloth course over the country; and of those he seemed the one who is winning and not the one who loses.

> Nel quale io vivo ancora; e più non cheggio. 120
> Poi si rivolse, e parve di coloro
> Che corrono a Verona il drappo verde
> Per la campagna; e parve di costoro
> Quegli che vince e non colui che perde.

that in respect both of framework and of incidents Dante was indebted to it for many suggestions. It is quite worth reading. Other works ascribed to Brunetto are certainly apocryphal.

[120] **vivo ancora.** On this text Boccaccio launches forth into a long eulogy of the literary, and more especially the poetic life. One passage is worth quoting. After an encomium of 'mio maestro e padre Francesco Petrarca,' he proceeds: 'Non il presente nostro autore, la luce del cui valore per alquanto tempo [è] stata nascosa sotto la caligine del volgar materno, è cominciato da grandissimi letterati ad essere desiderato e ad aver caro?' These words must have been written (or spoken) in 1375; and it would appear from them that Dante's fame had undergone a temporary diminution after Villani's famous chapter (ix. 136) was written.

[122] All that seems to be known is that on the first Sunday in Lent it was the custom at Verona for a footrace to be run outside the city by naked men; the prize being a piece of green cloth. In later times the competitors appear to have been women. See Comm. Cass.

[124] Observe the use of **colui**, properly the oblique case, as exactly equivalent to the nom. **quegli**.

CANTO XVI

ARGUMENT

Dante talks with certain Florentines, who in the world had been men of renown. Afterwards they come to a brink, where the water falls over. They cast down a cord for signal, and a shape comes up.

I WAS already in a place where was heard the booming of the water which was falling into the next circle, like to that humming which the beehives make; when three shades together separated as they ran from a troop which was passing under the rain of the bitter torment. They came toward us, and each was crying: 'Stay thee, thou who by thy garb seemest to us to be one of our perverted land.'

> Già era in loco ove s' udia il rimbombo
> Dell' acqua che cadea nell' altro giro,
> Simile a quel che l' arnie fanno rombo:
> Quando tre ombre insieme si partiro,
> Correndo, d' una torma che passava
> Sotto la pioggia dell' aspro martiro.
> Venian ver noi, e ciascuna gridava:
> Sostati tu, che all' abito ne sembri
> Essere alcun di nostra terra prava.

⁹ Puossi in queste parole comprendere che quasi ciascuna città aveva un suo singolar modo di vestire . . . perciocchè ancora non eravam divenuti inghilesi nè tedeschi, come oggi agli abiti siamo.— Bocc. Benvenuto has a similar lamentation.

Ah me! what wounds saw I on their limbs, fresh and old, burnt in by the flames; still does it grieve me thereof, only to remember them. To their cries my Teacher gave heed: he turned his face toward me, and 'Wait now' said he; 'to these one would be courteous. And were there not the fire which the nature of the place darts, I would say that haste suited better to thee than to them.'[1] They began again, when we halted, their former stave; and when they were come up to us, all three made a wheel of themselves. As the champions, naked and oiled, are wont to do, looking out for their grip and their advantage, before they beat and punch each other; so in wheeling each directed his visage

> Aimè, che piaghe vidi nei lor membri 10
> Recenti e vecchie dalle fiamme incese!
> Ancor men duol, pur ch' io me ne rimembri.[2]
> Alle lor grida il mio Dottor s' attese,
> Volse il viso ver me, ed: Ora aspetta,
> Disse; a costor si vuole esser cortese:
> E se non fosse il foco che saetta
> La natura del loco, io dicerei,
> Che meglio stesse a te, che a lor, la fretta.
> Ricominciar, come noi ristemmo, ei
> L' antico verso; e quando a noi fur giunti, 20
> Fenno una rota di se tutti e trei.
> Qual soleano i campion far nudi ed unti,
> Avvisando lor presa e lor vantaggio,
> Prima che sien tra lor battuti e punti:
> Così, rotando, ciascuno il visaggio

[1] It would better become you to hasten to meet persons of their quality, than to let them come to you.

[2] **ei**: Benvenuto, Bargigi, Landino, and several of the early edd. read *hei*. The former explains 'idest heu, adverbium dolentis.' This

toward me so that the neck made a continual journey in opposite wise to the feet. And, 'If wretchedness of this unstable place brings us and our prayers into contempt,' one began, 'and our aspect stained and stripped, let our renown bend thy mind to tell us who thou art, who thus secure draggest thy living feet through Hell. This one whose footprints thou seest me trample, albeit he go naked and flayed, was of greater degree than thou deemest. He was grandson of the good Gualdrada; Guidoguerra had he

> Drizzava a me, sì che in contrario il collo
> Faceva ai piè continuo viaggio.
> E, Se miseria d' esto loco sollo ^a
> Rende in dispetto noi e nostri preghi,
> Cominciò l' uno, e il tinto aspetto e brollo;   30
> La fama nostra il tuo animo pieghi
> A dirne chi tu sei, che i vivi piedi
> Così sicuro per lo inferno freghi.
> Questi, l' orme di cui pestar mi vedi,
> Tutto che nudo e dipelato vada,
> Fu di grado maggior che tu non credi.
> Nepote fu della buona Gualdrada:
> Guido Guerra ebbe nome, ed in sua vita

^a *Deh, se* Gg.: *Eh, se* W.

does not seem very probable; but those who prefer it may compare Purg. v. 27.

³³ **freghi**: lit. 'rubbest,' i.e. on the ground. The feet of the shades would of course, as is elsewhere noticed, make no mark. The **orme** of the next line cannot therefore be taken literally.

³⁸ Guido Guerra belonged to the powerful family known as the Conti Guidi, whom we shall find frequently referred to in the poem (e.g. Par. xvi. 98, 99). See the note of Philalethes, and the family tree there given. He led the Florentine Guelfs at the battle of Grandella; his cousin Guido Novello, the head of the family, being at the same time Vicar-General of Tuscany for Manfred. Their grandfather Guido

for name, and in his life he did much with his wisdom and
with his sword. The other who after me treads the sand is
Tegghiaio Aldobrandi, the voice of whom ought to have been
accepted in the world above. And I, who am placed upon

> Fece col senno assai e con la spada.
> L' altro che appresso me l' arena trita, 40
> È Tegghiaio Aldobrandi, la cui voce
> Nel mondo su dovria esser gradita.
> Ed io, che posto son con loro in croce,

(called Il Vecchio †1213) married Inghirdruda, or Gualdrada, the daughter of Bellincione Berti (see Par. xv. 112). The story went that the Emperor Otto IV. being in Florence, was struck with the beauty of the girl, and asked who she was. Bellincione replied, 'The daughter of a man who will be proud to let you kiss her.' 'No man alive shall kiss me, but he who is to be my husband,' said the young lady. The emperor was so delighted with her spirit, that he urged Guido, who was nothing loth, to ask her in marriage, and dowered them with lands in the Casentino (Vill. v. 37, Bocc., Benv.) German criticism has found difficulties of chronology to stand in the way of accepting this pretty story.

[41] Tegghiaio Aldobrandi, of the Adimari, appears in Villani vi. 77 as the spokesman of the Guelf nobles, at whose head was Guido Guerra, and who, knowing more of the conditions of war, tried to dissuade the people from undertaking against the banished Ghibelines and their Sienese allies, aided as they were by a body of German mercenaries, the expedition which ended so disastrously at Montaperti. Villani's comments on this incident (here and ch. 81) are worth reading as showing that the Guelfs as a party were in no sense the democratic party, but contained aristocrats as much inclined (and in this case with reason) to despise the 'popolani' as any Ghibeline noble. Dante was, as appears from ll. 46 sqq. below, at any rate when he wrote this, in full social and intellectual sympathy with such men as these, however he might condemn them morally. Later on, when he wrote of Tegghiaio's family in the words of Par. xvi. 115, he had perhaps had personal reason to dwell on their pride rather than on their sagacity in counsel.

[42, 43] The older commentators merely understand 'whose fame ought to be well received.' But there would be nothing specially

the torture with them, was James Rusticucci; and of a truth my proud wife more than aught else is my bane.'

If I had been covered from the fire, I should have thrown me down among them; and I believe that the Teacher would have suffered it; but for that I should have been burned and roasted, fear overcame my good will, which had made me greedy of embracing them. Then I began: 'Not contempt, but grief did your condition fix within me in such measure that slowly is it all shaken off,

> Jacopo Rusticucci fui; e certo
> La fiera moglie più ch' altro mi nuoce.
> S' io fussi stato dal foco coperto,
> Gittato mi sarei tra lor disotto,
> E credo che il Dottor l' avria sofferto.
> Ma perch' io mi sarei bruciato e cotto,
> Vinse paura la mia buona voglia,   50
> Che di loro abbracciar mi facea ghiotto.
> Poi cominciai: Non dispetto, ma doglia
> La vostra condizion dentro mi fisse
> Tanto, che tardi tutta si dispoglia.

appropriate to Tegghiaio in this; and therefore I have, in spite of some grammatical difficulty (for we should have rather expected *dorette*, cf. Gr. ὤφελε), followed Philalethes, Witte, and Scartazzini.

44 Of Jacopo Rusticucci nothing seems to be known, except that he did not belong to the nobles. It will be observed that in Canto vi., where Dante is inquiring of Ciacco as to the fate of certain Florentines, this Jacopo is the only one whose surname is given; which would seem to imply that he was not specially distinguished. Lubin indeed says that he was of the Cavalcanti, but gives no authority.

45 Here Boccaccio translates several pages from Theophrastus; Benvenuto more tersely observes: Vere acerbior poena inferni est suavis respectu malae mulieris; per diem non habes bonum, per noctem pejus.

54 **dispoglia**: for this use of the present cf. Purg. vii. 96, xiv. 66.

so soon as this my Lord said to me words through the
which I thought to myself that such folk as ye are was
coming. Of your land I am; and ever yet the work and
the honoured names of you have I with affection recounted
and heard. I am leaving the gall, and going after sweet
fruits promised to me by my truthful Leader; but to the
very centre it is meet that I first go down.'

'So may thy soul yet long guide thy limbs,' answered
he, 'and so may thy fame shine after thee, say if courtesy
and worth dwell in our city as they are wont, or if they are
wholly gone forth thereof? For William Borsiere, who has

  Tosto che questo mio Signor mi disse
   Parole, per le quali io mi pensai,
   Che qual voi siete, tal gente venisse.
  Di vostra terra sono; e sempre mai
   L' opre di voi e gli onorati nomi
   Con affezion ritrassi ed ascoltai.   60
  Lascio lo fele, e vo per dolci pomi
   Promessi a me per lo verace Duca:
   Ma fino al centro pria convien ch' io tomi.
  Se lungamente l' anima conduca
   Le membra tue, rispose quegli, ancora,
   E se la fama tua dopo te luca,
  Cortesia e valor, di', se dimora
   Nella nostra città, sì come suole,
   O se del tutto se n' è gita fuora?
  Chè Guglielmo Borsiere, il qual si duole   70

---

 fele: the bitterness of a sinful life; cf. i. 7.

 cortesia e valor may be said to cover the whole duty of man.
Cf. Purg. xvi. 116.

 Guglielmo Borsiere is the hero of a story in the Decameron (Day
1, Nov. 8) which Benvenuto repeats at length. He further mentions
that Guglielmo was originally a manufacturer of purses; but afterwards

been in woe with us since lately, and goes yonder with his companions, grieves us full sore with his words.' 'The new folk and the sudden gains have begotten pride and excess in thee, Florence, so that already thou art wailing therefore.' Thus I cried with my face uplifted; and the three who heard that for answer looked one at another, as one gazes at [hearing] the truth. 'If the other times it costs thee as little,' answered they all, 'to satisfy another, happy thou, if thou speak so at thy desire. Therefore, if thou escapest from these gloomy places, and returnest to see

> Con noi per poco, e va là coi compagni,
>   Assai ne cruccia con le sue parole.
> La gente nuova, e i subiti guadagni,
>   Orgoglio e dismisura han generata,
>   Fiorenza, in te, sì che tu già ten piagni
> Così gridai colla faccia levata:
>   E i tre, che ciò inteser per risposta,
>   Guardar l' un l' altro, come al ver si guata.[b]
> Se l' altre volte sì poco ti costa,
>   Risposer tutti, il satisfare altrui,
>   Felice te, se sì parli a tua posta.
> Però se campi d' esti lochi bui,

[b] *Guatar* W.

left his trade and became 'homo curialis,' travelling about and making the acquaintance of distinguished people: Boccaccio says too, doing social services.

71 **per poco**: Benv. 'per parvum tempus,' which is undoubtedly right. He is mentioned as having brought the latest news.

73 Cf. again Cacciaguida's denunciations, esp. Par. xv. 100 sqq., xvi. 67 sqq.

74 Pride is opposed to *valor*, true worth; lack of moderation to *cortesia*, τὸ ἐπιεικές or *modestia* (Philippians iv. 5).

79 sq. It will be well for you if you can always, in answering a question, speak your mind with as little fear of hurt to yourself.

again the fair stars; when it shall please thee to say: I have been; see that thou talk of us to the people.' Then they broke their wheel, and at flying their legs seemed wings in swiftness.

An *amen* could not have been said so quickly as they disappeared; wherefore to the Master it seemed good to depart.

I followed him, and little way had we gone, when the sound of the water was so close to us that for speaking should we scarce have been heard. As that river which from Monte Viso eastward first has a course of its own on

> E torni a riveder le belle stelle,
>   Quando ti gioverà dicere: Io fui,
> Fa che di noi alla gente favelle.
>   Indi rupper la rota, ed a fuggirsi
>   Ali sembiar le gambe loro snelle.
> Un ammen non saria potuto dirsi
>   Tosto così, com' ei furo spariti:
>   Perchè al Maestro parve di partirsi. 90
> Io lo seguiva, e poco eravam iti,
>   Che il suon dell' acqua n' era sì vicino,
>   Che, per parlar, saremmo appena uditi.
> Come quel fiume, ch' ha proprio cammino
>   Prima da monte Veso in ver levante

---

[86] **per parlar**: this use of *per* explains that of *perchè*—'although,' as in Purg. v. 58, where see note.

[95] I.e. is the first which, rising on the north side of the Apennines, does not flow into the Po. This would now be the Lamone; but in Dante's time that river ended in the swamps about the mouths of the Po (Witte). He means the Montone, which rising near San Casciano, flows through Forli, and into the sea just south of Ravenna.

the left flank of Apennine, which is called Acquacheta above,
before that it goes valewards down to its low bed, and at
Forli is emptied of that name, booms there above San
Benedetto from its alp, through falling at a descent where
it ought to be received by a thousand; so shaken downward

      Dalla sinistra costa d' Apennino,
   Che si chiama Acquaqueta suso, avante
    Che si divalli giù nel basso letto,
    Ed a Forlì di quel nome è vacante,
  Rimbomba là sopra san Benedetto   100
     Dell' alpe, per cadere ad una scesa,
     Ove dovea per mille esser ricetto;
    Così, giù d' una ripa discoscesa,

[99] Because it loses its name of the Stillwater, and becomes the Ram (from its violence after its fall, say the commentators). Cf. Purg. v. 97.

[100] Near the monastery of St. Benedict on the frontier of Tuscany and Romagna the river makes a great fall from the high ground to the plain.

[102] 'I was long in doubt,' says Boccaccio, 'what the author meant here: till once finding myself in the monastery of St. Benedict I was told by the abbot that the counts (Guidi) who are the lords of that mountain-land had it in mind to build a castle at that spot, and enclose within it many of the neighbouring homesteads occupied by their vassals'; for whom, it may be supposed, this river would have served as water-supply. Afterwards, he says, the count principally interested died, and the scheme fell through. If, as Philalethes suggests, the count in question was Roger of Dovadola, great nephew of Guido Guerra, who was living in 1322 (Vill. ix. 183, the scheme must still have been afoot when Dante wrote. According to another view, Dante means to imply that the monastery ought to have had a larger number of occupants than the luxury of its abbots cared to see there. Thus the Latin version of D'Aquino: 'Sacri rarescunt ubi vasta in mole sodales.' See also Daniello.

from a bank we found that stained water resounding, so that in short while it would have numbed the ear.

I had a cord girt about, and with it I thought at one

> Trovammo risonar quell' acqua tinta,
> Si che in poc' ora avria l' orecchia offesa.
> Io aveva una corda intorno cinta,
> E con essa pensai alcuna volta

[106] Perhaps the most perplexing piece of symbolism in the whole poem. The oldest commentators, from P. di Dante onward (with the exception of Boccaccio, who, alas! puts the point off for consideration with the allegory of Geryon generally), have, with a grotesque confusion between a sin itself and the material of it, taken the catching of the leopard (i.e. the sin of unchastity) to mean the seduction of women. Buti (towards the end of the fourteenth century) produced a statement that Dante had in his youth joined the Franciscan order, but had never got beyond the novitiate. Landino mentions this, but rejects it; but it has been adopted by most modern commentators from Lombardi onward, though it rests on nothing but Buti's assertion, while, if it were true, one would expect to find mention of it earlier. It seems on the whole best, whether the Franciscan story be correct or not, to refer to Isaiah xi. 5: Erit justitia cingulum lumborum ejus, et fides cinctorium renum ejus. To object with Scartazzini that Dante was not likely to strip himself of a virtue just when he was going to the depths of Hell seems to be an over-insistence on allegorical consistency. Nor was he likely, another objector of similar spirit might add, to take off any part of his clothing when he was going to walk on the ice of Cocytus. Something is wanted to throw, in order to attract Geryon. 'I have this cord, the cord of righteousness,' says Dante. 'Once I thought to capture Florence (which, it will be remembered, is also signified by the pard) with it, and put an end to faction; let us throw that down—it is of no further use to me—and see if the unwonted sight will bring Geryon.' Observe that Isaiah continues, v. 6: Habitabit lupus cum agno: et pardus cum hoedo accubabit: vitulus et leo et ovis simul morabuntur, etc. Another objection of Scartazzini's, that you cannot throw a metaphorical cord, is rather comic; though it is a testimony to Dante's power of impressing his readers with a sense of reality. But the *burrato* is no doubt as metaphorical, or rather allegorical, as the *corda*, or as Geryon himself.

time to catch the ounce with the painted skin. After I had wholly loosed it from me, in such wise as my Leader had commanded me, I reached it to him knotted and wrapped together. Whereupon he turned him toward the right side, and to some little distance from the edge he threw it down into that deep ravine. It is meet indeed that a new thing should answer, said I within myself, to the new signs which the Master is following so with his eye. Ah, how cautious should men be near to those who see not

> Prender la lonza alla pelle dipinta.
> Poscia che l' ebbi tutta da me sciolta,
> Si come il Duca m' avea comandato, 110
> Porsila a lui aggroppata e ravvolta.
> Ond' ei si volse inver lo destro lato,
> Ed alquanto di lungi dalla sponda
> La gittò giuso in quell' alto burrato.
> E' pur convien che novità risponda,
> Dicea fra me medesmo, al nuovo cenno
> Che il Maestro con l' occhio si seconda.
> Ahi quanto cauti gli uomini esser denno
> Presso a color, che non veggon pur l' opra,

[112] No doubt going a little way along the edge of the pit, to be clear of the falling water. But there is probably some symbolism in every word here. See next Canto, l. 31.

[118-129] The reflections contained in these lines, and in 124-126, seem intended to attune the reader's mind to what is coming. Henceforth Dante is going to deal with sins opposed to that good faith between man and man on which the whole fabric of society rests. He gives here two maxims of caution against relying too fully on that good faith. Man is not perfect; it is therefore advisable in our intercourse even with good men not to reveal our minds too fully, and not to try their confidence in us too severely. One seems to see almost the germs of the statecraft which in later days attained such perfection in Italy.

only the act, but look within the thoughts by their wisdom!
He said to me: 'Soon will come up that which I await;
and what thy thought is brooding must needs be shortly
discovered in thy visage.' Ever to that truth which has
the face of falsehood should the man close his lips so far as
he can, because it brings shame without a fault; but here I
cannot keep it silent; and by the strains of this Comedy,
reader, I swear to thee, so may they not be void of long-
enduring grace, that I saw through that gross and gloomy
air a figure come swimming upwards, wondrous to every
heart at ease; just as he returns who goes down at times to
free the anchor, which is grappling either a rock or something

> Ma per entro i pensier miran col senno!   120
> Ei disse a me: Tosto verrà di sopra
>   Ciò ch' io attendo, e che il tuo pensier sogna
>   Tosto convien ch' al tuo viso si scopra.
> Sempre a quel ver ch' ha faccia di menzogna
>   De' l' uom chiuder le labbra finch' ei puote,
>   Però che senza colpa fa vergogna:
> Ma qui tacer nol posso: e per le note
>   Di questa commedia, lettor, ti giuro.
>   S' elle non sien di lunga grazia vote,
> Ch' io vidi per quell' aer grosso e scuro   130
>   Venir notando una figura in suso.
>   Maravigliosa ad ogni cor sicuro,
> Si come torna colui che va giuso
>   Talora a solver l' ancora, ch' aggrappa

---

[122] **al tuo viso**: most understand 'to thy sight'; but the rendering I have given seems to accord better with the preceding *terzina*.

[127] **note**. Others, e.g. Land. and Vell., understand merely 'words'; Benv., 'i.e. literas.'

[127] Cf. xxviii. 113-115.

else that is hidden in the sea, when he stretches himself
upward, and draws himself up at foot.

> O scoglio od altro che nel mare è chiuso,
> Che in su si stende, e da piè si rattrappa.

[136] Benvenuto oddly takes this as of a man climbing up a rope, though it seems certainly intended of a swimmer. Is it possible that he conceived of Geryon as *climbing* up the cord?

CANTO XVII

ARGUMENT

A monster appears and stays at the brink. While Virgil is parleying with it, Dante speaks with certain that are sitting a little way off, who are those that have practised usury. They mount on the back of the monster, which Virgil addresses as Geryon; and it bears them downwards; whereat Dante is in fear.

'BEHOLD the beast with the pointed tail that passes the mountains and breaks walls and weapons; behold that which makes all the world to stink!' So did my Leader

> Ecco la fiera con la coda aguzza,
>   Che passa i monti, e rompe muri ed armi;
> Ecco colei che tutto il mondo appuzza:
> Sì cominciò lo mio Duca a parlarmi,

[1 sqq.] The figure which now appears is presently addressed by Virgil, and spoken of, as Geryon. The story of the mythological Geryon slain by Hercules is well known, but there is nothing in it, as told by the usual authorities, to account for his selection for his present office. His methods indeed seem rather to have been those of violence. He is coupled with Tityus by Horace (Odes, ii. 14. 8), and by Virgil with Centaurs, Gorgons, and Harpies (if he be denoted by the 'forma tricorporis umbrae' of Aen. vi. 289), and the other forms which haunt the entrance of the infernal regions. Possibly the description of him as *threefold* (which Dante appears to have misunderstood, or to have modified to suit his purpose) may have seemed to make him an appropriate symbol of fraud. The representation of him as a kind of serpent or dragon is parallel to the treatment of Minos and Cerberus ('il gran vermo'); perhaps with some suggestions from the monsters of Rev. ix. The symbolism of the various details is pretty evident.

begin to speak to me; and beckoned it to come to shore, near to the bound of the marble we had crossed. And that filthy image of fraud came on, and brought its head and body to bank, but on to the bank it did not draw its tail. Its face was the face of a righteous man, so benign the skin it had outside; and of a serpent all the rest of its trunk. Two arms it had, hairy to the armpits; it had its back and breast and both its sides painted with knots and little rings. With more colours, groundwork or design, did never Turks and Tartars make their cloths, nor were such webs set on

> Ed accennolle che venisse a proda,
>   Vicino al fin dei passeggiati marmi:
> E quella sozza imagine di froda
>   Sen venne, ed arrivò la testa e il busto;
>   Ma in sulla riva non trasse la coda.
> La faccia sua era faccia d' uom giusto;
>   Tanto benigna avea di fuor la pelle,
>   E d' un serpente tutto l' altro fusto.
> Due branche avea pilose infin l' ascelle:
>   Lo dosso e il petto ed ambo e due le coste
>   Dipinte avea di nodi e di rotelle.
> Con più color sommesse e soprapposte
>   Non fer ma' i drappi Tartari nè Turchi,

10

by Arachne. As at times the shallops stand on the shore, when they are part in the water and part on the land; and as out there among the German gluttons the beaver squats to wage his warfare, so did the vilest beast stand on the edge which, made of stone, encloses the sand. All in the

> Nè fur tai tele per Aragne imposte.
> Come tal volta stanno a riva i burchi,
>   Che parte sono in acqua e parte in terra,   20
>   E come là tra li Tedeschi lurchi
> Lo bevero s' assetta a far sua guerra ;
>   Così la fiera pessima si stava
>   Sull' orlo che, di pietra, il sabbion serra.

to be wanted. We must, I think, take **sommesse** and **soprapposte** as nouns, and in a kind of apposition with **colori**; for Blanc's theory that they are adjectives in agreement with it, the final *i* being *e* for the rhyme, will hardly hold water.

At this point we part company with Boccaccio, whose commentary ends abruptly—doubtless by reason of his death in December 1375—in the middle of the explanation of these lines. No doubt his faithful and admiring disciple, Benvenuto, has preserved a good deal of the information which he would have given; and no doubt he is prolix and garrulous, and never forgets that he is a reformed character, and has a reputation to maintain as such; but he is a scholar and a man of the world, and we feel that to have the rest of his less than half-told story we would willingly surrender a wilderness of 15th-century pedantry.

²² The beaver's habit of sitting with his tail in the water (see his portrait in Bewick's Natural History) seems to have been regarded as an artifice for catching fish. P. di Dante informs us that oily particles exude from the tail, by which the fish are attracted. Benv. merely says, 'caudam tenet sub aqua et parat insidias piscibus.' He also mentions that beavers are found near Ferrara. It is curious that none of the older authorities on natural history, such as Aristotle or Pliny, say anything of this supposed habit; nor do Dante's contemporaries, Brunetto and Cecco d'Ascoli. As a matter of fact, the beaver is a vegetable feeder.

void it was twitching its tail, twisting up the venomous fork, which armed the point in fashion of a scorpion.

My Leader said: 'Now it is meet that our way turn a little so far as that evil beast which is couching yonder.' Therefore we descended towards the right pap, and ten paces we made upon the edge, to bring quite to an end the sand and the flame; and when we are come to it, a little further I see folk sitting on the sand near to the place

> Nel vano tutta sua coda guizzava,
>   Torcendo in su la venenosa forca
>   Che, a guisa di scorpion, la punta armava.
> Lo Duca disse: Or convien che si torca
>   La nostra via un poco infino a quella
>   Bestia malvagia che colà si corca.   30
> Però scendemmo alla destra mammella,
>   E dieci passi femmo in sullo stremo,
>   Per ben cessar la rena e la fiammella:[b]
> E quando noi a lei venuti semo,
>   Poco più oltre veggio in sulla rena
>   Gente seder propinqua al loco scemo.

[b] *cansar* Benv. Vell.

[26] His tail is forked to indicate the two kinds of fraud referred to in xi. 52-54. So Bargigi, whom Scartazzini follows. Benv. finds the same symbolism in the two *arms* of Geryon.

[32] Once before they have gone a few paces in the contrary direction to their usual course; see ix. 132. It is true, as Witte points out, that the slight digression to the right is made necessary here by Geryon's position; but Dante need not have put him into that position, unless he had wished to lead up to this movement. Probably in both cases the intention is to suggest a formal act of adhesion to goodness at the moment of entering on a fresh division of sin and its punishment. The 'ten paces' may well allude to God's commandments, and the whole will be illustrated by such passages as Ps. cxix. (Vulg. cxviii.) 29, 30, 32.

where it is cut off. Here the Master: 'To the end that thou mayest bear all full experience of this circle,' said he to me, 'go and behold their demeanour. Let thy converse there be brief; until thou returnest will I parley with this thing, that it may grant us its strong shoulders.' Thus further over the uttermost headland of that seventh circle all alone I went, where the sorrowful folk were sitting. Through their eyes their woe was bursting forth; on this side and on that they sheltered with their hands now against the exhalations and now against the hot soil. Not otherwise

> Quivi il Maestro: Acciocchè tutta piena
>   Esperienza d' esto giron porti,
>   Mi disse, va, e vedi la lor mena.^c
> Li tuoi ragionamenti sian là corti: 40
>   Mentre che torni parlerò con questa,
>   Che ne conceda i suoi omeri forti.
> Così ancor su per la strema testa
>   Di quel settimo cerchio, tutto solo
>   Andai, ove sedea la gente mesta.
> Per gli occhi fuori scoppiava lor duolo:
>   Di qua, di là soccorrien con le mani,
>   Quando ai vapori, e quando al caldo suolo.

^c *or vu Ald. IV.*

³⁷ Note that whereas hitherto Virgil has adopted a tone of authority, sometimes of defiance, with the guardians of the various circles, he has henceforth to use persuasion.

⁴³⁻⁴⁵ The usurers, as Benvenuto points out, form a link between the sins of violence and those of deceit. In the abstract, as has been explained, usury does violence to natural laws; but in practice, and as between man and man, it is often attended by fraud. Scart. remarks upon the fact that their position is out of Dante's direct road, and that in order to see them he has to make a digression, unaccompanied by Virgil.

do the dogs in summer, now with their snout, now with their paws, when they are bitten by fleas or by gnats or by gadflies.

After I had directed my gaze toward the countenance of certain upon which the woeful fire is streaming, I recognised not any of them, but I was aware that from the neck of each hung a purse which had a certain colour and certain design, and therewith it seems that their eye is fed. And as I came among them gazing, on one yellow pouch I saw blue, which had face and outline of a lion. Thereafter proceeding the course of my gaze, I saw that another of them

> Non altrimenti fan di state i cani,
>   Or col ceffo or coi piè, quando son morsi   50
>   O da pulci o da mosche o da tafani.
> Poi che nel viso a certi gli occhi porsi,
>   Nei quali il doloroso foco casca,
>   Non ne conobbi alcun; ma io m' accorsi
> Che dal collo a ciascun pendea una tasca,
>   Che avea certo colore e certo segno,
>   E quindi par che il loro occhio si pasca.
> E com' io riguardando tra lor vegno,
>   In una borsa gialla vidi azzurro,
>   Che d' un leone avea faccia e contegno.   60
> Poi procedendo di mio sguardo il curro
>   Vidine un' altra come sangue rossa

---

54 As with the avaricious, perhaps because usury involved avarice, their very features are obliterated, and they are only recognisable by the arms on their money bags; which in a kind of bitter mockery they are permitted to have with them. All seem to be of good family.

59, 60 These are the arms of the Gianfigliazzi, a family belonging to the Black Guelfs; Vill. viii. 39.

62, 63 The Ubriachi, a Ghibeline house, heads of the party in Oltrarno, banished with the rest in 1258: Vill. vi. 65.

as red as blood showed a goose more white than butter. And one who had his white satchel marked with a sow blue and lusty, said to me: 'What doest thou in this foss? Go now thy way; and since thou art still alive, know that my neighbour Vitaliano will sit here on my left flank. With these Florentines am I a Paduan; oftentimes do they thunder in my ears, crying, "Let the supreme cavalier come who will bring the purse with three he-goats."' Then he distorted his mouth, and drew out his tongue, like

> Mostrare un' oca bianca più che burro.
> Ed un, che d' una scrofa azzurra e grossa
>   Segnato avea lo suo sacchetto bianco,
>   Mi disse: Che fai tu in questa fossa?
> Or te ne va; e perchè sei vivo anco,
>   Sappi che il mio vicin Vitaliano
>   Sederà qui dal mio sinistro fianco.
> Con questi Fiorentin son Padovano;   70
>   Spesse fiate m' intronan gli orecchi,
>   Gridando: Vegna il cavalier soprano,
> Che recherà la tasca con tre becchi:
>   Qui distorse la bocca, e di fuor trasse ᵈ

ᵈ *la faccia* Gg. Cass. 1234.

The commentators say that this is one Rinaldo de' Scrovegni of Padua. He is said to have been father of the man who was just now building the 'Arena' Chapel, where people go to see Giotto's frescoes.

Vitaliano: del Dente, say the older commentators; but recent investigations have discovered that an early Paduan chronicler identifies him with a Vit. de' Vitaliani, whose house, as a matter of fact, was near that of the Scrovegni. See Scart. *ad loc*. Bargigi curiously refuses to name any of the others, out of regard for the feelings of their families, and this more than a hundred years later.

becchi: or 'beaks.' The person alluded to is said to be Messer Giovanni Buiamonte de' Bicci of Florence. Nothing else seems to be known about him.

an ox licking its nose. And I, fearing lest my longer stay should anger him who warned me to stay little, turned me back from the weary souls.

I found my Leader who had mounted already on the croup of the fierce animal, and said to me: 'Now be strong and bold. Now is the descent by stairs thus-fashioned; get up in front, for I wish to be between, so that the tail may be unable to do harm.' Like him who is taken in the shivering-fit of the quartan, that has his nails already pallid, and trembles all over only looking at the shade, such became I at the proffered words; but his menaces wrought shame in me, which in the presence of a good lord makes the slave

  La lingua, come bue che il naso lecchi.^e
Ed io, temendo nol più star crucciasse
  Lui che di poco star m' avea monito,
  Tornai mi indietro dall' anime lasse.
Trovai lo Duca mio ch' era salito
  Già in sulla groppa del fiero animale,   80
  E disse a me: Or sii forte ed ardito.
Omai si scende per sì fatte scale:
  Monta dinanzi, ch' io voglio esser mezzo,
  Sì che la coda non possa far male.
Qual è colui, ch' ha sì presso il riprezzo
  Della quartana, ch' ha già l' unghie smorte,
  E trema tutto, pur guardando il rezzo,
Tal divenn' io alle parole porte;
  Ma vergogna mi fer le sue minacce,
  Che innanzi a buon signor fa servo forte.   90

^e *come il bue* 14 ll'.

⁸⁹ **minacce** must be taken in the wider sense of 'fear of his displeasure,' for Virgil has uttered no threat. Benv. puts an imaginary harangue into his mouth, and illustrates by a story of Julius Caesar:

strong. I seated myself on those broad shoulders; so would
I have said—but the voice came not as I deemed—'See
that thou embrace me.' But he, who other time helped me
at other perplexity, as soon as I was up, bound me and
sustained me with his arms; and said: 'Geryon, now set
forth; let thy wheels be wide and thy descent slow; think
on the new burthen which thou hast.' As the little bark
goes out of its place backing, backing; so did he take himself thence; and when he felt himself wholly in play, he
turned his tail round where his breast had been, and moved
it tense, like an eel, and with his arms drew in the air to

> Io m' assettai in su quelle spallacce:
>   Sì volli dir (ma la voce non venne
>   Com' io credetti): Fa, che tu m' abbracce.
> Ma esso che altra volta mi sovvenne
>   Ad altro forse, tosto ch' io montai,
>   Con le braccia m' avvinse e mi sostenne:
> E disse: Gerion, moviti omai:
>   Le rote larghe, e lo scender sia poco:
>   Pensa la nuova soma che tu hai.
> Come la navicella esce del loco   100
>   In dietro, in dietro, sì quindi si tolse:
>   E poi ch' al tutto si sentì a giuoco,
> Là ov' era il petto, la coda rivolse,
>   E quella tesa, come anguilla, mosse,
>   E con le branche l' aria a sè raccolse.

[f] *l'alto G.* 5: *alto forte* Cass. Ald.: *alto tosto fort* 3: *alti fort* 124.

⁹⁵ **ad altro forse**: more especially on the back of the Centaur, notes Benv. **forse**, as in viii. 110. For a discussion of the various readings, see Moore, 'Textual Criticism.'

¹⁰² **a giuoco**: we say 'had free play.' It is curious that here and elsewhere Benvenuto speaks as if he imagined Geryon to be really swimming in water.

himself. Greater fear I do not think there was when Phaethon let go the reins, whereby the heaven, as is still seen, was scorched ; nor when Icarus unhappy felt his back lose its wings through the melted wax, his father crying to him : 'Thou takest an ill path'; than was mine when I saw that I was in the air on all sides, and saw every view gone except of the monster. It goes its way, swimming slowly, slowly ; it wheels and descends, but I take no note thereof,

> Maggior paura non credo che fosse,
> > Quando Fetòn abbandonò li freni,
> > Per che il ciel, come pare ancor, si cosse :
> Nè quando Icaro misero le reni
> > Sentì spennar per la scaldata cera, 110
> > Gridando il padre a lui : Mala via tieni,
> Che fu la mia, quando vidi ch' i' era
> > Nell' aer d' ogni parte, e vidi spenta
> > Ogni veduta, fuor che della fiera.
> Ella sen va nuotando lenta lenta ;
> > Rota e discende, ma non me n' accorgo,

[107, 108] Ar. Meteor. i. 8 (345 a) : Τῶν καλουμένων Πυθαγορείων φασί τινες ὁδὸν εἶναι ταύτην, οἱ μὲν τῶν ἐκπεσόντων τινὸς ἄστρων, κατὰ τὴν λεγομένην ἐπὶ Φαέθοντος φθοράν. Conv. ii. 15: Li Pittagorici dissero che 'l sole alcuna fiata errò nella sua via ; e passando per altre parti non convenienti al suo fervore, arse il luogo per lo quale passò, e rimasevi quell' apparenza dell' arsura. Cf. Par. xiv. 97 sqq. This is the first of Dante's many allusions to the fable of Phaethon, which seems to have had a special attraction for him.

[109 ff.] Ov. Met. viii. 223 sqq., especially—

> Altius egit iter : rapidi vicinia Solis
> Mollit odoratas, pennarum vincula, ceras.
> . . . . .
> At pater infelix, nec jam pater, 'Icare' dixit,
> 'Icare' dixit 'ubi es ? qua te regione requiram,
> Icare ?'

save that the wind blows in my face and from below. I heard already on the right hand the torrent make beneath us a horrible splashing; wherefore I crane my head with downturned eyes. Then was I more fearful in regard to the alighting; because I saw fires and heard wailings; whereat all trembling I crouch me down again. And then I saw, for I had not seen it before, the descent and the

> Se non ch' al viso e disotto mi venta.
> Io sentia già dalla man destra il gorgo
> Far sotto noi un orribile stroscio;
> Per che con gli occhi in giù la testa sporgo. 120
> Allor fu' io più timido allo scoscio:
> Perocch' io vidi fochi, e sentii pianti;
> Ond' io tremando tutto mi raccoscio.
> E vidi poi, chè nol vedea davanti,
> Lo scendere e il girar, per li gran mali

[118] That is, they had, as Philalethes points out, made half a circuit; not the whole, as Witte puts it, which of course would bring the fall on their left hand again. We must imagine Geryon as descending in large circles, but always remaining on the side of the pit whence they had set out. It would hardly be possible to hear the sound of the fall from the other side, since we know by comparison of xxix. 9 and xxx. 86 (where see the note of Philalethes) that Malebolge must have been some 35 miles wide.

We hear no more of Phlegethon; and Philalethes supposes that it must be conceived as passing through a subterranean channel (if the term be allowed) to join Cocytus in the ninth circle.

[121] **scoscio**: a word of very uncertain meaning. Benv. 'idest ad motum, ad movendum me.' Land., Vell., Dan. take it to be the fall of the water. Others of the Italian commentators, and Philalethes, think it is 'the precipice,' or rather the 'drop' below. Witte, 'Anprall.' I am inclined to take it as 'the shock of alighting': see Glossary.

[123] **raccoscio**. Benv. and Lomb. think this means 'grip with the thigh,' as in riding; but it seems better to understand 'cower.' Cf. xviii. 132.

circling, by the great evils that were approaching on divers sides. As the falcon that has stayed enough on the wing, that without seeing lure or bird makes the falconer say: 'Alack, thou stoopest'; it descends wearily whence it starts swiftly through a hundred wheels, and alights at a distance from its master, disdainful and surly; so did Geryon set us down at the bottom on foot at the foot of the splintered rock, and, our bodies discharged, vanished as arrow from bowstring.

> Che s' appressavan da diversi canti.
> Come il falcon ch' è stato assai sull' ali,
>   Che senza veder logoro o uccello,
>   Fa dire al falconiere: Oimè tu cali:
> Discende lasso, onde si move snello,   130
>   Per cento rote, e da lungi si pone
>   Dal suo maestro, disdegnoso e fello:
> Così ne pose al fondo Gerione
>   A piè, a piè della stagliata rocca,
>   E, discarcate le nostre persone,
> Si dileguò, come da corda cocca.

[127] Dante's delight in similes from falconry has often been remarked upon. We have seen one in iii. 117. Here he supposes the falcon to descend, without any lawful cause, being tired or sulky. A more cheerful image might perhaps be too complimentary to Geryon, whom Dante seems to hold in more loathing than any other denizen of hell.

[128] **logoro**: the object roughly resembling a bird, which the falcon was taught to associate with her feeding-time, so that she might be recalled by the sight of it.

CANTO XVIII

ARGUMENT

They dismount in a place called Malebolge, the form of which is described. Here they come among folk whom fiends are scourging as they go, and learn that they are pandars. Next they come to some who are covered with filth; these are the flatterers.

THERE is a place in Hell, called Malebolge, all of stone and of an iron colour, like the circle which compasses it around. Right in the middle of the malign plain sinks a pit fairly

> LUOGO è in inferno, detto Malebolge,
> Tutto di pietra e di color ferrigno,
> Come la cerchia che d' intorno il volge.
> Nel dritto mezzo del campo maligno

---

[1] The eighth circle in which are punished the first division of the deceivers—those who have sinned against no special natural ties—is imagined as a plain sloping not very steeply on all sides towards the centre (xxiv. 38), and intersected with ten concentric ravines, over which a number of rock ribs, running from the circumference to the central orifice, make a series of bridges. Each of these is called a *bolgia*, originally 'wallet' or 'pouch'; Benvenuto says that it was a regular Florentine term for a hollow valley. Each is occupied by some particular class of sinners, fraud being of many kinds. The following list shows the order. Pandars and seducers of women, Flatterers, Simoniacs, Diviners, Jobbers of public offices, Hypocrites, Thieves, Evil counsellors, Schismatics and other makers of strife, Alchemists and coiners.

[2] Cf. Purg. xiii. 9.

[3] N.B. **volge** with acc. in the sense of 'turns round it.'

wide and deep, whereof in its place I will tell the arrangement. That belt which remains then is round, between the pit and the foot of the hard high bank, and it has its bed divided into ten trenches. Such figure as, when for defence of the walls more and more fosses gird the castles, the part where they are displays, such an appearance did those there make. And as in such fortresses from their thresholds to the outermost bank are little bridges, so from the bottom of

   Vaneggia un pozzo assai largo e profondo,
    Di cui *suo loco* dicerò l' ordigno.[a]
  Quel cinghio che rimane adunque è tondo,
    Tra il pozzo e il piè dell' alta ripa dura,
    Ed ha distinto in dieci valli il fondo.
  Quale, dove per guardia delle mura,   10
    Più e più fossi cingon li castelli,
    La parte dov' ei son rende figura:[b]
  Tale imagine quivi facean quelli:
    E come a tai fortezze dai lor sogli
    Alla ripa di fuor son ponticelli,

  [a] *dicerà* Gg. 1234; *conterà* Ald.
  [b] *rendon fig.* Gg.: *rende figura* Cass.: *dov' è il sol* Ald.

 [5] **vaneggia**: here from *vano* in the sense which it has in xvii. 25, or Purg. x. 22, the only sense which has passed into our 'vanish.'

 [6] **suo loco** must, I think, be taken as Latin, like *coram patre*, Par. xi. 62, or *sine causa*, ib. xxxii. 59. Bianchi, taking it as Italian, compares the Fr. *quelque part*, but there seems no example of this omission of the prep. in Italian. Witte, without much authority, inserts *in*. Others read *dicerà*, making **loco** the subject. Benv., reading both *in* and *dicerà*, takes **ordigno** in the sense of 'the course of my story,' as the subject to the latter.

 [11] **li castelli**: castles in general. So *i valloni*, Purg. vii. 66.

 [12] A large number of MS. copyists, puzzled by a sentence which is, as Benvenuto says, 'valde intricata,' give here *rende* or *rendon figura*. See Moore, Text. Crit., for a full discussion.

the cliff rocks went, which cut across the embankments and the fosses up to the pit, which cuts them short and brings them together.

In this place, when dropped from the back of Geryon, we found ourselves; and the Poet held to the left, and I started after him. On the right I saw new grief, new torments, and new slashers, of which the first pit was full. At the bottom were the sinners naked; on this side the middle they were coming with their face towards us; on the other side with us, but with longer steps; as the Romans, by reason of the great host, in the year of the Jubilee took

> Cosi da imo della roccia scogli
>> Movien, che recidean gli argini e fossi
>> Infino al pozzo, che i tronca e raccogli.
> In questo loco, dalla schiena scossi
>> Di Gerion, trovammoci: e il Poeta 20
>> Tenne a sinistra, ed io dietro mi mossi.
> Alla man destra vidi nuova pieta;
>> Nuovi tormenti e nuovi frustatori,
>> Di che la prima bolgia era repleta.
> Nel fondo erano ignudi i peccatori:
>> Dal mezzo in qua ci venian verso il volto,
>> Di là con noi, ma con passi maggiori:
> Come i Roman, per l' esercito molto,
>> L' anno del Giubbileo, su per lo ponte

[16] It seems clear from this description that Dante conceived several rius radiating from the centre, and forming systems of bridges. Indeed farther on, in Canto xxiii., we shall find that they pass from one line of bridges to another. It would seem impossible, if it had not been done, to hold the opposite view that there was only one line.

[29] For some account of the Jubilee, ordered by Boniface VIII. in 1300, see Villani viii. 36; where we learn incidentally that it was the reflection on the history of Rome, induced by the sight of the mighty

measures for the passing of the folk over the bridge, that on one side all have their front toward the castle, and go to St. Peter's, on the other rim they go toward the mount. On this side, on that, over the dingy stone I saw horned demons with great whips who were beating them cruelly in rear. Ah! how they made them stir their stumps at the first strokes; and none awaited longer the second or the third.

> Hanno a passar la gente modo colto: 30
> Che dall' un lato tutti hanno la fronte
>   Verso il castello, e vanno a santo Pietro;
>   Dall' altra sponda vanno verso il monte.
> Di qua, di là, su per lo sasso tetro
>   Vidi Demon cornuti con gran ferze,
>   Che li battean crudelmente di retro.
> Ahi come facean lor levar le berze
>   Alle prime percosse! e già nessuno
>   Le seconde aspettava nè le terze.

concourse, that gave the historian the first idea of compiling that of his own city. Whether Dante was there or not we do not know. This description seems like that of an eyewitness, and he alludes to the Jubilee more than once (see Par. xxxi. 35); but it was the year in which he was Prior, and taking a prominent part in public affairs, which must just then have been very absorbing, at Florence.

[30] **passar** may be transitive, as we use 'to pass'; but I should prefer to take the construction like 'a salir persona' in Purg. xi. 51.

[32] **il castello**: that of Sant' Angelo; once the mole of Hadrian.

[33] **il monte**: San Pietro in Montorio, the old 'Janiculum,' which, though on the same side of the river as the castle, is, owing to a bend, almost exactly in face of any one coming away from it. Monte Giordano, which some take to be meant, is an artificial mound, possibly of medieval formation.

[35] The first appearance of fiends as regular officials of hell. The special mention of *horns* in this case is doubtless intended to have a significance which our forefathers would have well understood.

While I was going my eyes were arrested upon one, and I quickly said thus: 'Of seeing this one ere now have I had my fill.' Therefore I stayed my feet to make him out; and the kind Leader halted with me, and gave leave for me to go back somewhat. And that slashed one thought to conceal himself by lowering his face, but it availed him little; for I said: 'Thou that castest thine eye to earth, if the fashion that thou bearest is not false, Venedico Caccianimico

> Mentr' io andava, gli occhi miei in uno   40
>   Furo scontrati; ed io sì tosto dissi:
>   Di già veder costui non son digiuno.ᶜ
> Perciò a figurarlo i piedi affissi:
>   E il dolce Duca meco si ristette,
>   Ed assentì ch' alquanto indietro gissi:
> E quel frustato celar si credette
>   Bassando il viso, ma poco gli valse:
>   Ch' io dissi: Tu che l' occhio a terra gette,
> Se le fazion che porti non son false,
>   Venedico sei tu Caccianimico: 50

ᶜ *Già di* 2 *Ald.*

⁴² **digiuno**: cf. xxviii. 87. Benv. hints at some personal quarrel between Venedico and Dante.

⁴⁸ Observe that henceforth Dante has no more words of love or honour or even respect for those to whom he speaks, even in the cases (e.g. that of Ulysses) where he inspires a kinder feeling in his readers.

⁵⁰ Venedico Caccianimico appears to have been a gentleman of Bologna, who is said to have acted as intermediary in an intrigue between his own sister and Azzo VIII. (according to Benvenuto's reckoning, III.) of Este. There is some difficulty about the story, as Azzo was at the time at war with Bologna. On the other hand, it is said that Ghisola was married to one of the Aldighieri of Ferrara (Par. xv. 137), so that the affair may have been transacted there, where the Esti were powerful.

thou art; but what brings thee to so stinging Salse?' And he to me: 'Unwillingly do I tell it; but thy clear words compel me, which make me remember the ancient world. I was the one that brought the fair Ghisola to do the will of the Marquis, however the unseemly tale be told. And not only I wail here from Bologna; rather is this place so full of us that not so many tongues are now learned to say *sipa* between Savena and the Reno; and if of this thou wishest

> Ma che ti mena a sì pungenti salse?
> Ed egli a me: Mal volentier lo dico:
> Ma sforzami la tua chiara favella,
> Che mi fa sovvenir del mondo antico
> Io fui colui, che la Ghisola bella
> Condussi a far la voglia del Marchese,
> Come che suoni la sconcia novella.
> E non pur io qui piango Bolognese:
> Anzi n' è questo loco tanto pieno,
> Che tante lingue non son ora apprese   60
> A dicer *sipa* tra Savena e il Reno:⁴
> E se di ciò vuoi fede o testimonio,

^d *e Reno* 3 W.: *e 'l Rheno* Ald.

⁵¹ The Salse was a ravine near Bologna, where the bodies of criminals were thrown; but there is an obvious play on *salsa*, 'sauce,' or 'pickle.'

⁵⁹, ⁶⁰ Benvenuto, who lived in Bologna, and liked the place and people, does not think this estimate at all extraordinary, and says that any place ('not to mention Paris') would easily furnish hell with more of this class than would equal the existing population of Bologna.

⁶¹ **sipa**: Bolognese provincialism for *sia*. So Benv., who must have known. Blanc refers to Tassoni, Secch. Rap. xii. st. 50: *fina che l'uno Sipa vittorios, e l'altro mora*. In Vulg. El. i. 15 Dante speaks favourably of the Bolognese dialect.

Savena and Reno are two rivers which flow past Bologna at a distance of about two miles on the east and west respectively.

proof or testimony, bring to thy mind our money-loving breast.' As he thus talked a demon smote him with his scourge, and said: 'Get on, pimp; here are no women on hire.' I joined myself again with my escort; afterwards with few paces we came where a rock jutted from the bank. Easily enough we mounted that, and turning to the right along the spur of it we departed from these eternal circlings.

> Recati a mente il nostro avaro seno.
> Cosi parlando il percosse un demonio
>   Della sua scuriada, e disse: Via,
>   Ruffian, qui non son femmine da conio.
> Io mi raggiunsi con la scorta mia:
>   Poscia con pochi passi divenimmo,
>   Là dove un scoglio della ripa uscia.
> Assai leggieramente quel salimmo,   70
>   E volti a destra su per la sua scheggia,
>   Da quelle cerchie eterne ci partimmo.

⁶⁶ Not that they were miserly, but they wanted money for their pleasures, and were not scrupulous as to the way in which they earned it. Fazio degli Uberti (Dittam. iii. 5) gives a picture of life in Bologna:

> Intra Savena e Ren città si vede,
>   Si vaga e piena di tutti i diletti,
>   Che tal vi va a caval che torna a piede.
> Quivi son donne di leggiadri aspetti,
>   E il nome della terra segue il fatto,
>   Buona ne' studi e sottil d' intelletti.

Benv. suggests that Dante knew all about it when he was a student there.

⁷¹ **scheggia**: the reefs of rock which form the lines of bridges are regarded as split off from the main mass which walls the pit.

⁷² **cerchie**, from *cerchiare*, as e.g. *circa*, Par. xvi. 63, from *circare*. This seems much the simplest explanation. Dante had been walking a little way with Venedico; now he crosses the line of march.

When we were at the place where it is hollow below to give a passage to the flogged ones, the Leader said: 'Wait, and let the sight of these other misbegotten strike on thee, of whom thou hast not yet viewed the face, seeing that they have been going together with us.' From the old bridge we looked at the train which was coming toward us on the other border, and which the lash in like manner chases. The good Master, without my asking, said to me: 'Look at that great one who is coming, and for woe seems to shed

> Quando noi fummo là, dov' ei vaneggia
>   Di sotto, per dar passo agli sferzati,
>   Lo Duca disse: Attienti, e fa che feggia
> Lo viso in te di questi altri mal nati,
>   Ai quali ancor non vedesti la faccia,
>   Peroechè son con noi insieme andati.
> Dal vecchio ponte guardavam la traccia,
>   Che venia verso noi dall' altra banda,   80
>   E che la ferza similmente scaccia.
> Il buon Maestro, senza mia domanda,
>   Mi disse: Guarda quel grande che viene,
>   E per dolor non par lagrima spanda:

---

[73] **vaneggia**, as in l. 5. Here it refers to the opening of the arch.

[76] These are the seducers and betrayers of women. Why they go in the usual direction while the others go counter to it is not clear; unless it be to indicate that their sin, being in the first instance prompted by natural passion, is less contrary to the ordinary instincts of human nature.

[79] **vecchio**: 'qui [?quia] est veterior quam pons vetus Arni de Florentia.'—Benv.

[81] **per dolor.** Blanc is probably right in taking *per* here = *prae*. His suffering is too great to let him weep. Cf. xxxiii. 49. Witte's 'Was er auch leide,' 'for all his grief,' would require rather *per dolor*, for which there seems no authority.

no tear; what a kingly aspect does he yet retain! That is Jason, who through courage and through wisdom made the Colchians bereaved of their sheep. He passed by the isle of Lemnos, after that the bold women ruthless gave all their males to death. There with tokens and with words tricked-out he cheated Hypsipyle, the girl who already had cheated all the others. He left her there great with child and lonely; such fault condemns him to such torment; and also for Medea is vengeance wrought. With him goes along

> Quanto aspetto reale ancor ritiene!
>   Quelli è Jason, che per core e per senno
>   Li Colchi del monton privati fene.
> Egli passò per l' isola di Lenno,
>   Poi che le ardite femmine spietate
>   Tutti li maschi loro a morte dienno.   90
> Ivi con segni e con parole ornate^e
>   Isifile ingannò, la giovinetta,
>   Che prima avea tutte l' altre ingannate.
> Lasciolla quivi gravida e soletta:
>   Tal colpa a tal martiro lui condanna;
>   Ed anco di Medea si fa vendetta.

^e *con senno Cass.*

86 sqq. The murder by the Lemnian women of their husbands, and the subsequent desertion of Hypsipyle by Jason, is told at length in Stat. Theb. v. 404-485. Apollodorus, Bibl. i. 17, relates the stories briefly. Dante, however, was doubtless most familiar with Ovid's version, in the cases of both Hypsipyle and Medea. Heroides, vi. and xii.

91 The reading *senno* is, as Dr. Moore points out (Text. Crit. p. 321 sqq.), decidedly preferable from a literary point of view; but **segni** has the great weight of authority, and gives a sufficiently good sense.

93 When she contrived to save her father from the general massacre of males.

whoso cheats in such a matter; and let this suffice to know concerning the first vale, and concerning those whom it holds in its fangs.'

By this we were at the point where the narrow path forms a cross with the second embankment and makes of that abutments to a second arch. Thence we heard folk whimpering in the second trench, and grouting with the muzzle, and beating themselves with their palms. The banks were caked with a mould by reason of the exhalation from below which sticks there, so that it made strife with the eyes and with the nose. The bottom is so hollow that space suffices not to see without mounting on the crown

> Con lui sen va chi da tal parte inganna
>> E questo basti della prima valle
>> Sapere, e di color che in sè assanna.
> Già eravam là 've lo stretto calle   100
>> Con l' argine secondo s' incrocicchia.
>> E fa di quello ad un altro arco spalle.
> Quindi sentimmo gente che si nicchia
>> Nell' altra bolgia, e che col muso scuffa.¹
>> E sè medesma con le palme picchia.
> Le ripe eran grommate d' una muffa
>> Per l' alito di giù che vi si appasta,
>> Che con gli occhi e col naso facea zuffa.
> Lo fondo è cupo sì, che non ci basta
>> Loco a veder senza montare al dosso   110

¹ *sbuffa* Ald. W.; *stuffa* 4.

⁹⁷ **da tal parte**: lit. on that side.
¹⁰³ The flatterers, and those who entice others with smooth words.
¹⁰⁹ **cupo**: not so much deep as hollowed at the sides. In the former case there would be no particular advantage in the view from the crown of the bridge.

of the arch, where the rock stands highest. There we came, and from thence I saw down in the foss folk immersed in a dungheap that seemed brought from the privies of mankind. And while I was searching down there with my eye, I saw a head so foul with dung that it was not apparent whether it was lay or cleric. He cried out to me: 'Why art thou so greedy to look at me more than at the other brutes?' And I to him: 'Because, if I remember right, I have seen thee ere now with thy hair dry, and thou art Alessio Interminei of Lucca; therefore I eye thee more than all the rest.' And he then, beating his pate: 'My flatteries have submerged me down here, whereof I never

> Dell' arco, ove lo scoglio più soprasta.
> Quivi venimmo, e quindi giù nel fosso
>   Vidi gente attuffata in uno sterco,
>   Che dagli uman privati parea mosso:
> E mentre ch' io là giù con l' occhio cerco,
>   Vidi un col capo sì di merda lordo,
>   Che non parea s' era laico o cherco.
> Quei mi sgridò: Perchè sei tu sì ingordo
>   Di riguardar più me, che gli altri brutti?
>   Ed io a lui: Perchè, se ben ricordo,   120
> Già t' ho veduto coi capelli asciutti,
>   E sei Alessio Interminei da Lucca:
>   Però t' adocchio più che gli altri tutti.
> Ed egli allor, battendosi la zucca:
>   Quaggiù m' hanno sommerso le lusinghe.

[122] The Interminelli were a house at Lucca, prominent in the faction of the time, wherein they took the 'White' side. The famous partisan leader Castruccio Castracane was sprung from them; on the mother's side, says Benvenuto, but he seems to have borne their name. Nothing further is known of this Alessio.

had my tongue cloyed.' After that my Leader said to me: 'See thou urge thy glance a little onward, so that thou mayest with thine eyes duly reach the face of that unclean dishevelled wench, who is scratching herself there with her nails befouled, and now squats down, now is standing on her feet. Thais it is, the harlot, who answered her paramour, when he said, *Have I great thanks with thee?—Nay, marvellous.* And herewith let our sight have had enough.'

Ond' io non ebbi mai la lingua stucca.
Appresso ciò lo Duca: Fa che pinghe,
   Mi disse, il viso un poco più avante,
   Sì che la faccia ben con gli occhi attinghe
Di quella sozza e scapigliata fante,   130
   Che là si graffia con l' unghie merdose,
   Ed or s' accoscia, ed ora è in piede stante.
Taide è la puttana, che rispose
   Al drudo suo, quando disse: Ho io grazie
   Grandi appo te? Anzi meravigliose.
E quinci sien le nostre viste sazie.

_{130 sqq.} Benv. observes that some people were scandalised at the coarse and low terms employed by Dante in this passage; but holds that language should be adapted to the matter. Cf. xxv. 144.

_{133, 134.} The allusion is to the opening words of the third act of Terence's 'Eunuchus.' As a matter of fact, the word 'ingentes' is that of the parasite who brings the message from Thais to her suitor. The introduction by Dante of a person who is merely a character in a play is very curious, and suggests that he probably only knew the passage as a quotation, and assigned it to the historical Thais: or, like Benvenuto, confused the real and the fictitious persons of that name.

CANTO XIX

ARGUMENT

They reach the next pit, and find therein folk thrust head downwards into holes, with their feet on fire, who are the simoniacs. The author speaks with Pope Nicolas, and upbraids the ill-doing of certain Bishops of Rome.

O Simon Magus! O unhappy followers! because the things of God, which of goodness ought to be spouses, and ye in

> O Simon mago, o miseri seguaci,
> Che le cose di Dio, che di bontate
> Deono essere spose, e voi rapaci^a

^a *spose voi* Cass. 13 *Ald. IV.*

[1] *Simony*, so called from Simon the sorcerer (Acts viii.), is the sin of trafficking in spiritual things: see S. T. ii. 2. Q. 100. It is to sacrilege what theft is to violent robbery; and stands in opposition to *religion*, which is a branch of *justice*.

[a] **e voi**. On the whole it seems better to retain **e**. MS. authority is almost exactly divided; but its value is reduced by the fact of the previous word ending in *e*. With either reading the sentence is an 'anacoluthon,' for **che**—though in order to make the sentence intelligible I have rendered it 'because'—can hardly be anything but the relative, and in that case it is a subject without a verb, while **cose** is an object with nothing to govern it. Dr. Moore's suggestion that **e** is 'a sort of interjection' hardly helps. *E* no doubt has often a kind of demonstrative or intensive force in the apodosis of a conditional sentence, to which class all his instances belong (see also note, i. 28); but there is nothing of that sort here. Dante, I imagine, intended to write

your greed make to commit whoredom for gold and for silver—now it is meet that for you the trumpet sound, seeing that in the third pit ye are stationed. We were now at the next-ensuing tomb, having mounted on that part of the rock which plumbs exact above the middle of the foss. O highest Wisdom, how great is the skill that thou showest in heaven, in earth, and in the evil world, and how great justice does thy power distribute! I saw over the sides and over the bottom the livid stone full of holes, all of one size, and each was round. They seemed not to me less wide nor larger than those which in my fair Saint John's are made

> Per oro e per argento adulterate;
>   Or convien che per voi suoni la tromba,
>   Perocchè nella terza bolgia state.
> Già eravamo alla seguente tomba,
>   Montati dello scoglio in quella parte,
>   Che appunto sopra mezzo il fosso piomba.
> O somma Sapienza, quanta è l' arte   10
>   Che mostri in cielo, in terra e nel mal mondo,
>   E quanto giusto tua virtù comparte!
> Io vidi per le coste e per lo fondo
>   Piena la pietra livida di fori
>   D' un largo tutti, e ciascuno era tondo.
> Non mi parean meno ampi nè maggiori,
>   Che quei che son nel mio bel San Giovanni

something like this: 'Who have *misused* the things of God which ought to be . . . and (or but) which you have . . .,' and then, either forgetting, on account of the double relative, to finish the sentence, or judging that an aposiopesis would be more effective, left out the main verb. The omission of **e** does not make matters better, for 'che voi,' which the Germans can glibly render by 'die ihr,' is not an Italian idiom.

  12 **quanto giusto**: I have followed Benvenuto's rendering.

  17 **San Giovanni**: the Baptistery, originally the Cathedral of Florence.

for a place of the baptizers; one of which, it is not many
years since, I broke for the sake of one who was suffocating
therein: and let this be a sign to undeceive every man.
Out from the mouth of each was projecting of a sinner the
feet, and of the legs up to the thick part, and all the rest
stood within. The soles of all were on fire, both of them;
whereby they twitched their joints so hard that they would
have burst asunder twisted ropes and withes. As the flaming

>   Fatti per loco dei battezzatori;
> L' un delli quali, ancor non è molt' anni.
>   Rupp' io per un che dentro vi annegava: 20
>   E questo sia suggel ch' ogni uomo sganni.[b]
> Fuor della bocca a ciascun soperchiava
>   D' un peccator li piedi, e delle gambe
>   Infino al grosso, e l' altro dentro stava.
> Le piante erano a tutti accese intrambe;
>   Per che si forte guizzavan le giunte,
>   Che spezzate averian ritorte e strambe.

[b] *fia V.*

---

[18] The old font (removed in 1576) had in the thickness of its outer wall circular holes, such as may still be seen in that at Pisa, in which the officiating priest stood, to escape the pressure of the crowd. During Dante's Priorate, says Benvenuto, he happened to find a boy who had got stuck—presumably head downwards—in one of these holes, and was forced to break the marble to free him.

[19] **è—anni.** For the constr. see Diez iii. 180.

[20] **annegava**, intrans., as in Purg. vi. 15. The word (from Lat. *ad necem*) need not imply death by drowning only. So Fr. *noyer* in early times seems to have been used for any form of slaying; but especially by fatigue or suffocation.

[21] **sganni**: lest they should think it an act of wanton mischief on my part.

of oiled things is wont to move only on the outermost skin, so was it there from the heels to the points.

'Who is that, Master, that is wrathful, twitching more than the others his consorts,' said I, 'and whom a ruddier flame licks?' And he to me: 'If thou wilt that I carry thee down there by that bank which lies lowest, from him shalt thou know of himself and of his errors.' And I: 'All is good to me that pleases thee; thou art lord, and thou knowest that I depart not from thy will, and thou knowest that which is not said.' Then we came upon the fourth embankment; we turned and descended to the left hand,

> Qual suole il fiammeggiar delle cose unte
>   Moversi pur su per l' estrema buccia;
>   Tal era lì dai calcagni alle punte.   30
> Chi è colui, Maestro, che si cruccia,
>   Guizzando più che gli altri suoi consorti,
>   Diss' io, e cui più rozza fiamma succia?
> Ed egli a me: Se tu vuoi ch' io ti porti
>   Laggiù per quella ripa che più giace,
>   Da lui saprai di sè e dei suoi torti.
> Ed io: Tanto m' è bel, quanto a te piace:
>   Tu sei signore, e sai ch' io non mi parto
>   Dal tuo volere, e sai quel che si tace.
> Allor venimmo sull' argine quarto;   40
>   Volgemmo, e discendemmo a mano stanca

[29] **estrema buccia**: the same words in a rather different sense will be found in Purg. xxiii. 25.

[35] As the general level of Malebolge descends towards the centre, while the floor of each pit is horizontal, the wall on the side towards the centre will be lower than the other. There is here no question, as some commentators hold, of a difference in slope, such as, in xxiii. 31, *giacere* does seem to imply.

down into the bottom, pitted and narrow. The good
Master set me not yet down from his haunch, so he brought
me to the breach where he was who was bewailing himself
with his shank. 'Oh, whoso thou art, who holdest thy
upper part downward, sorry soul, like a stake in place,' I began to say, 'if thou canst, speak.' I was standing like the friar

> Laggiù nel fondo foracchiato ed arto.
> Lo buon Maestro ancor della sua anca
> Non mi dipose, sì mi giunse al rotto
> Di quel che si piangeva con la zanca.
> O qual che sei, che il dì su tien di sotto,
> Anima trista, come pal commessa,
> Comincia' io a dir, se puoi, fa motto.
> Io stava come il frate che confessa

[44] There seems no need to read *sin* here, or to suppose that **sì** is used in the sense of it. The use is like that in Purg. xxi. 12.

[45] **si piangeva**, almost in the original sense of *plangere*, 'to beat' (Lomb.). Benv. appears to read *pingeva*; but his comment is ambiguous: qui ita agitabat crura percutiens illa invicem.—The person is John Guatani (Vill. vii. 54), of the Orsini family, who as Nicolas III. held the Papal see from November 1277 to August 1281. His personal character seems to have been good, and as an Italian in a series of French popes, Dante might have been expected to favour him, especially as he offered some opposition to Charles of Anjou. But even Villani, who was no scandalmonger, supports the charge of simony, telling us that he made James Colonna a cardinal in order to get the support of that powerful house. This would bring him under the description of simony formulated by Aquinas, S. T. ii. 2. Q. 100. A. 5: Sicut contrahitur simonia accipiendo pecuniam . . . ita etiam contrahitur per munus in lingua vel ab obsequio. Probably his real offence in Dante's eyes was the transaction by which he obtained from Rudolf the lordship of Romagna, as a kind of penalty for neglect to go on crusade. It may be noted here that in the opinion of some a Pope could not commit simony. See S. T. ii. 2. Q. 100. A. 1. St. Thomas rejects this view, and considers that, on the contrary, it is a graver sin in a Pope than in any other man.

who confesses the treacherous assassin that after he is fixed
calls him back, whereby he delays his death. And he cried:
'Art thou already upright here, art thou already upright
here, Boniface? by several years did the writing lie to me.
Art thou so soon sated of that possession, for the which

> Lo perfido assassin, che poi ch' è fitto, 50
> Richiama lui, per che la morte cessa :
> Ed ei gridò : Sei tu già costì ritto,
> Sei tu già costì ritto, Bonifazio ?
> Di parecchi anni mi mentì lo scritto.
> Sei tu sì tosto di quell' aver sazio,

[50] Burying alive with the head downwards appears to have been a recognised punishment in the Middle Ages for aggravated murder.

[53] Boniface VIII., Pope from December 1294 to October 1303. His name was Benedict Guatani (or Gaetani), and he was therefore probably a kinsman of Nicolas. He procured the abdication of the incapable Celestin V. (iii. 60), and having gained the support of Charles II. (of Anjou and Naples) by promising to co-operate with him—which would be an act of simony of the converse kind to that with which Nicolas is charged—secured by his aid the votes of both Orsini and Colonna cardinals (including the James Colonna mentioned above), and thereby his own election. See Villani viii. 5, 6 ; and for his end and a study of his character, chaps. 63, 64 ; or the summary of Villani's account given by Benvenuto. He may be called the last of the great Popes ; a man whom even Dante, who hated him, felt to be an antagonist worth fighting. Allusions to him will be found throughout the poem—see more especially xxvii. 70 ; Purg. xx. 87 ; Par. xvii. 49 ; and xxx. 148—so that no more need be said here ; but an excellent sketch of his career is given by Philalethes in a note to this Canto. Some of the early commentators, notably Landino, are much struck by the ingenuity of the artifice employed to bring a still living man under the lash. But, as will be seen later, this does not exhaust Dante's resources.

[54] **scritto**, like *volume* in Par. xv. 50, is generally taken to mean merely the knowledge of the future which all the spirits possess ; but there may well be an allusion to some well-known prophecy, such as that of Abbot Joachim, Par. xii. 140.

thou fearedst not to carry off by deceit the fair Lady, and afterward to make havoc of her?' I became such as are those who stand, through not comprehending that which is answered to them, as it were baffled, and know not how to answer. Then Virgil said: 'Tell him quickly, I am not he, I am not he that thou deemest'; and I answered as it was enjoined to me. Wherefore the spirit writhed his feet all over; then sighing, and with voice of weeping he said to me: 'Then what askest thou of me? If thou carest so much to know who I am that thou hast for this run down the bank, know that I was clad with the great mantle; and

> Per lo qual non temesti torre a inganno
> La bella Donna, e poi di farne strazio?
> Tal mi fec' io, quai son color che stanno,
> Per non intender ciò ch' è lor risposto,
> Quasi scornati, e risponder non sanno.   60
> Allor Virgilio disse: Digli tosto,
> Non son colui, non son colui che credi:
> Ed io risposi come a me fu imposto.
> Per che lo spirto tutti storse i piedi:*
> Poi sospirando, e con voce di pianto,
> Mi disse: Dunque che a me richiedi?
> Se di saper chi io sia ti cal cotanto,
> Che tu abbi però la ripa corsa,
> Sappi ch' io fui vestito del gran manto:

* *tutto 2 H'.*

" **la bella Donna**: the Church.

" Some, not understanding the use of **tutti**, and thinking that the word was incorrectly applied to *two* feet, have wished to read *tutto* (adv.). Even Blanc, in his Dict., seems to take this reading: though in his Erklärungen he defends *tutti*, comparing xxxi. 15. Cf. Fr. *à toutes jambes*.

" **il gran manto**: cf. Purg. xix. 104.

verily I was a child of the bear; so eager to advance the whelps, that above I pocketed wealth, and here myself. Below my head have the others been drawn, who went before me in committing simony, flattened out through the cracks of the rock. Down there shall I drop in turn, when he shall come who I deemed that thou wast, when I made my sudden inquiry. But more is the time that I have already roasted my feet, and that I have stood thus upside down, than he shall stand planted with his feet red; for after him

> E veramente fui figliuol dell' orsa,　　　　　　　　70
> 　　Cupido sì, per avanzar gli orsatti,
> 　　Che su l' avere, e qui me misi in borsa.
> Di sotto al capo mio son gli altri tratti
> 　　Che precedetter me simoneggiando,
> 　　Per le fessure della pietra piatti.
> Laggiù cascherò io altresì, quando
> 　　Verrà colui ch' io credea che tu fossi,
> 　　Allor ch' io feci il subito domando.
> Ma più è il tempo già che i piè mi cossi,
> 　　E ch' io son stato così sottosopra,　　　　　　　80
> 　　Ch' ei non starà piantato coi piè rossi:

⁷⁰ **orsa**: with allusion of course to his house.

⁷¹ See Villani vii. 54: Tolse alla Chiesa castello Santangiolo, e diello a messer Orso suo nipote . . . Incontanente che ebbe privilegio di Romagna, sì ne fece conte messer Bertoldo degli Orsini suo nipote . . . e con lui per legato messer frate Latino di Roma cardinale ostiense suo nipote. See also chap. 58.

⁷² **più tempo**: because Nicolas had to wait more than twenty years for Boniface to take his place; but Boniface only eleven for Clement, who died in 1314 (Vill. ix. 59), not, as Philalethes misled by the old legend which made his death follow immediately on Philip's, according to the prophecy of the dying Grand Master of the Templars says, in 1307.

⁸¹ **piè rossi**: perhaps with allusion to the red shoes worn by Popes in life.

shall come, of fouler works, from the westward a lawless pastor, such as is meet should cover up him and me. A new Jason shall he be, whereof we read in the Maccabees; and as to that one his king was easy, so shall be to him he who rules France.'

I know not if I was here too foolhardy, that I answered him only in this strain: 'Tell me now, I pray, how much

> Chè dopo lui verrà, di più laid' opra,
>   Di ver ponente un pastor senza legge,
>   Tal che convien che lui e me ricopra.
> Nuovo Iason sarà, di cui si legge
>   Nei Maccabei: e come a quel fu molle
>   Suo re, così fia a lui chi Francia regge.
> Io non so s' io mi fui qui troppo folle,
>   Ch' io pur risposi lui a questo metro:
>   Deh or mi di', quanto tesoro volle   90

[84] This refers to Bertrand (called by Villani 'Ramondo') de Goth, Archbishop of Bordeaux, who by the intrigues of Philip the Fair with the French party among the cardinals, got elected Pope on the death of Benedict XI. in 1305. By him the Papal see was removed to Avignon. See Par. xvii. 82; xxvii. 58; and Villani viii. 90, 91.

[85] The dealings of Jason with Antiochus Epiphanes, when, as our version has it, he 'laboured underhand to be high priest,' recorded in 2 Macc. iv., form a curious parallel to what the contemporary historians tell us of Clement's with Philip. According to what Villani tells of Clement's character, there seem to have been other points of resemblance between him and Jason. The historian relates at the same time a story, which may be noticed here, that Clement, wishing to know the fate of a nephew of his, procured by magic arts that one of his chaplains should visit Hell; and that the chaplain was there shown a palace, and in it a fiery bed on which lay the soul of the nephew, and was told that he was thus punished for simony: his informant adding that a similar place was being prepared for Clement himself. The Pope on hearing this became melancholy and died soon after; and while his body was lying in state, a fire broke out in the church, and consumed it from the waist downwards.

treasure craved our Lord at first from Saint Peter, that He should give him the keys in his stewardship? Surely He asked nought but—Follow me. Nor did Peter nor the others ask of Matthias gold or silver, when he was chosen by lot to the place which the guilty soul lost. Therefore stay, for thou art rightly punished; and be sure thou keep the ill-raised money which made thee daring against Charles. And were it not that still forbids it to me my reverence for the supreme keys which thou heldest in the glad life, I would use words yet more grievous; for your avarice makes the world sad,

> Nostro Signore in prima da san Pietro,
> > Che ponesse le chiavi in sua balìa?[d]
> > Certo non chiese se non: Viemmi retro.
> Nè Pier nè gli altri chiesero a Mattia
> > Oro od argento, quando fu sortito
> > Al loco che perdè l' anima ria.
> Però ti sta, che tu sei ben punito;
> > E guarda ben la mal tolta moneta,
> > Ch' esser ti fece contra Carlo ardito.
> E se non fosse, che ancor lo mi vieta   100
> > La riverenza delle somme chiavi,
> > Che tu tenesti nella vita lieta,
> I' userei parole ancor più gravi;
> > Chè la vostra avarizia il mondo attrista,

[d] *Che li ponesse . . in sua b.* Cass. 1234; *che ponesse* Ald.: *in balìa* W.

[99] Nicolas, it appears, had wished to ally himself with Charles of Anjou by marrying his niece to Charles's nephew. Charles returned a scornful answer, implying that scarlet shoes did not make noble blood; and from that time the Pope was his enemy. He deprived him of the honours which he had conferred on him, and favoured the intrigue of John of Procida, which led up to the 'Sicilian Vespers,' and the loss of Sicily to the house of Anjou. It was said that he received money from the Eastern Emperor in aid of this scheme.

trampling the good and exalting the wicked. Of you pastors was the Evangelist aware, when she who sits above the waters was seen of him to commit whoredom with the kings; she that was born with the seven heads, and had equipment from the ten horns so long as virtue was pleasing

> Calcando i buoni e sollevando i pravi.
> Di voi pastor s' accorse il Vangelista,
>   Quando colei, che siede sopra l' acque,
>   Puttaneggiar coi regi a lui fu vista:
> Quella che con le sette teste nacque,
>   E dalle dieci corna ebbe argomento,   110
>   Fin che virtute al suo marito piacque.

[109 sqq.] This was another of the passages which was required by the Spanish Inquisition in its flourishing days to be cancelled, before the poem could be introduced into Spanish territory. Fortunately for modern readers and collectors, the Holy Office was less able to make its power felt elsewhere. The passage is probably the earliest instance in literature of the identification, which has since become so popular, of the 'scarlet woman' of Rev. xvii. with the Papal power. The commentators have charged Dante with inaccuracy in attributing the seven heads and ten horns to the woman herself; but this need not follow from his words. **Con le sette teste nacque** need not mean more than 'came into existence at the same time with the seven heads,' i.e. with the beginning of the Empire—the heads denoting, as in the original (see vv. 9, 10), 'kings,' i.e. according to the most plausible interpretation, the early emperors. It must be said, however, that Dante's treatment of the prophecy is confused, for in l. 111 he seems to conceive a time when the 'harlot' had not fallen from virtue, of which there is no suggestion in the Apocalypse. Is it possible that he understood by the 'horns' the ten persecutions, as they are generally reckoned? The mention of Constantine, with whose conversion persecutions came to an end (cf. Brunetto, Trésor. i. 87: quant l'emperères dona si grant honor a Silvestre et as pastors di sainte Eglise, toutes persecutions furent définees), rather suggests this. In that case **argomento** must mean 'proof' or 'trial.'

to her husband. Ye have made a god of gold and silver, and what else is there between you and the idolater save that he worships one, and you a hundred. Ah, Constantine, of how great ill was mother, not thy conversion, but that dowry which the first rich pope got from thee!' And whiles that I was chanting him such notes, whether it were anger or conscience that pricked him, he kicked hard with both feet. I deem well that it pleased my Leader, with mien so content did he attend all the time to the sound of the true words uttered. Therefore he took me with both his arms, and after that he had got me up wholly on his breast,

> Fatto v' avete Dio d' oro e d' argento :
> E che altro è da voi all' idolatre,
> Se non ch' egli uno, e voi n' orate cento?
> Ahi, Constantin, di quanto mal fu matre,
> Non la tua conversion, ma quella dote
> Che da te prese il primo ricco patre !
> E mentre io gli cantava cotai note,
> O ira o coscienza che il mordesse,
> Forte spingava con ambo le piote.   120
> Io credo ben che al mio Duca piacesse,
> Con si contenta labbia sempre attese
> Lo suon delle parole vere espresse.
> Però con ambo le braccia mi prese,
> E poi che tutto su mi s' ebbe al petto,

---

[112] Hosea viii. 4: argentum suum et aurum suum fecerunt sibi idola.

[115] For the history of the fictitious donation of the 'States of the Church' by Constantine to Pope Silvester, see Gibbon, chap. xlv. notes 68-76. Cf. also xxvii. 94; Purg. xxxii. 128; and De Mon. iii. 10. Milton, 'Of Reformation in England,' quotes these lines, but seems to have no doubt about the genuineness of the donation.

[119] For the construction, see Diez iii. 335.

he mounted again by the way whence he came down; nor did he weary of holding me clasped to him, till so carried he me on to the crown of the arch which is the passage from the fourth to the fifth embankment. Here gently he laid down the burden, gently by reason of the untrimmed and steep reef, which would be a hard track for the goats. Thence another valley was disclosed to me.

> Rimontò per la via onde discese:
> Nè si stancò d' avermi a sè distretto,
> Sì mi portò sopra il colmo dell' arco,
> Che dal quarto al quinto argine è tragetto.
> Quivi soavemente spose il carco, 130
> Soave per lo scoglio sconcio ed erto,
> Che sarebbe alle capre duro varco:
> Indi un altro vallon mi fu scoperto.

[129] **sì**, as in l. 44.

[131] **soave**: the commentators who notice this use of the word are almost unanimous in regarding it as a repetition of the adverb, and not as an adj. agreeing with **carco**. It may easily be a survival from the time when the termination *mente* was recognised (as it still is to some degree in Spanish) as an independent word. Land. Vell. and Dan. pass it without notice.

CANTO XX

ARGUMENT

In the third pit they find soothsayers and diviners who go with their faces turned backwards. Virgil points out Tiresias, Manto, and others, and tells of the founding of his own city.

OF a new penalty it behoves me to make verses, and to give matter for the twentieth chant of my first canticle, which is of the sunken ones. I was already wholly in position to gaze into the uncovered depth, which was bathed with tears of anguish; and I saw folk, throughout the circular valley, come silent and weeping, at the pace which the litany-processions make in this world. As my sight went

> Di nuova pena mi convien far versi,
>   E dar materia al ventesimo canto
>   Della prima canzon, ch' è dei sommersi.
> Io era già disposto tutto e quanto
>   A riguardar nello scoperto fondo,
>   Che si bagnava d' angoscioso pianto :
> E vidi gente per lo vallon tondo
>   Venir tacendo e lagrimando, al passo
>   Che fan le letanie in questo mondo.

[1] I.e. he was on the highest point of the bridge, cf. xviii. 110.

[5] **scoperto**: because in the last pits the sinners had been more or less concealed, in one case by filth, in the other by the holes in which they were planted.—Benv.

[7] **gente**: soothsayers and diviners.

lower down among them, strangely did each one appear twisted round between the chin and the beginning of the chest; for the face was turned on the side of the reins, and it behoved them to go backward, because seeing forward was taken from them. Haply ere now by force of palsy has some one been thus twisted right round, but I never saw it, nor do I believe that it is so. So may God grant thee, reader, to take profit of thy reading, think now for thyself how I could keep my visage dry when I saw close at hand our form so turned round, that the weeping of the eyes

> Come il viso mi scese in lor più basso,   10
>   Mirabilmente apparve esser travolto
>   Ciascun tral mento e 'l principio del casso :[a]
> Chè dalle reni era tornato il volto,
>   Ed indietro venir gli convenia,
>   Perchè il veder dinanzi era lor tolto.
> Forse per forza già di parlasia
>   Si travolse così alcun del tutto;
>   Ma io nol vidi, nè credo che sia.
> Se Dio ti lasci, Lettor, prender frutto
>   Di tua lezione, or pensa per te stesso,   20
>   Com' io potea tener lo viso asciutto,
> Quando la nostra imagine da presso
>   Vidi sì torta, che il pianto degli occhi

[a] *dal mento al pr. Ald.*

12 Modern edd. mostly read *dal mento al prin.* The meaning would be the same, but the reading in the text has the most MS. authority. On the other hand it must be said that *da—a* is slightly *lectio difficilior*.

19 Benvenuto has some observations here on the futility of astrology, summing up with 'Certe fateor quod astra non mentiuntur, sed astrologi bene mentiuntur de astris.'

22 **nostra imagine**: the human figure.

bathed the buttocks by their division. Of a truth I began to weep leaning against one of the rocks of the hard cliff, so that my Escort said to me: 'Art thou yet among the other foolish ones? Here pity lives when it is right dead. Who is more wicked than he who brings passion to the

> La natiche bagnava per lo fesso.
> Certo i' piangea, poggiato ad un dei rocchi
>   Del duro scoglio, sì che la mia scorta
>   Mi disse: Ancor sei tu degli altri sciocchi?
> Qui vive la pietà quando è ben morta.
>   Chi è più scellerato che colui
>   Che al giudizio divin passion comporta?[b]   30

[b] *compassion porta* Gg. (*alt.*) *Benv. W.*: *passion porta Ald.*

[28] Cf. xxxiii. 150. Here there is a further play on the two meanings of **pietà**, 'piety' and 'pity.'

[30] Of the various readings which are found here, the one in the text has, according to Dr. Moore's collations, much more MS. authority than the others put together, besides being that of all edd. before 1480; *passion porta* (for which it is hard to understand his preference) the least. The meaning obviously is 'who allows himself to be influenced by feeling when considering God's judgements,' 'imports feeling into his view of them'; and either *porta* or *comporta* will bear this signification, though the latter word, in the few places where Dante uses it, seems to mean rather 'bear with' or 'endure.' It was, however, quite possible for Dante to go back to the original meaning of the word. Still his use of it is sufficiently uncommon to account for the very early change to *compassion porta*, which fits in with certain expressions used by St. Augustine and St. Thomas (e.g. S. T. ii. 1. QQ. 19. 39); and is adopted by Benvenuto among others. Dr. Moore's suggestion that if *passion porta* were written as one word, the *c* might be mistaken for an abbreviated *com* will hardly commend itself to paleographers; the only abbreviation for *com*, so far as I know, being 9, for which *c* is as unlikely to be mistaken as any letter well could be. It may be added that, though not without parallel, *passion* as a trisyllable would be unusual. Why Dante should be so affected by the sight of the punishment of this class of sinners as to require a caution of the kind here, and here only, it is hard to see.

judgement of God? Lift, lift thy head, and see him for whom the earth opened in the sight of the Thebans, whereby they all cried: Whither rushest thou, Amphiaraus; why leavest the war? And he stayed not from dashing downward even to Minos, who fetters each one. Look how he has made a breast of his shoulders; because he wished to see too far in front, he looks behind and goes a backward road. See Teiresias, who changed semblance when from

> Drizza la testa, drizza, e vedi a cui
>   S' aperse agli occhi dei Teban la terra,
>   Per ch' ei gridavan tutti: Dove rui,
> Anfiarao? perchè lasci la guerra?
>   E non restò di ruinare a valle
>   Fino a Minòs, che ciascheduno afferra.
> Mira, che ha fatto petto delle spalle:
>   Perchè volle veder troppo davante,
>   Diretro guarda, e fa retroso calle.
> Vedi Tiresia, che mutò sembiante,   40

[31] The story of Amphiaraus the seer, how he was swallowed up by the earth in the midst of the battle, will be found in Stat. Theb. vii. ad fin.

[32-34] There is not a word in Statius of any mocking cries on the part of the Thebans towards Amphiaraus; but the remark made by Pluto as he enters the lower world is something like that in the text, especially if we may suppose that Dante read it cursorily, and took 'Manes' for a verb:

> At tibi quos, inquit, Manes, qui limite praeceps
> Non licito per inane ruis? . . .

[35] Minos is specially mentioned, Theb. viii. 27, 103: but curiously enough as tempering by merciful counsels the too great severity of Pluto.

[40] Tiresias was the Theban augur, as Amphiaraus the besiegers'. The story here referred to is in Ov. Met. iii. 318 sq.

male he became female, shifting all his members; and afterwards he needed again to strike with his rod the two entwined serpents, before he regained his manly plumes. Aruns is he who turns his back to this one's belly; who in the mountains of Luni, where hoes the man of Carrara who dwells below, had among white marbles the cave for his lodging; whence to gaze on the stars and the sea his view was not shortened. And she who covers her breasts, which thou seest not, with her unbound tresses, and has on the further side all skin which bears hair, was Manto, who sought

> Quando di maschio femmina divenne,
>   Cangiandosi le membra tutte quante;
> E prima poi ribatter gli convenne
>   Li due serpenti avvolti con la verga,
>   Che riavesse le maschili penne.
> Aronta è quel che al ventre gli s' atterga,
>   Che nei monti di Luni, dove ronca
>   Lo Carrarese che di sotto alberga,
> Ebbe tra bianchi marmi la spelonca
>   Per sua dimora; onde a guardar le stelle   50
>   E il mar non gli era la veduta tronca.
> E quella che ricopre le mammelle,
>   Che tu non vedi, con le trecce sciolte,
>   E ha di là ogni pilosa pelle,

---

46 Aruns, a soothsayer of later times, consulted by the authorities, according to Lucan, before the outbreak of the civil war. See Phars. i. 586: 'incoluit desertae moenia Lunae.' Dittamondo iii. 6:

> E il monte ancora e la spelonca propia
> Là dove stava lo indovin di Aronta.

Dante seems to have confused him with his colleague Figulus, for it was he, 'quem non stellarum Aegyptia Memphis aequarat visu'; while the business of Aruns lay more in the inspection of entrails.

through many lands; afterward she settled in the place where I was born; wherefore it is my pleasure that thou hear me a little. After that her father issued from life, and the city of Bacchus came to servitude, she went a long time about the world. Above in fair Italy lies a lake at the foot of the Alp which over Tirol locks Germany, and it has

> Manto fu, che cercò per terre molte,
>   Poscia si pose là dove nacqu' io;
>   Onde un poco mi piace che m' ascolte.
> Poscia che il padre suo di vita uscio,
>   E venne serva la città di Baco,
>   Questa gran tempo per lo mondo gio. 60
> Suso in Italia bella giace un laco
>   Appiè dell' alpe, che serra Lamagna
>   Sopra Tiralli, ch' ha nome Benaco.

⁵⁵ Manto, daughter of Tiresias, appears frequently in the 'Thebais' (see especially iv. 463 sqq), but there is no hint there of her wanderings after the death of her father; which indeed did not take place till ten years after the action of the poem ends, that is, at the capture of Thebes by the Epigoni (Apollod. Bibl. iii. 7). It must be to this, and not to any servitude under Theseus or Creon, that l. 59 refers. Dante has probably taken the idea of her travels about the world merely from Virgil's statement, Aen. x. 199, that she was the mother of Ocnus, the founder of Mantua—if indeed that be not, as some commentators hold, another Manto altogether. It will be seen, however, that he departs from his authority, and ignores Ocnus; the latter part of the legend being, it would seem, entirely of his own invention. The reference to Benacus and the Mincio is obviously suggested by Virgil's mention of them in the same passage.

⁶³ **Tiralli**: 'unus comitatus in introitu Alemanniae ubi regnant hodie quidam comites theutonici, qui vocantur Turones,' says Benv. writing very soon after the transfer of the province from the old line of Counts to the Hapsburgs. ('Turon' is found with 'Tirol' in a grant dated 1242, probably meaning Dürrenstein, a village near Schloss Tirol, of which the Counts were lords.)

name Benacus. Through a thousand springs, I think, and more the Pennine is washed, between Garda and Val Camonica, by the water which lies in the aforesaid lake.

> Per mille fonti, credo, e più si bagna,
> Tra Garda e Val Camonica, Pennino ᶜ
> Dell' acqua che nel detto lago stagna.

ᶜ *Vale e Apennino* Cass.; *e V. e Ap.* 35; *Apennino* Gg. 124 Ald. W.

⁶⁴⁻⁶⁶ The difficulty of these lines is the word *Apennino* or *Pennino*. The first has the great weight of authority; but the fact of the previous word ending in *a* makes MS. authority of less importance than it usually is. Neither one nor the other name, however, belongs to the district which is here referred to. It is true that Herr Witte, who had rather a gift for discovering mountains where he wanted them (see e.g. his note to xv. 9), found a mountain called Apennino to the north of Gargnano, on the west coast of the lake; but this, if it exists, is far too obscure to be introduced at the outset of such a grand piece of topography, and too small to be washed 'per mille fonti e più.' Benvenuto reads *e Pennino*, but seems (for his note is obscure—probably the text is corrupt) to understand the Apennine. Bargigi sees the difficulty, but turns it by assuming that Dante said Apennine when he meant Alp, as in xvi. 101 he has used *alpe* for a part of the Apennine. Vellutello reads *Valdimonica* under some misunderstanding as to the position of Val Camonica, but accepts *Pennino* without difficulty. Cass. has *e Apennino*, and the annotator takes the three names as indicating the provinces of Verona, Brescia, and Trent. The second *e* is clearly wrong, as it involves taking **laco** as subject to **si bagna**. On the whole, I am inclined to think that Dante took *Pennino* in a wide sense, as applying to any part of the central Alps, and (possibly) did not clearly distinguish it from *Apennino*. No doubt the Pennine Alps, according to modern usage, do not come within 120 miles of Val Camonica: but the term seems to have been very loosely used. Josias Simler, writing in 1574, tells us (de Alpibus Commentarius) that according to one system of nomenclature, the name was given to the mountains at the head of the Vinstgau, or valley of the Adige. The district here referred to is that drained by the Sarca, which is fed by the glaciers and snows of the Adamello and Brenta groups. **Garda** is of course the place of that name on the east shore of the lake.

There is a place in the middle there where the pastor of
Trent, and he of Brescia, and the Veronese, might give their
blessing, if they made that journey. Peschiera sits, a fair
and mighty armament, to make head against Brescians and
Bergamasks, where the surrounding shore comes lowest.
There it behoves that all that pour forth which cannot stay
in the bosom of Benacus, and it becomes a river down
through green pastures. As soon as the water starts to
flow, no longer Benacus but Mincio it is called, even to
Governo where it falls into Po. It has no long course when
it finds a hollow into which it spreads itself, and turns it to

> Loco è nel mezzo là, dove il Trentino
>   Pastore, e quel di Brescia, e il Veronese
>   Segnar potria, se fesse quel cammino.[d]
> Siede Peschiera, bello e forte arnese   70
>   Da fronteggiar Bresciani e Bergamaschi,
>   Ove la riva intorno più discese.
> Ivi convien che tutto quanto caschi
>   Ciò che in grembo a Benaco star non può,
>   E fassi fiume giù per verdi paschi.
> Tosto che l' acqua a correr mette co,
>   Non più Benaco, ma Mincio si chiama
>   Fino a Governo, dove cade in Po.
> Non molto ha corso, che trova una lama,
>   Nella qual si distende e la impaluda,   80

[d] *fusse a quel Cass.; sel fusse* 2 ; *fosse* 1345.

The point on the lake, towards the north end, where the dioceses of the three bishops meet.

co = *capo* as in xxi. 64, Par. iii. 96 (where it means 'the completion' instead of as here 'the beginning.' Either may of course be regarded as the 'head'.

Governo: now called Governolo.

Any one who has been at Mantua in summer will recognise the truth of this.

a marsh, and it is wont in summer at times to be hurtful. Passing thence the savage maid saw land in the midst of the swamp, without cultivation and bare of dwellers. There to escape all society of men she abode with her servants to work her arts, and lived, and left there her empty corpse.

'Afterward the men who were scattered around assembled themselves to that place, for it was strong by reason of the swamp which it had on all sides; they made their city above those dead bones; and for her sake who first chose out the spot they called it Mantua, without further lot. Its folk within were once thicker than now, before the folly of Casalodi

> E suol di state talora esser grama.
> Quindi passando la vergine cruda
>   Vide terra nel mezzo del pantano,
>   Senza cultura, e d' abitanti nuda.
> Li, per fuggire ogni consorzio umano,
>   Ristette coi suoi servi a far sue arti,
>   E visse, e vi lasciò suo corpo vano.
> Gli uomini poi, che intorno erano sparti,
>   S' accolsero a quel loco, ch' era forte
>   Per lo pantan che avea da tutte parti.   60
> Fer la città sopra quell' ossa morte;
>   E per colei, che il loco prima elesse,
>   Mantova l' appellar senz' altra sorte.
> Già fur le genti sue dentro più spesse,
>   Prima che la mattia di Casalodi

^{senz' altra sorte}: without casting lots or taking auguries.

A little before Dante's time Pinamonte de' Buonaccorsi, wishing to get the government of Mantua into his hands, had got rid, by playing them off one against the other, of all the other leading houses except the Casalodi, a Brescian family. He then took himself the popular side, and after persuading Alberto da Casalodi, under pretext of pacifying the people, to consent to the temporary banishment of any of the

received fraud from Pinamonte. Therefore I do thee to wit that if thou ever hear that my land had origin otherwise, no lie may cheat the truth.' And I: 'Master, thy reasonings are to me so certain, and hold so my belief, that the others will be to me extinct coals. But tell me of the folk that goes onward, if thou seest of them any worthy of note, for only on that does my mind strike.' Then he said to me: 'He who from his cheek spreads his beard over his brown shoulders was, when Greece was so void of males that hardly were any left for the cradles, an augur; and gave with Calchas the moment for cutting the first cable in

> Da Pinamonte inganno ricevesse.
> Però t' assenno, che se tu mai odi
>   Originar la mia terra altrimenti,
>   La verità nulla menzogna frodi.
> Ed io: Maestro, i tuoi ragionamenti   100
>   Mi son sì certi, e prendon sì mia fede,
>   Che gli altri mi sarian carboni spenti.
> Ma dimmi della gente che procede,
>   Se tu ne vedi alcun degno di nota;
>   Chè solo a ciò la mia mente rifiede.
> Allor mi disse: Quel, che dalla gota
>   Porge la barba in sulle spalle brune,
>   Fu, quando Grecia fu di maschi vota
> Sì che appena rimaser per le cune,
>   Augure, e diede il punto con Calcanta   110
>   In Aulide a tagliar la prima fune.

remaining nobles who showed any energy, finally raised the people against those who were left, including the Casalodi, and got rid of them, banishing some and slaughtering others.

[97] It is curious, as the commentators point out, that Dante should make Virgil contradict with so much energy his own account of the origin of Mantua.

Aulis. Eurypylus had he name, and thus does my lofty Tragedy chant it in a certain place; well knowest thou it, for thou knowest that throughout. That other who is so scant in the flanks was Michael Scot, who of a truth knew the game of the magic frauds. Behold Guido Bonatti,

> Euripilo ebbe nome, e così il canta
> > L' alta mia Tragedia in alcun loco:
> > Ben lo sai tu, che la sai tutta quanta.
> Quell' altro che nei fianchi è così poco,
> > Michele Scotto fu, che veramente
> > Delle magiche frode seppe il gioco.
> Vedi Guido Bonatti, vedi Asdente,

---

[113] Aen. ii. 114.

[116] Michael Scot of Balwearie is known to every reader of 'The Lay of the Last Minstrel.' As a matter of fact, he lived almost entirely in Italy, at the court of Frederick II. Honorius III. wished to make him Archbishop of Cashel; and Gregory IX. favoured him; but some of his more learned contemporaries seem to have thought him an impostor. He translated from Averroes and Avicenna, and commented on Aristotle. The prophecies ascribed to him enjoyed a great reputation for a long time; Villani in his later books quotes several. (See Oliphant, Frederick II. vol. i. 449.) He is mentioned, Dittamondo ii. 27, as 'che per sua arte sapeva Simon mago contraffare'; probably with allusion to the legend current about both of them, that they could dispose as they pleased of their shadows. Other stories are told of him which seem in later times to have been transferred to Dr. Faustus.

[118] **Guido Bonatti** of Forlì, a roofer by trade, seems to have acted as domestic prophet to Guido da Montefeltro (Vill. vii. 81). Benvenuto tells with reference to him the pleasant story of the rustic, who by noticing the movements of his donkey was able to foretell the weather with more accuracy than the regular prophet.

Asdente, a shoemaker of Parma, was a famous character about the middle of the 13th century. Fra Salimbene takes him very seriously, and believes in his prophetic gifts. In Conv. iv. 16 he is mentioned, but only as a type of the man of low birth who had made himself notorious.

behold Asdente, who now would wish to have given heed to his leather and to his thread, but repents too late. Behold the sorry ones who left the needle, the shuttle, and the distaff, and became diviners; they wrought charms with herbs and with an image.

'But come away now, for already Cain and his thorns hold the boundary of both the hemispheres, and touch the waves beyond Seville. And even yesternight was the moon full; well oughtest thou to remember it, for it did thee no harm on a time amid the deep wood.' So he talked to me, and we were going the while.

> Che avere inteso al cuoio ed allo spago
> Ora vorebbe, ma tardi si pente. 120
> Vedi le triste che lasciaron l' ago,
> La spuola e il fuso, e fecersi indivine;
> Fecer malie con erbe e con imago.
> Ma vienne omai, chè già tiene il confine
> D' amendue gli emisperi, e tocca l'onda
> Sotto Sibilia, Caino e le spine.
> E già iernotte fu la luna tonda:
> Ben ten dee ricordar, chè non ti nocque
> Alcuna volta per la selva fonda.
> Sì mi parlava, ed andavamo introcque. 130

E pur 3 W.

124 *sqq.* I.e. it is a little after sunrise, or about 6 A.M. on Easter Eve. **iernotte** means, of course, the night before the one which has just ended, i.e. the night which preceded Dante's meeting with Virgil.

126 **Caino**: cf. Par. ii. 51.

130 **introcque**: a Florentine word, which Benv. says was obsolete in his time, cf. Vulg. El. i. 13.

CANTO XXI

ARGUMENT

In the fourth pit they find pitch seething, wherein are plunged those who have traded in public offices. They fall in with a troop of demons; and they learn that the next bridge is broken down. The captain of the troop assigns ten to them as an escort.

THUS from bridge to bridge, talking of else than my Comedy cares to chant, did we come; and we were holding the summit when we stayed to see the next fissure of Malebolge, and the next idle lamentations; and I beheld it wondrously dark. As in the Arsenal of the Venetians boils in winter the sticky pitch, to pay afresh their unsound craft, for they cannot sail: and in place of that one makes his new craft, and one

> Cosi, di ponte in ponte, altro parlando
>   Che la mia commedia cantar non cura,
>   Venimmo, e tenevamo il colmo, quando
> Ristemmo per veder l' altra fessura
>   Di Malebolge, e gli altri pianti vani;
>   E vidila mirabilmente oscura.
> Quale nell' Arzanà dei Viniziani
>   Bolle l' inverno la tenace pece
>   A rimpalmar li legni lor non sani,
> Che navicar non ponno, e in quella vece   10
>   Chi fa suo legno nuovo, e chi ristoppa

[1] **in quella vece:** instead of sailing. So Purg. xvi. 36.

recaulks the sides of that which has made many voyages;
one hammers forward and one aft; another makes oars and
another twists cordage; one patches mizzen and mainsail.
So, not by fire, but by divine craft, was boiling there below
a thick pitch, which slimed the bank on every side. I saw
it, but I saw nought in it save the bubbles which the boiling

> Le coste a quel che più viaggi fece;
> Chi ribatte da proda e chi da poppa;
>   Altri fa remi, ed altri volge sarte;
>   Chi terzeruolo ed artimon rintoppa:
> Tal, non per foco, ma per divina arte
>   Bollia laggiuso una pegola spessa
>   Che inviscava la ripa da ogni parte.
> Io vedea lei, ma non vedeva in essa
>   Ma che le bolle che il bollor levava,   20

---

[13] One is much tempted to read *ribade*, 'rivets,' as in xxv. 8; but there seems no trace of it in MSS.

[17] Benvenuto thinks that the boiling pitch is specially appropriate to the punishment of *barataria* or jobbery, as we should now call it. He quotes Solomon on the effect of touching pitch, and adds, 'So contagious is this jobbery that if a saint entered public office about the court, he would fall into it, as I have in fact seen in many cases.' The whole description of the operation of the arsenal he thinks to be typical, down to the smallest detail, of the *baratarius* and his procedure! (It may be as well to mention here that the word 'barratry' has a special legal sense in English, quite different from what is intended here, and therefore I have avoided its use. The sin here punished is to secular offices exactly what simony is to sacred, and has the same kind of ramifications. Thus Villani (vii. 148) speaks of the *baratteria* of some officers, who received pay for a certain force, and maintained a smaller; no doubt pocketing the difference. It is somewhat curious that Aquinas nowhere deals with it specifically. He assumes in one place, as a matter of course, that a judge must not take money for giving judgement or a witness for his evidence; but he never mentions this sin under any special name, nor gives any regular discussion to it.)

raised, and the whole swelling, and settling again, pressed together.

While I was gazing down fixedly, my Leader saying: 'Look, look,' drew me to him from the place where I was standing. Then I turned like the man who is in a hurry to see that which it behoves him to flee, and whom sudden fear makes void of mirth, so that he delays not his departure for seeing; and I beheld behind us a black devil running to come up on to the rock. Ah, how fierce was he in his aspect! and how cruel he seemed to me in his demeanour, with his wings spread and light upon his feet! His shoulder, which was sharp and high, a sinner freighted with both

> E gonfiar tutta, e riseder compressa.
> Mentr' io laggiù fisamente mirava,
>   Lo Duca mio, dicendo: Guarda, guarda,
>   Mi trasse a sè del loco dov' io stava.
> Allor mi volsi come l' uom cui tarda
>   Di veder quel che gli convien fuggire,
>   E cui paura subita sgagliarda,
> Che, per veder, non indugia il partire:
>   E vidi dietro a noi un diavol nero
>   Correndo su per lo scoglio venire.   30
> Ahi quanto egli era nell' aspetto fiero!
>   E quanto mi parea nell' atto acerbo,
>   Con l' ale aperte, e sopra il piè leggiero!
> L' omero suo, ch' era acuto e superbo,
>   Carcava un peccator con ambo l' anche.

[25] **cui tarda**: as in xiii. 119. To read *chi tarda* as some, including apparently Benvenuto, do, exactly reverses the meaning.

[34] **superbo** appears to = *superbus* in its primary meaning, almost lost in classical Latin. Lombardi compares Plautus Amph. i. 1. 261; we may perhaps add Virg. Georg. ii. 461.

haunches, and he was holding the sinew of the feet gripped. From our bridge he said: 'O Malebranche, here is one of the Elders of Santa Zita; put him under, since I am returning for more to that land which is well furnished with them; every man there is a barrator, except Bonturo; *No* becomes

> E quei tenea dei piè ghermito il nerbo.
> Del nostro ponte, disse, o Malebranche,
> Ecco un degli anzian di santa Zita:
> Mettetel sotto, ch' io torno per anche
> A quella terra che n' è ben fornita:[a]   40
> Ognun v' è barattier, fuor che Bonturo:

[a] *chio ben* Cass. 3; *ch' i' n' ho* W.

[38] I.e. of Lucca. Santa Zita is said to have been a woman of humble origin, who for her good deeds and religious life was canonised by Nicolas III. Her body is still shown on her festival, in the Church of San Frediano at Lucca. The *Anziani* of that city held the same kind of position as the Priors at Florence. This particular one is said by Buti and other early commentators to have been one Martin Bottaio, who was in office in 1300, and died during his term.

[39] **anche**: used somewhat like the Fr. *davantage*. See Diez iii. 137.

[40] The v. l. *ch' io n' ho* is very possibly an original variant; at least it is hard to see why either reading should have been substituted by a copyist for the other.

[41] Bonturo Dati seems to have been, as Benvenuto says, the 'arch-barrator' of Lucca, and to have carried on his operations on so large a scale that nearly all the officials of the commune owed their appointments to him. Once when he was on a mission to Boniface, the Pope in playful anger at some piece of unscrupulousness, shook him by the arm; whereon Bonturo remarked, 'Holy Father, do you know that you have shaken half Lucca?' The irony of the words which Dante puts into the demon's mouth may be compared with xxix. 125. It is curious that the Lucchese commentators, Vellutello and Daniello, pass over these attacks on their city in silence; though the former is usually ready enough to protest. See also Purg. xxiv. 44.

Yes there for the paying.' Down he shot him, and turned round over the hard rock; and never was mastiff unloosed with such speed to follow the thief. That one dipped in, and came up again turned round; but the demons who had cover of the bridge cried: 'Here the holy Face has no place; here it is other sort of swimming than in the Serchio, therefore if thou dost not want any of our hooks, do not make any uprising above the pitch.' Then they nicked him with more than a hundred prongs; they said:

> Del no, per li denar, vi si fa ita.
> Laggiù il buttò, e per lo scoglio duro
>   Si volse, e mai non fu mastino sciolto
>   Con tanta fretta a seguitar lo furo.
> Quei s' attuffò, e tornò su convolto;[b]
>   Ma i demon, che del ponte avean coperchio,
>   Gridar: Qui non ha loco il santo volto;
> Qui si nuota altrimenti che nel Serchio;
>   Però, se tu non vuoi dei nostri graffi,　　　　50
>   Non far sopra la pegola soperchio.
> Poi l' addentar con più di cento raffi;

[b] *col volto* Gg. Cass. Benv.

⁴⁶ **convolto**: as a man coming up after a 'header.' Others take it as 'twisted together,' or 'writhing.' Lombardi thinks it means 'lowed,' head and feet down; but if his head was under the demons would hardly think it worth while to mock him. Dict. Crusc. takes it as 'rolled in the pitch,' 'befouled.' The word no doubt can bear this meaning, but it is rather feeble here. The reading *col volto*, which the majority of MSS. have, though it gives the sense well enough, is barred by the inadmissibility of *volto* twice in rhyme with the same meaning.

⁴⁸ The Holy Face of Lucca is a crucifix of great antiquity and especial sanctity, carved, as its legend relates, by Nicodemus. It was usual for people of Lucca to invoke it when in trouble; and its renown is proved by the fact that our king William II. was wont to swear by it.

⁴⁹ **Serchio**: the river which flows by Lucca.

'Here it behoves that thou dance under cover, so that, if thou canst, thou mayest do thy grabbing secretly.' Not otherwise do the cooks make their underlings dip the meat into the middle of the caldron with their hooks, so that it may not float.

The good Master said to me: 'To the end that it appear not that thou art here, squat thee down behind a splinter, that thou mayest have some screen to thee; and fear thou not for any rebuff that may be wrought to me, since I have knowledge of the matter, seeing that aforetime I have been at such traffic.' Then he passed beyond the head of the

> Disser: Coperto convien che qui balli,
> Sì che, se puoi, nascosamente accaffi.
> Non altrimenti i cuochi ai lor vassalli
> Fanno attuffare in mezzo la caldaia
> La carne cogli uncin, perchè non galli.
> Lo buon Maestro: Acciocchè non si paia
> Che tu ci sii, mi disse, giù t' acquatta
> Dopo uno scheggio, che alcun schermo t' haia; 60
> E per nulla offension che mi sia fatta,
> Non temer tu, ch' io ho le cose conte,
> Perchè altra volta fui a tal baratta.
> Poscia passò di là dal co del ponte,

[62] **conte**: see note x. 39. Here the sense of *cognitus* seems to predominate; but there is an idea of 'order' involved. 'I know the proper course to take in the circumstances,' Virgil would say.

[63] **baratta**: he uses the word in its ordinary meaning (cf. Bratti Ferravecchi in 'Romola'), but of course with a special allusion. The occasion referred to is no doubt that mentioned in ix. 26, 27. Benvenuto, who for some reason, possibly as having suffered at the hands of corrupt officials, which indeed he tells us he did, is exceedingly alert throughout all this part, thinks that there must be a further allusion to the trouble which Virgil doubtless had with court-officials, when seeking to get back his confiscated lands from Augustus.

bridge, and when he came upon the sixth bank, need was for him to have a fearless front. With that madness and that storm wherewith dogs come out upon the poor man, who suddenly begs where he stops, issued those beneath the little bridge, and turned towards him all their bills; but he cried: 'Let none of you be savage. Before your hook takes hold of me, let one of you draw forward to hear me, and then counsel may be taken about clawing me.' All cried out: 'Let Malacoda come'; wherefore one moved, while the rest stood still, and came to him, saying 'What brings them?' 'Deemest thou, Malacoda, that thou seest me

> E com' ei giunse in su la ripa sesta,
>   Mestier gli fu d' aver sicura fronte.
> Con quel furor e con quella tempesta
>   Ch' escono i cani addosso al poverello,
>   Che di subito chiede ove s' arresta;
> Usciron quei di sotto al ponticello,   70
>   E volser contra lui tutti i roncigli;
>   Ma ei gridò: Nessun di voi sia fello.
> Innanzi che l' uncin vostro mi pigli,
>   Traggasi avanti alcun di voi che m' oda,
>   E poi d' arroncigliarmi si consigli.
> Tutti gridaron: Vada Malacoda;
>   Perchè un si mosse, e gli altri stetter fermi;
>   E venne a lui dicendo: Che gli approda?
> Credi tu, Malacoda, qui vedermi

---

⁷⁸ **approda** transitive, as *arrivò* in xvii. 8. Benv. and others, taking it as from *prodesse*, interpret, 'What good will parleying do them?' But Malacoda knows that he will have to give way, though he does what he can to hinder them. On the other hand, the muttered grumble 'What brings them here?' is very dramatic.

come hither,' said my Master, 'safe already from all your obstacles, without will divine and propitious fate? Let me go, for in heaven it is willed that I show to another this wild road.' Then was his pride so brought down that he let his hook drop at his feet, and said to the rest: 'Now let him not be struck.' And my Leader to me: 'O thou who art sitting all squatted down among the splinters of the bridge, return now securely to me.' Wherefore I moved, and came quickly to him; and the devils all put themselves in front, so that I feared they would not keep compact. And thus saw

> Esser venuto, disse il mio Maestro, 80
> Sicuro già da tutti vostri schermi,
> Senza voler divino e fato destro?
> Lasciane andar, chè nel cielo è voluto
> Ch' io mostri altrui questo cammin silvestro.
> Allor gli fu l' orgoglio sì caduto,
> Che si lasciò cascar l' uncino ai piedi,
> E disse agli altri: Omai non sia feruto.
> E il Duca mio a me: O tu, che siedi
> Tra gli scheggion del ponte quatto quatto,
> Sicuramente omai a me tu riedi. 90
> Perch' io mi mossi, ed a lui venni ratto:
> E i diavoli si fecer tutti avanti,
> Sì ch' io temetti ch' ei tenesser patto.^c

^c *temetti che non t*. Cass.: *temetti non t*. W.

⁸⁶ The reading *non tenesser* is clearly wrong. It could only mean 'I feared that they would keep.' See, for example, ii. 35; iii. 80. This seems to be the only example of the converse construction in the D.C., and many editors and copyists have been puzzled by it, and have substituted the more familiar *non*.

I on a time the footmen fear, who were coming under compact out of Caprona, when they saw themselves among so many foes. I drew up with my whole frame to my Leader's side, and turned not my eyes from their countenances, which were not good. They began to lower their prongs, and 'Wilt thou, that I touch him,' one was saying to the next, 'over the rump?' And they answered: 'Yes, see that thou notch it for him.' But that demon who was holding discourse

> E così vid' io già temer li fanti
>   Ch' uscivan patteggiati di Caprona,
>   Veggendo sè tra nimici cotanti.
> Io m' accostai con tutta la persona
>   Lungo il mio Duca, e non torceva gli occhi
>   Dalla sembianza lor ch' era non buona.
> Ei chinavan gli raffi, e, Vuoi che il tocchi,   100
>   Diceva l' un con l' altro, in sul groppone?
>   E rispondean: Sì, fa che gliele accocchi.
> Ma quel demonio che tenea sermone

---

[95] In August 1289 the Lucchese, with some help from Florence, invaded the territory of Pisa, and captured various forts, among them that of Caprona (Vill. vii. 137). The usual view is that Dante refers here to the departure of the Pisan garrison. Buti, however, who lectured at Pisa, avers that the place was soon afterwards recaptured by the Pisans under Guy of Montefeltro, and that as the Lucchese troops marched out, cries were raised of 'Hang them! hang them!' It is no doubt probable that an invading force in a hostile country would go more in fear of their lives than the original native garrison would have done; but, on the other hand, Villani and other historians make no mention of the recapture, nor is it likely that any Florentine Guelf would have been present unless he had formed part of the occupying force; which we can hardly suppose that Dante did.

[102] I do not feel at all sure that we ought not to read *E ei ponderai, Fa*, etc. It is a sort of 'aside' between two of the demons, and the plural is a little awkward. 'The answer would come' is certainly neater. In MSS. of course there would be little difference.

with my Leader, turned round quite sharply, and said:
'Quiet, quiet, Scarmiglione.' Then he said to us: 'To go
further by this rock will not be possible, seeing that the
sixth arch lies all in pieces at the bottom; and if it still is
your pleasure to go forward, go your way over this ridge;
hard by is another rock which makes a way. Yesterday, five
hours later than this, completed one thousand two hundred

> Col Duca mio, si volse tutto presto
> E disse: Posa, posa, Scarmiglione.
> Poi disse a noi: Più oltre andar per questo
> Scoglio non si può, perocchè giace
> Tutto spezzato al fondo l' arco sesto:
> E se l' andare avanti pur vi piace,
> Andatevene su per questa grotta;
> Presso è un altro scoglio che via face.
> Ier, più oltre cinqu' ore che quest' otta,
> Mille dugento con sessanta sei

110

[111] This, as will presently appear, is a lie; and, so far as can be seen, a perfectly useless one. There is a touch about Malacoda of the plausible official who prophesies smooth things.

[112-114] He refers the destruction of the bridges to the earthquake which took place at our Lord's death, and fixes the moment of speaking to 10 A.M. on the morning of Easter Eve (cf. xii. 37 sqq.; Conv. iv. 23.—In this latter passage I assume *ora quasi sesta* to mean 'in the period of three hours beginning with the sixth hour.' It is impossible that Dante can have supposed St. Luke's words (xxiii. 44) to mean that the sixth hour was the actual moment of our Lord's death, in the face of the statement of the other Evangelists that it was the ninth hour. And in any case the reference here is to the *earthquake*. There has been a good deal of controversy over the lines, and the exact date indicated. We know, however, on many other grounds that Dante intends us to suppose his journey to be taking place at Easter 1300—that is, at the end of the year 1299 and beginning of 1300, according to the Florentine (and pretty general) method of reckoning 25th March as New Year's Day. The date of our Lord's death similarly would be the end of 33 or beginning of 34. There seems no need to go into refinements

and sixty-six years since the way here was broken. I am
sending in that direction some of my lot here to see if
any one is emerging; go with them, for they will not be
wicked.—Come forward thou Alichino, and Calcabrina,' he
began to say, 'and thou Cagnazzo; and let Barbariccia lead
the ten. Let Libicocco come besides, and Draghignazzo,
Ciriatto with the tusks, and Graffiacane, and Farfarello, and
mad Rubicante. Search around the boiling bird-lime; let

>   Anni compiè, che qui la via fu rotta.^d
> Io mando verso là di questi miei
>   A riguardar s' alcun se ne sciorina:
>   Gite con lor, ch' ei non saranno rei.
> Tratti avanti, Alichino e Calcabrina,
>   Cominciò egli a dire, e tu, Cagnazzo,
>   E Barbariccia guidi la decina.   120
> Libicocco vegna oltre, e Draghignazzo,
>   Ciriatto sannuto, e Graffiacane,
>   E Farfarello, e Rubicante pazzo.
> Cercate intorno alle boglienti pane;

^d *compier Cass. Ald.*

as to the exact day of the month, or the date of the real Easter in 1300
A.D. Dante clearly neglects facts of the calendar, and adapts everything to an imaginary date of his own, lying close to the spring equinox.
Just as in Purgatory he makes Venus a morning-star at a time when
she was really behind the sun, so here he fixes his own Easter and his
own moon. Those who care to see the point fully discussed may read
Moore, 'Time References of the D. C.' and Philalethes' note.

114 If we read **compiè**, the subject to it must be **ieri**. The reading
compier gives a better sense, whether we make **ore** the subject (it being
the hours, rather than the 'yesterday,' which completed the years) or,
better, take it as intransitive with **anni**. But it lacks authority.

118 *sqq.* The German renderings of the devils' names given by Philalethes are most ingenious.

these be safe so far as the next splinter which goes all unbroken over the dens.' 'Ah me! Master, what is that I see?' said I; 'prithee, go we alone without escort, if thou knowest the course, for I crave it not for myself. If thou art as heedful as thou art wont, seest thou not how they are grinding their teeth, and with their brows are threatening woe to us?' And he to me: 'I will not that thou be afraid; let them grind just as they list, for they do that for the sake of the woeful ones who are stewing.' Along the left embankment they made a turn; but first each had pressed his tongue with his teeth towards their leader as a sign; and he had made a trumpet of his rear.

> Costor sien salvi insino all' altro scheggio
>   Che tutto intero va sopra le tane.
> O me! Maestro, che è quel che io veggio?
>   Diss' io: deh! senza scorta andiamci soli,
>   Se tu sai ir, ch' io per me non la chieggio.
> Se tu sei sì accorto come suoli,   130
>   Non vedi tu ch' ei digrignan li denti.
>   E colle ciglia ne minaccian duoli?
> Ed egli a me: Non vo che tu paventi:
>   Lasciali digrignar pure a lor senno,
>   Ch' ei fanno ciò per li lessi dolenti.
> Per l' argine sinistro volta dienno;
>   Ma prima avea ciascun la lingua stretta
>   Coi denti verso lor duca per cenno,
> Ed egli avea del cul fatto trombetta.

[137] The same offensive gesture is made by the usurer in xvii. 74.

CANTO XXII

ARGUMENT

They set out with the demons, and witness a strange sport. One of the sinners is drawn out, and answers their questions; after which the demons fall to quarrelling among themselves, and two are themselves trapped in the pitch.

I HAVE seen ere now horsemen strike camp, and begin a charge, and make their display, and at times depart for their retreat; I have seen scouts about your land, men of Arezzo, and I have seen raids ridden, tournaments stricken, and jousts run, now with trumpets, now with bells; with drums

> Io vidi già cavalier mover campo,
>   E cominciare stormo, e far lor mostra,
>   E talvolta partir per loro scampo:
> Corridor vidi per la terra vostra,
>   O Aretini, e vidi gir gualdane,
>   Ferir torneamenti, e correr giostra,
> Quando con trombe, e quando con campane,

4, 5 There is no need to take this as referring particularly to the battle of Certomondo or Campaldino, at which some of his later biographers say that Dante was present. Hostilities between Florence and Arezzo were pretty persistent after the expulsion of the Guelfs from the latter city in June 1287 (Vill. vii. 115, and the rest of the book).

7 **con**: 'started to the sound of.'—**campane**: Philalethes cites as an example the 'Martinella' of Florence, which went on the *carroccio* of that city. Benvenuto thinks rather of the ringing of the bells in times of civil commotion.

and with castle-signals, and with things of our own land and with foreign things; but never yet with so uncouth a shawm did I see horsemen start, or footmen; nor ship by the mark of land or of star.

We were going with the ten demons—ah, fierce company! but in church with the saints and in tavern with the gluttons. Ever on the pitch was my attention, to see every aspect of the pit, and of the folk that was burning therewithin. As the dolphins, when they give a sign to the sailors with the arch of their backs, so that they set to work

> Con tamburi e con cenni di castella,
>   E con cose nostrali e con istrane;
> Nè già con sì diversa cennamella   10
>   Cavalier vidi mover, nè pedoni,
>   Nè nave a segno di terra o di stella.
> Noi andavam con li dieci dimoni:
>   Ahi fiera compagnia! ma nella chiesa
>   Coi santi, ed in taverna coi ghiottoni.
> Pure alla pegola era la mia intesa,
>   Per veder della bolgia ogni contegno,
>   E della gente ch' entro v' era incesa.
> Come i delfini, quando fanno segno
>   Ai marinar con l' arco della schiena,   20

⁷ **cenni di castella**: fire-signals, or flags.

¹⁷ **contegno**: 'the contents,' say some of the older commentators; and this also gives a good sense, if we take it in the second clause in the sense of 'individual members.' But it seems better to understand it as in xvii. 60. Eng. 'countenance' has the same force.

¹⁹ The Italian version of the 'Trésor' says of the dolphins: Cognoscono lo mal tempo, quando dee essere, e vanno contro alla fortuna che dee essere. (This last statement, which is not in the original French, is the opposite of Pliny's view. He says, Nat. Hist. xviii. 87: praesagiunt . . . delphini . . . flatum, ex qua veniant parte.) Et quando li marinari veggiono ciò, sì si anteveggiono de la fortuna.

to save their vessel, thus at times, to alleviate the pain, some one of the sinners would show his back, and hide it in less time than it lightens. And as at the edge of the water of a ditch the frogs stand with just the snout outside, so that they conceal their feet and the rest of their bulk, so were the sinners standing on every hand; but as Barbariccia came near, so they would draw back beneath the boiling. I saw, and my heart still shudders at it, one wait in such wise as it happens when one frog remains and the other springs. And Graffiacane, who was most over against him, hooked his pitch-smeared locks, and drew him up, that he seemed to

  Che s' argomentin di campar lor legno :
 Talor così ad alleggiar la pena
  Mostrava alcun dei peccatori il dosso,
  E nascondeva in men che non balena.
 E come all' orlo dell' acqua d' un fosso
  Stanno i ranocchi pur col muso fuori,
  Sì che celano i piedi e l' altro grosso ;
 Sì stavan d' ogni parte i peccatori :
  Ma come s' appressava Barbariccia,
  Così si ritraean sotto i bollori.   30
 Io vidi, ed anco il cor me n' accapriccia,
  Uno aspettar così, com' egli incontra
  Che una rana rimane, ed altra spiccia.
 E Graffiacan, che gli era più d' incontra,
  Gli arronciglìò le impegolate chiome,
  E trassel su, che mi parve una lontra.

---

 24 **che non balena** : a good instance of the negative in the second clause of a comparative sentence, which all the Romance languages affect. Diez iii. 395.
 32 **egli**, with impersonal verb. Diez iii. 279. Cf. Par. xiii. 118.

me an otter. I knew by this time the names of all, so did
I mark them, when they were chosen, and after, when they
called each other, I listened how. 'O Rubicante, do thou put
thy claws on to the back of him, so as to flay him,' began all
the accursed to cry at once. And I: 'My Master, study if
thou canst to know who is that ill-starred one come into the
hand of his adversaries.' My Leader then came close
beside him, asked him whence he was; and he replied: 'I was
of the kingdom of Navarre by birth. My mother put me to
serve a lord; for she had borne me of a scamp, a spendthrift of himself and of his chattels. Afterwards I was a
domestic of the good king Tybalt; there I set myself to

> Io sapea già di tutti e quanti il nome,
>   Sì li notai, quando furono eletti,
>   E poi che si chiamaro, attesi come.
> O Rubicante, fa che tu gli metti 40
>   Gli unghioni addosso sì che tu lo scuoi,
>   Gridavan tutti insieme i maledetti.
> Ed io: Maestro mio, fa, se tu puoi,
>   Che tu sappi chi è lo sciagurato
>   Venuto a man degli avversari suoi.
> Lo Duca mio gli s' accostò allato,
>   Domandollo ond' ei fosse, e quei rispose:
>   Io fui del regno di Navarra nato.
> Mia madre a servo d' un signor mi pose,
>   Chè m' avea generato d' un ribaldo 50
>   Distruggitor di sè e di sue cose.
> Poi fui famiglia del buon re Tebaldo;^a

^a *famiglio* 3 *W*.

" The commentators call this person 'Ciampolo' (not a very
Spanish-looking name), but add nothing else to what Dante tells us.
" The reading **famiglia** has the less authority; but it is far more

work jobbery, whereof I give account in this heat.' And Ciriatto, from whose mouth issued on either side a tusk as of a pig, let him feel how one of them ripped. Among ill cats was the mouse come; but Barbariccia enclosed him in his arms, and said: 'Keep away, while I bestride him.' And he turned his face to my Master; 'Ask him,' said he, 'further, if thou desirest to know more of him, before

> Quivi mi misi a far baratteria,
> Di che io rendo ragione in questo caldo.
> E Ciriatto, a cui di bocca uscia
> D' ogni parte una sanna come a porco,
> Gli fe sentir come l' una sdrucia.
> Tra male gatte era venuto il sorco;
> Ma Barbariccia il chiuse con le braccia,
> E disse: State in là, mentr' io lo inforco.   60
> Ed al Maestro mio volse la faccia:
> Domanda, disse, ancor se più desii
> Saper da lui, prima ch' altri il disfaccia.

likely to have been altered to *famiglio* than *vice versa*. The feminine form need give no trouble. We may compare such words as *scorta*, *guida*, or *reda*, Purg. vii. 118, or *guardia*, ib. xxxii. 95.—**Tebaldo**: no doubt the second of that name, who went on crusade with Saint Lewis in 1270.

54 **rendo ragione**: doubtless intended to recall the words of the parable of the Unjust Steward, 'redde rationem villicationis tuae.'

60 **mentr' io lo inforco.** This might mean 'till *I* fork him'; the leader claiming the right of priority. But it seems best to take *inforco* in the sense in which it is used elsewhere by Dante, e.g. Purg. vi. 99. (Here the 'bestriding' is done with the arms.) Also it is a little doubtful whether *mentre* ever means simply 'until,' when the action awaited is momentary.

63 It is tempting to take **disfaccia** in the sense of 'deface,' 'spoil his looks'; but the subjunctive is necessary after *prima che* (Diez iii. 320), so the word must be from *disfare*, 'unmake,' 'pull to pieces.'

another spoil him.' My Leader: 'Then tell now of the other criminals; knowest thou any that is a Latin beneath the pitch?' And he: 'I parted not long ago from one, who was on the other side a neighbour; so would I were still with him covered up, for I should not fear claw nor flesh-hook.' And Libicocco: 'Too much have we endured,' said he; and seized his arm with his hook, so that, tearing, he carried away a muscle of it. Draghignazzo too wished to give him a grip down in the legs; wherefore their decurion turned him round about with evil mien. When they were a little pacified again, of him who was still gazing at his wound my Leader asked without delay: 'Who was that from whom

> Lo Duca: Dunque or di' degli altri rii:
>   Conosci tu alcun che sia Latino
>   Sotto la pece? E quegli: Io mi partii
> Poco è da un, che fu di là vicino;
>   Così foss' io ancor con lui coperto,
>   Che io non temerei unghia, nè uncino.
> E Libicocco: Troppo avem sofferto,   70
>   Disse, e presegli il braccio col ronciglio,
>   Sì che, stracciando, ne portò un lacerto.
> Draghignazzo anco i volle dar di piglio
>   Giuso alle gambe; onde il decurio loro
>   Si volse intorno intorno con mal piglio.
> Quand' elli un poco rappaciati foro,
>   A lui che ancor mirava sua ferita,
>   Domandò il Duca mio senza dimoro:

---

65. **Latino**: the name which would suit both Virgil and Dante.

67. **di là**: on earth; the person referred to having, as will appear, lived in Sardinia, and so been a neighbour of the 'Latins.' 'Sardos . . . qui non Latini sunt, sed Latinis associandi videntur.' *Vulg. El.* i. 11.

thou sayest that thou madest an ill parting to come to shore?' And he answered: 'It was friar Gomita, he of Gallura, a vessel of every fraud; who had the enemies of his lord in hand, and dealt so with them, that each one has a good word for it; money he took, and left them on smooth ground, as he says; and in the other offices too he was no small trafficker, but supreme. With him consorts Lord

> Chi fu colui, da cui mala partita
> > Di' che facesti per venire a proda? 80
> > Ed ei rispose: Fu frate Gomita,
> Quel di Gallura, vasel d' ogni froda,
> > Ch' ebbe i nimici di suo donno in mano,
> > E fe si lor, che ciascun se ne loda:
> Denar si tolse, e lasciolli di piano,
> > Sì come dice: e negli altri offizi anche
> > Barattier fu non picciol, ma soprano.
> Usa con esso donno Michel Zanche

[82] Gallura was one of the four districts into which Sardinia was divided by the Pisans. The governors of them were called judges, and for the most part were great Pisan nobles, who lived at home, taking part in the turbulent political life of the mother-city, and leaving their provinces to be managed by deputies. This Friar Gomita is said to have been lieutenant to Nino de' Visconti (Purg. viii. 53); and ultimately to have been hanged by him for malversation. Of the transaction here alluded to nothing further seems to be known.

[84] The word **donno** comes naturally from the lips of the half-Spanish Navarrese. It may, as the commentators say, be also a Sardinian word, but that would hardly be a reason for its use. Similarly **di piano**, in l. 85, may be regarded as a native idiom of his own put into the mouth of the other.

[84] **se ne loda**: so ii. 74.

[84] The commentators are confused about Michael Zanche. He was steward of Logodoro (another Sardinian judgeship) under King Enzio, son of Frederick II.; who came into possession of Sardinia by his marriage with Adelasia, widow of Ubaldo Visconti, Judge of Gallura.

Michael Zanche of Logodoro; and to tell of Sardinia their tongues do not feel weary. O me! see the other who is grinding his teeth; I would say more, but I fear that he is making ready to scratch my scurf for me.' And the great provost, turning to Farfarello, who was rolling his eyes for a blow, said: 'Keep on this side, bird of mischief!' 'If ye wish to see or hear,' began again the frightened man thereafter, 'Tuscans or Lombards, I will make some of them

> Di Logodoro: ed a dir di Sardigna
> Le lingue lor non si sentono stanche.　　　90
> O me! vedete l' altro che digrigna:
> Io direi anco; ma io temo ch' ello
> Non s' apparecchi a grattarmi la tigna.
> E il gran proposto, volto a Farfarello
> Che stralunava gli occhi per ferire,
> Disse: Fatti in costà, malvagio uccello.
> Se voi volete vedere o udire,
> Ricominciò lo spaurato appresso,
> Toschi o Lombardi, io ne farò venire.

After the death of Enzio, Michael is said to have married her. J. della Lana and Benv., however, followed by Land. and Vell., say that it was Enzio's *mother* whom he married (but they at least do not, like the commentators referred to, though not named, by Scartazzini, confuse her with Bianca Lancia, the mother of Manfred). This is a very unlikely story, as Enzio's mother was probably a German, and in any case had nothing to do with Sardinia. If he married Adelasia, it could not have been by her that he had, as P. di Dante asserts, the daughter who married Branca d' Oria; for Enzio only died, aged over fifty, in 1271, and his own murder by Branca d' Oria (xxxiii. 137), who is said to have been his son-in-law, took place in 1275.

[93] **grattarmi la tigna**: the low and vulgar expression is in keeping with the behaviour of this class of sinners, and the fiends who look after them.

come. But let the Evilclaws stand a little aloof, so that
they may not fear their vengeance, and I sitting in this very
place, for one that I am will make seven of them come when
I whistle, as our way is to do when any one gets outside.'
Cagnazzo at such speech raised his snout, wagging his head,
and said: 'Hear a trick that he has devised to throw himself down.' Wherefore he, who had artifices in great plenty,
answered: 'Too tricky am I, when I am earning greater
sorrow for my friends.' Alichino did not contain himself,
and in the teeth of the others said to him: 'If thou drop, I
shall not come after thee at a gallop, but I shall flap my
wings over the pitch; let us leave the top and let the bank

  Ma stien le male branche un poco in cesso,   100
   Sì ch' ei non teman delle lor vendette:
   Ed io, sedendo in questo loco stesso,
  Per un ch' io son, ne farò venir sette,
   Quand' io sufolerò, com' è nostr' uso
   Di fare allor che fuori alcun si mette.
  Cagnazzo a cotal motto levò il muso,
   Crollando il capo, e disse: Odi malizia
   Ch' egli ha pensata per gittarsi giuso.
  Ond' ei ch' avea lacciuoli a gran divizia,
   Rispose: Malizioso son io troppo,   110
   Quand' io procuro ai miei maggior tristizia.
  Alichin non si tenne, e di rintoppo
   Agli altri, disse a lui: Se tu ti cali,
   Io non ti verrò dietro di galoppo,
  Ma batterò sopra la pece l' ali:
   Lascisi il colle, e sia la ripa scudo

_b *che non temi* Cass.: *io non tema* 23.
_c *a me* Cass.: *a mia* 3 Add.

be a screen, to see if thou alone availest more than we.' O thou that readest, thou shalt hear a new sport. Each one turned his eyes toward the other side; he first who had been most unready to do that. The Navarrese chose his time well; he steadied his feet on the ground, and in a moment leaped, and freed himself from their design. Whereof each one was on the instant grieved, but he most who had been cause of the blunder; therefore he started up and cried: 'Thou art caught!' But little it availed him, for his wings could not overtake terror; that one went under, and he as he flew turned his breast upward. Not otherwise the

> A veder se tu sol più di noi vali.
> O tu che leggi, udirai nuovo ludo;
>   Ciascun dall' altra costa gli occhi volse;
>   Quei prima, ch' a ciò fare era più crudo.   120
> Lo Navarrese ben suo tempo colse,
>   Fermò le piante a terra, ed in un punto
>   Saltò, e dal proposto lor si sciolse.
> Di che ciascun di colpa fu compunto,
>   Ma quei più, che cagion fu del difetto;
>   Però si mosse, e gridò: Tu sei giunto.
> Ma poco i valse: chè l' ali al sospetto
>   Non potero avanzar: quegli andò sotto,
>   E quei drizzò, volando, suso il petto:
> Non altrimenti l' anitra di botto,   130

---

[1] No doubt Cagnazzo. **crudo**, as in Par. ix. 48.

[2] **proposto.** Blanc, in his Erklärungen (but not in his Dict.), follows Benv. in taking this as in l. 94. But Barbariccia, who had been holding the sinner, would of course have retired with the rest; not to mention the improbability of his allowing anything that he had gripped to escape him.

[3] Alichino, whose counsel (ll. 116, 117) had persuaded the others.

duck of a sudden when the falcon comes near dips down; and he returns up cross and routed. Calcabrina, angered by the jape, held after him in flight, longing that that one might get off, so as to have his quarrel. And when the trafficker was out of sight, right so he turned his claws on his mate, and was at grips with him over the foss. But the other was a well-grown sparrow-hawk indeed to claw him well, and both fell into the midst of the boiling swamp. The heat was quickly an ungrappler; but for all that there was no way to get up, so had they limed their wings. Barbariccia, with his other fellows in distress, made four fly off on the

> Quando il falcon s' appressa, giù s' attuffa,
>   Ed ei ritorna su crucciato e rotto.
> Irato Calcabrina della buffa,
>   Volando dietro gli tenne, invaghito
>   Che quei campasse, per aver la zuffa.
> E come il barattier fu disparito,
>   Così volse gli artigli al suo compagno,
>   E fu con lui sopra il fosso ghermito.
> Ma l' altro fu bene sparvier grifagno
>   Ad artigliar ben lui, ed ambo e due   140
>   Cadder nel mezzo del bogliente stagno.
> Lo caldo sghermitor subito fue:[d]
>   Ma però di levarsi era niente,
>   Sì aveano inviscate l' ali sue.
> Barbariccia, con gli altri suoi dolente,
>   Quattro ne fe volar dall' altra costa

[d] *schermitor* (or *-dor*) *Gg. Cass.* 1234 *Ald.*

[132] **crucciato** is not derived from *crux*; but our word renders it well.

[139] Benv. says that the sparrow-hawk is called 'grifagno' in his third year.

other side, with hooks and all, and smartly enough they descended on either hand to their post; they stretched their hooks out toward those in the bird-lime, who were already baked within the crust; and we left them thus entangled.

> Con tutti i raffi, ed assai prestamente
> Di qua, di là discesero alla posta:
>   Porser gli uncini verso gl' impaniati,
>   Ch' eran già cotti dentro dalla crosta: 150
> E noi lasciammo lor così impacciati.

[149] **impaniati**: cf. xxi. 124. *Pania* is bird-lime: the derivation seems to be unknown, but it may have been originally a paste made from bread.

CANTO XXIII

ARGUMENT

They leave the demons, and escape by descending into the fifth pit, where they meet folk clad in leaden cloaks, gilt outwardly. These are the hypocrites. Dante speaks with two who had borne office in his own city.

SILENT, lonely, without company, we went our way, one in front and the other behind, as Friars Minor go along a road. My thought through the strife before me had turned upon the fable of Aesop, where he spoke of the frog and of

> TACITI, soli, senza compagnia,
> N' andavam l' un dinanzi e l' altro dopo,
> Come frati minor vanno per via.
> Volto era in sulla favola d' Isopo
> Lo mio pensier per la presente rissa,
> Dov' ei parlò della rana e del topo :

---

[1] **soli**: the demons having remained behind, and the sinners being all concealed under the pitch (Scart.) It may be added that this solitude is a new experience. Hitherto, except in passing from one circle to another, they have always been in sight of some person or persons.

[4] The fable—not in the original Aesop (Cary)—is that of the frog who invited a mouse to go into the water with him, attached for safety to his leg. The mouse was drowned, and in course of time his body, floating or lying on the shore, with the frog still tethered to it, attracted the notice of a bird of prey, which swallowed both the friends. So say the modern commentators, but the parallel with the recent scene does not seem very close.

the mouse; for *now* and *this minute* are not more matched
than is the one with the other, if one rightly couples beginning
and end with the mind attentive. And as the one thought
bursts out from the other, so from that another afterward
had birth, which made my first fear double. I was thinking
thus: "These by our means have been befooled, and with
loss and with derision of such fashion that much I ween it
annoys them. If wrath is woven upon their ill-will, they
will come after us more cruel than a dog upon the hare
which he seizes.' Already was I feeling my hairs stand all
on end with the fear, and was stayed to watch to rearward,
when I said: 'Master, if thou hidest not thyself and me
quickly, I have fear of the Evilclaws; we have them now

> Chè più non si pareggia mo ed issa,
>   Che l' un con l' altro fa, se ben s' accoppia
>   Principio e fine con la mente fissa:
> E come l' un pensier dell' altro scoppia,   10
>   Così nacque di quello un altro poi,
>   Che la prima paura mi fe doppia.
> Io pensava così: Questi per noi
>   Sono scherniti, e con danno e con beffa
>   Sì fatta, ch' assai credo che lor noi.
> Se l' ira sopra il mal voler s' aggueffa,
>   Ei ne verranno dietro più crudeli
>   Che il cane a quella levre ch' egli acceffa.
> Già mi sentia tutti arricciar li peli
>   Della paura, e stava indietro intento,   20
>   Quando io dissi: Maestro, se non celi
> Te e me tostamente, i' ho pavento
>   Di Malebranche: noi gli avem già dietro:

---

[7] **mo** (*modo*), used frequently by Dante, e.g. in line 28, is Tuscan; for **issa** (*ipsa*, sc. *hora*), see xxvii. 21.

in rear: I imagine them so that already I feel them.' And he: 'If I were of leaded glass, I should not draw thy outward image more quickly to me than I obtain the one within. But now thy thoughts were coming among mine, with like behaviour and with like mien, so that of both I made one single counsel. If it be that the slope on our right lies so that we may be able to descend into the next pit, we shall escape thy imagined chase.'

He had not yet made an end of rendering such counsel, when I saw them coming with wings outstretched, not very far off, with will to seize us. My Leader of a sudden seized

> Io gl' immagino sì, che già gli sento.
> E quei: S' io fossi d' impiombato vetro,
>   L' imagine di fuor tua non trarrei
>   Più tosto a me, che quella d' entro impetro.
> Pur mo venian li tuoi pensier tra i miei
>   Con simile atto e con simile faccia,
>   Sì che d' intrambi un sol consiglio fei.   30
> S' egli è che sì la destra costa giaccia,
>   Che noi possiam nell' altra bolgia scendere,
>   Noi fuggirem l' immaginata caccia.
> Già non compiè di tal consiglio rendere,
>   Ch' io gli vidi venir con l' ali tese,
>   Non molto lungi, per volerne prendere.
> Lo Duca mio di subito mi prese,

---

[25] **impiombato vetro**: 'come specchio, che è vetro terminato con piombo' (Conv. iii. 9).

[31] **giaccia**: or perhaps more definitely, 'slopes gently,' as in Purg. iii. 76. Virgil is not improbably expecting to find as before a way down by the 'geroll' which the shattering of the rocks, spoken of in xii. 10, 45; and xxi. 106 sqq., will have left.—**destra**: because, as they turned to the left (xxi. 136) with the demons, the next (sixth) *bolgia* will be on their right.

me, as a mother who is aroused at the uproar and sees close to her the flames alight, when she seizes her boy and flies and stays not, caring more for him than for herself, insomuch that she puts on only a smock. And down from the ridge of the hard bank he committed himself supine to the slanting rock which blocks one of the sides of the next pit. Never so fast did water run through a leat to turn the wheel of an overshot mill when it approaches nearest to the paddles, as did

> Come la madre ch' al romore è desta,
> E vede presso a sè le fiamme accese,
> Che prende il figlio e fugge e non s' arresta, 40
> Avendo più di lui che di sè cura,
> Tanto che solo una camicia vesta:
> E giù dal collo della ripa dura [a]
> Supin si diede alla pendente roccia,
> Che l' un dei lati all' altra bolgia tura.
> Non corse mai sì tosto acqua per doccia
> A volger rota di mulin terragno,
> Quand' ella più verso le pale approccia,

[a] *colle Gg. W.*

45. Benvenuto's reading is curious: 'ch' è l' un dei lati all' altra bolgiatura.' *Tura*, which is an ἅπαξ λεγόμενον here, so far as D.C. is concerned, is certainly unusual in this sense, meaning generally rather 'to stop a hole.'

47. **mulin terragno**: a 'mill on land,' turned, as one may often see in mountain countries, by a small shoot, bringing the water from the hillside; as opposed to the mills which are seen in great rivers (like the Po, says Benvenuto), where the stream flows below the wheel. Virgil seems to make a kind of *glissade* down the slope, lying on his back, and to let himself, with Dante, shoot over the drop (which we must suppose a low one) to the bottom.

my Master over that rim, carrying me off upon his breast, like his son and not like a companion.

Hardly had his feet reached the bed of the bottom below when they arrived upon the ridge right over us; but there was no fear of them, for the Providence on high that willed to place them as ministers of the fifth foss, took away power from all of separating themselves from it.

Below these did we find a painted folk, who were going round with paces slow enough, weeping and in their semblance weary and beaten. They had cowls with hoods down in front of their eyes, shaped of the cut which is made for the monks in Cologne. Outwardly they are gilded so

> Come il Maestro mio per quel vivagno,
>   Portandosene me sopra il suo petto,   50
>   Come suo figlio, e non come compagno.
> Appena fur li piè suoi giunti al letto
>   Del fondo giù, ch' ei furono in sul colle
>   Sopresso noi: ma non gli era sospetto;
> Chè l' alta provvidenza, che lor volle
>   Porre ministri della fossa quinta,
>   Poder di partirs' indi a tutti tolle.
> Laggiù trovammo una gente dipinta,
>   Che giva intorno assai con lenti passi
>   Piangendo, e nel sembiante stanca e vinta.   60
> Egli avean cappe con cappucci bassi
>   Dinanzi agli occhi, fatti della taglia
>   Che in Cologna per li monaci fassi.[b]

[b] *Cologni Gg.* 14; *Colognin Cass.: per li m. in Cel. Ald.: Ciugni W.*

58. The hypocrites. Aquinas, it may be noted, considers that hypocrisy, as not being opposed to charity, is not among the gravest sins. S. T. ii. 2. Q 111.

63. **Cologna.** So all, or nearly all of the older commentators. Witte and Philalethes, perhaps on patriotic grounds, prefer the reading

that it dazzles; but within all are lead and so heavy that what Frederick put on were of straw. O mantle to eternity wearisome! We turned again ever to the left hand along with them, intent on their sad wailing; but through the weight that weary folk were coming so slowly that we were new in company at every movement of the leg. Therefore I to my Leader: 'See that thou find some one who is known by deed

> Di fuor dorate son, sì ch' egli abbaglia;
>   Ma dentro tutte piombo, e gravi tanto,
>   Che Federico le mettea di paglia.
> O in eterno faticoso manto!
>   Noi ci volgemmo ancor pure a man manca
>   Con loro insieme, intenti al tristo pianto:
> Ma per lo peso quella gente stanca   70
>   Venia sì pian, che noi eravam nuovi
>   Di compagnia ad ogni mover d' anca.
> Perch' io al Duca mio: Fa che tu trovi
>   Alcun, ch' al fatto o al nome si conosca,

Clugni, which has less authority. Benv. and others mention that the hoods worn by the monks of Cologne were noted for the badness of their fit. Landino adds a story (told by Buti) that this was owing to special instructions from Rome, in consequence of the presumption of a certain abbot, who had asked that his monks might wear scarlet cowls, and other fineries. However this may be, it seems very likely that Dante, who more than once (e.g. xvii. 21) has a fling at the Germans, intends some sarcastic allusion here.

⁶⁴ **di fuor dorate.** P. di Dante derives *hypocrisis* from 'epi quod est supra, et *crisis* aurum' (!) So Comm. Cass.

⁶⁶ One of the 'lingering and humorous' punishments invented by Frederick II., especially for persons guilty of treason, was the investing of the criminal in a leaden tunic or cope; which 'weighed them down until death came to the rescue' (Oliphant, Hist. Fred. II. vol. i. p. 475). Others say that the tunic and the criminal were put into a great vessel, and melted together.

or by name, and as thou goest thus, move thine eyes around.'
And one who paid heed to my Tuscan speech cried behind
us: 'Stay your feet, ye who speed so through the murky air;
maybe that thou wilt have by me him whom thou seekest.'
Wherefore my Leader turned, and said: 'Wait; and then
go on according to his pace.' I stopped, and saw two display great haste, of the mind, with their visages, to be with
me; but their burthen and the narrow way delayed them.
When they were come up, with their dim eyes they gazed
their fill at me without uttering a word; then they turned to
each other, and said with themselves: 'This one seems
alive by the action of his throat; and if they are dead, by

> E gli occhi sì andando intorno movi.
> Ed un, che intese la parola Tosca,
>   Diretro a noi gridò: Tenete i piedi,
>   Voi, che correte sì per l' aura fosca:
> Forse ch' avrai da me quel che tu chiedi.
>   Onde il Duca si volse, e disse: Aspetta,   80
>   E poi secondo il suo passo procedi.
> Ristetti, e vidi due mostrar gran fretta
>   Dell' animo, col viso, d' esser meco;
>   Ma tardavagli il carco e la via stretta.
> Quando fur giunti, assai con l' occhio bieco
>   Mi rimiraron senza far parola:
>   Poi si volsero in sè, e dicean seco:
> Costui par vivo all' atto della gola:

---

76 It must have been Dante's accent that attracted notice, for there seems to be no specially Tuscan idiom in his words.

85 Blanc observes that though the spirits in Hell do not breathe (which is a special sign of life, says Philalethes; but from xiii. 122 they would appear to be able to *pant*), they are yet palpable—e.g. xxxii. 97. In Purgatory, however, they are impalpable. See notes Purg. vi. 75; vii. 54.

what immunity do they go uncovered with the heavy robe?'
Then they said to me: 'O Tuscan, who to the college of
the sorry hypocrites art come, hold it not in despite to say
who thou art.' And I to them: 'I was born and bred up
upon the fair stream of Arno at the great town, and I am
with the body which I have always had. But who are ye,
in whom grief, so great as I see, drips down over the cheeks,
and what penalty is it that so sparkles on you?' And one of
them answered me: 'The orange copes are so gross with
lead that the weights make their scales creak thus. We
were Joyous Friars, and of Bologna, I Catalan and this man

> E s' ei son morti, per qual privilegio
>   Vanno scoperti della grave stola?   90
> Poi disser me: O Tosco, ch' al collegio
>   Degl' ipocriti tristi sei venuto,
>   Dir chi tu sei non avere in dispregio.
> Ed io a loro: Io fui nato e cresciuto
>   Sopra il bel fiume d' Arno alla gran villa,
>   E son col corpo ch' i' ho sempre avuto.
> Ma voi chi siete, a cui tanto distilla,
>   Quant' io veggio, dolor giù per le guance,
>   E che pena è in voi che sì sfavilla?
> E l' un rispose a me: Le cappe rance   100
>   Son di piombo sì grosse, che li pesi
>   Fan così cigolar le lor bilance.
> Frati Godenti fummo, e Bolognesi,
>   Io Catalano, e questi Loderingo

---

tristi: perhaps with allusion to Matt. vi. 16.

The wearers are the scales, their weeping the creaking.

These personages were famous in Florentine history. In 1266, after the defeat of Manfred by Benevento, the commons of Florence, who

Lorrainer by name; and taken together by thy land, as a solitary man is wont to be brought, to keep its peace, and of such sort we were as still may be seen about the Gar-

> Nomati, e da tua terra insieme presi,
> Come suole esser tolto un uom solingo
> Per conservar sua pace, e fummo tali,
> Ch' ancor si pare intorno dal Gardingo.

were mainly Guelf, began to be turbulent. The governing Ghibelines, seeing the need of making some kind of terms, agreed to send to Bologna for two members of the body known as Frati Godenti, Catalano de' Catalani and Loderingo degli Andalò (their surnames are variously given—Villani, for example, calls the former 'de' Malavolti' and the latter 'Roderigo (sic) de Landolo'), who belonged the one to the Guelf the other to the Ghibeline party, that they might hold the office of *podestà* jointly. Being installed, says Villani, 'under cover of false hypocrisy they acted in harmony, more for their own gain than for that of the commonwealth.' Nothing that he tells us of their doings, however, points to anything but an honest attempt to keep the peace. They set up the 'Council of Thirty-six,' selected from both parties and both classes; but before long the demands of Guido Novello and his *condottieri* became intolerable, the Ghibelines were forced by popular pressure to leave the city, a Guelf *podestà* was established by Charles of Anjou, and the 'Frati' disappeared (Vill. vii. 14-16).

Frati Godenti were a military order. They were authorised by Urban IV., under the name of Knights of Our Lady, the Loderingo mentioned here being one of the founders. Their vows were not very strict, whence the nickname of 'Jolly Friars' which they soon acquired. 'It was not long,' says Villani, 'before they brought their conduct into agreement with the name.' In later times the history of the name seems to have been forgotten, and we find Erasmus talking of friars 'qui dicuntur Gaudentes,' meaning merely those who were lax in their lives.

[104] He is no doubt jesting on the fact that both their Christian names were national names as well. (See note Par. xi. 43, as to 'Francesco.')

[105] **solingo**: because it was usual to have one *podestà* only. 'Et non exponas *solingo* idest solitarius, sicut aliqui exponunt.'—Benv.

[108] **Gardingo**: the part of Florence in which stood the palace of the

dingo.' I began: 'O friars, your ills——' but more I said not; for to my eyes sped one, crucified to earth with three stakes. When he saw me he writhed all over, blowing in his beard with his sighs. And friar Catalan, who noted this, said to me: 'That impaled one, at whom thou art looking, gave counsel to the Pharisees that it was expedient to put one man to the torments for the people. He is stretched across naked in the way, as thou seest; and it is necessary that he first feel how every passer-by weighs; and in such wise his father-in-law is stretched in this foss, and the others of the council, which was an ill seed for the Jews.' Then

> Io cominciai: O frati, i vostri mali . . .
>   Ma più non dissi: ch' all' occhio mi corse
>   Un crocifisso in terra con tre pali.
> Quando mi vide, tutto si distorse,
>   Soffiando nella barba coi sospiri:
>   E il frate Catalan, ch' a ciò s' accorse,
> Mi disse: Quel confitto, che tu miri,
>   Consigliò i Farisei, che convenia
>   Porre un uom per lo popolo ai martiri.
> Attraversato e nudo è nella via,
>   Come tu vedi, ed è mestier ch' ei senta
>   Qualunque passa com' ei pesa pria:
> Ed a tal modo il suocero si stenta
>   In questa fossa, e gli altri del concilio
>   Che fu per li Giudei mala sementa.

Uberti, which after the expulsion of the Ghibelines was wrecked by the people. So Benvenuto and P. di Dante. Villani says nothing of this.

There is nothing to show what was to follow. The commentators supply 'are the due reward of your deeds,' or words to that effect.

116, 117 John xi. 50.

saw I Virgil marvel over him who was distended in a cross, so vilely in the eternal banishment. Afterwards he addressed to the friar these words: 'Let it not displease you, if it be permitted you, to tell us if to the right hand any entry lies, whereby we two can issue without constraint of the black angels that they come to get us away from this bottom.' He answered then: 'Nearer than thou art hoping comes a rock which starts from the great circle, and crosses all the wild valleys, except that at this one it is broken, and covers it not. You will be able to climb up by its ruin, for it lies

> Allor vid' io maravigliar Virgilio
>   Sopra colui ch' era disteso in croce
>   Tanto vilmente nell' eterno esilio.
> Poscia drizzò al frate cotal voce:
>   Non vi dispiaccia, se vi lece, dirci
>   Se alla man destra giace alcuna foce,
> Onde noi ambo e due possiamo uscirci   130
>   Senza costringer degli angeli neri,
>   Che vegnan d'esto fondo a dipartirci.
> Rispose adunque: Più che tu non speri
>   S' appressa un sasso, che dalla gran cerchia
>   Si move, e varca tutti i vallon feri,
> Salvo ch' a questo è rotto, e nol coperchia:*
>   Montar potrete su per la ruina,

* che questo Cass. Gg. 1234 Ald.

[124] Because Virgil would naturally be unfamiliar with the Gospel history.

[136] It is nowhere explained why the bridges over this particular division of Malebolge should have specially felt the shock of the Crucifixion; nor does any commentator until Landino appear to notice the point. He says: Intendendo per questo, che in quel tempo fu disgregata la sinagoga de i Giudei, e la fraude de la hipocrisia de i sacerdoti. Vellutello follows him; and looking to the presence of Annas and Caiaphas in this *bolgia*, their interpretation may be correct.

low on the side and rises up in the bottom.' My Leader stood awhile with head bowed; then he said: 'Ill did he recount the business who hooks the sinners on the other side.' And the friar: 'I have heard tell ere now at Bologna faults enough of the devil, among which I heard that he is a liar and father of falsehood.' After that my Leader went on with great steps, troubled a little with anger in his countenance: wherefore I parted from the burthened ones after the prints of his dear feet.

>   Chè giace in costa, e nel fondo soperchia.
> Lo Duca stette un poco a testa china,
>   Poi disse: Mal contava la bisogna   140
>   Colui, che i peccator di là uncina.
> E il frate: Io udi' già dire a Bologna
>   Del Diavol vizii assai, tra i quali udi'
>   Ch' egli è bugiardo, e padre di menzogna.
> Appresso il Duca a gran passi sen gì,
>   Turbato un poco d' ira nel sembiante:
>   Ond' io dagl' incarcati mi parti'
> Dietro alle poste delle care piante.

[140] When he told them (xxi. 111) that only the one bridge was broken, and that they would find a sound one to cross by.

CANTO XXIV

ARGUMENT

They climb the side of the pit, and come to the next, wherein are the thieves, who are tormented in divers ways by serpents. Dante talks with one of Pistoia, who foretells evils to come upon his party.

IN that part of the youthful year, when the Sun is tempering his locks under the Waterman, and the nights are already

> IN quella parte del giovinetto anno,
>   Che il sole i crin sotto l' Aquario tempra,
>   E già le notti al mezzo dì sen vanno :

---

[1] *sqq.* The time indicated is the latter half of January or beginning of February. The sun enters Aquarius on Jan. 20; which in Dante's time would have been called the 10th.

[3] It is curious that scarcely any commentator has taken this line in what is clearly its proper meaning. With only one exception, so far as I have seen, they render it 'the nights are getting to equal the day,' or 'are getting towards half the day' (sc. of 24 hours). But this ignores the meaning of **sen vanno** ('are going *away*'); the time indicated is still many weeks from the equinox; and it may be doubted if *il mezzo dì* ever means 'half the day.' What it does constantly mean (e.g.—if an example is needed—Conv. iii. 5) is 'the south.' *Notte* is frequently used by Dante (e.g. Purg. ii. 4) for the point in the heavens opposite to the sun, which of course at this time of year is getting further and further towards the south, as the sun comes to the north. It has been doing so ever since the solstice, but one does not begin to be very conscious of the fact, particularly in the morning, much before the end of January. Possibly the plural **notti**, which, however, need give no trouble (cf.

passing away to the south; when the rime on the ground portrays the likeness of her white sister, but short while does temper endure in her pen; the churl, to whom substance is lacking, gets up and looks, and sees the countryside all white, wherefore he smites on his thigh; he returns to his house, and grumbles here and there, like the poor wretch who knows not what is to be done; then he comes back, and again stores up hope seeing the world to have changed countenance in little while; and takes his crook, and drives forth his flock to pasture. Thus did my Master make me

> Quando la brina in sulla terra assempra
>   L' imagine di sua sorella bianca,
>   Ma poco dura alla sua penna tempra;
> Lo villanello, a cui la roba manca,
>   Si leva e guarda, e vede la campagna
>   Biancheggiar tutta, ond' ei si batte l' anca:
> Ritorna in casa, e qua e là si lagna,   10
>   Come il tapin che non sa che si faccia;
>   Poi riede, e la speranza ringavagna,
> Veggendo il mondo aver cangiata faccia
>   In poco d' ora, e prende suo vincastro,
>   E fuor le pecorelle a pascer caccia:
> Così mi fece sbigottir lo Mastro,

Georg. ii. 481, 482, where *noctes* is opposed to *soles*), was the cause of the mistake, and this once made was as usual adopted without criticism by the early interpreters and copied from them by the moderns. The only place where I found what I believe to be the true interpretation is the Ottimo Comento: Perocchè la notte, ch' è opposita del sole, cade in quello tempo verso la parte di mezzo giorno. Ashburnham MS. L 832, 'Dr. Moore's I', in which this is copied, reads 'la parte di meridie.'

"Having used the word **assempra**, 'draws' (cf. V. N. § 1, where also we find v. l. *esempli*, or *pri*), he continues the metaphor by ascribing to the rime the use of a pen, doubtless the reed pen of those days.

[11] **non sa**, etc., sc. whether to turn his sheep out or not. Benv.

to be out of countenance, when I saw his brow so troubled; and thus quickly did the salve come to the hurt. For as we came to the ruined bridge, my Leader turned him to me with that sweet mien which I saw at first at the foot of the mount. He opened his arms, after certain counsel adopted with himself, first looking well at the fallen mass, and took hold of me. And as the man who is working and reckoning, in that he always seems to be making provision ahead, so while lifting me up to the top of one crag, he was taking note of another splinter, saying: 'Hook thyself next on to that one; but try first if it is of such sort as to bear thee.' It was not a road for one clad in a cope; for we with diffi-

>Quand' io gli vidi sì turbar la fronte,
> E così tosto al mal giunse lo impiastro:
>Chè come noi venimmo al guasto ponte,
> Lo Duca a me si volse con quel piglio   20
> Dolce, ch' io vidi prima a piè del monte.
>Le braccia aperse, dopo alcun consiglio
> Eletto seco, riguardando prima
> Ben la ruina, e diedemi di piglio.
>E come quei che adopera ed estima,
> Che sempre par che innanzi si proveggia:
> Così, levando me su ver la cima
>D' un ronchion, avvisava un' altra scheggia,
> Dicendo: Sopra quella poi t' aggrappa:
> Ma tenta pria s' è tal ch' ella ti reggia.   30
>Non era via da vestito di cappa,

21, 23 **prima**: note the different uses of the word. In l. 21 it means 'for the first time,' in l. 23 'beforehand.' Our 'first' renders both.

22-30 Mr. Freshfield (Alpine Journal, vol. x. p. 404) has called attention to the mountaineering experience which this description reveals.

31 With allusion to the leaden copes of the hypocrites.

culty, he light, and I pushed forward, were able to climb up from ledge to ledge. And if it had not been that towards that circumference the hill was shorter than towards the other, I do not know about him, but I should certainly have been beaten. But whereas Malebolge all slopes toward the opening of the lowest pit, the position of each valley brings about that one side is high and the other low; we at any rate came at last above the point whence the last stone is rent away.

The breath was so drawn from my lungs when I was up, that I could go no further, nay, I sate me down at my first

> Chè noi a pena, ei lieve, ed io sospinto,
> Potevam su montar di chiappa in chiappa.
> E se non fosse, che da quel precinto
> Più che dall' altro era la costa corta,
> Non so di lui, ma io sarei ben vinto.
> Ma perchè Malebolge in ver la porta
> Del bassissimo pozzo tutta pende,
> Lo sito di ciascuna valle porta
> Che l' una costa surge e l' altra scende: 40
> Noi pur venimmo alfine in sulla punta
> Onde l' ultima pietra si scoscende.
> La lena m' era del polmon sì munta
> Quando fui su, ch' io non potea più oltre,
> Anzi mi assisi nella prima giunta.

²⁹ One does not quite see why Virgil should have had any difficulty. But Dante seems to conceive his spirits as retaining a part of such physical properties as gravity, though in a reduced measure. Cf. xxxiv. 78.

³⁴ **quel precinto**: the inner circumference of the *bolgia*, where, as we have already seen (xix. 35), the depth, for the reason explained in the following lines, is less at its lower rim. Benv. supposes that each *bolgia* is in itself shallower than the last, all their floors being on the same level; but there is no need to assume this. See Scartazzini's diagram. I read *precinto*, not *procinto*, as Dante probably followed the Latin use.

coming. 'Henceforward it behoves that thou brace thyself thus,' said the Master; 'for not by sitting on feathers does one come into fame, nor under quilts; without the which whoso consumes his life leaves such trace on earth of himself as smoke in air or its froth on water. And therefore lift up, conquer the task with the mind that wins every battle, if with its heavy body it throw not itself down. A longer stair has need to be ascended; it is not enough to have got away from those. If thou understandest me, now see that it avail thee.'

> Omai convien che tu così ti spoltre,
>   Disse il Maestro, chè, sedendo in piuma
>   In fama non si vien, nè sotto coltre,
> Senza la qual chi sua vita consuma,
>   Cotal vestigio in terra di sè lascia, 50
>   Qual fummo in aer ed in acqua la schiuma:
> E però leva su, vinci l' ambascia
>   Con l' animo che vince ogni battaglia,
>   Se col suo grave corpo non s' accascia.
> Più lunga scala convien che si saglia:
>   Non basta da costoro esser partito:
>   Se tu m' intendi, or fa sì che ti vaglia.

47-51 It seems almost superfluous to refer to Lycidas:

> Fame is the spur that the clear spirit doth raise
>   .   .   .   .   .   .
> To scorn delights and live laborious days.

51 **la schiuma**: the article is required because the foam is a part of, or belongs to, the water; **fumo** is no part of the air.

53 **vince ogni battaglia**: so *la pugna*, ix. 7: *tutto*, Purg. xvi. 78.

55 Either the climb from the centre back to the surface of the Earth, or (more probably) that of the purgatorial mountain.

56 It is not enough to abandon sins; there must be a striving after positive goodness.

I lifted myself then, making myself seem better furnished with breath than I felt; and said, 'Go, for I am strong and bold.' We took our way over the rock, which was craggy, narrow, and ill to compass, and far steeper than the foregoing. I was talking as I went, so as not to appear feeble; whereat a voice issued from the next foss, ill-suited to form words. I know not what it said, albeit I was already upon the crown of the arch which crosses there; but he who was talking appeared moved to wrath. I had turned downward; but my living eyes could not reach the bottom through the gloom, wherefore I: 'Master, see that thou

> Leva' mi allor, mostrandomi fornito
>   Meglio di lena ch' io non mi sentia;
>   E dissi: Va, ch' io son forte ed ardito.   60
> Su per lo scoglio prendemmo la via,
>   Ch' era ronchioso, stretto e malagevole,
>   Ed erto più assai che quel di pria.
> Parlando andava per non parer fievole,
>   Onde una voce uscìo dall' altro fosso,^a
>   A parole formar disconvenevole.
> Non so che disse, ancor che sopra il dosso
>   Fossi dell' arco già che varca quivi;
>   Ma chi parlava ad ira parea mosso.
> Io era volto in giù; ma gli occhi vivi   70
>   Non potean ire al fondo per l' oscuro:
>   Perch' io: Maestro, fa che tu arrivi

^a *Ed una v. W.*

⁶¹ **scoglio**: the rib of rock forming the bridge over the seventh *bolgia*.
⁶⁴ A human touch. Few climbers have not done the same.
⁶⁵ **onde**: here, as elsewhere, the sound of his voice sets a spirit talking.
⁶⁶ Benv. appears to take **disconvenevole** as plural, agreeing with **parole**, and interprets 'idest inhonesta.' But Dante has not heard the words.

arrive at the next ring, and let us go down the wall; for as I hear where I am, and do not comprehend, so I look down, and make out nothing.' 'Other answer,' said he, 'I return thee not, save to do it; for a fair demand ought to be followed with silent action.' We descended the bridge on the side of the head, where it is joined with the eighth bank; and then was the pit manifest to me, and there I saw within a terrible pack of serpents, and of so uncouth kind that the memory yet thins my blood. Let Libya with her sand boast

> Dall' altro cinghio, e dismontiam lo muro;
>   Chè com' i' odo quinci e non intendo,
>   Così giù veggio, e niente affiguro.
> Altra risposta, disse, non ti rendo,
>   Se non lo far: chè la domanda onesta
>   Si dee seguir coll' opera tacendo.
> Noi discendemmo il ponte dalla testa
>   Dove s' aggiunge coll' ottava ripa,   80
>   E poi mi fu la bolgia manifesta:
> E vidivi entro terribile stipa
>   Di serpenti, e di sì diversa mena,
>   Che la memoria il sangue ancor mi scipa.
> Più non si vanti Libia con sua rena;

---

[79] Though he does not expressly state it, it would appear from xxvi. 13-15 that they descended not only the bridge, but also the rocks forming the inner side of the seventh *bolgia*; stopping, however, as is indicated in xxv. 35, before they reached the bottom. It must be remembered that each *bolgia*, with its encircling wall of rock, has a breadth of about a mile and three-quarters. How this is divided appears in xxx. 87, from which we find that half a mile is allotted to the *bolgia* itself, so that the passage of the bridge would be a work of some labour. Philalethes thinks that each bridge is steeper than the last.

[82] **stipa**: so xi. 3.

her no more; for if she produces watersnakes, whipsnakes, and asps, and diamond-snakes with amphisbaena, plagues so many and so cruel never yet did she display, with all Ethiopia, nor with that which is above the Red Sea. Among this savage and most joyless swarm folk were running, naked and terrified, without hope of hiding-hole or heliotrope. With serpents they had their hands tied behind; these fixed through the loins their tail and head, and were

> Chè, se chelidri, iaculi e faree [b]
> Produce, e cencri con amfisibena,
> Nè tante pestilenzie nè sì ree
> Mostrò giammai con tutta l' Etiopia,
> Nè con ciò che di sopra il mar rosso ee.   90
> Tra questa cruda e tristissima copia
> Correvan genti nude e spaventate,
> Senza sperar pertugio o elitropia.
> Con serpi le man dietro avean legate:
> Quelle ficcavan per le ren la coda
> E il capo, ed eran dinanzi aggroppate.

[b] *Che sì* Cass.; *che se lidri* 14; *cherse chel* 3.

85, 86 These names of serpents are all taken from Lucan Phars. ix, 711, 712; 719-721.

92 **genti**: thieves; not the violent robbers who were lying in the boiling blood higher up, but stealthy plunderers.

93 **elitropia**. The stone called heliotrope had the property of making its wearer invisible, when rubbed with the juice of the plant of the same name; which, according to P. di Dante, seems to been a sort of endive, not the flower to which we now give that appellation. Fazio degli Uberti says of it Dittam. v. 18: *Util si crede a colui che fura*: whence no doubt the allusion here. A pleasant story, turning more or less on the supposed virtues of the stone, will be found in the Decameron, Day viii. Nov. 3.

94 Benv. reads *dietro aggr*. as if the serpent had tied himself in a knot behind the man. He is aware of the usual reading; according to

bunched in front. And lo, to one who was toward our bank, a serpent came up, which transfixed him in the place where the neck is knotted to the shoulders. And never was O or I so quickly written, as he took fire and burned, and falling down must needs become all ashes; and after that he had thus been destroyed to the ground, the ash gathered together of itself, and returned of a sudden into that same man. Thus by the great sages it is professed that the Phoenix dies and then is born again, when she draws near to her fivehundredth year. In her life she feeds not on herb nor corn,

> Ed ecco ad un, ch' era da nostra proda,
>   S' avventò un serpente, che il trafisse
>   Là dove il collo alle spalle s' annoda.
> Nè O sì tosto mai nè I si scrisse, 100
>   Com' ei s' accese ed arse, e cener tutto
>   Convenne che cascando divenisse:
> E poi che fu a terra sì distrutto,
>   La polver si raccolse per sè stessa,
>   E in quel medesmo ritornò di butto:
> Così per li gran savi si confessa,
>   Che la Fenice more e poi rinasce,
>   Quando al cinquecentesimo anno appressa.
> Erba nè biado in sua vita non pasce,

which we must suppose the body of the serpent twisted and knotted in front of the man, a coil thrown round his arms, and the head and tail pinned into the loins. This property of *piercing* is ascribed by Lucan to the snake he calls Jaculus.

   99–101 Ov. Met. xv. 393, 394:

> non fruge neque herbis
> Sed turis lacrimis et suco vivit amomi;

and 398–400:

> Quo simul ac casias et nardi lenis aristas
> Quassaque cum fulva substravit cinnama myrrha,
> Se superimponit, finitque in odoribus aevum.

but only on tears of incense and of amomum; and nard and myrrh are her last winding-sheet. And as is he who falls, and does not know how, by force of a demon which drags him to earth, or of other obstruction which binds the man, when he rises and looks around him, all bewildered with the great anguish which he has undergone, and as he gazes, sighs; so had that sinner risen thereafter. Oh! power of God how stern it is, when it lashes such strokes for ven-

  Ma sol d' incenso lagrime ed amomo: 110
 E nardo e mirra son l' ultime fasce.
E qual è quei che cade, e non sa como,
 Per forza di demon ch' a terra il tira,
 O d' altra oppilazion che lega l' uomo,
Quando si leva, che intorno si mira
 Tutto smarrito dalla grande angoscia
 Ch' egli ha sofferta, e guardando sospira:
Tal era il peccator levato poscia.
 O potenzia di Dio quant' è severa,
 Che cotai colpi per vendetta croscia.   120

^c quanto ... vera Cass. Gg. 23; quanto severa 14; quanto è vera W.

[114] **oppilazion**: the regular term for an obstruction in any internal organ.

[119] **potenzia** seems to have much more authority than *giustizia*, and it suits the sense equally well. This cannot, however, be said of the reading which Witte prefers, *quanto se' vera*. In the first place it is hard to see how the *nature* of the punishment can be any evidence of the *truth* of the power which inflicts it, though it is of its severity. Then, though **croscia** might possibly be the second person, the form is extremely rare. It need hardly be said that as between *se' vera* and *severa*, MS. authority goes for nothing; and whichever was understood by the scribe would decide the form of the previous word. On the other hand Dante only uses *severa* once elsewhere in D. C.

geance! My Leader then asked him who he was; wherefore he answered: 'I dropped from Tuscany little while ago, into this wild gully. A beast's life pleased me, and not a man's, like a mule that I was; I am Vanni Fucci, a beast, and Pistoia was a fit den for me.' And I to my Leader: 'Tell him not to run away, and ask him what fault drove him down here, for I saw him a man of blood and quarrels.' And the sinner, who heard, made no feigning, but directed his mind and his face towards me, and took on him the hue of sad shame; then he said: 'It is more woe to me that thou hast caught me in the wretchedness wherein thou seest

> Lo Duca il domandò poi chi egli era:
>   Perch' ei rispose: Io piovvi di Toscana,
>   Poco tempo è, in questa gola fera.
> Vita bestial mi piacque, e non umana,
>   Sì come a mul ch' io fui: son Vanni Fucci
>   Bestia, e Pistoia mi fu degna tana.
> Ed io al Duca: Digli che non mucci,
>   E domanda qual colpa quaggiù il pinse:
>   Ch' io il vidi un uomo di sangue e di crucci.
> E il peccator, che intese, non s' infinse,   130
>   Ma drizzò verso me l' animo e il volto,
>   E di trista vergogna si dipinse:
> Poi disse: Più mi duol che tu m' hai colto
>   Nella miseria, dove tu mi vedi,

[125] **Vanni Fucci** was a natural son of one of the Lazzari of Pistoia, and a turbulent partisan on the 'Black' side. In 1295 he plundered the treasury of the Church of St. James, and contrived to get another man hanged for the crime. Benv. and Land. give the story at length, and Philalethes adds some further particulars.

[126] Pistoia seems to have had a reputation for lawlessness and savagery. It will be remembered that the factions of Whites and Blacks sprang out of a family quarrel there. See note xxxii. 63.

[127] **mucci**: a Lombard colloquialism, according to Benvenuto.

me, than when I was taken from the other life. I cannot refuse that which thou askest; I have been sent down thus far, because at the sacristy I was a thief of the fair ornaments, and falsely was it once laid upon another. But to the end that thou mayest not rejoice at such sight, if thou art ever forth of the places of darkness, open thine ears to my announcement and hear. First Pistoia thins herself of

> Che quando fui dell' altra vita tolto.
> Io non posso negar quel che tu chiedi;
> In giù son messo tanto, perch' io fui
> Ladro alla sacrestia dei belli arredi;
> E falsamente già fu apposto altrui.
> Ma perchè di tal vista tu non godi, 140
> Se mai sarai di fuor dei lochi bui,
> Apri gli orecchi al mio annunzio, ed odi:
> Pistoia in pria di Neri si dimagra,[d]

[d] *in prima di ner s.d.* Cass.; *in pria di nigri* 2; *Negri* Ald. W.

[143 sqq.] In May 1301 the Whites of Pistoia, with the aid of the same party, who were then in power, at Florence, banished the Blacks (Villani viii. 45). In November of the same year Charles of Valois entered Florence, and drove out the Whites (ib. 48). For some years after this Pistoia remained the only stronghold in Tuscany of the White-Ghibeline party, and as such was an object of special hostility to the Florentines, who attacked it more than once, in conjunction with the Lucchese (ib. 52, 65), and finally captured it and destroyed its fortifications in 1306 (ib. 82). The particular battle here foretold appears to have been an incident in the attack of 1302, when the combined Florentines and Lucchese took the stronghold of Serravalle. The 'mist from Valdimagra' is Moroello Malaspina, lord of the Lunigiana (see note Purg. viii. 118), who was at that time in command of the attacking force: a fact of which Villani, who curiously ignores the Malaspina family, makes no mention, nor does he record this engagement. Dante, on the other hand, who received much kindness from the family during the latter part of his life, loses no opportunity of an allusion to them. See on the subject of the

the Blacks; then Florence renews folk and fashions. Mars draws a mist from Val di Magra, which is wrapt in turbid clouds, and with a tempest violent and bitter is the battle fought upon the Picene plain; whence he will suddenly rend in pieces the cloud, so that every White shall be smitten therewith. And I have told it thee to the end that thou mayest need to grieve therefore.'

>   Poi Fiorenza rinnuova genti e modi.
>   Tragge Marte vapor di val di Magra
>   Ch' è di torbidi nuvoli involuto.
>   E con tempesta impetuosa ed agra
>   Sopra campo Picen fia combattuto:
>   Ond' ei repente spezzerà la nebbia,
>   Sì ch' ogni Bianco ne sarà feruto: 150
>   E detto l' ho, perchè doler ti debbia.

family, the Appendix to the sixth volume of Prof. Bartoli's 'Storia della Letteratura Italiana.' **Campo Piceno** appears to mean the country near Serravalle. Why it had this name (see also Villani i. 32, where it is *Campo a Picno*) does not clearly appear. It is at some distance from the ancient Picenum. In Sallust's account of the defeat of Catiline we read that when Metellus Celer, who was commanding 'in agro Piceno,' heard of Catiline's move 'in agrum Pistoriensem,' he succeeded by rapid marches in blocking the mountain route from Pistoia into 'Gaul,' as it would appear, on the north of the mountains. Some misunderstanding of this passage may have led medieval writers to imagine that the subsequent battle with Petreius was fought on Picene territory. Thus John of Serravalle: Ille campus qui est prope Pistorium in quo devictus fuit Cathellina vocatur Picenus a Sallustio. It is a little curious that his Serravalle, near Rimini, is only just outside of the old Picenum.

CANTO XXV

ARGUMENT

They continue by the same folk, and see new and horrible torments inflicted by the serpents. Dante recognises five persons of his own city.

At the end of his speech the robber raised his hands with both their figs, crying, 'Take them, God, for at thee I show them.' From that time to this have the serpents been my friends, seeing that one wound itself then about his neck, as though it said: 'I will not that thou say more'; and another about his arms, and bound him, clenching itself so in front that he could not give a quiver with them.

> Al fine delle sue parole il ladro
> Le mani alzò con ambedue le fiche,
> Gridando: Togli, Iddio, chè a te le squadro.
> Da indi in qua mi fur le serpi amiche,
> Perch' una gli s' avvolse allora al collo,
> Come dicesse: Io non vo' che più diche:
> Ed un' altra alle braccia, e rilegollo,
> Ribadendo sè stessa si dinanzi,[a]
> Che non potea con esse dare un crollo.

[a] *Ribatendo* G.: *Rebattendo* Cass.: *Rilattento* 2 Ald.

* **le fiche**: the coarse gesture is well known. It is attributed with special propriety to a sinner from Pistoia, because a century before the Pistoiese had displayed it in two marble hands on their fortress of Carmignano, in mockery of Florence. See Villani vi. 5.

Ah, Pistoia, Pistoia, why dost thou not determine to make thyself ashes, so that thou endure no more, since thou dost surpass thy begetting in ill deeds? Through all the murky circles of Hell I saw not a spirit so proud toward God, not he who fell at Thebes down from the walls. He fled, so that he spake no word more; and I saw a Centaur full of rage come crying: 'Where is he, where is the savage?' I do not believe that Maremma holds as many snakes as he had up over his croup, to the point where our face begins.

    Ahi Pistoia, Pistoia, chè non stanzi   10
      D' incenerarti, sì che più non duri,
      Poi che in mal far lo seme tuo avanzi.
    Per tutti i cerchi dell' inferno oscuri
      Non vidi spirto in Dio tanto superbo,
      Non quel che cadde a Tebe giù dai muri.
    Ei si fuggì, che non parlò più verbo:
      Ed io vidi un Centauro pien di rabbia
      Venir chiamando: Ov' è, ov' è l' acerbo?
    Maremma non cred' io che tante n' abbia,
      Quante bisce egli avea su per la groppa,   20
      Infin dove comincia nostra labbia.

---

[10] Compare the apostrophe to Pisa in xxxiii. 79 sqq. It is worth notice, as bearing on Dante's political views, that these two cities, which he treats with such, almost savage, indignation, were two of the stoutest supporters of the Ghibeline cause. Faction was hateful to him, on one side no less than on the other.

[11] **incenerarti**: as had just befallen the citizen of Pistoia.

[12] Probably an allusion to the story that Pistoia was founded by the Catilinarians who survived their defeat at the hands of Petreius (Vill. i. 32).

[15] Capaneus, whom we saw in Canto xiv.

[19] **Maremma**: the same district as is referred to in xiii. 7-9.

[21] **labbia**: as in xix. 122, Purg. xxiii. 47. Most modern commentators take this as meaning the human part generally; but this seems a

Above his shoulders behind the nape a dragon with open wings was lying on him and that sets fire to whosoever comes in his way. My Master said: 'He is Cacus, that beneath the rock of Mount Aventine made oftentimes a lake of blood. He goes not upon one road with his brethren, for the theft which he treacherously wrought of the great herd, that he had to his neighbour; wherefore his stealthy dealings ceased under the club of Hercules, who gave him haply a hundred, and did not feel ten.' While he

> Sopra le spalle, dietro dalla coppa,
>   Con l' ale aperte gli giacea un draco,
>   E quello affoca qualunque s' intoppa.
> Lo mio Maestro disse: Quegli è Caco,
>   Che sotto il sasso di monte Aventino
>   Di sangue fece spesse volte laco.
> Non va coi suoi fratei per un cammino,
>   Per lo furto che frodolente fece^h
>   Del grande armento, ch' egli ebbe a vicino: 30
> Onde cessar le sue opere biece
>   Sotto la mazza d' Ercole, che forse
>   Gliene diè cento, e non senti le diece.

^h *lo furar* 2 ; *lo furar frod. che* Ald. II.

very wide extension of the sense of the word, and the next line shows that he had them up to his neck.

²⁵ For Cacus, see Aen. viii. 190 sqq. Of course he was not a Centaur, only a fire-breathing monster; but Dante seems to have been misled by the epithet 'semihominis' which Virgil applies to him.

²⁷   Semperque recenti
      Caede tepebat humus.

³¹ **biece**: 'underhand'; much as in Par. vi. 136.

³³ **gliene**: *n.*, sc. blows, implied in **mazza**.—**senti**: the subject to this is usually taken to be Cacus: 'he did not feel ten of them,' because

was speaking thus, so he ran by; and three spirits came beneath us, of whom neither I nor my Leader took note, save when they cried: 'Who are ye?' wherefore our story was stayed, and then we gave heed only to them. I did not know them, but it followed, as is wont to follow in certain cases, that one had occasion to name another, saying: 'Where will Cianfa have stayed?' Wherefore I, in order that my Leader might stand attentive, laid my finger from the chin up to the nose. If thou art now, reader, slow

> Mentre che si parlava, ed ei trascorse,
>   E tre spiriti venner sotto noi,
>   Dei quai nè io nè il Duca mio s' accorse,
> Se non quando gridar: Chi siete voi?
>   Per che nostra novella si ristette,
>   Ed intendemmo pure ad essi poi.
> Io non gli conoscea: ma ei seguette,   40
>   Come suol seguitar per alcun caso,
>   Che l' un nomare un altro convenette,
> Dicendo: Cianfa dove fia rimaso?
>   Perch' io, acciocchè il Duca stesse attento,
>   Mi posi il dito su dal mento al naso.
> Se tu sei or, Lettore, a creder lento

---

he was dead. But it seems better both in grammar and sense to understand it of Hercules: 'he gave ten blows for one that he got.' In Virgil, Hercules strangles Cacus.

34 **ed**: see note l. 28; and cf. l. 50.

35 **sotto noi**: from which it appears that in this case they did not descend to the bottom of the pit.

40 **ei seguette**: so *egli incontra* Par. xiii. 118. See note Purg. xxviii. 37. Daniello to this passage gives several good examples of the idiom.

42 Lit. 'the other had occasion to name the one.'

43 **Cianfa** de' Donati, say the commentators: but nothing more.

to believe that which I am going to say, it will be no marvel, for I who saw it hardly allow it to myself. As I was holding my eyelids lifted toward them, lo a serpent with six feet launches itself in front of one, and clings to him all over. With its middle feet it bound his paunch, and with its forefeet seized his arms, then it bit him on one and the other cheek; its hind feet it spread out upon his thighs, and put its tail between the two of them, and stretched up over his loins behind. Ivy was never yet so clasped to a tree, as the horrible beast entwined over the other's limbs its own.

> Ciò ch' io dirò, non sarà maraviglia,
>   Chè io, che il vidi, appena il mi consento.
> Com' io tenea levate in lor le ciglia,
>   Ed un serpente con sei piè si lancia   50
>   Dinanzi all' uno, e tutto a lui s' appiglia.
> Coi piè di mezzo gli avvinse la pancia,
>   E con gli anterior le braccia prese;
>   Poi gli addentò e l' una e l' altra guancia.
> Gli diretani alle cosce distese,
>   E miseli la coda tr' ambe e due,
>   E dietro per le ren su la ritese.
> Ellera abbarbicata mai non fue
>   Ad arbor sì, come l' orribil fiera
>   Per l' altrui membra avviticchiò le sue: 60

levate le ciglia: so x. 45; but here it merely denotes a steady gaze.

The descriptions which follow are more or less based on those in Lucan Phars. ix. of what befell Cato's soldiers in the Libyan desert; but Dante undoubtedly surpasses his master in fertility of horrible invention.

serpente. The commentators say that this is the missing Cianfa in serpent form; but there is no evidence in the text for this view.

li must be omitted in modern English. Our forefathers might have said 'put *him* its tail between,' etc.

Then they stuck together, as if they had been of hot wax, and mingled their hues, nor did the one nor the other appear any more what he had been; like as in front of the burning proceeds a brown colour upward over the paper, which yet is not black, and the white fades. The two others looked on, and each cried: 'O me, Agnello, how thou dost change! see how already thou art neither two nor one.' Already

> Poi s' appiccar, come di calda cera
>   Fossero stati, e mischiar lor colore;
>   Nè l' un nè l' altro già parea quel ch' era:
> Come procede innanzi dall' ardore
>   Per lo papiro suso un color bruno,
>   Che non è nero ancora, e il bianco more.
> Gli altri due riguardavano, e ciascuno
>   Gridava: O me, Agnel, come ti muti!
>   Vedi che già non sei nè due nè uno.

64-66 One would have supposed that the description of a piece of paper burning was too obvious to be doubted; but some commentators, noticing that *carta* is the usual Italian word for paper, and that papyrus pith was used for the wicks of lamps, have rather perversely supposed this to be intended, in the face of the fact that a wick usually burns down and not up. Landino takes this view, and in more recent times Lombardi adopts it; adducing a passage (which Scart. quotes after him without acknowledgement) on the papyrus from Dante's contemporary Peter Crescentius, a writer on farming (or rather from Sansovino's translation of him) in support of it. But if he had read a little further he would have seen that Crescentius proceeds, 'Se ne fanno anche carte, nelle quale si scrive'; in the original Latin, 'de papirio etiam sunt cartae in quibus scribitur.' J. della Lana takes it as meaning paper; so Dict. Cruse. Daniello calls it a Gallicism. Benv. is undecided; candelae, vel intellige de carta bombicinea alba (showing that the meaning had extended from paper made of *papyrus*, nam . . . papyrus habet ista diversa significata.

68 **Agnel** de' Brunelleschi, the commentators tell us.

had the two heads become one, when there appeared to us two figures mixed in one face, where two were lost. From four bands their arms became two; the thighs with the legs, the belly and the chest turned to members which have never been seen. Every original feature was there undone; two and none the distorted image appeared; and so he went his way with slow pace.

As the lizard, under the mighty lash of the dog-days

> Già eran li due capi un divenuti,   70
>   Quando n' apparver due figure miste
>   In una faccia, ov' eran due perduti.
> Fersi le braccia due di quattro liste;
>   Le cosce con le gambe, il ventre e il casso
>   Divenner membra che non fur mai viste.
> Ogni primaio aspetto ivi era casso:
>   Due e nessun l' imagine perversa
>   Parea, e tal sen gìa con lento passo.
> Come il ramarro, sotto la gran fersa

[79] *sqq.* It will be observed that there are three distinct froms of punishment by means of the serpents. Vanni Fucci is burnt up by the bite of a serpent, and comes to his own shape again; Agnello blends with a serpent; and now we shall find man and serpent exchanging shapes. There is no doubt some reason for these variations, and the commentators speculate much on their symbolism; but in the absence of any knowledge as to the persons introduced, it is impossible that such speculations can be profitable.— **fersa** is variously explained; the most usual, though not very satisfactory, view being that it is merely *sferza*, altered for the rhyme. 'La ferza del sole' is, however, a phrase used by contemporary writers. Others connect it with *ferrea*, but it is not easy to see how it can be derived from this. Daniello says the word means 'a lace' as of bed-curtains or sails, and is used here for the sun's path above the horizon, which is greater in the summer. No trace of this meaning is to be found in Dict. Crusc. No one seems to have suggested that the word is merely the German *ferse*, though this would not give a bad sense.

changing hedges, seems a flash of lightning if it crosses the
road, so seemed as it came towards the paunches of the
other two a serpent inflamed, livid and black as a pepper-
corn. And that part whence first is drawn our nourishment,
it transfixed in one of them; then it fell down in front of
him stretched out. The one transfixed gazed at it but said
nought; rather with halted feet he began to yawn, just as if
drowsiness or fever were attacking him. He kept looking
at the serpent and it at him; the one through the wound
and the other through its mouth began to smoke abundantly,
and the smoke met. Now let Lucan hold his peace, where
he touches on the wretched Sabellus and on Nasidius, and

> Dei dì canicular cangiando siepe, 80
> Folgore par, se la via attraversa:
> Così parea, venendo verso l' epe
> Degli altri due, un serpentello acceso,
> Livido e nero come gran di pepe.
> E quella parte, donde prima è preso
> Nostro alimento, all' un di lor trafisse;
> Poi cadde giuso innanzi lui disteso.
> Lo trafitto il mirò, ma nulla disse:
> Anzi coi piè fermati sbadigliava,
> Pur come sonno o febbre l' assalisse. 90
> Egli il serpente, e quei lui riguardava:
> L' un per la piaga, e l' altro per la bocca
> Fumavan forte, e il fummo si scontrava.
> Taccia Lucano omai, là dove tocca
> Del misero Sabello e di Nassidio,

83 **quella parte**: the navel. Cf. note Purg. vii. 15.
94 **tocca di**: so vii. 68.
95 The end of Sabellus and Nasidius is described Phars. lib. cit. 762-804. The former is bitten by a *seps* and becomes, to borrow a

let him give heed to hear what is now coming forth. Let Ovid
hold his peace about Cadmus and about Arethusa; for if
he turns him into a serpent and her into a fountain in his
poem, I do not grudge it him; for never two natures front
to front did he transmute, in such wise that both the forms
should be prompt to exchange their matter. At the same
time they corresponded with each other after such order
that the serpent split its tail into a fork, and the stricken
man drew his feet together. The legs with the thighs of

> Ed attenda ad udir quel ch' or si scocca.
> Taccia di Cadmo e d' Aretusa Ovidio:
> Chè se quello in serpente, e quella in fonte
> Converte poetando, io non l' invidio;
> Chè due nature mai a fronte a fronte 100
> Non trasmutò, sì ch' ambo e due le forme
> A cambiar lor materia fosser pronte.
> Insieme si risposero a tai norme,
> Che il serpente la coda in forca fesse,
> E il feruto ristrinse insieme l' orme.
> Le gambe con le cosce seco stesse

phrase from Poe, 'a mass of loathsome putrescence'; the latter, struck by a *proster*, swells up till his corslet bursts, and dies miserably.

97 The change of Cadmus and Harmonia into snakes (from which Dante has borrowed several touches in the following description) is related Ov. Met. iv. 576-603. The tale of Arethusa is in the following book, 632 sqq. Here the 'form' = almost the personal identity; the 'matter' is the body in which it resides. Cf. Purg. xxv. 88 sqq. S. T. i. Q. 66. A. 2: Materia, secundum id quod est, est in potentia ad formam; oportet ergo quod materia secundum se considerata sit in potentia ad formam omnium illorum quorum est materia communis. Per unam autem formam non fit in actu, nisi quantum ad illam formam; remanet ergo in potentia quantum ad omnes alias formas.

103, 105 The first **insieme** is of time, the second of place.—**orme**: lit. footprints.

106 **stesse**: when the feet had been brought together, the fusion of the legs followed automatically.

themselves stuck so to each other, that shortly the joining made no mark that could be seen. The split tail took the shape which was lost in the other, and its skin grew soft and the other's hard. I saw the arms draw in at the armpits, and the two feet of the beast that were short lengthen out in proportion as those shortened. Afterwards the hind feet, twisted together, became the member which man conceals, and the wretch from his had two such produced. While the smoke was veiling the one and the other with a new tint, and causing the hair to grow upward over the one part, and stripping it off from the other, the one lifted himself and the other fell down, not therefore distorting the

> S' appiccar sì, che in poco la giuntura
> Non facea segno alcun che si paresse.
> Toglica la coda fessa la figura
> Che si perdeva là, e la sua pelle   110
> Si facea molle, e quella di là dura.
> Io vidi entrar le braccia per l' ascelle,
> E i due piè della fiera, ch' eran corti,
> Tanto allungar, quanto accorciavan quelle.
> Poscia li piè diretro, insieme attorti,
> Diventaron lo membro che l' uom cela,
> E il misero del suo n' avea due porti.
> Mentre che il fummo l' uno e l' altro vela
> Di color nuovo, e genera il pel suso
> Per l' una parte, e dall' altra il dipela,[c]   120
> L' un si levò, e l' altro cadde giuso,

[c] e per l' altra Gg.; parte da l' altra Cass.; parte e l' altro 2.

117 **ne**: i.e. legs.
118 **Mentre** with indic. like Lat. *dum*.

evil lamps, below which each was exchanging snouts. He
that was upright drew his up towards the temples, and of
the excess of material which came into that part, issued the
ears from the smooth cheeks; that which did not run to the
back, but stayed, of that surplus made a nose to the face,
and thickened the lips so much as was fitting. He that
was prostrate shoots his snout forward, and draws in his ears
by his head, as the snail does its horns; and his tongue
which he had before united and quick to speak, is split; and
the forked one in the other is closed; and the smoke is
stayed. The soul which was become a beast flies hissing
through the vale, and the other after him in his talk sputters.

> Non torcendo però le lucerne empie,
>   Sotto le quai ciascun cambiava muso.
> Quel ch' era dritto, il trasse ver le tempie,
>   E di troppa materia che in là venne,
>   Uscir gli orecchi delle gote scempie:
> Ciò che non corse in dietro e si ritenne,
>   Di quel soperchio fe naso alla faccia,
>   E le labbra ingrossò quanto convenne.
> Quel che giacea il muso innanzi caccia,   130
>   E gli orecchi ritira per la testa,
>   Come face le corna la lumaccia:
> E la lingua, che avea unita e presta
>   Prima a parlar, si fende, e la forcuta
>   Nell' altro si richiude, e il fummo resta.
> L' anima, ch' era fiera divenuta,
>   Si fuggì sufolando per la valle,
>   E l' altro dietro a lui parlando sputa.

[122] The eyes are the only feature which remains unaltered. — **torcendo**: so vi. 91.

[134] **il**: sc. *muso*, i.e. the nose and mouth, or part below the eyes.

[138] **sputa**: not, I think, as Witte renders, 'spits after him,' but

Afterwards he turned on him his newly-made shoulders, and said to the other: 'I will that Buoso run, as I did, groveling along this path.'

Thus did I see the seventh ballasting change and shift; and here let the strangeness be my excuse if my pen strays a little. And albeit that my eyes were confused somewhat, and my mind dismayed, those could not escape so hidden

> Poscia gli volse le novelle spalle,
>   E disse all' altro: Io vo' che Buoso corra,   140
>   Com' ho fatt' io, carpon, per questo calle.
> Così vid' io la settima zavorra
>   Mutare e trasmutare; e qui mi scusi
>   La novità, se fior la penna abborra.[d]
> Ed avvegnachè gli occhi miei confusi
>   Fossero alquanto, e l' animo smagato,
>   Non poter quei fuggirsi tanto chiusi,

[d] *la vita ab.* 2; *la lingua Ald.*

merely to indicate that he has not yet got the full use of his human mouth. Benv. appears to take it as an imperative: as though he were mockingly challenging his metamorphosed companion to perform an act only possible to a man.

140 **Buoso** degli Abati (P. di Dante) or de' Donati (Benv.). Whichever he may have been, nothing further is known of him.

142 **zavorra**, Lat. *suburra*, coarse sand or gravel used for ballast. The use of the word is probably suggested by the fact that Dante evidently imagines the floor of this *bolgia* to be gravelly, like the Libyan desert, which he has had in his mind throughout. The term thus occurs to him as a good one to denote the worthless occupants of the place.

144 There is some little uncertainty as to the exact meaning of **fior** and **abborra**; but it seems best to take the former as in xxxiv. 26: it would seem a recognised use; and regard the latter as the Lat. *aberrat*. The *abborre* of Par. xxvi. 73 (though the context is somewhat similar, so far as the following lines go) must be considered a different word altogether, from *abborrere*. Dante is apologising possibly for certain supposed crudities of expression not only in this Canto, but elsewhere.

that I did not mark Puccio Sciancato well; and he it was
who alone of the three companions that came first, was not
changed; the other one was he whom thou, Gaville, be-
wailest.

> Ch' io non scorgessi ben Puccio Sciancato:
> Ed era quei che sol, dei tre compagni
> Che venner prima, non era mutato: 150
> L' altro era quel che tu, Gaville, piagni.

[148] **Puccio Sciancato** (the Lame) de' Galigai.

[149, 150] Agnello having been blended with a serpent, and Buoso metamorphosed into one.

[151] This is said to be one Francesco Guercio (the Squinter) de Cavalcanti. He was killed by some people of Gaville near Florence, and in revenge his family made a raid upon the place and slew many. For the form of expression cf. Purg. vii. 136.

CANTO XXVI

ARGUMENT

They come to the next pit, and find flames moved therein, in which are enwrapped those who had given evil counsel. They speak with the spirit of Ulysses, who recounts to them the manner of his end.

REJOICE, Florence, since thou art so great that over sea and over earth thou beatest thy wings, and through Hell is thy name spread. Among the robbers found I five such, thy citizens, whence to me comes shame, and thou dost not thence rise to great honour. But if close upon the morn one

> Godi, Fiorenza, poi che sei sì grande,
>   Che per mare e per terra batti l' ali,
>   E per l' inferno il tuo nome si spande.
> Tra li ladron trovai cinque cotali
>   Tuoi cittadini, onde mi vien vergogna,
>   E tu in grande onranza non ne sali.
> Ma se presso al mattin del ver si sogna,

---

⁴ **cinque**: Cianfa, Agnello, Buoso, Puccio, Francesco; all belonging to families of distinction, and of various parties.

⁷ The belief that morning dreams are true is too well known to require much illustration. Perhaps the most familiar allusion to it is Horace's 'Post mediam noctem visus, cum somnia vera' (1 Sat. x. 33). Aristotle, though in the Parva Naturalia he discusses the question of divination by dreams, says nothing on this point. An explanation of the phenomenon is indicated Purg. ix. 16-18. Here of course the point of its introduction is merely to give force to the words which follow: 'my forecast is as certain as a morning dream.'

dreams of the truth, thou wilt be aware within a little while of that which Prato, not to name others, is wishing thee. And if it were already, it would not be betimes; so might it be, since verily it has to be! for it will be more grievous to me, the more I wait.

We departed, and up over the stairs which the slabs had before made for us to descend, my Master mounted again,

> Tu sentirai di qua da picciol tempo
> Di quel che Prato, non ch' altri, t' agogna.
> E se già fosse, non saria per tempo.   10
> Così foss' ei, da che pure esser dee;
> Chè più mi graverà, com' più m' attempo.
> Noi ci partimmo, e su per le scalee,
> Che n' avean fatte i borni a scender pria,[a]

[a] *fatti i borni* Gg. Cass. 12345; *fatto borni* Land.; *Che il buior n' avea f. sc.* Barg.

[8] **di qua da picciol tempo**: lit. 'on this side of a little time.'

[9] The allusion is not very clear. The little city of Prato, between Florence and Pistoia, seems to have been, save for a short quarrel over an extradition question in 1293, generally in sympathy with its powerful neighbour. Dante may mean 'even Prato, generally your friend, is now desiring your hurt.' This appears to be P. di Dante's interpretation. Many commentators, ancient and modern, think that by the name of his native town the Cardinal Nicolas of Prato is indicated. He was the right-hand man of Benedict XI., and was sent by him in 1304 to reconcile the factions in Tuscany; but he was known to have Ghibeline sympathies, and his efforts were defeated by the intrigues of the Black Guelfs, who stirred up tumults against him in various places, and especially in his own city of Prato. After three months' futile endeavours, he laid Florence under an interdict and departed. Various disasters which followed, such as the fall of the Ponte alla Carraja, a great fire, etc., were regarded as the effect of the Church's censure. See Villani viii. 69-71.

[14] **borni**: it is curious that many of the early commentators, including Benv., read *n' avea fatti borni*, and take the word as 'dim-sighted'

and drew me. And pursuing our solitary way among the splinters and among the rocks of the crag, the foot without the hand could not clear itself. Then I grieved, and now I grieve afresh when I divert any thought to that which I saw, and I bridle my wit more than I am wont so that it run not where virtue does not guide it; so that if a lucky star or aught better have given me the good, I may not grudge it to myself. In such numbers as the countryman who is

> Rimontò il mio Maestro, e trasse mee.[b]
> E proseguendo la solinga via
>   Tra le schegge e trai rocchi dello scoglio,
>   Lo piè senza la man non si spedia.
> Allor mi dolsi, ed ora mi ridoglio,
>   Quand' io drizzo la mente a ciò ch' io vidi: 20
>   E più lo ingegno affreno ch' io non soglio,
> Perchè non corra, che virtù nol guidi;
>   Sì che se stella buona, o miglior cosa
>   M' ha dato il ben, ch' io stesso nol m' invidi.
> Quante il villan, ch' al poggio si riposa,[c]

---

[b] *il Duca mio* Add. W.
[c] *Quandel* v. Gg. (?) Cass. 2.

Fr. *borgne*. Its real meaning may be gathered from the modern Fr. *borne*, 'a stone placed at the angle of a piece of land, or at a street corner.' Mountaineers nowadays use the German *Platten* to denote rocks of this kind.

22 **che** may be the general relative here (see i. 3); but perhaps it is better to understand 'may not run so as not to be guided by virtue.' It is not easy to see why this aspiration is made specially here; but it will be observed that in the division which they are about reaching, those who are suffering are not, like most of the tenants of Malebolge, sinners of a sordid and mean type, but men of great talents and high renown in the world, who had abused their gifts of intellect.

24 Here **che** appears to be 'pleonastic.'

resting on the hillside, at the season when he who illumines the world keeps his face hidden from us the least, when the fly gives place to the gnat, sees fireflies below throughout the valley, perhaps in the place where he gathers his grapes and ploughs: with so many flames was all the eighth pit shining according as I perceived so soon as I was at the point where the bottom came into view. And as he who avenged himself by means of the bears saw the chariot of Elijah at its departing when the horses erect toward heaven lifted themselves—for he could not so follow it with his eyes, as to see aught else but the flame alone rising on high like a cloud,—so was each moving through the gully of the

>   Nel tempo che colui che il mondo schiara
>   La faccia sua a noi tien meno ascosa,
> Come la mosca cede alla zenzara,
>   Vede lucciole giù per la vallea,
>   Forse colà dove vendemmia ed ara: 30
> Di tante fiamme tutta risplendea
>   L' ottava bolgia, sì com' io m' accorsi,
>   Tosto ch' io fui là 've il fondo parea.
> E qual colui che si vengiò con gli orsi,
>   Vide il carro d' Elia al dipartire,
>   Quando i cavalli al cielo erti levorsi:
> Chè noi potea sì con gli occhi seguire,
>   Ch' ei vedesse altro che la fiamma sola,
>   Sì come nuvoletta, in su salire:
> Tal si movea ciascuna per la gola   40

    When the days are longest.
  tal. Note the two relatives to the one antecedent, **qual** in l. 34 and **che** in l. 41; and cf. i. 4, 7 (where see note).

foss, that none displays its theft, and every flame steals away a sinner. I was standing upon the bridge, having risen up to look, so that, if I had not taken hold of a crag, I should have fallen down without being pushed. And the Leader who saw me thus intent said: 'Within the fires are the spirits; each is swathed of that wherewith he is kindled.' 'My Master,' I answered, 'through hearing thee I am more sure; but already I was advised that so it was, and already I was meaning to say to thee, who is in that fire, which comes so divided at the top that it seems to rise from the pyre where Eteocles was placed with his brother?' He answered me: 'Therewithin are tormented Ulysses and

  Del fosso, che nessuna mostra il furto,
   Ed ogni fiamma un peccatore invola.
  Io stava sopra il ponte a veder surto,
   Sì che, s' io non avessi un ronchion preso,
   Caduto sarei giù senza esser urto.
  E il Duca, che mi vide tanto atteso,
   Disse: Dentro dai fochi son gli spirti:
   Ciascun si fascia di quel ch' egli è inceso.
  Maestro mio, rispos' io, per udirti
   Son io più certo: ma già m' era avviso   50
   Che così fusse, e già voleva dirti:
  Chi è in quel foco, che vien sì diviso
   Di sopra, che par surger della pira,
   Ov' Eteòcle col fratel fu miso?
  Risposemi: Là entro si martira

 48 **inceso**: perhaps with allusion to James iii. 6: Lingua ignis est; these 'evil counsellors' having sinned with the tongue.
 54 Stat. Theb. xii. 431, 432:
   exundant diviso vertice flammae
   Alternosque apices abrupta luce coruscant.
 55 **martira**: a good instance of an idiom frequent in early Italian,

Diomede, and thus do they go together in their punishment as in their wrath; and within their flame is lamented the ambush of the horse which made the breach whence issued the noble seed of the Romans. Within there is bewailed the art through which dead Deidamia yet has woe for Achilles, and there is punishment borne for the Palladium.'

> Ulisse e Diomede, e così insieme
> Alla vendetta vanno come all' ira:
> E dentro dalla lor fiamma si geme
> L' aguato del caval, che fe la porta
> Ond' uscì dei Romani il gentil seme.   60
> Piangevisi entro l' arte, per che morta
> Deidamia ancor si duol d' Achille,
> E del Palladio pena vi si porta.

and not unknown in other Romance languages; two nouns (even in rare cases, as here, proper names) coupled by *e* and followed by a verb in the singular. Conversely, nouns coupled by *con* will often be found to take the plural verb. See Diez iii. 273, 274.

⁶¹ Aeneas and his followers. Virgil does not say that they issued from the breach by which the horse entered; indeed from Aen. ii. 716 it would appear that they left the city by various ways. All that is meant here is that the entry of the horse was the cause of their departure.

⁶² Deidamia, daughter of Lycomedes, king of Scyros, with whom Achilles, disguised in woman's clothes, was left by his mother, that he might not go to Troy. The craft of Ulysses penetrated the disguise, and his persuasions induced Achilles to join the other chiefs. See Statius' Achilleis.

⁶³ Aen. ii. 165: Impius ex quo
> Tydides sed enim, scelerumque inventor Ulixes,
> Fatale aggressi sacrato avellere templo
> Palladium, etc.

The intrigue of Ulysses and Diomede with Antenor in regard to the Palladium (for which the last gives his name to a division of the lowest circle of Hell) is told at great length by Guido dalle Colonne; from

'If they are able to speak within those flashes,' said I,
'Master, I pray thee much, and I pray again that the prayer
have the strength of a thousand, that thou make me not
refusal of waiting until the horned flame come here; thou
seest how of my desire I lean toward it.' And he to me:
'Thy prayer is worthy of much praise, and I therefore
accept it; but see that thy tongue hold itself back. Leave
talking to me, for I have conceived that which thou dost
wish; since they would be shy perchance, seeing that they
were Greeks, of thy speech.' After the flame was come

> S' ei posson dentro da quelle faville
>   Parlar, diss' io, Maestro, assai ten prego
>   E riprego, che il prego vaglia mille,
> Che non mi facci dell' attender nego,
>   Finchè la fiamma cornuta qua vegna:
>   Vedi che del disio ver lei mi piego.
> Ed egli a me: La tua preghiera è degna   70
>   Di molta lode, ed io però l' accetto;
>   Ma fa che la tua lingua si sostegna.
> Lascia parlare a me: ch' io ho concetto
>   Ciò che tu vuoi: ch' ei sarebbero schivi,
>   Perch' ei fur Greci, forse del tuo detto.
> Poichè la fiamma fu venuta quivi,

whose account (or that of his authority, Dictys Cretensis), rather than from Virgil's, Dante would seem to have formed his idea of the heroes of the Trojan war.

74, 75 Why should they object to being addressed by the Tuscan Dante more than by the Lombard Virgil? asks Benvenuto; and decides that it was because Virgil knew Greek—though he does not appear to have spoken it in this case—and had written of Greek heroes. It will be noticed that this is the only occasion on which they hold any converse with a person belonging to a period earlier than the establishment of the Roman Empire, unless we reckon the Centaurs of Canto xii.

there where it seemed to my Leader time and place, I heard him speak in this fashion: 'O ye who are two within one fire, if I merited of you while I lived, if I merited of you much or little, when in the world I wrote my lofty verses, do not move, but let one of you say where, having lost himself, he came to die.' The greater horn of the ancient flame began to shake and murmur, just like one which a wind is disturbing. Then working its top to and fro, as it were a tongue to speak, it cast a voice abroad and said:

> Dove parve al mio Duca tempo e loco,
> In questa forma lui parlare audivi:
> O voi, che siete due dentro ad un foco,
> S' io meritai di voi mentre ch' io vissi, 80
> S' io meritai di voi assai o poco,
> Quando nel mondo gli alti versi scrissi,
> Non vi movete; ma l' un di voi dica
> Dove per lui perduto a morir gissi.
> Lo maggior corno della fiamma antica
> Cominciò a crollarsi mormorando,
> Pur come quella cui vento affatica.
> Indi la cima qua e là menando,
> Come fosse la lingua che parlasse,
> Gittò voce di fuori, e disse: Quando 90

Literally, 'where it was by him, when lost, gone to death.'

lo maggior corno. Guido dalle Colonne gives, after Dares, a full account of the personal appearance of the Greek chiefs; but of these two it is Diomede whose stature he insists upon.

Whence Dante derived the idea of Ulysses' end which he has expanded into the magnificent passage which follows remains obscure. The regular medieval authorities on the subject give the story, to which Horace alludes, of his meeting his death at the hands of his own son Telegonus. Benvenuto concludes that he invented it, as a picture of what a brave man's end should be. To us it is interesting as having

'When I departed from Circe, who had drawn me away more than a year there hard by Gaeta, before that Aeneas named it so, neither the sweetness of my son, nor my affection for my old father, nor the due love which ought to have made Penelope happy, could conquer within me the ardour which I had to become experienced in the world, and in the vices of men and in their goodness; but I set me forth upon

> Mi diparti' da Circe, che sottrasse
>   Me più d' un anno là presso a Gaeta,
>   Prima che si Enea la nominasse;
> Nè dolcezza di figlio, nè la pieta
>   Del vecchio padre, nè il debito amore,
>   Lo qual dovea Penelope far lieta,
> Vincer poter dentro da me l' ardore
>   Ch' i' ebbi a divenir del mondo esperto,
>   E degli vizii umani e del valore:
> Ma misi me per l' alto mare aperto   100

suggested a theme to Lord Tennyson. The germ of it may perhaps be looked for in the well-known passage of the Odyssey xi. 134, in which Tiresias prophesies for Ulysses 'a death from the sea.' A MS. note of about 1600 in my copy of the Sessa edn. of 1578 takes a similar view, defending Dante from the charge of speaking 'tanto a sproposito come veggasi a molti.' The writer also refers to Tac. Germ. ch. 1, as showing a widespread belief in Ulysses' later journey. Though Dante knew little or no Greek, there were clearly old translations, now lost, of Greek works, to which he had access; and the Odyssey was undoubtedly very widely known in the 13th century, for we find evidence of its study in early Irish literature no less than in the 'Thousand and One Nights.'

⁹¹ If this is to be taken literally, it would imply that Ulysses never went home at all. But he may mean that the desire of wandering took him then, and that he gratified it in later years. It would seem from l. 106 that a long period is supposed to pass between his leaving Circe and his last voyage.

⁹³ See Aen. vii. 1 sqq.

the open deep sea lonely with one bark, and with that little company, by the which I was not deserted. The one coast and the other I saw as far as Spain, even to Morocco, and the isle of the Sards, and the others which that sea washes round about. I and my companions were old and slow when we came to that narrow passage where Hercules marked his backward looks, to the end that man should not set himself further; on the right hand I left Seville, on the other I had already left Ceuta. O brothers, I said, who through a hundred thousand perils are come to the West, to this waking-time of our senses so little as it is which our

> Sol con un legno e con quella compagna
> Picciola, dalla qual non fui deserto.
> L' un lito e l' altro vidi infin la Spagna,
> Fin nel Morrocco, e l' isola dei Sardi,
> E l' altre che quel mare intorno bagna.
> Io e i compagni eravam vecchi e tardi,
> Quando venimmo a quella foce stretta,
> Ov' Ercole segnò li suoi riguardi,
> Acciocchè l' uom più oltre non si metta:
> Dalla man destra mi lasciai Sibilia, 110
> Dall' altra già m' avea lasciata Setta.
> O frati, dissi, che per cento milia
> Perigli siete giunti all' occidente,
> A questa tanto picciola vigilia
> Dei nostri sensi, ch' è del rimanente,^d

^d *vostri* All. W.

¹⁰⁸ Others take **riguardi** as 'things to call attention,' i.e. that here was the limit of the habitable world. Others say that the word is used in Romagna for 'boundaries.'

¹¹⁵ **ch' è del rimanente**: lit. 'which belongs to your remnant.'

remaining life possesses, desire not to deny the experience, in wake of the sun, of the unpeopled world. Consider your begetting; ye were not made to live as brutes, but to follow virtue and knowledge.— I made my fellows with this short speech so keen for the journey, that hardly thereafter should I have held them back. And, our poop turned toward the sunrise, we made of our oars wings to our mad flight, ever bearing to the left side. All the stars of the other pole did the night already see, and our own so low that it did not rise forth of the ocean floor. Five times kindled, and as often put out had been the light below the

> Non vogliate negar l' esperienza,
>   Diretro al sol, del mondo senza gente.
> Considerate la vostra semenza:
>   Fatti non foste a viver come bruti,
>   Ma per seguir virtute e conoscenza.   120
> Li miei compagni fec' io sì acuti,
>   Con questa orazion picciola, al cammino,
>   Che appena poscia gli avrei ritenuti.
> E, volta nostra poppa nel mattino,
>   Dei remi facemmo ali al folle volo,
>   Sempre acquistando dal lato mancino.
> Tutte le stelle già dell' altro polo
>   Vedea la notte, e il nostro tanto basso,
>   Che non surgeva fuor del marin suolo.
> Cinque volte racceso, e tante casso   130

[125] **folle volo**: so *varco folle*, Par. xxvii. 82, 83.

[130] Five months had passed. From the Pillars of Hercules to the Mountain of Purgatory (if, as most commentators hold, we must understand it to be that which Ulysses sighted) would represent one-fourth of the circumference of the earth, or, according to Dante's reckoning, something less than 5000 miles. This would make their daily course about 33 miles.

moon since we entered upon the passage of the deep, when there appeared to us a mountain, dun through its distance, and it seemed to me high in such measure as none had been seen by us. We were blithe, but soon it turned to wailing, for from the new land a whirlwind had birth, and smote the foremost angle of our vessel. Three times it caused it to whirl round with all the waves, at the fourth it made the poop lift on high, and the prow go downward, as it pleased Another, even till the sea had closed again over us.'

> Lo lume era di sotto dalla luna,
> Poi ch' entrati eravam nell' alto passo,
> Quando n' apparve una montagna bruna
> Per la distanza, e parvemi alta tanto,
> Quanto veduta non n'aveva alcuna.
> Noi ci allegrammo, e tosto tornò in pianto;
> Chè dalla nuova terra un turbo nacque,
> E percosse del legno il primo canto.
> Tre volte il fe' girar con tutte l' acque,
> Alla quarta levar la poppa in suso,   140
> E la prora ire in giù, com' altrui piacque,
> Infin che il mar fu sopra noi richiuso.

[131] Or possibly 'on the lower side of the moon,' the side toward the earth.

[132] The notion of a great mountain in the Ocean, west of Gibraltar, is very ancient, probably based on early reports of Teneriffe. See the description of 'Atlas' in Pliny, Hist. Nat. v. 1.

[141] **com' altrui piacque**: so Purg. i. 133. As has been elsewhere remarked, the name of God is never uttered in Hell, save in blasphemy.

CANTO XXVII

ARGUMENT

Another spirit accosts them out of its flame, and enquires for news of Romagna. The author replies, and the spirit reveals himself for the Count of Montefeltro, and relates how he had been brought to that pass.

ALREADY was the flame erect on high and at rest for saying no more, and already was going its way from us, with the leave of the sweet Poet; when another which was coming behind it made us turn our eyes towards its top by reason of a confused sound which issued forth from it. As the Sicilian bull that bellowed first with the plaint of him (and

> Già era dritta in su la fiamma e queta,
> Per non dir più, e già da noi sen gìa
> Con la licenza del dolce Poeta:
> Quando un' altra, che dietro a lei venìa,
> Ne fece volger gli occhi alla sua cima,
> Per un confuso suon che fuor n' uscìa.
> Come il bue Ciciliàn che mugghiò prima
> Col pianto di colui (e ciò fu dritto)

   ³ **con la licenza**: the actual words are given presently.

   ⁷ The story of the brazen bull which Perillus made for Phalaris, tyrant of Syracuse, to roast criminals in, and which was first tested on the person of the artificer himself, is a commonplace of classical antiquity.

that was just) who had moulded it with his file, used to bellow with the voice of the tormented one, so that albeit it was of brass it still appeared pierced through with the pain—so through not having at the first a way nor opening, the grim words were turned in the fire into its language. But after that they had taken their course up through the point, giving to it in their passage that vibration which a tongue had given, we heard say: 'O thou to whom I address my voice, and who but now spakest Lombard, saying, Now go

> Che l' avea temperato con sua lima,
> Mugghiava con la voce dell' afflitto,   10
>   Si che, con tutto ch' ei fosse di rame,
>   Pure e' pareva dal dolor trafitto:
> Cosi per non aver via nè forame
>   Dal principio, nel fuoco in suo linguaggio[a]
>   Si convertivan le parole grame.
> Ma poscia ch' ebber colto lor viaggio
>   Su per la punta, dandole quel guizzo
>   Che dato avea la lingua in lor passaggio,
> Udimmo dire: O tu, a cui io drizzo
>   La voce, e che parlavi mo Lombardo,   20

[a] *del foco* G, &c. Cass. 2 Ald.

[14] **dal principio nel fuoco**: Witte renders 'from their origin in the fire.' But it seems best to follow Benvenuto's 'idest intra flammam praedictam,' connecting **fuoco** closely with **suo linguaggio**, i.e. the roaring of the flame. It is, however, very doubtful whether the right reading be not *del fuoco*. This has, if anything, superior MS. authority, and is adopted by many (though not, as Scartazzini says, 'quasi tutti') of the early commentators and editors, being also perhaps 'lectio difficilior.' If that reading be taken, we must understand **principio** as in Par. ii. 71, 'the formative principle.' The words while they were passing through the fire were subject to the operation of the 'form' of fire, and only perceptible as its language.

thy way, I urge thee no more—though I be come haply somewhat late, let it not irk thee to stay to talk with me; thou seest that it irks not me, and I am on fire. If thou but now hast fallen into this blind world from that sweet Latin land whence I bring all my sin, tell me if the men of Romagna have peace or war; for I was of the hill-country

> Dicendo: Issa ten va, più non t' adizzo:[b]
> Perch' io sia giunto forse alquanto tardo,
>   Non t' incresca restare a parlar meco:
>   Vedi che non incresce a me, ed ardo.
> Se tu pur mo in questo mondo cieco
>   Caduto sei di quella dolce terra
>   Latina, ond' io mia colpa tutta reco,
> Dimmi se i Romagnuoli han pace, o guerra;
>   Ch' io fui dei monti là intra Urbino

[b] *Istra* Gg. 124; *Ista* Cass. 3 Ald.

[21] These are the words of Virgil dismissing Ulysses, and are appropriately couched, if we may believe the commentators, in the Lombard dialect. But the readings are uncertain. The great majority of MSS. have *istra*, which I venture to think Dr. Moore is somewhat hasty in dismissing as 'a word without any meaning at all.' Is it certain that the Teutonic invaders of North Italy, when they began to talk Latin, did not confuse *extra* and *ultra*? On the other hand, it is by no means sure that *issa* is peculiarly Lombardic. In xxiii. 7 Dante uses it apparently as a word familiar to all readers; and in Purg. xxiv. 55 it is put into the mouth of a man of Lucca. It may be added that **adizzo** is undoubtedly of Teutonic origin. **Mo** is said to be in use in Romagna. It is thrice put into the mouth of the present speaker (ll. 20, 25, 109), and once (xxxiii. 136) into that of another Romagnole; and it may be noted that Dante himself uses it oftener in the Paradise, written during and after his stay in Romagna and the adjacent tract of Tuscany, than in all the rest of the poem. In Inf. and Purg. it is generally, though not always, found in the combination *pur mo*.

[22] The speaker is Guy, Count of Montefeltro, the hill-country about the part where Tuscany, Romagna, and the Marches meet, so called

there between Urbino and the ridge from which Tiber is

E il giogo di che il Tever si disserra.   30

from Mons Feretrus, the ancient name of the present San Leo, which is still preserved in the affix 'Feltria' which the names of some of the towns bear. He is mentioned with praise (for his social qualities) in Conv. iv. 28. The politics of Romagna, in which he took a prominent part in the latter half of the 13th century, are terribly involved, and Villani does not give us much help. This arises, doubtless, in the first place, from the fact that no city of that province held a commanding position like that of Florence in Tuscany. Witte thinks, too, that the comparative weakness of the commons in the cities left matters more in the hands of the great nobles; who for their part did not scruple to change sides on the main question as suited their interests at the moment. Then again the Popes laid claims to an authority in Romagna of a much more immediate kind than any which they ventured to assert in Tuscany, thus estranging their own supporters, and weakening the Guelf principle, which had quite as much to do with a desire for local autonomy as with any enthusiasm in the cause of the Church. Dante recurs to the subject again in Purg. xiv. An account, as clear as is consistent with compression, will be found in the Historical Sketch given by Philalethes at the end of the present Canto. The chief facts in Guido's history, as Villani gives them, are as follows. In 1274 he was summoned by the Lambertazzi, or Ghibelines of Bologna, who had just been expelled, to take command of them (vii. 44). In 1282 he held Forli against the Papal party, defeating Martin IV.'s nominee the Count of Romagna, a Frenchman whom Villani calls Gianni de Pa, others John of Appia; only to be turned out in the following year by the inhabitants, who seem to have been bought over by the other side (ib. 80-82). In 1286 he submitted to Honorius IV., and was banished to Piedmont (ib. 108); and about three years later returned from exile (for which he was excommunicated) at the summons of the Ghibelines of Pisa, where his arrival was followed by the murder of Count Ugolino, of which we shall hear more (ib. 128). Under his leadership the Pisans gained some successes against the Florentines, but on peace being made between the cities in 1293 he was dismissed (viii. 2). Some time between this date and 1298 he joined the Franciscan order, and in the latter year he gave the counsel to Boniface which is referred to below. He must have died soon after. His son Buonconte was killed at the battle of Campaldino, June 1289, when fighting on the Ghibeline side (Purg. v.).

³⁰ Called *gran giogo*, Purg. v. 116.

unlocked.' I was still listening and bent downward, when my Leader touched me on the side, saying: 'Speak thou, this one is Latin.' And I, who had already my answer at hand, without delay began to speak: 'O soul that art hidden down there, thy Romagna is not and never was without war in the hearts of its tyrants, but now I left none there declared. Ravenna stands as she has stood many years; the eagle of Polenta so broods there that it covers Cervia with its pinions. The land which made erewhile the long trial, and

> Io era ingiuso ancora attento e chino,
>   Quando il mio Duca mi tentò di costa,
>   Dicendo: Parla tu, questi è Latino.
> Ed io ch' avea già pronta la risposta,
>   Senza indugio a parlare incominciai:
>   O anima, che sei laggiù nascosta,
> Romagna tua non è, e non fu mai,
>   Senza guerra nei cor dei suoi tiranni:
>   Ma in palese nessuna or vi lasciai.
> Ravenna sta, come stata è molti anni: 40
>   L' aquila da Polenta la si cova,
>   Sì che Cervia ricopre co' suoi vanni.
> La terra che fe già la lunga prova,

---

41 The Polenta (see note, v. 97) had been lords of Ravenna for many years, and long remained so. The head of the house at the present time was Guido Novello, Dante's future patron. They were on the Guelf side. Their arms an eagle, silver and blue on a red and gold field (Philal.)

42 Cervia, a small town on the coast, about 15 miles from Ravenna. It seems to have been more or less the key to the more important Forli.

43-45 Forli, from which Guido repelled the Papal (French) forces in 1282. A green lion on a gold field was the banner of the Ordelaffi. A member of this family led the Whites and Ghibelines on the occasion of

of the French a bloody heap, finds itself beneath the green claws. And the old Mastiff and the young one of Verrucchio who took the ill order with Montagna, there as they are wont make of their teeth a wimble. The cities of Lamone and of Santerno the lion-cub from the white nest governs, who changes side between summer and winter.

> E dei Franceschi sanguinoso mucchio,
>   Sotto le branche verdi si ritrova.
> E il Mastin vecchio e il nuovo da Verrucchio,
>   Che fecer di Montagna il mal governo,
>   Là dove soglion, fan dei denti succhio.
> Le città di Lamone e di Santerno
>   Conduce il leoncel dal nido bianco,   50
>   Che muta parte dalla state al verno:

their unlucky attempt to force their way back to Florence in 1302. The actual ruler of Forli at this time was Sinibaldo. A generation later, his son was lord of Forli.

[46-48] The house of Malatesta is here meant. They came originally, according to Benvenuto, from Pennabilli, in Montefeltro, and received the fief of Verrucchio as a reward for services rendered to the commonwealth of Rimini. Gradually they acquired the lordship of the place, after conflicts with the Count of Montefeltro and other Ghibeline chiefs. The last of these, Montagna de' Parcitati, was captured by them in 1295 by means of a truly medieval artifice, and murdered in prison. See also note, v. 97.

[49] Faenza and Imola, respectively on the rivers named, were under the lordship of Maghinardo Pagani: see note, Purg. xiv. 118. He took the former place in 1290, the latter in 1296.

[51] **state** and **verno** are taken by all the early commentators, doubtless correctly, to mean the south and the north. Serravalle says, 'tenebat in alpibus (i.e. the mountain country) partem gebbellinam, et in romandiola gelfam'; the opposite of the fact, but showing how he took the words.

And she whose flank the Savio bathes, in like manner as she stands between the plain and the mountain, passes her life between tyranny and a free state. Now I pray thee that thou recount to us who thou art; be not more hard than another has been; so may thy name make head in the world.'

After that the fire had roared somewhat according to its fashion, the sharp point moved on this side, on that, and then gave forth breath on this wise: 'If I believed that my reply was to a person who should ever return to the world, this flame would stand without more shaking. But seeing

> E quella cui il Savio bagna il fianco,^c
>   Così com' ella sie' tra il piano e il monte,
>   Tra tirannia si vive e stato franco.
> Ora chi sei ti prego che ne conte:
>   Non esser duro più ch' altri sia stato,
>   Se il nome tuo nel mondo tegna fronte.
> Poscia che il foco alquanto ebbe rugghiato
>   Al modo suo, l' acuta punta mosse
>   Di qua, di là, e poi diè cotal fiato: 60
> S' io credessi che mia risposta fosse
>   A persona che mai tornasse al mondo,
>   Questa fiamma staria senza più scosse:

^c *quella a cui 2 W.*

[52] The city of Cesena, on the Savio, just at the foot of the hills, on which its suburb of Murata stands.

[54] Benv. reads *in stato franco*; but the comparison of the previous line shows that the usual reading is correct. As a matter of fact, it would seem to have been constantly changing hands between the houses of Malatesta and Montefeltro. It may be noted that in this part of the world the Guelfs seem to have represented the power of the local tyrants, the Ghibelines to have been the party of popular rights; the converse of what obtained in Tuscany.

that from this gulf none has returned alive, if I hear the truth, I answer thee without fear of infamy. I was a man of arms, and then was a cordelier, deeming that thus girded I made amends; and of a surety my deeming had come to pass wholly, if there had not been the great Priest, whom ill befall, that set me back in my former sins; and how and wherefore I will that thou understand me. While that I was a shape of bones and flesh which my mother gave me, my works were not lion-like, but of a fox. Cunning things and hidden ways I knew them all; and so I wielded the arts of them that the sound went forth to the end of the earth. When I saw myself come to that part of my age at

>   Ma perocchè giammai di questo fondo ⁽ᵈ⁾
>   Non tornò vivo alcun, s' i' odo il vero,
>   Senza tema d' infamia ti rispondo.
>   Io fui uom d' arme, e poi fui cordelliero,
>   Credendomi, sì cinto, fare ammenda:
>   E certo il creder mio veniva intero,
>   Se non fosse il gran Prete, a cui mal prenda,   70
>   Che mi rimise nelle prime colpe;
>   E come, e quare voglio che m' intenda.
>   Mentre ch' io forma fui d' ossa e di polpe,
>   Che la madre mi diè, l' opere mie
>   Non furon leonine, ma di volpe.
>   Gli accorgimenti e le coperte vie
>   Io seppi tutte; e sì menai lor arte,
>   Ch' al fine della terra il suono uscìe.
>   Quando mi vidi giunto in quella parte

ᵈ perioche All. W.

* Villani calls him 'savio e sottile ingegno di guerra più che niuno che fosse al suo tempo.'

which every man ought to strike his sails and coil up his ropes, that which formerly pleased me was then irksome to me, and penitent and confessed I surrendered myself, alas miserable! and it should have been my help. The Prince of the new Pharisees having a war hard by Lateran—and not with Saracens nor with Jews, for every foe of his was

> Di mia etade, ove ciascun dovrebbe 80
> Calar le vele e raccoglier le sarte,
> Ciò che pria mi piaceva, allor m' increbbe,
> E pentuto e confesso mi rendei:
> Ahi miser lasso! e giovato sarebbe.
> Lo Principe dei nuovi Farisei,
> Avendo guerra presso a Laterano,
> E non con Saracin, nè con Giudei;
> Chè ciascun suo nimico era Cristiano,

[81] Dante uses precisely the same metaphor in Conv. iv. 28, when speaking of Guido.

[84] **giovato sarebbe**: this curious use of the auxiliary *essere* where we should expect *avere* is passed over without much notice by the grammarians. We may compare *eran piaciute*, Purg. xx. 28.

[86] Alluding to the feud between Boniface VIII. and the house of Colonna, which existed throughout his reign, but came to a head in 1297. In that year they left Rome and defied him from their strongholds of Palestrina and Nepi, and he actually proclaimed a crusade against them. Nepi was taken, but Palestrina held out, and then the Pope, after failing to induce the Count of Montefeltro to take command of his forces, received from him the advice here quoted. The Colonnesi capitulated, on promise of a complete amnesty; and the Pope, having got Palestrina into his hands, razed it, and gave them nothing but absolution, revoking even this before long, and practically banishing the family for the remainder of his reign. They had their revenge when Sciarra Colonna, acting for Philip the Fair, captured him at Anagni (see Purg. xx. 86). Villani (viii. 21, 23) gives the story much as Dante does; indeed, so similar is his account, that one is a little inclined to doubt its independence.

Christian, and none had been to conquer Acre, nor a trader in the land of the Soldan—heeded neither his supreme office nor holy orders in himself, nor in me that halter which was wont to make those girt with it more lean; but as Constantine sought Silvester within Soracte to heal him of his leprosy, so did this man seek me for a master to heal him of his fever of pride. He asked advice of me, and I held my peace because his words seemed drunken. And

  E nessuno era stato a vincer Acri,
  Nè mercatante in terra di Soldano: 90
Nè sommo offizio, nè ordini sacri
  Guardò in sè, nè in me quel capestro
  Che solea far li suoi cinti più macri.
Ma come Constantin chiese Silvestro
  Dentro Siratti a guarir della lebbre,
  Così mi chiese questi per maestro
A guarir della sua superba febbre:
  Domandommi consiglio, ed io tacetti,
  Perchè le sue parole parver ebbre.

[89] The capture of Acre by the Saracens in 1291 was the last blow in the struggle for the Holy Land. After the final expulsion of the Christians, the Pope forbade all men, under pain of excommunication, to trade with Alexandria or Egypt, then the headquarters of the Mussulman power. See Villani vii. 145. It is curious that the chief regret of the historian in the loss of Acre seems to be the closing to the West of a valuable trade route.

[92] **capestro**: cf. Par. xi. 87.

[94] The medieval legend ran that Constantine, smitten with leprosy for his persecution of the Christians, recalled Pope Silvester, who had taken refuge in the caverns of Soracte, and obtained from him remission and healing, making the 'Donations' as recompense. See xix. 115: De Mon. iii. 10. Dante probably took the story from Brunetto, Trésor, Bk. i. Pt. 2, Ch. 87: Or avint chose que Silvestres o grant compaignie de crestiens s' en estoient foi sos une haute montaigne por eschuer les persecutions; et Constantius li emperers, qui estoit malades d'une lepre, l'envoia querre, etc.

then he said to me, Let not thy heart suspect; I absolve thee from this moment, and do thou teach me to act so that I may hurl Palestrina to earth. I have power to lock and unlock Heaven, as thou knowest; since two are the keys which my forerunner held not dear. Then did his weighty arguments urge me to that point where silence was to my thinking the worst, and I said, Father, since thou dost wash me from that sin wherein I have now to fall, long promise with short keeping shall make thee triumph on thy high throne. Francis came afterward, when I was dead, for me; but one of the black Cherubim said to him: Take not: do

> E poi mi disse: Tuo cor non sospetti: 100
>   Finor t' assolvo, e tu m' insegna fare
>   Sì come Penestrino in terra getti.
> Lo ciel poss' io serrare e disserrare,
>   Come tu sai; però son due le chiavi,
>   Che il mio antecessor non ebbe care.
> Allor mi pinser gli argomenti gravi
>   Là 've il tacer mi fu avviso il peggio,
>   E dissi: Padre, da che tu mi lavi
> Di quel peccato, ov' io mo cader deggio.
>   Lunga promessa con l' attender corto 110
>   Ti farà trionfar nell' alto seggio.
> Francesco venne poi, com' io fui morto,
>   Per me; ma un dei neri Cherubini
>   Gli disse: Non portar: non mi far torto.[e]

[e] *nol portar W.*

[105] See note iii. 60.

[107] **mi fu avviso**: cf. Fr. *m'est avis*.

[113] **Cherubini**: Philalethes observes that as the Cherubim were specially connected (see note Par. xxviii. 98) with the eighth heaven, so the fallen members of that order are fitly put in charge of the eighth circle of Hell. There may be also an allusion to the fact that the Cherubim excel in knowledge (Par. xi. 37).

me no wrong. He has got to come along down among my wretches, because he gave the counsel of fraud, since which till now I have been at his hair; for absolved he cannot be, who does not repent; nor is it possible to repent and to will at the same time, by reason of the contradiction which agrees not in it. O woeful me! what an awaking had I when he seized me, saying to me: Perhaps thou didst not think that I was a logician. To Minos he carried me; and he twisted his tail eight times about his hard back, and after he had bitten it through great rage, he said: This man is of the criminals of the thievish fire; wherefore I am lost where thou seest, and as I go thus clad, I grieve.'

When he had thus completed his say, the flame in woe departed, twisting and lashing its pointed horn. We passed

> Venir se ne dee giù trai miei meschini,
>> Perchè diede il consiglio frodolente,
>> Dal quale in qua stato gli sono ai crini;
> Ch' assolver non si può, chi non si pente,
>> Nè pentere e volere insieme puossi,
>> Per la contradizion che nol consente.   120
> O me dolente! come mi riscossi,
>> Quando mi prese, dicendomi: Forse
>> Tu non pensavi ch' io loico fossi!
> A Minos mi portò: e quegli attorse
>> Otto volte la coda al dosso duro,
>> E, poi che per gran rabbia la si morse,
> Disse: Questi è dei rei del foco furo:
>> Perch' io là dove vedi son perduto,
>> E sì vestito andando mi rancuro.
> Quand' egli ebbe il suo dir così compiuto,   130
>> La fiamma dolorando si partio,
>> Torcendo e dibattendo il corno acuto.

further, both I and my Leader, over the crag until the next arch, which covers the foss wherein is paid the fee of those who gain a burthen by putting asunder.

> Noi passammo oltre, ed io e il Duca mio,
>   Su per lo scoglio infino in sull' altr' arco
>   Che copre il fosso, in che si paga il fio
> A quei che scommettendo acquistan carco.

[136] Philalethes thinks that there is a kind of play on words. Ordinarily, a burden is rendered lighter by division; in this case it is made heavier.

CANTO XXVIII

ARGUMENT

In the ninth pit are those who on earth caused strifes and dissensions. These as they pass along are cruelly mangled by a fiend. Mahommed speaks to them, and prophesies; also Peter of Medicina. They see Caius Curio, Mosca, and Bertrand of Born.

WHO would ever be able even in unfettered words to tell in full of the blood and of the wounds which I now saw, by dint of recounting many times? Every tongue for certain would fail, by reason of our speech and of his mind, which have too little room to embrace so much. If all the folk were yet again assembled who once upon the fortune-tossed land of Apulia were grieving for their own blood by reason

> Chi poria mai pur con parole sciolte
>   Dicer del sangue e delle piaghe appieno,
>   Ch' i' ora vidi, per narrar più volte?
> Ogni lingua per certo verria meno
>   Per lo nostro sermone e per la mente,
>   Ch' hanno a tanto comprender poco seno.
> S' ei s' adunasse ancor tutta la gente,
>   Che già in sulla fortunata terra
>   Di Puglia fu del suo sangue dolente

  fortunata: doubtless from *fortuna* in a sense like its technical one of 'a tempest.'

of the Trojans and by reason of the long war which of the
rings made such high-heaped booty, as Livy writes who goes
not astray; with that which felt smart of wounds through
resistance to Robert Guiscard; and the other whose bones
are still gathered up at Ceperano, where a traitor was each

>Per li Troiani, e per la lunga guerra^a   10
>   Che dell' anella fe sì alte spoglie,
>   Come Livio scrive, che non erra:
>Con quella che sentì di colpi doglie,
>   Per contrastare a Roberto Guiscardo,
>   E l' altra, il cui ossame ancor s' accoglie
>A Ceperan, là dove fu bugiardo

^a *Romani Cass.; Misserini* (1629), *and many modern edd.*

¹⁰ **Troiani**: this is the only reading of any authority. It may be explained either by taking 'Trojans' as equivalent to 'Romans,' Dante, as we know, following Virgil in tracing the descent of the latter from the former (cf. xxvi. 60); or, perhaps better, that Dante gave a somewhat extended meaning to 'Apulia,' including in it not only the 'kingdom,' but generally the country south of Rome. P. di Dante sees no difficulty, but says 'in illa parte Apuliae quae dicitur Laurentia.' So Jacopo della Lana: fa mentione di cinque grandi tagliate di uomini le quali furono tutte nello territorio di ytalia nella provincia di puglia. Neither Ceperano nor Tagliacozzo, it will be observed, is within the limits of Apulia in the strictest sense.

¹¹ The battle of Cannae: Livy xxii. 47.

¹² Notice that **Livio** has its full three syllables; the final *o*, which in similar words is usually merged in the preceding vowel, being, as in Latin, affected by the *scr* of the following word.

¹⁴ Robert Guiscard and his brother Humphrey obtained Apulia as a fief from Pope Leo IX., after defeating him in battle at Civitella in 1053. Humphrey died soon afterwards; but it took Robert a quarter of a century of continual fighting to get rid of the Lombards and Greeks, and secure undisputed authority over Southern Italy.

¹⁶ When Charles of Anjou was marching to meet Manfred at Benevento, the latter sent a force under his kinsman Count Giordano and the Count of Caserta to oppose the entry of the French into the kingdom at the point called the bridge of Ceperano, where the road crosses

Apulian; and there by Tagliacozzo where without arms the old Alardo conquered; and one should show his limb pierced, and one cut off, there would be nought to match the foul fashion of the ninth pit. Never yet was a cask, through losing middle-piece or stave, so opened as I saw one, split from his chin even to the place where the wind comes out. Between his legs were hanging the entrails;

> Ciascun Pugliese, e là da Tagliacozzo
> Ove senz' arme vinse il vecchio Alardo:
> E qual forato suo membro, e qual mozzo
>   Mostrasse, da equar sarebbe nulla [b]   20
>   Al modo della nona bolgia sozzo.
> Già veggia per mezzul perdere o lulla,
>   Com' io vidi un, così non si pertugia,
>   Rotto dal mento infin dove si trulla:
> Tra le gambe pendevan le minugia;

[b] *d'agguagliar Crusc. and most modern edd.*

the Liris, at that part the frontier. On the approach of the enemy, the Count of Caserta first suggested to Giordano that some of them should be allowed to cross, so that they might be crushed in detail. When this had happened, he refused to attack, and withdrew with his Apulians, forcing Giordano and the Germans to retire also. It was supposed that his action was prompted by a private quarrel with Manfred (Vill. vii. 5). As a matter of fact, no lives were lost at Ceperano, and Dante has probably confused what happened there with the action at San Germano a few days later.

[17] The battle of Tagliacozzo (1268) was won mainly through the steadiness with which Charles, acting upon the advice of Alard de Valéry, kept his reserves in hand until Conradin's German and Spanish troops, who at the first onset had routed their opponents, were disordered by pursuit. On Charles showing his fresh troops, Conradin and the leaders fled almost without striking a blow (Vill. vii. 27).

[22] **mezzul**: the middle of the three pieces of which a cask-head is usually made.—**lulla** *lunula*) is one of the side-pieces, according to most commentators. Bargigi, however, takes it as 'doga alcuna,' and this gives a much better and more appropriate image.

the pluck appeared, and the sorry pouch, which makes dung of whatsoever is swallowed. While I was wholly fixed on seeing him he looked at me, and with his hands opened his breast, saying: 'Now look how I split myself, look how Mahommed has been mangled. In front of me Ali goes his way weeping, cloven in the face from the chin to the forelock. And all the others whom thou seest here were sowers of scandal and of schism in their life, and therefore are cloven thus. A devil is here behind who arranges us so cruelly, putting to the edge of

> La corata pareva, e il tristo sacco
>   Che merda fa di quel che si trangugia.
> Mentre che tutto in lui veder m' attacco,
>   Guardommi, e con le man s' aperse il petto,
>   Dicendo: Or vedi come io mi dilacco: 30
> Vedi come storpiato è Maometto.^c
>   Dinanzi a me sen va piangendo Ali
>   Fesso nel volto dal mento al ciuffetto:
> E tutti gli altri, che tu vedi qui,
>   Seminator di scandalo e di scisma
>   Fur vivi; e però son fessi così.
> Un diavolo è qua dietro che n' accisma
>   Sì crudelmente, al taglio della spada

^c *scoppiato* Land.

[34] As a matter of fact, Ali himself seems to have abstained from creating a schism, and allowed three caliphs to reign before claiming the succession to his father-in-law; but as the object of the special veneration of the schismatic Shiites he is regarded as their founder. The older commentators make him the teacher of Mahommed. Philalethes points out that he is less severely mangled than the founder of Islam, as having only caused a schism within a schism.

[37] Compare the punishment of the pandars in Canto xviii.

the sword again each one of this pack, when we have turned the woeful road; because the wounds are closed again before any one comes back in front of him. But who art thou that art musing upon the crag, perhaps through delaying to go to the punishment which has been adjudged upon thy crimes?'

'Death has not reached him yet, nor does fault bring him,' answered my Master, 'to torment him; but, to give him a full experience, me who am dead it behoves to bring him through Hell down here, from round to round, and this is true in such wise as I speak to thee.' More than a hundred were they who when they heard it stopped in the foss to look at me, through wonder forgetting the torture. 'Now say then to Fra Dolcino that he equip him-

> Rimettendo ciascun di questa risma,
> Quando avem volta la dolente strada; 40
> Perocchè le ferite son richiuse
> Prima ch' altri dinanzi gli rivada.
> Ma tu chi sei che in sullo scoglio muse,
> Forse per indugiar d' ire alla pena,
> Ch' è giudicata in sulle tue accuse?
> Nè morte il giunse ancor, nè colpa il mena,
> Rispose il mio Maestro, a tormentarlo;
> Ma per dar lui esperienza piena,
> A me, che morto son, convien menarlo
> Per lo inferno quaggiù di giro in giro: 50
> E questo è ver così com' io ti parlo.
> Più fur di cento che, quando l' udiro,
> S' arrestaron nel fosso a riguardarmi,
> Per maraviglia obbliando il martiro.
> Or di' a Fra Dolcin dunque che s' armi,

---

55 'Fra' Dolcino, so called because he was connected with a body

self, thou who perhaps wilt see the sun shortly, if he wishes
not quickly to follow me hither, with provisions in such
wise that strait of snow may not give the victory to him of
Novara; for otherwise to gain it would not be easy.' After
he had lifted one foot to go on his way Mahommed said
this word to me; then he laid it flat on the ground to
depart.

Another who had his throat pierced, and his nose cut

> Tu che forse vedrai lo sole in breve,
> S' egli non vuol qui tosto seguitarmi,
> Sì di vivanda, che stretta di neve
> Non rechi la vittoria al Noarese,
> Ch' altrimenti acquistar non saria lieve. 60
> Poi che l' un piè per girsene sospese,
> Maometto mi disse esta parola,
> Indi a partirsi in terra lo distese.
> Un altro, che forata avea la gola

known as the Apostolic Brothers, was born near Romagnano in Val
Sesia. He was one of the half-sincere, half-lawless fanatics who arose
frequently in the Middle Ages. He became famous about 1305 (though
his views as to the need of ecclesiastical reform had drawn the attention
of the clergy to him long before), when, at the head of some thousands
of followers, he occupied a strong position between Novara and Vercelli, and defied for a year all the efforts of the Church authorities of
those towns, aided by 'crusaders' from all parts, to dislodge him.
Finally he and his garrison were starved out, 'per difetta di vivanda, e
per le nevi che v' erano,' as Villani, copying Dante's words, puts it;
and he was put to death with every refinement of cruelty. 'Poterat
martyr dici, si poena faceret martyrium, et non voluntas,' says Benvenuto;
who, it may be added, having had special opportunities of getting
information, and not being in any marked way a clerical sympathiser,
confirms the reports as to the profligacy of Dolcino's teaching. Philalethes suggested that Mahommed's interest in him may be due to certain
points of similarity in their doctrines, particularly with regard to
women.

off even to beneath his brows, and had not more than one
ear only, having stayed to look, for wonder, with the others,
before the others opened his windpipe, which outwardly
was in every part crimson, and said: 'O thou, whom fault
condemns not, and whom I have seen up above on Latin
land, if much resemblance cheats me not, remember
thee of Peter of Medicina, if ever thou returnest to see the
sweet plain which slopes from Vercelli to Mercabò. And
do to wit the two best men of Fano, Messer Guido and

> E tronco il naso infin sotto le ciglia,
> E non avea ma ch' un' orecchia sola,
> Restato a riguardar per maraviglia
> > Con gli altri, innanzi agli altri aprì la canna
> > Ch' era di fuor d' ogni parte vermiglia:
> E disse: Tu cui colpa non condanna,   70
> > E cui io vidi su in terra Latina,
> > Se troppa simiglianza non m' inganna,
> Rimembriti di Pier da Medicina,
> > Se mai torni a veder lo dolce piano,
> > Che da Vercelli a Marcabò dichina.
> E fa saper ai due miglior di Fano,

[21] Perhaps *Ch' avea d. f. ogni*, i.e. had its inside out.

[73] This Peter belonged to Medicina, a small town near Bologna, and seems to have devoted his talents to keeping alive the strife between the houses of Polenta and Malatesta, by means of stealthy insinuations to each of mischief intended by the other. He belonged to the Cattani, the chief family of the place: by whom, says Benvenuto, Dante had once been hospitably entertained, which accounts for Peter's knowledge of him.

[75] Marcabò was a castle, built by the Venetians at the mouth of the Po, to hold the people of Ravenna in check, and was destroyed by the latter, after the victory of the Ferrarese over the former, in 1309. It marked the eastern, as Vercelli the western extremity of the Lombard plain.

[76] *sr.* Guido del Cassero and Angiolello da Carignano, two noblemen of Fano, were invited by the younger Malatesta to a conference at

also Angiolello, that if foresight here is not vain, they will be cast forth out of their vessel, and sunk near the Cattolica through treachery of a fell tyrant. Between the isle of Cyprus and Majorca never has Neptune seen so great a sin, not at the hand of pirates, not of Greek folk. That traitor who sees only with one eye, and holds the land whereof

> A messer Guido ed anco ad Angiolello,
> Che, se l' antiveder qui non è vano,
> Gittati saran fuor di lor vasello,
> E mazzerati presso alla Cattolica, 80
> Per tradimento d' un tiranno fello.
> Tra l' isola di Cipri e di Maiolica [d]
> Non vide mai sì gran fallo Nettuno,
> Non da pirati, non da gente Argolica.
> Quel traditor che vede pur con l' uno,
> E tien la terra, che tal è qui meco,

[d] *Cipro W.*

La Cattolica (a small town on the coast, where Romagna and the Marches meet, said to have been the refuge of the Catholic bishops who seceded from the Arian council of Rimini, A.D. 360), and by his orders drowned at sea off the promontory of Focara, as they were on their way to meet him.

82 From one end of the Mediterranean to the other.

84 **gente Argolica**: Benv. seems to see a special allusion to the Argonauts.

85 This Malatesta had lost an eye. He was half-brother to Gianciotto, the husband of Francesca, and to Paul, her lover.

86 **tal**. As will presently appear, this is Curio, who when Caesar was at Ariminum, after crossing the Rubicon, urged him to go on with his enterprise, as recorded in the first book of the Pharsalia. He 'wishes that he had never seen Rimini,' because it was there that he committed the sin for which he is punished. It is somewhat strange that Dante, while regarding Caesar as the divinely appointed chief of the Empire, should nevertheless treat as a crime the civil war which put

one is here with me would wish to be fasting from the sight, will make them come to a parley with him; then will he so do, that for the wind of Focara vow or prayer will not serve their turn.' And I to him: 'Show forth to me and declare, if thou wilt that I carry up news of thee, who is he to whom the sight was bitter.' Then laid he his hand upon the jaw of one his companion, and opened his mouth, crying: 'This is the very one, and he does not talk. This one, being banished, suppressed the doubt in Caesar, assuring him that the man who was prepared ever with harm endured delay.' O how abashed seemed to me,

>   Vorrebbe di vedere esser digiuno,
> Farà venirli a parlamento seco;
>   Poi farà sì, che al vento di Focara
>   Non farà lor mestier voto nè preco.   90
> Ed io a lui: Dimostrami e dichiara,
>   Se vuoi ch' io porti su di te novella,
>   Chi è colui dalla veduta amara.
> Allor pose la mano alla mascella
>   D' un suo compagno, e la bocca gli aperse
>   Gridando: Questi è desso, e non favella:
> Questi, scacciato, il dubitar sommerse
>   In Cesare, affermando che il fornito
>   Sempre con danno l' attender sofferse.
> O quanto mi pareva sbigottito   100

him in that position, and the incitement to it. Perhaps the fact that Curio had changed sides ('momentumque fuit mutatus Curio rerum') may have affected Dante's judgement of him.

⁹⁴ The squalls which came from the headland of Focara were thought especially dangerous. Benvenuto says that there was a proverb, 'Deus custodiat te a vento Focariensi!'

⁹⁸, ⁹⁹ 'Semper nocuit differre paratis.' Phars. i. 281.

his tongue cut off in his throat, Curio who was so bold to
speak! And one who had the one and the other hand
mutilated, lifting the stumps through the dim air, so that
the blood made his face foul, cried: 'Thou shalt recall too
Mosca, who said, alas! A thing done has an end; which
was a seed of woe for the Tuscan folk.' And I added
thereto: 'And death of thy stock'; wherefore he, heaping
woe on woe, went his way like a person sad and mad. But
I remained to look at the band, and saw a thing which I

   Con la lingua tagliata nella strozza,
  Curio, ch' a dire fu così ardito!
 Ed un ch' avea l' una e l' altra man mozza,
  Levando i moncherin per l' aura fosca,
  Sì che il sangue facea la faccia sozza,
 Gridò: Ricordera' ti anche del Mosca,
  Che dissi, lasso! Capo ha cosa fatta,
  Che fu mal seme per la gente tosca.
 Ed io gli aggiunsi: E morte di tua schiatta;
  Perch' egli accumulando duol con duolo,   110
  Sen gio come persona trista e matta.
 Ma io rimasi a riguardar lo stuolo,
  E vidi cosa ch' io avrei paura,

---

¹⁰² Perhaps with special allusion to Lucan's line: Audax venali
comitatur Curio lingua.

¹⁰⁶ Mosca de' Lamberti; see note Par. xvi. 133. 'Cosa fatta capo
ha' was the phrase which he used when suggesting the murder of Buondelmonte. With reference to the form of his punishment, it will be
remembered that a similar mutilation inflicted by one member of the
Cancellieri of Pistoia upon another, in the year 1300, was the immediate
cause which brought about the schism of the 'Black' and 'White'
parties. (Villani viii. 38.)

¹⁰⁹ The family of Lamberti seems to have become extinct before the
end of the 13th century.

113, 114 **che la.** Here *che* is clearly the relative, and *la* pleonastic.
See note v. 69.

should be afraid, without more proof, only to recount; if it were not that conscience secures me, the good consort which enfranchises a man, under the hauberk of the knowledge that it is pure. I saw of a certainty, and still it seems that I see it, a body without a head go as the rest of the sorry herd were going. And it held its head cut off, by the locks with its hand, dangling in the fashion of a lanthorn; and that was looking at us, and saying: 'O me!' Of itself it made a lamp to itself; and they were two in one and one in two; how it can be, He knows who so orders. When he was right at foot of the bridge, he lifted his arm

>   Senza più prova, di contarla solo;
> Se non che coscienza mi assicura,
>   La buona compagnia che l' uom francheggia
>   Sotto l' osbergo del sentirsi pura.
> Io vidi certo, ed ancor par ch' io il veggia,
>   Un busto senza capo andar, sì come
>   Andavan gli altri della trista greggia. 120
> E il capo tronco tenea per le chiome,
>   Pesol con mano a guisa di lanterna,
>   E quel mirava noi, e dicea: O me!
> Di sè faceva a sè stesso lucerna,
>   Ed eran due in uno, ed uno in due:
>   Com' esser può, quei sa che si governa.
> Quando diritto al piè del ponte fue.

[116] With **compagnia** for *compagno*, cf. *condotto* for *conduttore*, Purg. iv. 20, and words like *magistratus* in Latin, *justice* in English.

[117] Mr. Harrison, 'Oliver Cromwell,' p. 61, quotes from Whitelocke a passage which is a curious parallel to this. Speaking of Cromwell's men, he says: 'Thus being well armed within by the satisfaction of their own consciences . . . they would as one man stand firmly and charge desperately.'

on high, head and all, to bring his words near us, which were: 'Now see my baneful punishment, thou who breathing goest beholding the dead; see if any is great as this. And to the end that thou mayest bear news of me, know that I am Bertrand de Born, that man who gave the evil

> Levò il braccio alto con tutta la testa
>   Per appressarne le parole sue,
> Che furo: Or vedi la pena molesta   130
>   Tu che, spirando, vai veggendo i morti:
>   Vedi se alcuna è grande come questa;
> E perchè tu di me novella porti,
>   Sappi ch' io son Beltran dal Bornio, quelli
>   Che diedi al re giovane i mai conforti.ᶜ

   ᶜ *Giovanni* Gg. Cass. 12345 *Ald. W.*

¹³⁴ Bertrand de Born, lord of Hautefort in the Limousin, and one of the earliest troubadours, was born of a good family about 1140. His verse, which is remarkable for vigour and melody, deals mostly with political and martial subjects (cf. Vulg. El. ii. 2). He is praised in Conv. iv. 11. The charge that he stirred up the 'Young King,' Henry son of Henry II., Duke of Aquitaine and King of England, to rise against his father, is not borne out to any great extent by his poems. Indeed, none of the poems which we have seems to refer to the principal struggle between the father and the son (1172-1175); and though he celebrates the outbreak of 1183, it is against Richard rather than against their father that his fiercest attacks are directed. After the death of the younger Henry in the same year, it was from the father that he obtained redress for injuries done him by Richard. He seems to have lived for the future on fairly good terms with both, though his love, not so much of fighting as of cheering others on to fight, led him to exult in every prospect of a war, whether between Richard and Henry, or between the latter and Philip Augustus. He ended his days as a Cistercian monk, some time before 1215. (See 'Poésies Complètes de B. de B.' ed. A. Thomas.)

¹³⁵ The MSS. in the proportion of about ten to one, and all the earlier edd. and comm. read *Giovanni*, and Villani (v. 4) also makes *Giovanni* the name of Henry's elder son, some of them, e.g. Benvenuto,

support to the young king. I set the father and the son at war together; Ahithophel did no more for Absalom and David with his wicked incitements. Because I parted persons thus united I carry my brain, alas! parted from its origin, which is in this trunk. So is observed in me the retaliation.'

> Io feci il padre e il figlio in sè ribelli:
>   Achitofel non fe più d' Ansalone
>   E di David coi malvagi pungelli.
> Perch' io partii così giunte persone,
>   Partito porto il mio cerebro, lasso!   140
>   Dal suo principio ch' è in questo troncone.
> Così s' osserva in me lo contrapasso.

adding words to the effect that *John* was called 'the young king.' Dr. Moore has discussed the point very fully in his 'Textual Criticism,' and I so far agree with him as to think it probable that both readings may have existed in the autographs. But I feel pretty sure that if it was so, Dante wrote originally *Giovanni*, and later (perhaps as a result of reading Bertrand's poems) got the name right. There is no reason to think that his knowledge of the history of the 12th century was any better than Villani's, nor have we any evidence that he had read Bertrand's poems till long after this Canto was written. I have, however, given him the benefit of the doubt.

[141] **principio**: the heart, which is the origin of all other organs. Cf. Purg. xxv. 59, 60.

[142] I.e. 'in me is illustrated the law of τὸ ἀντιπεπονθός.' Ar. Eth. v. 5. S. T. ii. 2. Q. 61. A. 4: hoc quod dicitur contrapassum, importat aequalem recompensationem passionis ad actionem praecedentem.

CANTO XXIX

ARGUMENT

They come to the last of the pits, wherein are folk labouring under grievous and foul disorders. Dante speaks with two from Tuscany, who on earth were noted alchemists.

THE multitude of folk and their divers wounds had made my eyes so dizzy, that they were fain of staying to weep. But Virgil said to me: 'What still dost watch? Why is thy view stayed only down there among the sorry mutilated shades? Thou didst not do so at the other pits. Consider, if thou thinkest to count them, that the valley goes twenty-

> La molta gente e le diverse piaghe
>   Avean le luci mie sì inebriate,
>   Che dello stare a piangere eran vaghe:
> Ma Virgilio mi disse: Che pur guate?
>   Perchè la vista tua pur si soffolge
>   Laggiù tra l' ombre triste smozzicate?
> Tu non hai fatto sì all' altre bolge:
>   Pensa, se tu annoverar le credi,
>   Che miglia ventidue la valle volge:

⁹ For the first time Dante gives us a precise measurement. The number 22 is no doubt selected in order to bring the diameter to an exact number of miles, 22 : 7 being the accepted ratio between circumference and diameter. In the Trésor, Brunetto puts it at about 3 : 1, but the Italian translation, which was made not long after the appearance of the work itself, states it more precisely at 'six times the radius

two miles round, and by this the moon is beneath our feet. The time is little which henceforth is allowed to us, and there is else to see than thou seest.' 'If thou hadst,' answered I straightway, 'given heed to the reason for which I was gazing, perhaps thou wouldest yet have excused my stay.' My Leader meanwhile was going on, and I was going behind him already as I was making my answer, and subjoining: 'Within that hollow where I was keeping my

> E già la luna è sotto i nostri piedi: 10
>   Lo tempo è poco omai che n' è concesso,
>   Ed altro è da veder che tu non vedi.
> Se tu avessi, rispos' io appresso,
>   Atteso alla cagion perch' io guardava,
>   Forse m' avresti ancor lo star dimesso.
> Parte sen gia, ed io retro gli andava,
>   Lo Duca, già facendo la risposta,
>   E soggiungendo: Dentro a quella cava,
> Dov' io teneva or gli occhi sì a posta,

one-seventh of the diameter.' Dante's contemporary, Cecco d' Ascoli, also gives this proportion in his Treatise on the Sphere, so it was evidently well known. Philalethes, in a note to l. 87 of the next Canto, takes the highly probable view that the whole of Malebolge is to be reckoned on the same scale, which would give us a total of 35 miles for its width. (He adds something for the pit of the ninth circle, but we may consider that as bored out of the 'core' of the last *bolgia*.) The only objection to this is, that a *bolgia* being, as we gather from xxx. 87, half a mile wide, the intervening walls would have a thickness of 1¾ miles, giving a more appreciable distance than anything in the text (except perhaps l. 37 below) seems to indicate between one *bolgia* and the next. It adds, however, considerably to the interest of the scene at the beginning of Canto xxiii. if we suppose them to have had some distance of rough ground to cross before they were out of the demons' power.

That is, it is about 1¼ hours past noon; the moon being two days past the full.

parte: see Purg. xxi. 19.

eyes so on guard, I believe that a spirit of my race is weeping the sin which down here is so costly.' Then said the Master: 'Let not thy thought henceforth break on him; give heed to somewhat else, and let him remain there. For I saw him at the foot of the bridge point thee out, and menace greatly with his finger, and I heard name him Geri, son of Bello. Thou wast then so wholly fettered upon him who once held Hautefort, that thou didst not look that way; so he was gone.' 'O Leader mine, the violent death which is not yet avenged for him,' said I, 'by any one who is a partner in the disgrace, made him disdainful; wherefore he

> Credo che un spirto del mio sangue pianga 20
> La colpa che laggiù cotanto costa.
> Allor disse il Maestro: Non si franga
> Lo tuo pensier da qui innanzi sopr' ello:
> Attendi ad altro, ed ei là si rimanga;
> Ch' io vidi lui a piè del ponticello
> Mostrarti, e minacciar forte col dito,
> Ed udi 'l nominar Geri del Bello.
> Tu eri allor sì del tutto impedito
> Sopra colui che già tenne Altaforte,
> Che non guardasti in là; sì fu partito. 30
> O Duca mio, la violenta morte
> Che non gli è vendicata ancor, diss' io,
> Per alcun che dell' onta sia consorte,
> Fece lui disdegnoso; ond' ei sen gio

[22] **non si franga**: idest, non fatigetur.—Benv.

[27] Geri, son of Bello degli Alighieri, was first cousin to Dante's grandfather. He is said to have been a quarrelsome and turbulent person, and to have been slain by one of the Sacchetti, rather less than thirty years before this date. The vengeance was taken soon after this by his nephew.

[33] **sia**: the subjunctive, because there is a causal connection between relationship and the duty of vengeance.

went his way without speaking to me, as I judge; and therein has he made me more pitiful towards him.' Thus talked we as far as the first place which from the crag shows the next valley, if there had been more light, all to the bottom. When we were above the last cloister of Malebolge so that its brethren could appear to our view, divers laments smote me as arrows which had their shafts tipped with pity; wherefore I covered my ears with my hands.

Such woe as would be if of the spitals of Valdichiana

  Senza parlarmi, sì com' io stimo;
  Ed in ciò m' ha e' fatto a sè più pio.
Così parlammo infino al loco primo
  Che dello scoglio l' altra valle mostra,
  Se più lume vi fosse, tutto ad imo.
Quando noi fummo in sull' ultima chiostra   40
  Di Malebolge, sì che i suoi conversi
  Potean parere alla veduta nostra,
Lamenti saettaron me diversi,[a]
  Che di pietà ferrati avean gli strali:[b]
  Ond' io gli orecchi colle man copersi.
Qual dolor fora, se degli spedali[c]

[a] *La mente Gg.* (2); *me lor versi Gg.* (2) *Benv.*
[b] *di pietra Cass.: feruti* 2.
[c] *Qual d. esse fuor Gg. Benv.*

40 **chiostra**: cf. Purg. vii. 21.

41 **conversi**: lay-brethren. (The monks, Philalethes suggests, would be represented by the devils.) In this last *bolgia* are punished all kinds of falsifiers, such as coiners, impostors, alchemists, false-witnesses, etc.

43 Benvenuto has a curious variant: *la mente saettaron me lor versi*; *versi* being taken much as in xvi. 20. The text of 'Gg.,' to which, as I have mentioned elsewhere, a later hand has appended copious extracts from his commentary, has been altered to agree with his reading.

46 spr. The Chiana (Par. xiii. 23) flows southward from near Arezzo,

from July to September, and of Maremma and of Sardinia, the sick were in one foss all together—such was it there; and such a stench issued therefrom as is wont to come from their withered limbs. We descended upon the last bank from the long crag, ever to the left hand; and then was my view quicker downward toward the bottom, where the handmaid of the Lord on high, justice that cannot err, punishes the counterfeiters whom here it registers.

I do not believe that it was greater sadness to behold in

> Di Valdichiana tra luglio e il settembre,
> E di Maremma e di Sardigna i mali
> Fossero in una fossa tutti insembre;
> Tal era quivi, e tal puzzo n' usciva,   50
> Qual suol venir delle marcite membre.
> Noi discendemmo in sull' ultima riva
> Del lungo scoglio, pur da man sinistra,
> Ed allor fu la mia vista più viva
> Giù ver lo fondo, là 've la ministra
> Dell' alto Sire, infallibil giustizia,
> Punisce i falsator che qui registra.
> Non credo che a veder maggior tristizia

and joins the Tiber, or rather its tributary the Paglia, a little north of Orvieto. Witte says, on what authority does not appear, that it communicated at one time also with the Arno. In any case, the silting up of its bed rendered the whole valley swampy, and a byword for unhealthiness, till it was drained by a Grand Duke of Tuscany in the present century. Since then it has been remarkable for its fertility. There was a great hospital for fever patients at Altopasso.

49 The Maremma, or coast-land of Tuscany, and the lowlands of Sardinia have still a bad reputation for malaria.

58, 59 In strict syntax, **popol** must be the subject to **fosse**; **tristizia** being predicate. 'The sick folk was not a greater sadness (i.e. a sadder thing) to behold.' The implied adjective in **tristizia** would properly take **a**; as *caro a veder* (Purg. x. 99), *mirabile a veder* (Par. xxii. 96).

Aegina the people all ailing, when the air was so full of mischief that the animals, down to the small worm, all fell dead, and afterward the ancient folk, according as the poets hold for certain, were restored from seed of ants, than it was to behold throughout that gloomy vale the spirits languishing by divers heaps. One on his belly, and one on the shoulders of another they were lying; and one would shift himself groveling along the sorry path. Step by step we went on, without converse, looking at and listening to

> Fosse in Egina il popol tutto infermo,
>   Quando fu l' aer sì pien di malizia,   60
> Che gli animali infino al picciol vermo
>   Cascaron tutti, e poi le genti antiche,
>   Secondo che i poeti hanno per fermo,
> Si ristorar di seme di formiche;
>   Ch' era a veder per quella oscura valle
>   Languir gli spirti per diverse biche.
> Qual sopra il ventre, e qual sopra le spalle
>   L' un dell' altro giacea, e qual carpone
>   Si trasmutava per lo tristo calle.
> Passo passo andavam senza sermone,   70
>   Guardando ed ascoltando gli ammalati,

For the story of the devastation of Aegina by a plague, and its subsequent repeopling by the metamorphosis of ants into men (afterwards called Myrmidons), see Ov. Met. vii. 523 sqq.

⁶⁸ We should rather expect *giacean*. The singular is no doubt common enough after two nouns connected by *e*; but the verb must be taken here to refer to the spirits generally, the **qual - qual** only introducing specimens of their attitudes. None of Dr. Moore's MSS., however, appears to show any variant.—Some of the commentators rather whimsically see an allusion in this description to the ailments brought by the inhalation of poisonous fumes to which alchemists would be specially liable; but there is nothing to show that these only are intended, or that the various kinds of *falsatori* are kept apart from each other.

the afflicted ones, who were not able to lift up their frames.
I saw two sit propped on each other, as tile is propped on
tile to burn, from the head to the feet flecked with scabs;
and never saw I a currycomb wielded by a lad awaited of his
master, nor by one who against his will is staying awake, in
such wise as each was incessantly wielding the scrape of his
nails over himself, by reason of the great rage of the itching
which has no other refuge. And so the nails were drawing
down the scurf as a knife does the scales of a bream, or of
any fish which has them broadest.

  Che non potean levar le lor persone.
Io vidi due sedere a sè poggiati,
  Come a scaldar si poggia tegghia a tegghia,
  Dal capo al piè di schianze maculati:
E non vidi giammai menare stregghia
  Da ragazzo aspettato dal signorso,
  Nè da colui che mal volentier veggia;
Come ciascun menava spesso il morso
  Dell' unghie sopra sè per la gran rabbia   80
  Del pizzicor, che non ha più soccorso.
E sì traevan giù l' unghie la scabbia,
  Come coltel di scardova le scaglie,
  O d' altro pesce che più larghe l' abbia.

 74-83 Note the constant repetition of the sound *sc* in these ten lines.

 77 **signorso**. For this enclitic form of the possessive pronoun, peculiar to Italian, see Diez ii. 81. So we find in Sacchetti *mogliata*.

 78 I.e. who is in a hurry to get to bed. So the usual interpretation; but may not Dante, forgetting that the actual subject of his simile is the use of the *currycomb*, be thinking of the irritation which is apt to accompany sleeplessness?

 83 **scardova**: I have followed Longfellow and Philalethes. Crescentius mentions *scardoni* with *barbi* (barbel) as good fish to put into fish-ponds.

'O thou who with thy fingers are dismailing thyself,' began my Leader to one of them, 'and who makest of them at whiles pincers, tell us if any Latin is among those who are here within; so may thy nails suffice eternally to this task.' 'Latin are we whom thou seest thus despoiled here, both of us,' answered the one, weeping; 'but who art thou that inquirest of us?' And the Leader said: 'I am one who descend with this living man down from gallery to gallery, and I purpose to show Hell to him.' Then did their mutual support break, and trembling each turned him toward me, with others who overheard it by repetition. The good Master gathered himself wholly to me, saying: 'Say

> O tu che colle dita ti dismaglie,
>   Cominciò il Duca mio all' un di loro,
>   E che fai d' esse tal volta tanaglie,
> Dinne s' alcun Latino è tra costoro
>   Che son quinc' entro, se l' unghia ti basti
>   Eternalmente a cotesto lavoro.   90
> Latin sem noi, che tu vedi sì guasti
>   Qui ambo e due, rispose l' un piangendo:
>   Ma tu chi sei, che di noi domandasti?
> E il Duca disse: Io son un che discendo
>   Con questo vivo giù di balzo in balzo,
>   E di mostrar l' inferno a lui intendo.
> Allor si ruppe lo comun rincalzo:
>   E tremando ciascuno a me si volse
>   Con altri che l' udiron di rimbalzo.
> Lo buon Maestro a me tutto s' accolse,   100

A horribly comic touch which is truly Dantesque.

I.e. they started apart, having been leaning against each other, l. 74.

udiron di rimbalzo: lit. 'heard it on the rebound.'

The use of *accogliersi*, of one person only, is curious. The idea.

to them what thou wilt.' And I began, since he was willing: 'So may memory of you not be stolen away in the former world from the minds of men, but may it live under many suns, tell me who you are, and of what folk; let not your unseemly and loathsome punishment frighten you from making you known to me.' 'I was of Arezzo, and Albero of Siena,' replied one, 'had me put to the fire; but that for which I died brings me not here. True is it that I said to him, talking in jest, I should know how to raise myself in the air in flight; and he who had desire and little sense, would that I should show him the art; and only because I

> Dicendo: Di' a lor ciò che tu vuoli.
> Ed io incominciai, poscia ch' ei volse:
> Se la vostra memoria non s' imboli
> Nel primo mondo dall' umane menti,
> Ma s' ella viva sotto molti soli,
> Ditemi chi voi siete e di che genti:
> La vostra sconcia e fastidiosa pena
> Di palesarvi a me non vi spaventi.
> Io fui d' Arezzo, ed Albero da Siena,
> Rispose l' un, mi fe mettere al foco;
> Ma quel perch' io mori' qui non mi mena.
> Ver è ch' io dissi a lui, parlando a gioco,
> Io mi saprei levar per l' aere a volo:
> E quei che avea vaghezza e senno poco,
> Volle ch' io gli mostrassi l' arte; e solo

no doubt, is 'concentrated all his attention' or 'faculties.' (Cf. Purg. iv. 1 sqq.)

[109] This is said to be one Grifolino, who, having promised to teach Albero, son of the Bishop of Siena, to fly, and failing to do so, was burnt by the bishop on a charge of heresy, or magic.

did it not, a Daedalus, he made one who held him for son burn me. But to the last pit of the ten, for alchemy which I practised in the world, Minos condemned me, to whom it is not permitted to err.' And I said to the Poet: 'Now was ever a folk so vain as the Sienese? Certainly not so the French by far.' Wherefore the other leprous one, who heard me, answered to my speech: 'Except me Stricca, who knew how to make his expenses moderate; and Nicholas,

> Perch' io nol feci Dedalo, mi fece
>   Ardere a tal, che l' avea per figliuolo.
> Ma nell' ultima bolgia delle dieee
>   Me per alchimia che nel mondo usai,
>   Dannò Minos, a cui fallar non lece.   120
> Ed io dissi al Poeta: Or fu giammai
>   Gente sì vana come la sanese?
>   Certo non la francesca sì d' assai.
> Onde l' altro lebbroso che m' intese,
>   Rispose al detto mio: Trammene Stricca,
>   Che seppe far le temperate spese;
> E Niccolò, che la costuma ricca

---

[122] **vana** has a wider sense than our 'vain': 'empty-headed' or 'futile.' For its application to the Sienese cf. Purg. xiii. 151.

[123] Benvenuto has a little fling on his own account here at the habits and language of the French, and those in Italy who imitated them. He adds that there can hardly be any confusion, as some have thought, between Siena (Sena Julia) and Sinigaglia (Sena Gallica).

[125] A touch of irony, like the exception of Bonturo in xxi. 41.—Of Stricca nothing further appears to be known. Bianchi hears that he belonged to the Marescotti family; others otherwise.

[126] **le temperate spese**: for the order of the words cf. *il buon mondo*, Purg. xvi. 106.

[127] Niccolò de' Bonsignori is said to have roasted birds over a fire made of cloves.

who first discovered the rich fashion of the clove in the garden where such seed takes root; and except the gang in which Caccia of Asciano wasted his vineyard and his great wood, and Abbagliato set forth his own wisdom. But that thou mayest know who so backs thee against the Sienese, make thy eye keen toward me, so that my face may well make answer to thee; so wilt thou see that I am the shade of Capocchio, who falsified the metals by alchemy; and

> Del garofano prima discoperse
> Nell' orto, dove tal seme s' appicca:
> E tranne la brigata, in che disperse 130
> Caccia d' Ascian la vigna e la gran fronda,
> E l' Abbagliato il suo senno proferse.
> Ma perchè sappi chi sì ti seconda
> Contra i Sanesi, aguzza ver me l' occhio
> Sì, che la faccia mia ben ti risponda;
> Sì vedrai ch' io son l' ombra di Capocchio,
> Che falsai li metalli con alchimia,

130 **la brigata** sc. *spendereccia*. See note xiii. 120. They were, says Benv., a set of twelve young men, who managed to get through 216,000 florins in twenty months in fast living of all kinds. Two pleasant songs, he adds, were composed, relating their first and last state.

132 **Abbagliato** is generally taken as a nickname, the bearer of which is said to be one of the Folcachieri; or by others, the well-known poet Folgore da San Geminiano. Many MSS. and commentators, however, —among the latter Benvenuto—omitting **il**, treat **abbagliato** as an adjective, rendering 'and displayed his own muddled wits,' which seems almost preferable.

136 Capocchio was a Florentine artist who, according to some authorities, was burnt at Siena as an alchemist. Scartazzini gives documentary evidence, placing the date in 1293. Benvenuto relates that one Good Friday he depicted the story of the Passion on his fingernails, and then licked it off again; for which waste of his talents he was much reproved by Dante.

137 For the sin of alchemy, P. di Dante gives a reference to

thou oughtest to remember, if I eye thee aright, how I was a good ape of nature.'

> E ti dei ricordar, se ben t' adocchio,
> Com' io fui di natura buona scimia.

Aquinas, which is not to be found. As a matter of fact, St. Thomas holds (ii. 2. Q. 77. A. 2.) that there is no harm in dealing in gold produced by alchemy, if it be genuine.

CANTO XXX

ARGUMENT

They find that the pit contains all manner of counterfeiters; namely, such as have for wicked ends feigned to be other than themselves—false coiners, perjurers, and such like; who are punished with madness and sundry loathsome diseases. They speak with Master Adam; and the author, being intent on watching a quarrel, is reproved by Virgil.

In the time when Juno was wroth for Semele's sake against the Theban race, as she made manifest one and another time, Athamas became so mad that, seeing his wife with her two sons go, burthened on either hand, he cried: 'Let us stretch the nets, so that I may take the lioness and the lion-

> Nel tempo che Giunone era crucciata
> Per Semelè contra il sangue tebano,
> Come mostrò una ed altra fiata,
> Atamante divenne tanto insano,
> Che veggendo la moglie con due figli
> Andar carcata da ciascuna mano,
> Gridò: Tendiam le reti, sì ch' io pigli

---

[1] sqq. The story will be found in Ov. Met. iv. 420 sqq. Ino, sister of Semele, and wife of Athamas, brought up her nephew Bacchus, and thus incurred the anger of Juno.

[3] As when she caused Agave to murder her son Pentheus. See Met. iii. ad fin.

[7] Ov. Met. iv. 513 sqq.:

> Clamat, Io comites, his retia tendite silvis:
> Hic modo cum gemina visa est mihi prole leaena.

cubs in their passage;' and then stretched forth his pitiless claws, seizing one who had the name Learchus, and swung him and dashed him on a rock; and she drowned herself with her other burthen. And when fortune turned to abasement the haughtiness of the Trojans, which dared all things, so that together with his kingdom their king was brought to nought, Hecuba, sad, wretched, and captive, after that she had seen Polyxena dead, and of her Polydorus on the seashore was aware, the woeful one, being out of her wits, barked like a dog; so did her woe set her mind awry. But

> La leonessa e i leoncini al varco:
> E poi distese i dispietati artigli,
> Prendendo l' un che avea nome Learco,   10
> E rotollo, e percosselo ad un sasso;
> E quella s' annegò con l' altro carco.
> E quando la fortuna volse in basso
> L' altezza dei Troian che tutto ardiva,
> Sì che insieme col regno il re fu casso;
> Ecuba trista misera e cattiva,
> Poscia che vide Polissena morta,
> E del suo Polidoro in sulla riva
> Del mar si fu la dolorosa accorta,
> Forsennata latrò sì come cane;   20
> Tanto il dolor le fe la mente torta.

> Utque ferae sequitur vestigia conjugis amens;
> Deque sinu matris ridentem et parva Learchum
> Bracchia tendentem rapit, et bis terque per auras
> More rotat fundae, etc.

Then Ino leaps into the sea with her other son Melicerta.

[13 sqq.] See Ov. Met. xiii. 403-570. Several phrases are copied: e.g. l. 403: Troja simul Priamusque cadunt; l. 407: Ilion ardebat (did Dante connect *ardire* and *ardere*?); l. 535: Polydori in litore corpus.

furies neither of Thebes nor of Troy were ever seen so cruel in any, not to wound beasts, let alone human members, as I beheld in two shades, pallid and naked, who were running, biting in such manner as the boar when he is let out from the stye. One came to Capocchio and gored him upon the nape of the neck, so that, dragging, he made him scrape his belly on the hard ground. And the Aretine, who remained trembling, said to me: 'That mad imp is Gianni Schicchi, and he goes in his rage trimming others in such

> Ma nè di Tebe furie nè Troiane
> > Si vider mai in alcun tanto crude,
> > Non punger bestie, non che membra umane,
> Quant' io vidi in due ombre smorte e nude,
> > Che mordendo correvan di quel modo
> > Che il porco quando del porcil si schiude.
> L' una giunse a Capocchio, ed in sul nodo
> > Del collo l' assannò sì che, tirando,
> > Grattar gli fece il ventre al fondo sodo. 30
> E l' Aretin, che rimase tremando,
> > Mi disse: Quel folletto è Gianni Schicchi,
> > E va rabbioso altrui così conciando.

[24] **non punger**: idest, ad pungendum.—Benv. So Witte, Scartazzini, and Philalethes understand **si vider** to be repeated: 'never were seen beasts so wounded,' etc.

[32] Gianni Schicchi, of the Cavalcante family, had a remarkable gift of mimicry. He used this on one occasion, at the instance of one Simone, nephew of Buoso de' Donati (whom we have already met in Canto xxv. among the thieves), in order to secure to him Buoso's inheritance, there being reason to fear that he would leave his money to charitable institutions. As P. di Dante tells the tale, they first smothered Buoso, then Gianni took his place in the bed, and dictated such a will as Simone desired to the attendant notary, bequeathing to himself, as his commission on the transaction, a favourite mare (or, according to some authorities, she-mule) of Buoso's, famous for her beauty.

wise.' 'O,' said I to him, 'so may the other not fix his teeth on thy back, be it no weariness to thee to say who it is, before it flits from here.' And he to me: 'That is the ancient soul of Myrrha, accursed, who became dear to her father beyond lawful love. Thus came she to sin with him, dissembling herself in another's likeness; just as the other who goes his way yonder dared, in order to gain the lady of the stud, in his own person to simulate Buoso Donati, making a will, and giving to the will due form.' And after the two rabid ones were gone by, upon whom I had my

> O, diss' io lui, se l' altro non ti ficchi
>   Li denti addosso, non ti sia fatica
>   A dir chi è, pria che di qui si spicchi.
> Ed egli a me: Quell' è l' anima antica
>   Di Mirra scellerata, che divenne
>   Al padre, fuor del dritto amore, amica.
> Questa a peccar con esso così venne,   40
>   Falsificando sè in altrui forma,
>   Come l' altro, che là sen va, sostenne,
> Per guadagnar la donna della torma,
>   Falsificare in sè Buoso Donati,
>   Testando, e dando al testamento norma.
> E poi che i due rabbiosi fur passati,
>   Sopra cu' io avea l' occhio tenuto,

---

[*] The story of Myrrha (not a pleasant one) is told in Ov. Met. x. Dante refers to it again in the Letter to Henry of Luxemburg, § 7, where he uses it to illustrate his opinion of Florence.

41. "The apparent antithesis in these lines is hardly borne out by the sense: for both Myrrha and Gianni Schicchi counterfeited another person. Nor does Scartazzini's suggestion that while he pretended to be a particular person, she merely feigned to be not herself, make the case much better.

eye fixed, I turned it back to watch the others born to ill.
I saw one fashioned in shape of a lute, had he only had the
groin cut away in the quarter which man has forked. The
grievous dropsy which so unmates the limbs with the
humour which turns to bane, that the face does not correspond
to the paunch, made him hold his lips open as the
hectic does, that through thirst the one is turned towards
the chin, and the other upward.

'O ye, who without any penalty are (and I know not
wherefore) in the grim world,' said he to us, 'look and give
heed to the wretchedness of Master Adam. Living, I had

  Rivolsilo a guardar gli altri mal nati.
Io vidi un, fatto a guisa di liuto,
  Pur ch' egli avesse avuta l' anguinaia   50
  Tronca dal lato, che l' uomo ha forcuto.
La grave idropisì, che sì dispaia
  Le membra con l' umor che mal converte,
  Che il viso non risponde alla ventraia,
Faceva a lui tener le labbra aperte,
  Come l' etico fa, che per la sete
  L' un verso il mento e l' altro in su riverte.
O voi, che senza alcuna pena siete
  (E non so io perchè) nel mondo gramo,
  Diss' egli a noi, guardate ed attendete   60
Alla miseria del maestro Adamo:

"Adam of Brescia, a famous moneyer, was employed by the commonwealth of Florence to coin their gold florins. (Doubtless he was introduced by his fellow-townsman Filippo degli Ugoni, who was Podestà in 1252, when the gold florin was first struck.—Vill. v. 52.) The Counts of Romena, of the family of the Conti Guidi, induced him to manufacture coin containing one-eighth of alloy; and when he was detected, in 1281, the Florentines, jealous of the purity of their coinage, which had become a standard for the whole world, burnt him on the road to the Casentino, where the crime had been committed. St.

enough of that which I would, and now, alas! I crave a drop of water. The little brooks which from the green hills of the Casentino come down into Arno, making their channels cool and soft, ever stand before me, and not in vain; for their image parches me far more than the trouble by reason of which I am fleshless in the face. The unbending justice which goads me, draws occasion from the place where I sinned, to set my sighs flying the more. There is Romena, the place where I falsified the currency stamped with the Baptist, wherefore I left my body above

> Io ebbi, vivo, assai di quel ch' io volli,
> Ed ora, lasso! un gocciol d' acqua bramo.
> Li ruscelletti, che dei verdi colli
> Del Casentin discendon giuso in Arno,
> Facendo i lor canali freddi e molli,
> Sempre mi stanno innanzi, e non indarno;
> Chè l' imagine lor vie più m' asciuga,
> Che il male ond' io nel volto mi discarno.
> La rigida giustizia, che mi fruga, 70
> Tragge cagion del loco ov' io peccai,
> A metter più li miei sospiri in fuga.
> Ivi è Romena, là dov' io falsai
> La lega suggellata del Batista,
> Perch' io il corpo su arso lasciai.

Thomas appears only to mention the crime of coining in order to illustrate the lawfulness of putting heretics to death. 'Multo gravius,' he says (ii. 2. Q. 11. A. 3.), 'est corrumpere fidem, quam falsare pecuniam.'

[71] **Romena**: a castle in the Casentino, or upper Vale of Arno, on the road from Pratovecchio to Florence.

[74] **lega**: here in its original sense of *lawful* coin. When the addition of a certain proportion of inferior metal was found necessary, and fixed by law, it got the meaning of 'alloy,' as Par. ii. 139.—**il Batista**: cf. Par. xviii. 134.

burned. But if I might see here the sorry soul of Guy, or of Alexander, or of their brother, I would not give the sight for Branda spring. Within here is one already, if the raging shades that go about speak true; but what profits it me, who have my limbs bound? If I were yet only nimble so far that I could in a hundred years go an inch, I would ere this have set out along the road, seeking him among this

> Ma s' io vedessi qui l' anima trista
>   Di Guido, o d' Alessandro, o di lor frate,
>   Per fonte Branda non darei la vista.
> Dentro c' è l' una già, se l' arrabbiate
>   Ombre che van dintorno dicon vero :   80
>   Ma che mi val, ch' ho le membra legate?
> S' io fossi pur di tanto ancor leggiero,
>   Ch' io potessi in cent' anni andare un' oncia,
>   Io sarei messo già per lo sentiero,
> Cercando lui tra questa gente sconcia,

[77] The third brother was named Aghinolfo. They were great-grandsons of the original Guido, who married the 'good Gualdrada,' and their father was first cousin to Guido Guerra (xvi. 38).

[78] **Fonte Branda** is generally taken to mean the celebrated spring of that name at Siena. It seems, however, that another spring of the same name formerly existed near Romena, and it is possible that Bianchi and Scartazzini are right in supposing the allusion to be to this.

[79] **l' una.** It is unknown which of the brothers is here intended. Aghinolfo, it appears, is known to have died early in 1300 (but would not this, in any case, be *after* the date of Dante's journey, according to the old calendar?), while Alessandro seems to have lived till later. But there is much uncertainty as to all of them. The curious point is that Dante was on friendly terms during his exile with the Counts of Romena. We have, however, plenty of instances in which private friendship does not hinder him from branding misdeeds.

[83] **oncia.** Uncia Florentiae appellatur latitudo digiti grossi.—Benv. Our 'inch' is of course the same word.

deformed folk, albeit that it goes eleven miles about, and has not here less than half a mile of cross-measure. Through them I am among a household of such fashion; they led me on to strike the florins which had three carats of dross.'

And I to him: 'Who are the two lying low, who smoke like wetted hands in winter, lying hard by thy right-hand boundary?' 'I found them here, and since have they not turned,' he answered, 'when I dropped into this pot; and I do not think they will turn to all eternity. One is the liar who accused Joseph, the other is the lying Greek Sinon

> Con tutto ch' ella volge undici miglia,
> E men d' un mezzo di traverso non ci ha.
> Io son per lor tra sì fatta famiglia:
> Ei m' indussero a battere i fiorini,
> Che avean tre carati di mondiglia.
> Ed io a lui: Chi son li due tapini,
> Che fuman come man bagnate il verno,
> Giacendo stretti ai tuoi destri confini?
> Qui li trovai, e poi volta non dierno,
> Rispose, quand' io piovvi in questo greppo,
> E non credo che dieno in sempiterno.
> L' una è la falsa che accusò Joseppo:
> L' altro è il falso Sinon greco da Troia:

90

---

⁸⁶,⁸⁷ See note xxix. 9.

⁸⁹ **mondiglia**: strictly that which cleaning removes. Cf. Gr. καθάρμα.

⁹⁵ **greppo**: according to Benvenuto, a Florentine word for a damaged earthenware vessel, such as fowls might feed from. So Vellutello. Others say the side of a ditch.

⁹⁷ Potiphar's wife; introduced as a typical false-witness.

⁹⁸ Sinon belongs rather to the same class as Gianni Schicchi. He did not actually feign to be another person, but he described his position falsely. See Aen. ii. 57 sqq.

from Troy; through sharp fever they cast such a reek.' And the one of them who took in ill part, perhaps, to be so darkly named, with his fist smote him on the leathery paunch, that sounded as it had been a drum; and Master Adam smote him on the face with his arm, which seemed not less hard, saying to him: 'Even if I be deprived of my movement through my limbs, for they are heavy, I have an arm free for such office.' Wherefore he answered: 'When thou wast going to the fire, thou hadst it not so ready; but so and more thou hadst it when thou wast coining.' And the dropsical: 'Thou sayest true of this; but thou wast not so true evidence where thou wast asked of the truth at

>   Per febbre acuta gittan tanto leppo.
> E l' un di lor, che si recò a noia   100
>   Forse d' esser nomato sì oscuro,
>   Col pugno gli percosse l' epa croia:
> Quella sonò, come fosse un tamburo:
>   E mastro Adamo gli percosse il volto
>   Col braccio suo che non parve men duro,
> Dicendo a lui: Ancor che mi sia tolto
>   Lo mover per le membra, che son gravi,
>   Ho io il braccio a tal mestiere sciolto.
> Ond' ei rispose: Quando tu andavi
>   Al foco, non l' avei tu così presto;   110
>   Ma sì e più l' avei quando coniavi.
> E l' idropico: Tu di' ver di questo:
>   Ma tu non fosti sì ver testimonio,
>   Là 've del ver a Troia fosti richiesto.

---

¹² **croia**: see Glossary.
¹⁰⁷ Witte puts the comma at **muover**; but in that case we should surely require *che sian*, of which no trace appears in MSS.

Troy.' 'If I said false, so didst thou make false the coin,' said Sinon, 'and I am here for one fault, and thou for more than any other fiend.' 'Bethink thee, perjurer, of the horse,' answered he who had his paunch inflated, 'and be it thy bane that all the world knows it.' 'And thy bane be the thirst wherewith cracks thy tongue,' said the Greek; 'and the putrid water which thus makes thy belly a fence before thine eyes.' Then the moneyer: 'Thus gapes thy mouth to thy own ill as it is wont; for if I have thirst, and an humour bloats me out, thou hast thy burning, and thy head which pains thee; and to lap Narcissus his mirror, thou wouldest not wish many words of invitation.' To listen to

> S' io dissi 'l falso, e tu falsasti il conio,[a]
> Disse Sinone, e son qui per un fallo,
> E tu per più che alcun altro demonio.
> Ricorditi, spergiuro, del cavallo,
> Rispose quel ch' avea enfiata l' epa ;
> E siati reo, che tutto il mondo sallo. 120
> E te sia rea la sete onde ti crepa,
> Disse il Greco, la lingua, e l' acqua marcia
> Che il ventre innanzi a gli occhi si t' assiepa.
> Allora il monetier : Cosi si squarcia
> La bocca tua per suo mal come suole :
> Chè s' i' ho sete, ed umor mi rinfarcia,
> Tu hai l' arsura, e il capo che ti duole,
> E per leccar lo specchio di Narcisso,
> Non vorresti a invitar molte parole.

[a] om. *e W*.

[115] **e** : much as in xxv. 34, etc.
[128] **specchio di Narcisso**: merely 'running water.' See Ov. Met. iii. 351 sqq.

them I was wholly fixed, when the Master said to me: 'Now only see, for it lacks but little that I quarrel with thee.' When I heard him speak to me with anger, I turned me toward him with such shame, that it still revolves in my memory. And as is he who dreams his own hurt, that in his dream he longs to be dreaming, so yearns he for that which is as though it were not; such became I, not having power to speak, that I longed to excuse myself, and was excusing myself all the time, and deemed not I did it. 'Less shame washes a greater fault,' said the Master, 'than

> Ad ascoltarli er' io del tutto fisso, 130
>   Quando il Maestro mi disse : Or pur mira,
>   Che per poco è che teco non mi risso.
> Quand' io il senti' a me parlar con ira,
>   Volsimi verso lui con tal vergogna,
>   Ch' ancor per la memoria mi si gira.
> E quale è quei che suo dannaggio sogna,
>   Che sognando desidera sognare,
>   Sì che quel ch' è, come non fosse, agogna.
> Tal mi fec' io, non potendo parlare,
>   Che desiava scusarmi, e scusava 140
>   Me tuttavia, e nol mi credea fare.
> Maggior difetto men vergogna lava.
>   Disse il Maestro, che il tuo non è stato ;

[131] **or pur mira**: Benv. and others, e.g. Bianchi, understand the words to mean, 'Now just go on staring,' in irony. The former, by the way, is inclined to excuse Dante. 'Vere delectabile est,' he says, 'audire duos falsarios, lenones, baratarios, tanquam meretrices inter se contendentes'; a cynical view which Virgil could hardly be expected to endorse.

[132] **per poco**: see Diez ii. 442. The use is like, though not identical with, that in xvi. 71, where it refers to time.

[140, 141] Because the very fact of his being unable to express his shame showed its sincerity.

thine has been; therefore unload thyself of all sadness; and
make account that I am ever beside thee if it happens again
that fortune bring thee in company where folk are in a like
pleading; for to wish to hear that is a base will.'

> Però d' ogni tristizia ti disgrava:
> E fa ragion ch' io ti sia sempre allato,
>> Se più avvien che fortuna t' accoglia,
>> Ove sia gente in simigliante piato;
> Chè voler ciò udire è bassa voglia.

CANTO XXXI

ARGUMENT

Guided by the sound of a great horn, they reach the brink of the last descent, and find it guarded by giants. One of these, Antaeus by name, sets them down in the last circle of Hell.

ONE self-same tongue first wounded me, so that it tinged my one and the other cheek, and afterwards held out again the remedy to me. So do I hear that the spear of Achilles and

> UNA medesma lingua pria mi morse,
> Sì che mi tinse l' una e l' altra guancia,
> E poi la medicina mi riporse.
> Così od' io, che soleva la lancia

4, 5 Telephus, son of Hercules, and King of Mysia, was wounded by Achilles at the first landing of the Greeks. As his wound did not heal, he sought the oracle, and was told that only the wounder could cure him. Achilles accordingly applied his spear to the wound, and healed it. Ovid alludes to the story frequently. The particular passage which Dante had in mind was probably Rem. Am. 47:

> Vulnus in Herculeo quae quondam fecerat hoste
> Vulneris auxilium Pelias hasta tulit.

Dictys Cretensis, though he has a good deal about Telephus, and says that he was cured by Machaon and Podalirius with the help of Achilles, does not mention the actual method. Pliny, Nat. Hist. xxv. 19, rationalises the story.

of his father was wont to be an occasion first of a sorry largess and then of a good.

We turned our backs to the vale of misery, up over the bank which girdles it around, passing across without any converse. Here it was less than night and less than day, so that my sight went but little forward; but I heard sound a loud horn, such that it would have made every thunder feeble; so that as I followed its course against itself it directed my eyes wholly to one place. After the woeful rout when Charles the Great lost the holy enterprise, not so

> D' Achille e del suo padre esser cagione
> Prima di trista e poi di buona mancia.
> Noi demmo il dosso al misero vallone
>   Su per la ripa che il cinge dintorno,
>   Attraversando senza alcun sermone.
> Quivi era men che notte e men che giorno,   10
>   Sì che il viso m' andava innanzi poco:
>   Ma io senti' sonare un alto corno,
> Tanto ch' avrebbe ogni tuon fatto fioco,
>   Che, contra sè la sua via seguitando,
>   Dirizzò gli occhi miei tutti ad un loco:
> Dopo la dolorosa rotta, quando
>   Carlo Magno perdè la santa gesta,

---

* **cinge dintorno**: rather a curious way of indicating the *inner* bank.
14 In the opposite direction to the sound.
15 **gli occhi tutti**: so *tutti i piedi*, xix. 64.
16 *seq.* English readers need hardly be reminded of 'the blast of that dread horn, On Fontarabian echoes borne.' The story (from the Chronicle of Turpin) of the defeat of Charlemagne's rearguard by the Saracens at Roncesvalles appears to be purely legendary; but the allusion to it here, brought about as it was by the treachery of Ganelon, serves well to usher in the description of the lowest circle, in which traitors are punished.

terribly did Roland blow. A little while I bore my head
turned that way when I seemed to myself to see many lofty
towers; wherefore I: 'Master, say, what land is this?'
And he to me: 'Because thou speedest across through the
gloom from too far off, it befalls that thou afterward goest
astray in thy imagining. Thou wilt see well if thou drawest
near that place how much the sense is deceived at a distance;
therefore prick thyself on somewhat more.' Then in loving
wise he took me by the hand, and said: 'Before that we are
further forward, in order that the fact may seem less strange
to thee, know that they are not towers, but giants, and they
are in the gulf, around the bank, from the navel downward
all and each.' As when the cloud is dissipated the gaze

   Non sonò sì terribilmente Orlando.
 Poco portai in là volta la testa,
   Che mi parve veder molte alte torri;   20
   Ond' io: Maestro, di', che terra è questa?
 Ed egli a me: Però che tu trascorri
   Per le tenebre troppo dalla lungi,
   Avvien che poi nel 'maginare aborri.
 Tu vedrai ben, se tu là ti congiungi,
   Quanto il senso s' inganna di lontano:
   Però alquanto più te stesso pungi.
 Poi caramente mi prese per mano,
   E disse: Pria che noi siam più avanti,
   Acciocchè il fatto men ti paia strano.   30
 Sappi che non son torri, ma giganti,
   E son nel pozzo intorno dalla ripa
   Dall' umbilico in giuso tutti e quanti.
 Come, quando la nebbia si dissipa,

  [21] **terra** is often used in the sense of 'a town.'
  [26] Cf. Purg. xxix. 47.

little by little figures out whatsoever the vapour which packs the air is concealing; so piercing the gross and dim mist, approaching more and more to the brink, error fled from me and fear grew upon me. Because like as upon its round enclosure Montereggion is crowned with towers, so the bank which surrounds the pit were turreting, by half their frames, the horrible giants, whom Jove yet menaces from heaven when he thunders. And I began to perceive already of a certain one the face, the shoulders and the breast, and of the belly

> Lo sguardo a poco a poco raffigura
>   Ciò che cela il vapor che l' aere stipa:
> Così forando l' aura grossa e scura,
>   Più e più appressando in ver la sponda,
>   Fuggiemi errore, e cresceami paura.
> Perocchè come in sulla cerchia tonda   40
>   Montereggion di torri si corona;
>   Così la proda, che il pozzo circonda,
> Torreggiavan di mezza la persona
>   Gli orribili giganti, cui minaccia
>   Giove del cielo ancora, quando tuona.
> Ed io scorgeva già d' alcun la faccia,
>   Le spalle e il petto, e del ventre gran parte,

[40] **cerchia**: as in Par. xv. 97.

[41] The castle of Monte Reggione stands a few miles north-west of Siena.

[44] Nothing in Virgil seems to have suggested the introduction of the Giants among the warders of Hell. They appear, however, with the Furies, Centaurs, etc., in the account of Scipio's visit to the infernal regions, Silius Italicus, Punica xiii. 590. (Silius is generally supposed to have been 'lost,' and first rediscovered by Poggio at St. Gallen in the fifteenth century, nor does Dante, I believe, anywhere mention him; but there are in the passage referred to several points of resemblance to Dante's employment of classical legend almost too close to be mere coincidences: and MSS. of course were in existence somewhere.)

great part, and both the arms down by the sides. Nature surely did right well when she left the trick of animals so fashioned, to take away such ministers from Mars. And if of elephants and whales she does not repent her, whoso looks subtilly holds her therefore more just and more discreet; for where the equipment of the mind is joined to ill-will and to power, folk can make no rampart against it. His face appeared to me long and big as the pine-cone of

> E per le coste giù ambo le braccia.
> Natura certo, quando lasciò l' arte
>   Di sì fatti animali, assai fe bene,
>   Per torre tali esecutori a Marte: 50
> E s' ella d' elefanti e di balene [a]
>   Non si pente, chi guarda sottilmente,
>   Più giusta e più discreta la ne tiene:
> Chè dove l' argomento della mente
>   S' aggiunge al mal volere ed alla possa, [b]
>   Nessun riparo vi può far la gente.
> La faccia sua mi parea lunga e grossa,
>   Come la pina di san Pietro a Roma:

[a] *lionfanti* Gg.; *lifanti* Cass.
[b] *ha la possa* 2.

[54] Because elephants and whales, not possessing intelligence, are not such a danger to mankind.

[55] P. di Dante refers to Arist. Pol. i. 2 (1253 a): ὥσπερ γὰρ καὶ τελεωθὲν βέλτιστον τῶν ζώων ἄνθρωπός ἐστιν, οὕτω καὶ χωρισθὲν νόμου καὶ δίκης χείριστον πάντων. Χαλεπωτάτη γὰρ ἀδικία ἔχουσα ὅπλα.—**argomento**: as in xix. 110; Purg. ii. 31. But the meaning 'reason' is also suggested. See note Par. xv. 79.

[59] The gilt pine-cone, once on the Mausoleum of Hadrian, was put by Pope Symmachus in front of St. Peter's, where it stood in Dante's time. It is now in the Vatican. Philalethes gives its height at 10 palms = about 7½ English feet; and gives elaborate calculations as to the height of the giants. It will be sufficient to say that Dante must have imagined them to be about 70 English feet in stature.

St. Peter at Rome, and in proportion to it were the other bones; so that the bank which was a skirt from the middle downward, showed of him full so much above that to reach to his hair three Frisians would ill have boasted themselves, seeing that I saw of him thirty great spans down from the place where a man buckles his cloak. *Rafel mai amech zabi almi*

> Ed a sua proporzione eran l' altr' ossa: 60
> Sì che la ripa, ch' era perizoma
>   Dal mezzo in giù, ne mostrava ben tanto
>   Di sopra, che di giungere alla chioma
> Tre Frison s' averian dato mal vanto:
>   Perocch' io ne vedea trenta gran palmi
>   Dal loco in giù, dov' uomo affibbia il manto.
> Rafel mai amech zabi almi,

[64] If we put the Frisians at 6 ft. 6 in. each, and allow 2 ft. for the reach of the topmost, this will give $21\frac{1}{2}$ ft. to the ends of the giant's hair, which may be conceived as reaching to the same point as that indicated in l. 66, viz. the lower end of the neck. Allowing a few feet for his neck, we shall thus get 35 ft. for the half-giant.

[67] The labour which has been devoted to making sense of this jargon might have been spared if the would-be interpreters had taken the trouble to look a little further; for l. 81 clearly shows that Dante meant them to have no sense. If they can be twisted into a resemblance to any Arabic words (a question which, if I mistake not, the late Prof. E. H. Palmer answered with a decided negative), it is a mere coincidence. Dr. Scartazzini expends more space, and much more temper, than was at all necessary in reviewing and dismissing the various suggestions which have been made from Landino downwards, and which, with his comments, occupy seven closely-printed pages of small type. From these the reader turns with relief to the common-sense of Benvenuto: Ad cujus intelligentiam est hic notandum quod ista verba non sunt significativa, et posito quod in se aliquid significarent, sicut aliqui interpretari conantur, adhuc nihil significarent hic, nisi quod ponuntur ad significandum quod idioma istius non erat intelligibile alicui . . . Et haec est intentio autoris quam expresse ponit in litera. And so (in spite of his 'aliqui') all the commentators that we possess, till the end of the fifteenth century.

began the fierce mouth to cry, to which sweeter psalms were not convenient. And my Leader toward him: 'Silly soul, content thee with thy horn, and with that discharge thyself when anger or other passion touches thee. Search at thy neck, and thou shalt find the leash which holds it tied, O soul perplexed, and see it, how it hoops thy great breast.' Then said he to me: 'He accuses himself; this is Nimrod, through whose ill-weening only the world uses not one language. Let us leave him to stand, and not talk in vain, for so is each language to him as his to others, that it is

> Cominciò a gridar la fiera bocca,
>   Cui non si convenian più dolci salmi.
> E il Duca mio ver lui: Anima sciocca,   70
>   Tienti col corno, e con quel ti disfoga,
>   Quand' ira o altra passion ti tocca.
> Cercati al collo, e troverai la soga
>   Che il tien legato, o anima confusa,
>   E vedi lui che il gran petto ti doga.
> Poi disse a me: Egli stesso s' accusa;
>   Questi è Nembrotto, per lo cui mal coto
>   Pure un linguaggio nel mondo non s' usa.
> Lasciamlo stare, e non parliamo a voto:
>   Chè così è a lui ciascun linguaggio,   80
>   Come il suo ad altrui ch' a nullo è noto.

77 There is of course nothing in the Bible to suggest that Nimrod (Gen. x. 8, 9) was bigger than other people, and not much to connect him with the building of the tower. The giants indeed were extinct before the Flood; but in spite of this both Orosius (ii. 6) and St. Augustine (Civ. D. xvi. 3, 4) make Nimrod a giant; the latter (whom Dante doubtless followed) reading, for the 'potens in terra' of the Vulgate, 'gigas super terram'; and in the next verse, 'gigas venator' for 'robustus.' He also ascribes the building of Babel to him. Cf. Purg. xii. 34: Par. xxvi. 125, 126.

known to none.' We made then a longer journey, turned to the left; and at a crossbow's shot we found the next, far more fierce and larger. Who had been the master to bind him I cannot say; but he held the other arm bowed down in front and the right arm behind by a chain which he wore girt from the neck downward, so that on his uncovered part it was wound round even to the fifth coil. 'He in his pride would make trial of his strength against the most high Jove,' said my Leader, 'wherefore he has such recompense. Ephialtes he has to name, and he made his great trial when the giants caused fear to the gods; the arms which he wielded he moves nevermore.' And I to him: 'If it can

> Facemmo adunque più lungo viaggio
>   Volti a sinistra; ed al trar d' un balestro
>   Trovammo l' altro assai più fiero e maggio.
> A cinger lui, qual che fosse il maestro
>   Non so io dir, ma ei tenea succinto
>   Dinanzi l' altro, e dietro il braccio destro
> D' una catena, che il teneva avvinto
>   Dal collo in giù, sì che in sullo scoperto
>   Si ravvolgeva infino al giro quinto.   90
> Questo superbo voll' esser esperto
>   Di sua potenza contra il sommo Giove,
>   Disse il mio Duca, ond' egli ha cotal merto.
> Fialte ha nome; e fece le gran prove,
>   Quando i giganti fer paura ai Dei:
>   Le braccia ch' ei menò, giammai non move.
> Ed io a lui: S' esser puote, io vorrei

[94] It is not very clear whence Dante obtained the name of Ephialtes. The only mention of him by name in Latin literature is Claudian Bell. Get. 75; and it is doubtful if Dante knew Claudian. We must here, as in other instances, suppose that he had access to translations, now lost, of Greek authors, Homer or Apollodorus. See Odyssey λ 308.

be, I would that of Briareus the enormous my eyes might have experience.' Wherefore he replied: 'Thou shalt see Antaeus hard by here, how he speaks and is unbound, that shall place us at the bottom of all sin. He whom thou wishest to see is much further beyond, and he is tied and fashioned like this one, save that he appears in his countenance more fierce.' Never was an earthquake so violent to shake a tower thus mightily, as Ephialtes was quick to shake himself. Then I feared more than ever my death; and for it no more than the fear was needed, if I had not seen his bonds.

> Che dello smisurato Briareo
> Esperienza avesser gli occhi miei.
> Ond' ei rispose: Tu vedrai Anteo 100
> Presso di qui, che parla, ed è disciolto,
> Che ne porrà nel fondo d' ogni reo.
> Quel che tu vuoi veder, più là è molto,
> Ed è legato e fatto come questo,
> Salvo che più feroce par nel volto.
> Non fu tremoto già tanto rubesto,
> Che scotesse una torre così forte,
> Come Fialte a scotersi fu presto.
> Allor temett' io più che mai la morte,
> E non v' era mestier più che la dotta, 110
> S' io non avessi viste le ritorte.

---

⁹⁸ **smisurato**: the epithet is probably taken from the 'immensus Briareus' of Stat. Theb. ii. 596.

¹⁰² As Benvenuto remarks, Antaeus among the giants plays the same part as Chiron among the Centaurs, in helping them on their way: but it is less easy to see why he should be selected for it.

¹¹⁰ **dotta** strictly = 'doubt.' For the extension of meaning cf. Fr. *redouter*.

We proceeded then further in advance, and came to Antaeus, who issued full five ells without the head from out the rock. 'O thou who in the fortunate vale, which made Scipio an heir of glory when Hannibal with his men turned their backs, didst erewhile take a thousand lions for booty, and who if thou hadst been in thy brethren's war on high, methinks it still is deemed that the sons of the earth had won, set us down (and let no shyness thereof come to thee) where the cold locks up Cocytus. Make us not go to Tityus nor

> Noi procedemmo più avanti allotta,
>   E venimmo ad Anteo, che ben cinqu' alle,
>   Senza la testa, uscía fuor della grotta.
> O tu, che nella fortunata valle,
>   Che fece Scipion di gloria reda,
>   Quando Annibal coi suoi diede le spalle,
> Recasti già mille leon per preda,
>   E che, se fossi stato all' alta guerra
>   Dei tuoi fratelli, ancor par ch' e' si creda,   120
> Che avrebber vinto i figli della terra ;
>   Mettine giù (e non ten venga schifo)
>   Dove Cocito la freddura serra.
> Non ci far ire a Tizio, nè a Tifo :

115 sqq. The fight between Antaeus and Hercules is related by Lucan, Phars. iv. 593-660. To him also seems to be due the identification of the scene of the fight with the neighbourhood of Carthage. (It may be noted that it was in this same district, near Utica, that St. Augustine, as he records, Civ. D. xv. 9, saw the great molar tooth which he says would have cut up into a hundred such as we now have.)—**fortunata :** cf. xxviii. 8. Here too it may mean 'fortune-vexed.'

119 sq. Suggested no doubt by Lucan's

   Nec tam justa fuit terrarum gloria Typhon
   Aut Tityus Briareusque ferox ; caeloque pepercit (sc. Tellus)
   Quod non Phlegraeis Antaeum sustulit arvis.

It will be noticed that the three other giants named here are all referred to in the present passage.

to Typhoeus; this man can give thee of that which here is craved; therefore bend thyself, and writhe not thy muzzle. He can yet render thee fame in the world; for he lives and awaits long life yet, if grace calls him not to itself before the time.' Thus said the Master; and that one in haste stretched forth his hands, and took my Leader, the hands whence Hercules once felt a mighty constraint. Virgil, when he felt himself seized, said to me: 'Put thyself this way, that I may hold thee'; then did he so that he and I were one bundle. As appears the Carisenda to behold below its slant when a cloud goes over it in such wise that

> Questi può dar di quel che qui si brama:
> Però ti china, e non torcer lo grifo.
> Ancor ti può nel mondo render fama;
> Ch' ei vive, e lunga vita ancor aspetta,
> Se innanzi tempo grazia a sè nol chiama.
> Così disse il Maestro: e quegli in fretta   130
> Le man distese, e prese il Duca mio,
> Ond' Ercole sentì già grande stretta.
> Virgilio, quando prender si sentio,
> Disse a me: Fatti in qua, sì ch' io ti prenda:
> Poi fece sì, che un fascio er' egli ed io.
> Qual pare a riguardar la Carisenda
> Sotto il chinato, quando un nuvol vada

[125] **quel che qui si brama.** As elsewhere, Dante's power of conferring fame in the world above is held out as the inducement to help him. Philalethes observes that this is the last instance in which it is used with any effect. See xxxii. 94.

[136] **Carisenda**: the lesser of the two famous leaning towers at Bologna. It was built in the twelfth century by some members of the Carisendi family. It is now 130 feet high, and leans 8 feet out of the perpendicular; but Benv. avers that in Dante's time it was higher, a great part of it having been thrown down by Giovanni da Oleggio during his 'tyranny' (1355-1360).

it is hanging in the contrary way, such appeared Antaeus to me who was standing at gaze to see him stoop; and there was a moment when I had wished to go by another road. But lightly on the bottom, which swallows Lucifer with Judas, he set us down; nor so stooping did he make a pause there, but raised him like a mast in a ship.

> Sopr' essa sì, che ella incontro penda;
> Tal parve Anteo a me che stava a bada
>   Di vederlo chinare, e fu tal ora 140
>   Ch' io avrei voluto ir per altra strada:
> Ma lievemente al fondo, che divora
>   Lucifero con Giuda, ci sposò;
>   Nè sì chinato lì fece dimora,
> E come albero in nave si levò.

CANTO XXXII

ARGUMENT

They find themselves on a great plain of ice, wherein are immersed such as had dealt treacherously with those who trusted them. Of this there are four divisions; and first Caina, where those are who have betrayed their kinsfolk. The next is Antenora, where are the traitors to their city or land. Dante sees many of his own country; and at last two, of whom one is gnawing the other's head.

IF I had my rimes both rough and hoarse, as would be suitable to the sorry crevice over which all the other rocks thrust, I would express the sap of my conception more fully; but since I have them not, not without fear do I bring myself to speak. For it is not an enterprise to take up in jest, to describe a bottom to all the universe; nor for a tongue that utters childish prattle. But let those Dames aid my

> S' io avessi le rime ed aspre e chiocce,
> Come si converrebbe al tristo buco,
> Sopra il qual pontan tutte l' altre rocce,
> Io premerei di mio concetto il suco
> Più pienamente; ma perch' io non l' abbo,
> Non senza tema a dicer mi conduco.
> Chè non è impresa da pigliare a gabbo,
> Di scriver fondo a tutto l' universo,
> Nè da lingua che chiami mamma e babbo.
> Ma quelle Donne aiutino il mio verso,   10

[10] **Donne**: the Muses. Compare with this the invocation before the

verse who aided Amphion to enclose Thebes, so that the telling may not be diverse from the fact.

O rabble, created to ill above all, that stand in the place whereof to talk is hard, better had ye been here sheep or goats! When we were down in the gloomy pit, below the feet of the giant, far lower, and I was still gazing at the lofty wall, I heard say to me: 'Watch how thou pacest, go so that thou kick not with thy feet the heads of thy poor weary brethren.' Wherefore I turned me, and saw before me and

> Ch' aiutaro Amfion a chiuder Tebe,
>   Sì che dal fatto il dir non sia diverso.
> O sopra tutte mal creata plebe,
>   Che stai nel loco, onde il parlare è duro,
>   Me' foste state qui pecore o zebe.
> Come noi fummo giù nel pozzo scuro
>   Sotto i piè del gigante, assai più bassi,
>   Ed io mirava ancora all' alto muro,
> Dicere udimmi: Guarda, come passi;
>   Va sì, che tu non calchi con le piante^a   20
>   Le teste dei fratei miseri lassi.
> Perch' io mi volsi, e vidimi davante

^a *Fa sì* Ald. W.

closing scenes of Purgatory (Purg. xxix. 37 sqq.) The story of Amphion is of course a classical commonplace; though it is not easy to see any special propriety in the allusion to it here. The comparison of the last circle of Hell to a walled fortress (xxxi. 43) may have suggested it.

[13] **duro**: cf. i. 4.

[14, 15] **stai – foste**: note the change of number. One or two MSS. seem to read *fossi*, but there is not enough authority to warrant us in adopting it.

[17] Philalethes is doubtless right in supposing that the floor slopes downwards. One is tempted to wonder if Dante ever stood at the foot of the rock wall above some steep glacier.

[21] **miseri lassi**: the epithets are coupled again in Purg. x. 121.

beneath my feet a lake, which by reason of frost had semblance of glass and not of water. No such thick veil to its stream makes in winter the Danube in Austria, nor the Don there under its cold sky, as was there; which if Tabernicch had fallen thereon, or Pietrapana, would not even by the rim have given a crack. And as the frog stands to croak with its snout out of the water, what time the peasant-woman

> E sotto i piedi un lago, che per gelo
>   Avea di vetro e non d' acqua sembiante.
> Non fece al corso suo sì grosso velo
>   D' inverno la Danoia in Ostericchi,[b]
>   Nè Tanai là sotto il freddo cielo,
> Com' era quivi: chè, se Tabernicchi
>   Vi fosse su caduto, o Pietrapana,
>   Non avria pur dall' orlo fatto cricchi.   30
> E come a gracidar si sta la rana
>   Col muso fuor dell' acqua, quando sogna
>   Di spigolar sovente la villana:

[b] *Osterlicchi* Cass. 124; *Isterl.* Gg.; *Austerricchi* Ald.

[22] **lago.** The word *lacus* is used more than once in the Vulgate, where our version has 'pit'; e.g. Psalm lxxx. 5, 7 (in lacu inferiori, in tenebrosis, et in umbra mortis); Isai. xiv. 15. The notion may also have been suggested by the infernal lake of Plato, Phaedo 113.

[25] **fece**: a kind of 'aorist' use; which must be rendered in English by the present, unless we insert 'ever.'

[28] **Tabernicchi** has not been identified. There is a place called Tavornik, not far from the Danube, at the east of the Austrian province of Slavonia (of course far from anything that Dante would have known as Austria), with hills near it; and a mountain Tovarnica in Bosnia. The first part of the word is frequent in one form or another throughout the eastern Alps (it is probably identical with 'Tauern'), and *-nik* is a not uncommon termination of mountain names in Slavonic districts.

[29] **Pietrapana** is said to be a summit in the Carrara mountains. The true name seems to be Pietra Apuana—doubtless from the Ligurian tribe Apuani who formerly inhabited that part.

at whiles dreams of gleaning, livid, so far as the place where shame appears, were the shades woeful in the ice, setting their teeth to a stork's note. Every one was holding his face turned downward; by the mouth their chill, and by the eyes their sad heart provides testimony among them to itself. When I had looked round a little, I turned toward my feet, and saw two so close that they had the hair of their heads mingled together. 'Tell me, ye who hold your breasts so close,' said I, 'who you are.' And they bent their necks, and when they had turned up their faces toward me, their eyes which before were melted only inwardly, gushed over their lips, and the frost bound the tears between them and

>Livide insin là dove appar vergogna,
>>Eran l' ombre dolenti nella ghiaccia,
>>Mettendo i denti in nota di cicogna.
>Ognuna in giù tenea volta la faccia:
>>Da bocca il freddo, e dagli occhi il cor tristo
>>Tra lor testimonianza si procaccia.
>Quand' io ebbi d' intorno alquanto visto, 40
>>Volsimi ai piedi, e vidi due sì stretti,
>>Che il pel del capo avieno insieme misto.
>Ditemi voi, che sì stringete i petti,
>>Diss' io, chi siete. E quei piegaro i colli:
>>E poi ch' ebber li visi a me eretti,
>Gli occhi lor, ch' eran pria pur dentro molli,
>>Gocciar su per le labbra, e il gielo strinse *c*

---

c giù per 1245 : *super le braccia Cass.*

b **là dove**, etc., i.e. the face.
d Chattering as a stork with its bill.
e There seems no reason either (with a minority of MSS. and commentators) to read *giù*, or (with the most modern interpreters) to suppose that **labbra** is used in the uncommon, if not unexampled, sense of

locked them together again. Log with log never did clamp tie so hard; wherefore they, like two he-goats, butted together, such wrath overcame them. And one who had lost both his ears through the cold, ever with his face downward, said: 'Why dost mirror thyself so much on us? If thou wouldst know who are these two, the vale from which Bisen-

   Le lagrime tra essi, e riserrolli:
  Con legno legno spranga mai non cinse
    Forte così, ond' ei, come due becchi,   50
   Cozzaro insieme: tant' ira li vinse.
  Ed un, ch' avea perduti ambo gli orecchi
   Per la freddura, pur col viso in giue
   Disse: Perchè cotanto in noi ti specchi?[d]
  Se vuoi saper chi son cotesti due,
   La valle, onde Bisenzio si dichina.

    [d] *Mi disse perchè tanto ti*.

'eyelids.' **Su per** no doubt is equivalent, as in viii. 10, to Latin *super*, so that the objection that the tears flowed down and not up is futile. But *su* alone is used to mean 'from above'; e.g. Petr. Son. in Morte M. L. liv.: Spirto . . . c' hor su dal ciel tante dolcezze stille.

 [49] **essi**: doubtless their eyes, as indeed **riserrolli** shows. Their eyes had been opened for a moment by the change of attitude, but were closed again by the tears which froze as soon as they began to flow. The simile in the next line, however, affords some justification for the view which some have held that it was the face part of the sinners themselves which was locked, each to each. But in that case they could hardly have *butted* each other: though they might have pressed their foreheads hard together, to break the bond which joined the lower part of their faces.

 [51] **ira**: Scartazzini ingeniously suggests that the momentary sight which they had caught of each other would renew their rage.

 [52] The speaker names himself presently, l. 68.

 [54] As though he were looking at his own reflection in the ice.

 [56 sqq.] The Bisenzio is a small river which flows past Prato and joins the Arno near Signa. In its valley stood the castle of Mangona, belonging to the Counts Alberti. The two here mentioned are said to be

zio slopes down belonged to their father Albert and to them.
From one body came they forth; and all Caina thou
mightest search, and thou wilt not find a shade more worthy of
being fixed in jelly; not he who had his breast and his shadow
torn with one self-same blow by the hand of Arthur; not
Focaccia; not this one who encumbers me so with his head

> Del padre loro Alberto e di lor fue.
> D' un corpo usciro: e tutta la Caina
> Potrai cercare, e non troverai ombra
> Degna più d' esser fitta in gelatina: 60
> Non quelli, a cui fu rotto il petto e l' ombra
> Con esso un colpo, per la man d' Artù:
> Non Focaccia: non questi, che m' ingombra

Alessandro and Napoleone, sons of a Count Alberto. The castle seems to have belonged by right to Alessandro, the younger, and to have been unjustly seized by Napoleone. The Florentines, whose ward Alessandro was, in 1259 expelled Napoleone by force of arms, and eight years later reinstated the younger brother. Villani, who tells this (vi. 68), records nothing about any continuance of the feud between the brothers, but Benvenuto says that they killed each other. Soon after Dante's death, in 1325, Alberto, son of Alessandro, was murdered by two of his nephews.

[59] **gelatina**: our word having no longer any suggestion of *cold*, it is difficult to keep the full point of the bitter jest; which, in spite of the silence of the early commentators, who for the most part seem to think only *ice* is meant, we can hardly doubt that Dante intended to put into the speaker's mouth.

[61] **quelli**: Mordred. In the French romance it is related that Arthur thrust him through with so mighty a blow that the daylight could be seen through his body. The more sober Malory only says 'more than a fathom.' Notice *ombra* repeated in rhyme in a very slightly altered sense.

[63] As Benvenuto tells the story, Focaccia's father was one of three brothers belonging to the Cancellieri family at Pistoia. He had occasion one day to chastise one of his nephews for assaulting another boy with a snowball. The nephew struck his uncle, and was duly sent by his father to apologise. The uncle laughed the matter off, but Focaccia,

that I see no further, and was named Sassol Mascheroni; if thou art a Tuscan, well knowest thou now who he was. And to the end that thou set me not on further talk, know that I was Camicion of the Pazzi, and I await Carlino to excuse me.'

Afterward I saw a thousand faces grown dog-like with cold; whence a shudder comes to me and ever will come, of the frozen shallows. And while we were going toward

> Col capo sì, ch' io non veggio oltre più,
> E fu nomato Sassol Mascheroni:
> Se Tosco sei, ben sai omai chi fu.
> E perchè non mi metti in più sermoni,
> Sappi ch' io fui il Camicion dei Pazzi,
> Ed aspetto Carlin che mi scagioni.
> Poscia vid' io mille visi, cagnazzi   70
> Fatti per freddo: onde mi vien riprezzo,
> E verrà sempre, dei gelati guazzi.
> E mentre che andavamo in ver lo mezzo,

catching his young cousin as he left the house, dragged him into the stable, and cut off his hand on the manger. Afterwards he murdered the boy's father, his own uncle. Hence arose the feud of 'Blacks' and 'Whites' (see note xxiv. 143). Focaccia belonged to the latter party.

[65] Sassolo Mascheroni belonged to the Toschi, a Ghibeline family of Florence. He murdered his nephew in order to get his inheritance; and was rolled through the streets in a cask full of nails, and then beheaded.

[68, 69] All that seems to be known of Uberto Camicione, one of the Pazzi of Valdarno, is that he treacherously killed a cousin named Ubertino. Of his kinsman Carlino, Villani (viii. 53) records, that in 1302, being engaged with other 'Whites' and Ghibelines in defending the Pistoiese fortress of Piantrevigne against a force of Florentine Guelfs (see xxiv. 143 sqq.), he treacherously opened the gates to the enemy; whereby many of the best of the Florentine exiles (including, says Benvenuto, two relatives of his own) were captured or slain.—**mi scagioni**: may make my guilt seem light in comparison with his.

[70] **cagnazzi**: probably 'showing their teeth,' with the cold.

the centre, to which all gravity is collected, and I was shivering in the everlasting chill, whether it was will, or destiny, or chance I know not; but as I passed among the heads, I struck my foot hard upon the face of one. Wailing he cried out to me: 'Why dost thou batter me? If thou comest not to increase the vengeance of Monte Aperti, why dost molest me?' And I: 'My Master, now wait here for me; so that I may come out of a doubt by this one's means; after shalt thou make as much haste for me as thou wilt.' The Leader

> Al quale ogni gravezza si raduna,
> Ed io tremava nell' eterno rezzo:
> Se voler fu o destino o fortuna,
> Non so: ma passeggiando tra le teste,
> Forte percossi il piè nel viso ad una.
> Piangendo mi sgridò: Perchè mi peste?
> Se tu non vieni a crescer la vendetta   80
> Di Mont' Aperti, perchè mi moleste?
> Ed io: Maestro mio, or qui m' aspetta,
> Si ch' io esca d' un dubbio per costui:
> Poi mi farai, quantunque vorrai, fretta.

[76] We must not, with Scartazzini, understand **voler** to mean the will of God: though at first sight that interpretation seems tempting. But from the language of Aquinas (e.g. S. T. i. Q. 23) it would seem that destiny is only a particular case, so to speak, of the operation of the divine will; hence they could not be alternative to each other. More probably Dante was thinking of the αἰτία of Eth. Nic. iii. 5 (1112 a), among which are ἀνάγκη and τύχη, as well as νοῦς. He means merely 'I cannot now say whether I did it on purpose, or (if not) whether I was foreordained to do it, or constrained by some influence.'

[] **dubbio**: perhaps because the mention of Montaperti made him suspect who the speaker was; but more probably because he expected the reply to settle an undecided point as to the identity of the traitor in that battle. The name of the sinner whom he is addressing is given in l. 106.

stood; and I said to him who was still blaspheming stoutly:
'Of what sort art thou, that thus chidest another?' 'Now
who art thou, that goest through the Antenora,' said he,
'striking others' cheeks so that if thou wert alive, it would
be too much?' 'Alive am I, and precious can it be to
thee,' was my reply, 'if thou askest fame, that I put thy
name among my other notes.' And he to me: 'Of the
contrary have I a craving; take thyself hence, and give me
no more annoyance, for ill knowest thou how to entice in
this hollow.' Then I took him by the scalp, and said: 'It

>   Lo Duca stette; ed io dissi a colui
>   Che bestemmiava duramente ancora:
>   Qual sei tu, che così rampogni altrui?
>   Or tu chi sei, che vai per l' Antenora
>   Percotendo, rispose, altrui le gote
>   Sì, che se fossi vivo, troppo fora? 90
>   Vivo son io, e caro esser ti puote,
>   Fu mia risposta, se domandi fama,
>   Ch' io metta il nome tuo tra l' altre note.
>   Ed egli a me: Del contrario ho io brama:
>   Levati quinci, e non mi dar più lagna:
>   Chè mal sai lusingar per questa lama.
>   Allor lo presi per la cuticagna,

---

[88] The version of the Trojan story which makes the final capture of the city due to an act of treachery on the part of Antenor (whence the name given to this division of the lowest circle) was evidently unknown to Virgil. The so-called Dictys and Dares give it in somewhat varying forms; but both implicating Aeneas no less than Antenor. This of course Dante was obliged to suppress. Both these writers make Antenor remain at Troy as king after the final departure of the Greeks; but Guido dalle Colonne says that he too departed and no more was heard of him. Virgil's version (Aen. i. 242 sqq.) is of course quite different.

will behove that thou name thyself, or that no hair on here remain to thee.' Wherefore he to me: 'Though thou make me hairless, I will neither tell thee who I am nor show it to thee, if a thousand times thou tumble over my head.' I had already his locks twisted in my hand, and had drawn from them more than one shock, he howling with his eyes steadied downwards, when another cried: 'What ails thee, Bocca? Is it not enough for thee to sound with thy jaws without howling? What devil is touching thee?' 'After this,' said I, 'I will not that thou talk, foul traitor, for to thy shame will I bear true news of thee.' 'Go away,' he answered, 'and recount what thou wilt; but be not silent, if

    E dissi: Ei converrà che tu ti nomi,
        O che capel qui su non ti rimagna.
    Ond' egli a me: Perchè tu mi dischiomi,   100
        Nè ti dirò ch' io sia, nè mostrerolti,
        Se mille fiate in sul capo mi tomi.
    Io avea già i capelli in mano avvolti,
        E tratti glien' avea più d' una ciocca,
        Latrando lui con gli occhi in giù raccolti:
    Quando un altro gridò: Che hai tu, Bocca?
        Non ti basta sonar con le mascelle,
        Se tu non latri? qual diavol ti tocca?
    Omai, diss' io, non vo' che tu favelle,
        Malvagio traditor, chè alla tua onta   110
        Io porterò di te vere novelle.
    Va via, rispose, e ciò che tu vuoi, conta:

At the battle of Montaperti (see note x. 32), when the Florentine Guelfs were being hard pressed by the German cavalry, Bocca degli Abati, one of the Ghibelines who had remained in Florence, and was ostensibly on that side, treacherously cut off the hand of the standard-bearer; and the host, seeing the standard fall, took to flight (Vill. vi. 78).

thou issue from within this place, concerning him who now had his tongue so ready. He bewails here the silver of the French; I saw (thou mayest say) him from Duera, in the place where the sinners stand cool. If thou art asked of another who was there, thou hast beside thee him of Beccheria, whose gorget Florence slit. Gianni of the Soldanieri, I think,

> Ma non tacer, se tu di qua entr' eschi,
> Di quei ch' ebbe or così la lingua pronta.
> Ei piange qui l' argento dei Franceschi:
>   Io vidi, potrai dir, quel da Duera
>   Là dove i peccatori stanno freschi.
> Se fossi domandato, altri chi v' era,
>   Tu hai da lato quel di Beccheria,
>   Di cui segò Fiorenza la gorgiera. 120
> Gianni dei Soldanier credo che sia

[116] At the time of the entry of Charles of Anjou into Italy, when a force of Cremonese and others under the Marquis Pallavicino was prepared to block the advance of Guy of Montfort's division of the French army upon Parma, the way was opened by some piece of treachery, not clearly specified, on the part of Buoso da Duera, one of the Cremonese leaders, who was believed to have been bribed by Charles's wife (Vill. vii. 4).

[119] The Abbot of Vallombrosa, Tesauro de' Beccheria of Pavia, was beheaded in 1258 by the Florentines, on a charge of intriguing with the exiled Ghibelines; 'no regard being had to his dignity, nor to Holy Orders' (Vill. vi. 65). In spite of his confession, extracted by torture, many believed him to be innocent: and the good historian considers that the defeat of Montaperti was a judgement for the sacrilegious crime. The commentators point out that though by birth of Pavia, he was a Florentine by domicile; so that Dante is justified in putting him among traitors to their country.

[121] At the time of the expulsion of Guido Novello and the Ghibeline leaders in 1266 (see note xxiii. 103) Gianni de' Soldanieri, though belonging to a Ghibeline house (see note Par. xvi. 88), put himself at the head of the popular party. Villani, though he hints (vii. 14) that Gianni was moved by personal ambition, names him elsewhere (xii. 44)

is further on, with Ganelon, and Tribaldello, who opened Faenza when men slept.'

We had already departed from him, when I saw two frozen in one hole, so that the head of one was hood to the other. And as bread is chewed for hunger, so did the upper one fix his teeth on the other in the place where the brain is joined with the nape. Not otherwise did Tydeus gnaw the temples of Menalippus for despite, than he was doing

> Più là con Ganellone, e Tribaldello,
>   Ch' aprì Faenza quando si dormia.
> Noi eravam partiti già da ello,
>   Ch' io vidi due ghiacciati in una buca
>   Sì, che l' un capo all' altro era cappello:
> E come il pan per fame si manduca,
>   Così il sopran li denti all' altro pose
>   Là 've il cervel s'aggiunge colla nuca.
> Non altrimenti Tideo si rose   130
>   Le tempie a Menalippo per disdegno,

among those who had done good service to the state, and been treated with ingratitude.

[122] Ganelon of Mainz being sent by Charlemagne on an embassy to certain Moorish kings, took a bribe of them to destroy the Christian host. By his false counsel Charles was induced to retire across the Pyrenees, leaving only a small force under the command of Roland; which the infidels then attacked and destroyed at Roncesvalles. See note xxxi. 16.

Tribaldello de' Zambrasi (de' Manfredi Vill.) in 1282 opened the gates at Faenza to the Papal forces under John of Appia (Villani's Gianni de Pà), the Count of Romagna (Vill. vii. 81). According to another version he sent an impression of the key to the Geremei, the leaders of the Bologna Guelfs, in revenge for an injury done him by the opposite party, the Lambertacci. He was killed at the capture of Forlì by Guy of Montefeltro (see xxvii. 43).

[130, 131] The allusion is to the scene at the end of Stat. Theb. viii., where Tydeus, dying from the wound inflicted by Menalippus, gets the skull and the rest. 'O thou who showest by so bestial a sign hatred over him whom thou eatest, tell me the wherefore,' said I, 'on this condition, that if thou with reason complainest of him, knowing who you are, and his crime, in the world above I yet give thee requital therefore, if that with which I speak wither not.'

> Che quei faceva il teschio e l' altre cose.
> O tu che mostri per sì bestial segno
>   Odio sopra colui che tu ti mangi,
>   Dimmi il perchè, diss' io, per tal convegno.
> Che se tu a ragion di lui ti piangi,*
>   Sappiendo chi voi siete, e la sua pecca,
>   Nel mondo suso ancor io te ne cangi,
> Se quella con ch' io parlo non si secca.

       * *ai ragion* Cass. 124.

possession of his slain enemy's head. Minerva, coming to bear him to heaven, finds him so engaged:

> Atque illum eltracti perfusum tabe cerebri
> Adspicit et vivo scelerantem sanguine fauces.

si rose: a very curious instance of the quasi-reflexive form.

CANTO XXXIII

ARGUMENT

The sinner who gnaws the other bids them know that he is the Count Ugolino of Pisa, and tells how he came by his end. The next division is called Tolommea, in which are the souls of those who have betrayed their friends and companions. But their bodies are often still on earth, and a fiend dwells in them.

His mouth from the savage meal that sinner uplifted, wiping it on the hair of the head that he had ravaged in its rear part. Then he began: 'Thou wilt that I renew a hopeless woe which burthens my heart, already only in thinking, before I converse thereof. But if my words are to

> La bocca sollevò dal fiero pasto
> Quel peccator, forbendola ai capelli
> Del capo, ch' egli avea diretro guasto.
> Poi cominciò: 'Tu vuoi ch' io rinnovelli
> Disperato dolor che il cor mi preme,
> Già pur pensando, pria ch' io ne favelli.
> Ma se le mie parole esser den seme,

[1-9] Observe how the lines of this last great episode in the present division of the poem run parallel with those of the first, the story of Francesca. Each purports to contain a statement of details which can only have been known to the speaker, in a matter of which the general outlines were notorious. Even the phrases are constantly similar. We may compare this with v. 121-123. The actual words are of course here borrowed from Aen. ii. 3.

be a seed to bear fruit of infamy to the traitor whom I gnaw, thou shalt see me speak and weep at once. I know not who thou art, nor in what manner thou art come down here; but a Florentine thou seemest to me in truth when I hear thee. Thou must know that I was Count Ugolino,

>   Che frutti infamia al traditor ch' io rodo,
>   Parlare e lagrimar vedrai insieme.
>   I' non so chi tu sei, nè per che modo   10
>   Venuto sei quaggiù; ma Fiorentino
>   Mi sembri veramente, quand' io t' odo.
>   Tu dei saper ch' io fui Conte Ugolino,

⁹ Cf. v. 126.

¹² Blanc notes *convegno*, *sappiendo*, and the frequent reflexive forms, *ti mangi*, etc., as Florentine peculiarities.

¹³ **fui**: an example of the general rule (to which there are very few exceptions) that the spirits use the present when they indicate themselves by their names only, the past when they give their titles. Cf. Par. vi. 10. (Blanc, Erklärungen.)

¹³ sqq. At the time when the Guelf party, with the aid of Charles of Anjou, had got the upper hand in Tuscany, Pisa was almost the last city in which the Ghibelines had any hold. Even here, however, there was a powerful Guelf section, at the head of which (though belonging to a Ghibeline family, the Counts of Donoratico), from about 1280, was Ugolino dei Gherardeschi. He must have been advanced in years, for we find his sister's son, Nino dei Visconti, the Judge of Gallura (Purg. viii. 53), already an important personage. After the great defeat of Pisa by Genoa at Meloria, in 1284, to which he was strongly suspected of having, by untimely retreat, contributed, he contrived to get rid for a time of the Ghibelines, under pressure from a league formed by Genoa, Lucca, and Florence; but by a successful intrigue he detached Florence from her allies, and saved the city from destruction. At the same time he seems to have allowed the Lucchese to take possession of several outlying castles. By 1288 the Ghibelines were again strong, and the Guelfs divided, Ugolino leading one group, Nino the other. In July of that year Ugolino intrigued with the Ghibelines, at whose head was the Archbishop, Roger of the Ubaldini (see note Purg. xxiv. 29), and expelled Nino and his party. Then, having weakened the Guelfs, the Archbishop turned upon his accomplice, and, after some hard fighting, got

and this one is the Archbishop Roger; now will I tell thee why I am such a neighbour. How by the effect of his evil thoughts, trusting myself to him, I was taken and afterward slain there is no need to say. But that which thou canst not have heard, that is how cruel my death was, thou shalt hear, and shalt know if he was my stumbling-block.

'A scant opening in the mew which from me has the title "of hunger," and in which it yet behoves that another

> E questi è l' Arcivescovo Ruggieri:
> Or ti dirò perch' io son tal vicino.
> Che per l' effetto dei suoi ma' pensieri,
> Fidandomi di lui, io fossi preso
> E poscia morto, dir non è mestieri.
> Però quel che non puoi avere inteso,
> Ciò è come la morte mia fu cruda,   20
> Udirai, e saprai se m' ha offeso.
> Breve pertugio dentro dalla muda,
> La qual per me ha il titol della fame,
> E in che conviene ancor ch' altri si chiuda,

him imprisoned, with two sons and two grandsons. 'E cosi fu il traditore dal traditore tradito,' says Villani (vii. 121). In the following March the Pisans called in Guy of Montefeltro to command their armies; and, feeling perhaps that they could afford to despise public opinion, threw the keys of Ugolino's prison into the Arno, and left the old plotter and his descendants to starve. The incident created, Villani tells us, a widespread feeling of reprobation, and the Pisans were a good deal blamed. The historian does not ascribe the suggestion of the crime to any particular leader; but the Archbishop had private reasons for revenge. See Witte's note to this passage, and the Historical Sketch of Philalethes.

[21] **offeso**: cf. v. 102.

[22] **muda**: Ugolino's prison was a tower belonging to the Gualandi, then called, according to Benv., Aurea Muda. It exists no longer (though its site is known); but was long famous as Torre della Fame.

[24] This appears to be only a general prophecy; at all events Benvenuto says, 'I never heard if any one else was shut up there.'

be shut, had shown me through its orifice many moons already, when I had the evil dream which tore apart for me the veil of the future. This man appeared to me master and lord, chasing the wolf and its cubs on the mountain, by reason of which the Pisans cannot see Lucca. With bitches lean, eager, and trained, Gualandi with Sismondi and with Lanfranchi he had put forward in front of himself. In a short course weary appeared to me the father and the sons, and with the keen fangs meseemed I saw their flanks

> M' avea mostrato per lo suo forame
> Più lune già, quand' io feci il mal sonno,[a]
> Che del futuro mi squarciò il velame.
> Questi pareva a me maestro e donno,
> Cacciando il lupo e i lupicini al monte,
> Per che i Pisan veder Lucca non ponno.   30
> Con cagne magre, studiose e conte,
> Gualandi con Sismondi e con Lanfranchi
> S' avea messi dinanzi dalla fronte.
> In picciol corso mi pareano stanchi
> Lo padre e i figli, e con l' acute scane
> Mi parea lor veder fender li fianchi.

[a] *lune* Gg. 23 ; *lieve* 145.

[26] As to the v. ll. see Moore, Textual Criticism, to which little can be added, except to note that Benvenuto's statement that Ugolino was only a few days in prison is in direct opposition to Villani, who is his regular historical authority, and from whom his account of the previous events is transcribed almost *verbatim*. There can be little doubt that **lune**, though found in little more than a fourth of the MSS., is the correct reading. We may compare v. 79, 80.

[29] **monte**: called M. San Giuliano. Pisa and Lucca are only some ten miles apart.

[32] Three of the leading Ghibeline families of Pisa.

rent. When I was awake before the dawn, I heard my sons weeping in their sleep, who were with me, and demanding some bread. Right cruel art thou, if thou grievest thee not already, considering that which my heart was announcing to itself; and if thou weepest not, for what art thou wont to weep? Already they were awake, and the hour was drawing on when our food was wont to be brought to us, and each one was in doubt by reason of his dream; and I heard one nail up the lower door of the horrible tower; wherefore I looked in the face of my sons without saying a word. I was not weeping; so stony was I become within; they began to weep, and my boy Anselm said: "Thou lookest so,

> Quando fui desto innanzi la dimane,
>   Pianger senti' fra il sonno i miei figliuoli,
>   Ch' eran con meco, e domandar del pane.
> Ben sei crudel, se tu già non ti duoli,   40
>   Pensando ciò ch' il mio cor s' annunziava:
>   E se non piangi, di che pianger suoli?
> Già eran desti, e l' ora s' appressava
>   Che il cibo ne soleva essere addotto,
>   E per suo sogno ciascun dubitava:
> Ed io sentii chiavar l' uscio di sotto
>   All' orribile torre: ond' io guardai
>   Nel viso ai miei figliuoi senza far motto.
> Io non piangeva; sì dentro impietrai:
>   Piangevan elli: ed Anselmuccio mio   50

We must suppose that all had had a similar dream.

chiavare: though the chroniclers say nothing about *nailing*, it seems best, with Benv. and most modern commentators, to take the word in its usual sense, rather than as if from *clavis*. The sound of locking would hardly strike them as strange or specially significant.

Anselm was a grandson, probably brother to Nino called Brigata (see l. 89). His father was Guelfo, eldest son to Ugolino, and his

father; what ails thee?" I shed no tear for that, nor did I answer all that day, nor the night after, until the next sun came forth upon the world. When a little ray had made its way into the woeful prison, and I noted in four faces my very aspect, I gnawed both my hands for woe. And they, thinking that I did it through desire of eating, lifted themselves on a sudden, and said: "Father, far less woe to us will it be if thou eat of us; thou hast clad us with this wretched flesh, and do thou strip it off." I quieted me then, not to make them more sad; that day and the next we all stayed mute; ah! hard earth, why openest thou not thyself? After that

> Disse: Tu guardi sì, padre: che hai?
> Per ciò non lagrimai, nè rispos' io [b]
>   Tutto quel giorno, nè la notte appresso,
>   Infin che l' altro sol nel mondo uscio.
> Come un poco di raggio si fu messo
>   Nel doloroso carcere, ed io scorsi
>   Per quattro visi il mio aspetto stesso:
> Ambo le man per lo dolor mi morsi.
>   Ed ei, pensando ch' io il fessi per voglia
>   Di manicar, di subito levorsi,   60
> E disser: Padre, assai ci fia men doglia,
>   Se tu mangi di noi: tu ne vestisti
>   Queste misere carni, e tu le spoglia.
> Queta' mi allor per non farli più tristi:
>   Lo dì e l' altro stemmo tutti muti:
>   Ahi dura terra, perchè non t' apristi?

[b] *Però Ald. W.*

mother, according to Philalethes (who gives no authority, nor can I find any elsewhere), a daughter of King Enzo, natural son of Frederick II.

we were come to the fourth day, Gaddo threw himself outstretched at my feet saying: "My father, why aidest thou me not?" There he died, and as thou seest me, I saw the three fall one by one, between the fifth day and the sixth; wherefore I betook myself, already blind, to grope over each one, and two days I called on them after they were dead; then my fasting was more potent than my woe.' When he

> Posciachè fummo al quarto dì venuti,
>   Gaddo mi si gittò disteso ai piedi,
>   Dicendo: Padre mio, che non m' aiuti?
> Quivi morì: e come tu mi vedi,   70
>   Vid' io cascar li tre ad uno ad uno
>   Tra il quinto dì e il sesto: ond' io mi diedi
> Già cieco a brancolar sopra ciascuno,
>   E due dì li chiamai poi che fur morti:^c
>   Poscia, più che il dolor, potè il digiuno.

^c *tre dì Ald.*

⁶⁸ Gaddo and Uguccione (l. 89) were sons. Some relate that a third grandson was of the party.

^{72, 74} For the curious v. ll. (*quarto, quinto, tre*) which a few MSS. give, see Moore, Text. Crit.

⁷⁵ With the reticence of this line cf. v. 138. The meaning probably is 'hunger did what grief could not do, killed me'; or perhaps, as Landino seems to think, referring to a well-known physiological phenomenon, 'the natural end could no longer be delayed by the intensity of my emotion.' At the same time few readers will say with Scartazzini that the verse is quite clear; or treat as wholly inadmissible the interpretation which some have suggested, and even stoutly defended, that Ugolino at last, in the pangs of starvation, obeyed the request made by his sons while still alive. To say, at all events, that this, or any other conception, is too horrible for Dante is obviously absurd, as the occupation which he assigns to Ugolino in Hell (and which gives some colour to the theory in question) might show. But the real arguments against it are that (as Blanc points out) neither Villani nor the Pisan Buti says anything about what, if it had happened, must have been well known to

had said this, with his eyes turned aside he took the wretched skull again with his teeth, which were strong as a dog's on the bone.

Ah! Pisa, reproach of the peoples of the fair land where the *si* is spoken, since thy neighbours are slow to punish thee, may Capraia and Gorgona be removed and make a barrier to Arno at its mouth, so that it may drown in thee every person. For if the Count Ugolino had

> Quand' ebbe detto ciò, con gli occhi torti
>   Riprese il teschio misero coi denti,
>   Che furo all' osso, come d' un can, forti.
> Ahi Pisa, vituperio delle genti
>   Del bel paese là, dove il sì suona ;   80
>   Poi che i vicini a te punir son lenti,
> Movasi la Caprara e la Gorgona,
>   E faccian siepe ad Arno in sulla foce,
>   Sì ch' egli anneghi in te ogni persona.
> Chè se il Conte Ugolino aveva voce

every one in Florence and Pisa ; and that since, according to Buti, they were all dead when on the eighth day the doors were opened, it is clear that Ugolino could not on that day have employed this means of sustaining life.

79 Cf. with this the apostrophe to Pistoia, xxv. 10. No cities did more than these two to keep Tuscany in the state of faction and turbulence which prevailed throughout Dante's lifetime, and hindered the union of the Italian states which he desired to see.

81 **dove il sì suona**: cf. Vulg. El. i. 8, where languages are classified according to their particles of affirmation. 'Alii *oc*, alii *oil*, alii *sì* affirmando loquuntur ; ut puta Hispani [i.e. no doubt Languedoc], Franci et Latini.'

82 Capraia and Gorgona are two small islands lying between the mouth of the Arno and Sardinia. The former gave the title of count to a nephew of Ugolino's, whom he was currently believed to have poisoned (Vill. vii. 121).

report to have betrayed thee of thy castles, thou oughtest not to have put the sons to such torment. Their young age made innocent, thou new Thebes, Uguccione and Brigata, and the other two whom my song names above.

We passed beyond, there where the ice swathes urgently another folk; not turned downward but all reverted. Their very weeping lets them not weep, and the woe that finds a

> D' aver tradita te delle castella,
> Non dovei tu i figliuoi porre a tal croce.
> Innocenti facea l' età novella,
> Novella Tebe, Uguccione e il Brigata,
> E gli altri due che il canto suso appella. 90
> Noi passamm' oltre, là 've la gelata
> Ruvidamente un' altra gente fascia,
> Non volta in giù, ma tutta riversata.
> Lo pianto stesso lì pianger non lascia,
> E il duol, che trova in sugli occhi rintoppo,

---

[86] See note l. 13. Benvenuto considers the allusion to be to the gift by Ugolino of two Pisan castles as a dowry with his daughters to the Counts of Battifolle and Santafiore, by which the castles passed into the possession, or lordship, respectively of Lucca and Florence. Villani, however, mentions (ix. 78) a number of castles which Uguccione della Faggiuola in 1315 won back from the Lucchese, having been held by them 'from the time of Count Ugolino'; and probably Dante refers to these.

[87] As a matter of fact they were all grown men, even the grandsons (according to Troya, not a very trustworthy authority) being married. Nino il Brigata was at any rate old enough to have murdered one of the Visconti faction a short time before this.

[89] **Tebe**: the 'Thebaid' contains horrors and bloodshed sufficient to justify the comparison. There may be a suggestion that Pisa was to Florence as Thebes to Athens.

[90] Between this and the next line occurs in a very few MSS. an interpolation of eighteen lines, evidently inserted at a pretty early date, and as evidently quite spurious. See for a full account Moore, Text. Crit., Appendix III.

barrier over the eyes is turned inward to make their trouble increase, for the first tears form a lump, and like a visor of crystal, fill all the hollow beneath the eyebrow. And albeit that, as in a hardened skin, all feeling had, by reason of the cold, ceased its abode in my face, already I seemed to feel some wind; wherefore I: 'Master mine, who sets this in motion? Is not all vapour down here come to an end?' Wherefore he to me: 'Speedily shalt thou be where the eye shall make thee thy answer to this, when thou seest the cause that pours down the blast.' And one of the sorrowful ones of the cold crust cried to us: 'O souls so cruel that the

> Si volve in entro a far crescer l' ambascia:
> Chè le lagrime prime fanno groppo,
>   E, si come visiere di cristallo,
>   Riempion sotto il ciglio tutto il coppo.
> Ed avvegna che, si come d' un callo,   100
>   Per la freddura ciascun sentimento
>   Cessato avesse del mio viso stallo,
> Già mi parea sentire alquanto vento;
>   Perch' io: Maestro mio, questo chi move?
>   Non è quaggiù ogni vapore spento?
> Ond' egli a me: Avaccio sarai, dove
>   Di ciò ti farà l' occhio la risposta,
>   Veggendo la cagion che il fiato piove.
> Ed un dei tristi della fredda crosta
>   Gridò a noi: O anime crudeli   110

97-99 The description in these lines is clearly meant to suggest an aggravation of the torment; and is thus an argument against the rendering of *labbra* as 'eyelids' in xxxii. 47.

105 Aristotle (Meteor. ii. 4) regards winds as the result of exhalations from the earth.

110, 111 He supposes that they are spirits condemned to the last division, or Giudecca.

furthest place has been given to you, lift from my visage the hard veils, so that I may discharge a little the woe which impregnates my heart, before the tears are frozen up again.' Wherefore I to him: 'If thou wilt that I come to thy aid, tell me who thou art; and if I do not set thee at rest, may it be my lot to go to the bottom of the ice.' He answered therefore: 'I am Friar Alberigo, I am the man of the fruits

> Tanto, che data v' è l' ultima posta,
> Levatemi dal viso i duri veli,
>   Si ch' io sfoghi il duol che il cor m' impregna,[d]
>   Un poco, pria che il pianto si raggeli.
> Perch' io a lui: Se vuoi ch' io ti sovvegna,
>   Dimmi chi sei, e s' io non ti disbrigo,
>   Al fondo della ghiaccia ir mi convegna.
> Rispose adunque: Io son Frate Alberigo,
> Io son quel dalle frutta del mal orto,[e]

[d] *il dolor W.; i sfogi 'l dolor Ald.*
[e] *delle f. W.*

[117] Where he is going in any case.

[118] **Frate Alberigo**, of the order called Frati Godenti (see xxiii. 103), was a member of the powerful house of the Manfredi (to which the Tribaldello of xxxii. 122 also belonged) at Faenza. Having quarrelled with one of his kinsfolk, Manfredi of the same house, on account of a blow received from him, he dissembled his anger for a time, and then invited Manfredi, together with his young son, to dinner. At the end of the meal he called 'Bring in the fruit,' whereupon armed men rushed in and killed both the father and the son. This took place about 1286. When Frate Alberigo died seems not to be known. Villani (x. 27) alludes to the story, when relating the murder of a brother of Alberigo's by his nephew in 1327. 'Le male frutta di Frate Alberigo' became proverbial.

[119] Benv. and others reading *delle* make 'the garden' mean Faenza; but he would hardly call himself a fruit, the context being what it is— *quel dalle frutta* = exactly Fr. *l'homme aux fruits*, 'the fruit-man.'

of the evil garden, that here get back a date for a fig.'
'Oh,' said I to him, 'now art thou already dead?' And he
to me: 'How my body stands in the world above I receive
no tidings. Such privilege has this Tolomea, that oftentimes the soul falls here before that Atropos gives it
movement. And to the end that thou mayest more willingly brush the glazed tears from my face, know that so
soon as the soul betrays, as did I, its body is taken by a
demon, who afterward orders it until its time be fully come

> Che qui riprendo dattero per figo. 120
> O, diss' io lui: Or sei tu ancor morto?
> Ed egli a me: Come il mio corpo stea
> Nel mondo su, nulla scienza porto.
> Cotal vantaggio ha questa Tolomea,
> Che spesse volte l' anima ci cade
> Innanzi ch' Atropos mossa le dea.
> E perchè tu più volentier mi rade
> Le invetriate lagrime dal volto,
> Sappi che tosto che l' anima trade,
> Come fec' io, il corpo suo l' è tolto 130
> Da un demonio, che poscia il governa
> Mentre che il tempo suo tutto sia volto.

125 Benvenuto mentions a v. l. *riprendo* ('pay back'), which is good in itself, but seems not to occur in any of Dr. Moore's *codices*.—'Dates for figs,' the former being at that time much more costly in Italy (Witte).

124 **Tolomea**, the division in which those are punished who have murdered or betrayed under the mask of friendship and hospitality, is named from Ptolemeus, son of Abubus, the captain of Jericho, who slew Simon the Maccabee and his sons at a banquet he had made for them (1 Macc. xvi. 11 sqq.) The 'privilege' assigned to it is one of Dante's most original and terrible conceptions. P. di Dante seems to think that it may have been suggested by Ps. liv. 16: descendant in infernum viventes.

round. The soul rushes down into a receptacle of this fashion; and haply the body yet appears above of the shade which is wintering behind me on this side. Thou shouldest know him, if thou art but now come down here; he is Master Branca d' Oria, and many years have passed since he has been thus shut up.' 'I think,' said I to him, 'that thou deceivest me; for Branca d' Oria has never yet died, but eats and drinks and sleeps and wears clothes.' 'Into the foss above,' said he, 'of Malebranche, where the sticky pitch is boiling, Michael Zanche had not yet

  Ella ruina in sì fatta cisterna ;
   E forse pare ancor lo corpo suso
   Dell' ombra che di qua dietro mi verna.
  Tu il dei saper, se tu vien pur mo giuso :
   Egli è Ser Branca d' Oria, e son più anni
   Poscia passati, ch' ei fu sì racchiuso.
  Io credo, dissi lui, che tu m' inganni ;
   Chè Branca d' Oria non morì unquanche,   140
   E mangia e bee e dorme e veste panni.
  Nel fosso su, diss' ei, di Malebranche,
   Là dove bolle la tenace pece,
   Non era giunto ancora Michel Zanche,

---

[137] Branca d' Oria, of the famous Ghibeline house of that name at Genoa, with the aid of his nephew, murdered at a feast his father-in-law, Michael Zanche (xxii. 88). He appears to have been still living when Henry VII. went to Genoa in 1311; on the strength of which, and of an expression used by a Genoese chronicler, Troya invented and others have repeated a legend that Dante, going there with Henry, had a decidedly unfriendly reception from Branca and his associates. Of this story it is enough to say that none of the early commentators gives any hint of it. 'That is the way in which Dante's life is written,' remarks Professor Bartoli (Vita di D. Cap. xvi.)

arrived, when this man left a devil in his stead within his body, and that of one his kinsman who wrought the treachery together with him. But now stretch forth hither thy hand; open me my eyes.' And I opened him them not; and a courtesy it was to be a churl to him. Ah! Genoese, men uncouth of every custom, and full of every blemish, why are ye not scattered from the world? For with the worst spirit of Romagna I found one of you such that for his work already in soul he is steeped in Cocytus, and in body appears yet living above.

> Che questi lasciò un diavolo in sua vece
>   Nel corpo suo, e d' un suo prossimano
>   Che il tradimento insieme con lui fece.
> Ma distendi oramai in qua la mano,
>   Aprimi gli occhi: ed io non glie le apersi.
>   E cortesia fu, in lui esser villano. 150
> Ahi Genovesi, uomini diversi
>   D' ogni costume, e pien d' ogni magagna,
>   Perchè non siete voi del mondo spersi?
> Chè col peggiore spirto di Romagna
>   Trovai un tal di voi, che per sua opra
>   In anima in Cocito già si bagna,
> Ed in corpo par vivo ancor di sopra.

149 Note **e** = almost 'but.' Cf. Par. xvi. 124.

151, 152 **diversi d' ogni costume** may also be taken as 'strange to all good manners.' The Tuscans would naturally regard the Genoese as little better than barbarians; as was evidently Dante's view with regard to their dialect. See Vulg. El. i. 13. Here the invective is probably due to the same cause as that on Pisa above. It must be said, however, that they received Henry of Luxemburg well.

154 **col peggiore spirto**: i.e. with Friar Alberico.

CANTO XXXIV

ARGUMENT

The fourth and last division, called Giudecca, contains those who have betrayed their benefactors. These are wholly sunk in the ice. At the centre is Lucifer, who has three heads, and with every mouth gnaws a sinner. Having seen this, they return to earth by a strange road.

'*Vexilla Regis prodeunt Inferni* towards us; therefore look forward,' said my Master, 'if thou discern him.' As when a thick mist is exhaling, or when our hemisphere is growing dusk, appears afar off a mill which the wind is turning, such a structure it then seemed to me that I saw. Then by

> *Vexilla Regis prodeunt inferni*
> Verso di noi: però dinanzi mira,
> Disse il Maestro mio, se tu il discerni.
> Come quando una grossa nebbia spira,
> O quando l' emisperio nostro annotta,
> Par da lungi un molin che il vento gira:
> Veder mi parve un tal dificio allotta:

---

[1] 'The banners of the king of Hell go forth.' The words are modelled on the opening of the celebrated hymn written by Venantius Fortunatus (born near Treviso, 530; died Bishop of Poitiers, 609), and sung from Passion Sunday to Good Friday: Vexilla regis prodeunt, Fulget crucis mysterium. The time being now about sunset on Good Friday, the allusion is specially appropriate.

reason of the wind I shrank back to my Leader, for there was no rock else. Already was I (and with fear I put it into verse) in the place where the shades were wholly covered, and showed through like a mote in glass. Some have their station lying down; some stand erect, one with the head and one with the soles; another like a bow turns its face inward toward its feet. When we had brought ourselves so far onward that it pleased my Master to show me the creature which had the fair countenance, he took himself in front of me, and made me halt, saying: 'Lo! Dis, and lo! the place where it is meet that thou arm thyself

    Poi per lo vento mi ristrinsi retro
      Al Duca mio; chè non li era altra grotta.
  Già era (e con paura il metto in metro)   10
      Là, dove l' ombre eran tutte coperte,
      E trasparean come festuca in vetro.
  Altre sono a giacere, altre stanno erte,
      Quella col capo, e quella con le piante;
      Altra, com' arco, il volto ai piedi inverte.
  Quando noi fummo fatti tanto avante,
      Ch' al mio Maestro piacque di mostrarmi
      La creatura ch' ebbe il bel sembiante,
  Dinanzi mi si tolse, e fe restarmi,
      Ecco Dite, dicendo, ed ecco il loco,   20
      Ove convien che di fortezza t' armi.

  ⁹ **grotta**: perhaps suggested by Isai. xxxii. 2: Erit vir sicut qui absconditur a vento . . . et umbra petrae prominentis in terra deserta.

  ¹¹ It is not specified to what class of traitors these sinners belong, as, for obvious reasons, Dante is unable to have speech of any: but they are generally considered to be those in whom treachery was combined with ingratitude or disloyalty.

  ¹⁵ Cf. Purg. xii. 25.

with fortitude.' How I then became frozen and weak, do not ask, reader, for I do not write it, seeing that every speech would be too little. I did not die and did not remain alive; think now for thyself, if thou hast a grain of wit, what I became, being deprived of one and the other.

The Emperor of the realm of woe issued by half the breast forth out of the ice; and I compare more nearly with a giant than do giants with his arms; see now how great must be that whole which is conformed to a part of such fashion. If he was as fair as he is now foul, and raised his brows against his Maker, rightly should all sorrow

> Com' io divenni allor gelato e fioco,
>   Nol domandar, Lettor, ch' io non lo scrivo,
>   Però ch' ogni parlar sarebbe poco.
> Io non morii, e non rimasi vivo:
>   Pensa oramai per te, s' hai fior d' ingegno,
>   Qual io divenni, d' uno e d' altro privo.
> Lo imperador del doloroso regno
>   Da mezzo il petto uscia fuor della ghiaccia:
>   E più con un gigante io mi convegno,   30
> Che i giganti non fan con le sue braccia:
>   Vedi oramai quant' esser dee quel tutto
>   Ch' a così fatta parte si confaccia.
> S' ei fu sì bel com' egli è ora brutto,
>   E contra il suo Fattore alzò le ciglia,
>   Ben dee da lui procedere ogni lutto.

---

²² **fioco**: perdidi vigorem et vocem.—Benv. But it seems needless to confine it to the voice. See Gloss. Par. s.v.

²⁷ **d' uno e d' altro**: of death and of life, implied in the verbs of l. 25.

²⁸⁻²⁹ S. T. i. Q. 63. A. 8: Quia supremus angelus majorem habuit naturalem virtutem quam inferiores, intensiori motu in peccatum prolapsus est. Et ideo factus est etiam in malitia major.

come forth from him. O, how great a marvel appeared to me when I saw three faces to his head; one in front, and that was crimson. The other were two, which were joined to this right over the middle of either shoulder, and met at the place of the crest; and the right seemed between white and yellow; the left was such to look upon as come from

> O quanto parve a me gran maraviglia,
> Quando vidi tre facce alla sua testa!
> L' una dinanzi, e quella era vermiglia:
> L' altre eran due, che s' aggiungieno a questa   40
> Sopr' esso il mezzo di ciascuna spalla,
> E si giungieno al loco della cresta:
> E la destra parea tra bianca e gialla:
> La sinistra a vedere era tal, quali

[38] The symbolism of these three faces has been a good deal discussed. They are clearly intended as a kind of infernal counterpart to the Godhead in Trinity; and the early commentators are therefore probably correct when they see in them an image of the qualities antithetical to the divine attributes of power, wisdom, and love (see notes iii. 5, Par. x. 1). These will be impotence, ignorance, and hatred; denoted respectively by the sickly yellow tint, the black, and the red. The first two explain themselves; of the third it may be noted that red, which is rightly the colour of love, may stand for love turned to hate, as green, the colour of hope, serves equally (if my interpretation be right) in ix. 40 to symbolise despair. Note further that *vermiglio* is the word used to express the colour to which the Florentine lily was changed by party hatred, in Par. xvi. 154. This suggests that here, as elsewhere, there may be a political symbolism. The black face may be the 'Black' party; that 'between white and yellow' intended to call to mind the degradation of the original white lily of Florence by contact with the 'gigli gialli' (Par. vi. 100) of France. Another interpretation is suggested by S. T. ii. 2. QQ. 34, 35, 36, where three vices are opposed to *charitas*: viz. *odium, accidia, invidia*. It is possible to work out a fairly satisfactory result on this basis: but on the whole the older view seems the best. The view that the three divisions of the earth, as then known, are indicated, has not much to be said for it.

the place where the Nile flows down. Beneath each came out two great wings of such size as befitted so great a bird; sails at sea never saw I of such kind. They had not feathers, but their fashion was of a bat; and these he was flapping so that three winds set out from him. Hence Cocytus was all frozen. With six eyes he was weeping, and over three chins his tears and bloodstained slaver were dripping. At every mouth he was rending with his teeth a sinner, in fashion of a heckle, so that he was making three of them thus woeful. To the one in front the biting was nothing beside the clawing, whereby at whiles the back

> Vengon di là, onde il Nilo s' avvalla.
> Sotto ciascuna uscivan due grandi ali,
>   Quanto si convenia a tanto uccello;
>   Vele di mar non vid' io mai cotali.
> Non avean penne, ma di vipistrello
>   Era lor modo; e quelle svolazzava,   50
>   Sì che tre venti si movean da ello.
> Quindi Cocito tutto s' aggelava:
>   Con sei occhi piangeva, e per tre menti
>   Gocciava il pianto e sanguinosa bava.
> Da ogni bocca dirompea coi denti
>   Un peccatore, a guisa di maciulla,
>   Sì che tre ne facea così dolenti.
> A quel dinanzi il mordere era nulla,
>   Verso il graffiar, che tal volta la schiena

---

[45] I.e. Ethiopia.

[49] 'Vespertilio est animal ignobile,' says an early MS. Natural History in the University Library of Cambridge.

[51] Bargigi takes the three winds to be pride, luxury, and avarice. If this be correct, it would suitably link the end of this Cantica with the beginning.

remained all stripped of the skin. 'That soul up there which has the greatest punishment,' said the Master, 'is Judas Iscariot, who has his head inside and without is working his legs. Of the other two that have the head downwards, he who hangs from the black snout is Brutus; see how he writhes, and says not a word. The other is Cassius, that seems so large of limb. But the night is rising again, and by this it is time to be gone, for we have seen all.'

As it pleased him, I clasped his neck; and he took choice of time and place, and when the wings were enough opened, he clutched him to the shaggy sides; from tuft to

<blockquote>
Rimanea della pelle tutta brulla. 60
Quell' anima lassù che ha maggior pena,
Disse il Maestro, è Giuda Scariotto,
Che il capo ha dentro, e fuor le gambe mena.
Degli altri due ch' hanno il capo di sotto,
Quel che pende dal nero ceffo è Bruto :
Vedi come si storce, e non fa motto :
E l' altro è Cassio, che par sì membruto.
Ma la notte risurge ; ed oramai
È da partir, chè tutto avem veduto.
Com' a lui piacque, il collo gli avvinghiai ; 70
Ed ei prese di tempo e loco poste :
E, quando l' ali furo aperte assai,
Appigliò sè alle vellute coste :
</blockquote>

[65] Benvenuto rather oddly inclines to think that Decimus Brutus is meant.

[67] **membruto** : Shakespeare, more in accordance with the facts so far as they are known, makes Cassius have 'a lean and hungry look.' Philalethes thinks that Dante misunderstood Cicero's reference to ' L. Cassii adipem ' in the third Catilinarian Oration (§ 10).

[68] **la notte risurge** : i.e. the sun has again set ; the first time having been that recorded in ii. 1. For *notte* see note xxiv. 3, and Purg. ii. 4.

tuft he afterwards went down between the matted hair and the icy crusts. When we were at the place where the thigh turns exactly upon the thick of the haunches, my Leader with labour and with straining turned his head where he had had his legs, and grappled himself to the hair like one who climbs, so that I deemed we were returning again to Hell. 'Hold thyself on well, for by such stairs,' said the Master, panting as one weary, 'it behoves to set oneself free from so great evil.' Then he issued forth through the hole of a rock, and placed me on the edge to sit; afterwards he

> Di vello in vello giù discese poscia
> Tra il folto pelo e le gelate croste.
> Quando noi fummo là dove la coscia
>   Si volge appunto in sul grosso dell' anche,
>   Lo Duca con fatica e con angoscia
> Volse la testa ov' egli avea le zanche,
>   Ed aggrappossi al pel come uom che sale,   80
>   Sì che in inferno io credea tornar anche.
> Attienti ben, chè per cotali scale,[a]
>   Disse il Maestro, ansando com' uom lasso,
>   Conviensi dipartir da tanto male.
> Poi uscì fuor per lo foro d' un sasso,
>   E pose me in sull' orlo a sedere:

[a] *per sì fatte sc.* Cass. W.

[79] Blanc calls attention to Dante's oversight of the fact that at the centre the action of gravity would be *nil*; and that therefore no effort would be needed to change direction, or rather position. But, as may be seen from De Aq. et Ter. § xvi., Dante evidently followed Aristotle in looking upon gravity as a kind of force exerted by the centre specially, and not by the mass. Otherwise, as Dr. Whewell (Inductive Sciences, Bk. iv. Ch. 1, § 9) has pointed out, the general conception of this passage is more accurate than might have been expected.

[80] Note again an accurate bit of mountaineering practice. Virgil,

reached toward me his cautious step. I raised my eyes, and
thought to see Lucifer as I had left him, and saw him hold
his legs upwards. And if I then became perplexed, let the
dull folk consider it, who see not what is that point which
I had passed. 'Lift thee up,' said my Master, 'on foot;
the way is long and the road is bad, and already is the sun
returning to mid tierce.' No chimney of a palace was it

> Appresso porse a me l' accorto passo.
> Io levai gli occhi, e credetti vedere
>   Lucifero com' io l' avea lasciato,
>   E vidili le gambe in su tenere.   90
> E s' io divenni allora travagliato,
>   La gente grossa il pensi, che non vede
>   Qual è quel punto ch' io avea passato.
> Levati su, disse il Maestro, in piede:
>   La via è lunga, e il cammino è malvagio,
>   E già il sole a mezza terza riede.
> Non era camminata di palagio

like a careful guide, gets his traveller safely on to a ledge, and then
follows.

93 See below, ll. 110, 111.

96 **mezza terza**: half way from the beginning of the day (6 A.M.) to
the third hour (9 A.M.), as appears from Convito iii. 15, iv. 23. It was
just after sunset before they reached the centre; they are now in the
other hemisphere, and it is morning. See Moore, Time References,
pp. 51, 55. Dr. Moore is obviously right in holding that we must consider the time to have gone back twelve hours, and Easter Eve to be
beginning for the southern hemisphere. The word **riede** points to this;
and Dante would never have supposed himself to spend Easter Day in
climbing through the bowels of the earth. Note that this is the first
instance in which time has been indicated by the *sun* since they entered
Hell.

97 **camminata.** Although no commentator seems to recognise the
meaning, and Du Cange, s.v. *caminata*, speaks only of 'a room with a
hearth in it,' I can hardly doubt that Dante is using the word in the
sense of the French *cheminée*, a sense which it must have possessed, the

there where we were, but a natural cranny, which had bad ground and of light small store. 'Before I pluck myself away from the abyss, my Master,' said I, when I was upright, 'talk with me a little to draw me from error. Where is the ice? and how is this one fixed so upside-down? and how in so little time has the sun made a passage from evening to morning?' And he to me: 'Thou fanciest yet that thou art on that side of the centre, where I took hold on the hair of the worm of sin that pierces the world. On that side thou wast so long as I descended; when I turned, thou didst pass the point to the which from every part the weights are drawn; and thou art now come to the

> Là 'v' eravam, ma natural burella
> Ch' avea mal suolo, e di lume disagio.
> Prima ch' io dell' abisso mi divella,   100
> Maestro mio, diss' io quando fui dritto,
> A trarmi d' erro un poco mi favella.
> Ov' è la ghiaccia? e questi com' è fitto
> Si sottosopra? e come in sì poc' ora
> Da sera a mane ha fatto il sol tragitto?
> Ed egli a me: Tu immagini ancora
> D' esser di là dal centro, ov' io mi presi
> Al pel del vermo reo che il mondo fora.
> Di là fosti cotanto, quant' io scesi:
> Quando mi volsi, tu passasti il punto   110
> Al qual si traggon d' ogni parte i pesi:

----

word being found as early as the 13th century. The meaning usually given, 'a hall,' is altogether out of place here. Every Alpine climber knows what a 'Kamin' is. Benvenuto, it may be noted, takes it to be from cammino, *'a road.'*

 erro: said to be a Tuscanism.

 Ar. de Cælo, ii. 14, ἕκαστον γὰρ τῶν μορίων [sc. τῆς γῆς] βάρος ἔχει μέχρι πρὸς τὸ μέσον.

bottom of the hemisphere which is opposite to that which the great dry land covers, and beneath whose zenith was put to an end the Man who was born and lived without sin; thou hast thy feet upon a little sphere which the other face of the Giudecca forms. Here it is at morning when it is evening there; and this one who made a ladder for us with his hair is still fixed as he was at first. On this side he fell

> E sei or sotto l' emisperio giunto
>   Ch' è contrapposto a quel che la gran secca
>   Coperchia, e sotto il cui colmo consunto
> Fu l' uom che nacque e visse senza pecca:
>   Tu hai li piedi in su picciola spera
>   Che l' altra faccia fa della Giudecca.
> Qui è da man, quando di là è sera:
>   E questi che ne fee scala col pelo,
>   Fitto è ancora, sì come prim' era.   120
> Da questa parte cadde giù dal cielo:

113 **secca**: because the geography of that time imagined the inhabited hemisphere, beneath which Hell lies, to contain all the dry land of the globe, except (in Dante's view) the mountain of Purgatory.

114, 115 Jerusalem being regarded (doubtless, as Philalethes points out, on the authority of Ezekiel v. 5) as the central point of the inhabited hemisphere, its zenith (or perhaps rather, meridian) is the culminating point (or line) for the earth generally.

116, 117 The ice on one side, and the 'stone' of l. 85 on the other, make a small internal sphere, the diameter of which is somewhat less than the length of Lucifer.

118 **da man**: so *dal principio del mattino*, i. 37. But it is hard to resist the opinion that the true reading is *Di qua è man*.

121 sqq. It does not appear whence Dante got this theory of the creation of Hell. At first sight it seems inconsistent with iii. 7, but from Par. xxix. 49-51 we gather that the fall of Satan and the creation of the earth took place simultaneously. It may be noted that Aquinas, while holding (Suppl. Q. 97. A. 7) that 'conveniens locus tristitiae damnatorum est intimum terrae,' declines to commit himself to a definite

down from Heaven; and the earth which formerly was spread on this side, for fear of him made of the sea a veil, and came to our hemisphere; and haply to fly from him that which is seen on this side left its place here void, and fled upward.'

A place there is below, so far removed from Beelzebub as the tomb extends; which is not known by sight, but by the sound of a brook, which there descends through the cavity of a rock which it has gnawed by reason of the course

> E la terra che pria di qua si sporse,
> Per paura di lui fee del mar velo,
> E venne all' emisperio nostro; e forse
> Per fuggir lui lasciò qui il loco voto
> Quella che appar di qua, e su ricorse.
> Loco è laggiù da Belzebù remoto
> Tanto, quanto la tomba si distende,
> Che non per vista, ma per suono è noto
> D' un ruscelletto che quivi discende   130
> Per la buca d' un sasso, ch' egli ha roso

statement on the point; alleging St. Augustine's statement, Civ. Dei xx. 16: ignis aeternus in qua mundi vel rerum parte futurus si', hominem scire arbitror neminem.

[128] **di qua**: i.e. the opening through which they were going to ascend.—**su**: to make the Mount of Purgatory, the only dry land, as has been said, in that hemisphere.

[128] I.e. equal to the depth of Hell.

[129] **non per vista**: because it is dark.

[130] The brook is generally held to be the outflow of Lethe, which rises at the summit of the Mountain of Purification. The small inclination of its course must be due to its flowing spirally through the earth, for of course all straight lines to the centre would be equally steep. The account given by Philalethes of all this is difficult to follow. He seems to take **tomba** as the actual hole occupied by Lucifer; and to imagine a kind of great vault or dungeon on the other side, into which the stream enters through a fissure.

wherein it winds, and it slopes little. Through that hidden road my Leader and I entered to return into the bright world; and without having a care of any rest we mounted up, he first and I second, so far that I had sight of the fair objects which the Heaven bears, through a round opening; and thence we issued to see again the stars.

>   Col corso ch' egli avvolge, e poco pende.
> Lo Duca ed io per quel cammino ascoso
>   Entrammo a ritornar nel chiaro mondo:
>   E senza cura aver d' alcun riposo
> Salimmo suso, ei primo ed io secondo,
>   Tanto ch' io vidi delle cose belle
>   Che porta il ciel, per un pertugio tondo,
> E quindi uscimmo a riveder le stelle.

[139] **stelle**: as has often been noticed, each division of the poem ends with this word.

GLOSSARY[1]

ABBREVIATIONS: v. sub, 'see under'; s. v. 'under the word'; cf. 'compare'; O. E. 'Old English'; M. E. 'Middle English'; O. Fr. 'Old French'; O. G. 'Old German.' The rest explain themselves.

Accaffare, xxi. 54; 'to snap up,' 'pilfer.' From *caffo*, which means originally 'uneven' of numbers; whence 'giuocare a pari e caffo,' 'to play odd and even.' Lat. 'micare'; a game requiring quickness, and offering great facilities for cheating. Cf. Cic. de Off. iii. 77. Der. of *caffo* is obscure. It is generally referred to *caput*, and to this there is no phonetic objection; but evidence is lacking of any use of *caput* in this sense. However, the *head* being the one member which is conspicuously unpaired, the metaphor is *prima facie* a very natural one.

Accapricciare, xxii. 31; 'to cause shuddering.' From *capriccio*. This must almost certainly be from *capo* and *riccio*; the latter word being from Lat. *ericius*, 'a hedgehog,' Fr. *hérisson*, our *urchin*. The usual deriv. of *capriccio* from *caper*, 'a goat,' will no doubt suit the

---

[1] This Glossary does not profess to be exhaustive. I have given only such words as seemed interesting either from their obscure derivation, or from some peculiarity in their use, or else as being specially illustrative of some principle of Romance etymology. Still less is it final. I have neither the reading necessary to verify the rather crude conjectures occasionally put forth in it, nor leisure to supply this deficiency. At most, I can hope to stimulate other students. The term 'late Latin' is used in the case of such words as, though not in use in classical Latin, are to be found in Forcellinus. '*A* Latin' implies that the word, though not found, might have existed. 'Vigfússon' is used to denote Cleasby and Vigfússon's Icelandic Dictionary. It must not, of course, be supposed that any Italian words are derived from the Old Norse or Icelandic; but Gothic, which has supplied many words to Italian, is a closely-allied language, and we can in many cases use Icelandic to reconstruct forms which the Gothic probably possessed, but of which, through the scantiness of its remaining literature, all trace is now lost.

meaning 'caprice,' but will not account for that of 'shudder,' which both the original word, and still more its derivatives, express. *Riccio* has also the meaning of 'curly' as applied to hair. It is curious that *ericius*, Gr. χήρ, appears to contain the same root as *horreo* (Skeat).

Accismare, xxviii. 37 ; 'to arrange,' 'set in order.' Probably not connected with *cisma = schisma*. The Gr. σχίσμα does not appear to have passed into Lat. in its primary sense. It is better to connect the word with Prov. *acesmar*, 'to make ready,' 'put in place,' used e.g. of soldiers in battle. This is from *adaestimare* ; the original notion being 'to judge' or 'calculate,' and then 'to execute.' From *aestimare* come O. Fr. *esmer*, Eng. *aim* ; the transition between calculation and execution being well seen in the English word.

Adizzare, xxvii. 21 ; 'to urge,' 'excite.' Said to be properly used of setting dogs to fight. From Germ. *hetzen*. Also found in the form *aizzare* (which some read here).

Adonare, vi. 34 ; 'to beat down,' 'subdue.' From *donare*, the original sense, as in the reflexive form (Purg. xi. 19), being 'to surrender.' For the change of meaning Diez compares Sp. *rendir*, which means 'to subdue,' as well as 'to give up.' Possibly *domare* affected the sense.

Adontare, vi. 72 ; 'to shame.' From *onta*, Fr. *honte*. This from a vb. *onire*, Fr. *honnir*, from O. G. *hônen*, Germ. *höhnen*, 'to mock.'

Aggueffare, xxiii. 16 ; 'to add to,' 'lay upon.' Germ. *weben*, 'to weave,' ἅπαξ λεγόμενον. [Blanc, however, appears to read it xxxi. 56.]

Agognare, vi. 28, etc. ; 'to desire eagerly.' Through late Lat. *agonia*, from Gr. ἀγών, 'a contest.'

Allettare, ii. 122 ; ix. 93. Probably in these instances from *letto* : as it is hard to see what sense can be got if the usual meaning 'entice' (from *allectare*) be given to the word.

Anca, xix. 43, etc. ; 'haunch,' 'hip.' From O. G. *ancha* or *encha*. So Lat. *angulus*, *ancus*, *aduncus*, low Lat. *ankilus*, 'knee-joint,' Gr. ἄγκων, Eng. *ankle*, etc., the root being almost universal in the sense of 'bending.'

Appiccare, xxv. 61, 107 ; xxix. 129 ; 'to stick together,' 'cause to take hold.' Diez derives from *pix*, *picis*, 'pitch,' and though the vowel-change is somewhat unusual (and has probably been affected by a supposed connection with the root found in *picco*, *peak*, etc.), this seems on the whole most probable. The word no doubt is often used of attacking by means of something pointed : but a converse change is found in our *stick*, *sticky*, where a word which (as its cognates show) was originally proper only to the nail, has been transferred to the glue.

Arnia, xvi. 3; 'a beehive.' Of unknown origin; possibly, as the word is also found in Spanish, from Arabic.

Arrostare, xv. 39; 'to fan.' See **Rosta**.

Attuffare, viii. 53; xviii. 113, etc.; 'to submerge.' From Germ. *taufen*, 'to *dip*.'

Baratta, xxi. 63; 'traffic'; **barattiere**, ib. 41, etc.; 'a trafficker' or 'jobber.' Words of obscure origin, which have found their way into all the chief Romance languages, and in the form *barter* into modern English. (*Barratry* also exists, but as a technical term, taken it would seem directly from law-French.) There is also an older word *barrat*, obsolete apparently since 1500, in the sense both of 'fraud' and of 'quarrel' or 'fighting.' The latter meaning is given by many interpreters, including Dict. Crusc., to *baratta*; but in two of the instances, other than this, quoted in the Dict., it clearly means something which is *not* fighting; while in the other two, from the 'Dittamondo,' it looks very much as if Fazio had misunderstood Dante. Benvenuto evidently takes it here in the same sense as is found in its derivatives. It must, however, be said that there is an Icel. *baratta* (probably an imported word), meaning 'a fight,' and the English use of both *barrat* and *baratour* (see Murray) shows that the idea of 'contending' was conveyed by the word in other languages, if not in Italian. No doubt this idea is involved in that of buying and selling (especially as the process is conducted in the south of Europe), no less than in that of actual fighting or brawling. Diez suggests Gr. πράττειν, which is quite satisfactory phonetically, if any historical evidence were forthcoming. If so, the sense of 'dealing' would be the original one; and thence would easily come that of dealing or bandying blows. Fr. *baratter* = 'to churn butter,' the idea being no doubt of throwing to and fro. In Dittam. iii. 13, *barattarsi*, of the sea.

Belletta, vii. 124; 'mire.' According to Benv. a Florentine local term, denoting properly mud caused by rain or deposited by a swollen stream. He says that the forms *melma* and *melmetta* are also used. No doubt a jocose use of *belletto*, low Lat. *belletum*, 'paint for the cheeks,' 'cosmetic,' from *bellus*.

Berza, xviii. 37: 'heel' or 'leg.' Blanc's suggestion of Germ. *ferse* is open to the objection that initial *f* before a vowel does not seem to give *b*. Ménage seems more likely to be right in the view, quoted by Diez, that it is a slang word, and = *verza*, 'cabbage,' hence 'cabbage-stalk' or 'stalk' in general. Cf. 'gambale,' from 'gamba.' *Verza* is from *viridaria*, 'greens.'

Bica, xxix. 66; 'a heap'; and **abbicare**, ix. 78; 'to heap' or 'hunch up.' Said to be originally 'a sheaf,' from an O. G. *bíga* in the same sense: cf. mod. (South Germ.) *beige*, 'a woodstack,' *beigen*, 'to pile wood.' This appears to be connected with *beugen*, 'to bend,' and Grimm gives also *beigen*, 'to crook,' which brings us very near to the meaning required for *abbicare*. [The word, curiously like the Northern English *bike*, 'a crowd,' originally 'nest' or 'swarm of bees.' The meaning of 'montar sulla bica,' 'to get in a rage,' would fit the English word well. The origin of *bike* is unknown; so that a possible connection with *bica* need not be rejected.]

Biscazzare, xi. 44; 'to squander,' 'gamble away.' From *bisca*, 'a gaming-house.' Origin of this unknown; but it would seem to be akin to Fr. *bisque*, meaning 'odds given by one player to another at tennis.' [One would be inclined to see *bis* in the first syllable of this, as if the player should score twice for the same stroke. If so, the notion of 'odds' might be the original. But Littré gives no example of *bisque* before the 16th cent.]

Bizzarro, viii. 62; 'wrathful,' 'furious.' This appears to be the only sense which the word had before 1400. Villani (viii. 39) speaks of the 'bizzarra salvatichezza' of the Black Guelfs; Boccaccio, probably borrowing from Dante, uses it of Filippo Argenti. Later on it acquired the meaning of 'eccentric,' 'far-fetched'; with which it appears (but not till the 16th cent.) in Fr., and which alone it possesses in Fr. and Eng. (the latter not till 17th cent.) In Spanish it means 'brave,' 'high-spirited.' The sb. *bizarri* occurs in Basque with the same signification, and seems to be derived from *bizar*, 'beard,' which again may contain the same root as *guizon*, 'man.' If the passage of the word from West to East can be traced, this would give a satisfactory derivation, especially when the tendency of words towards deterioration in meaning is remembered.

Bolgia, xviii. 24, and *passim*; 'a bag,' 'pit.' O. Fr. *bouge* ('the mod. word signifies only 'a closet' or 'mean dwelling'), Eng. *budget*. From *bulga*, found as early as Lucilius, and said to be Gaulish. There is a Gaelic *builg*.

Borno or **-io**, xxvi. 14; 'a *bound*ary stone,' 'slab.' (This meaning is not recognised by Cruse., but there can hardly be any doubt of it here.) From Fr. *borne*, O. Fr. *bodne*, low Lat. *bodina*. This is found as early as the 7th cent. Its origin is unknown. [May not Germ. *boden*, our *bottom*, have originally meant merely 'end' or 'limit'? Wharton (Etyma Graeca), s. v. πυθμήν, connects this with Celtic *vonn*, from which the Fr. word has (though probably incorrectly) been derived. If this suggestion be tenable, we ought probably to see the same root in Fr. *bout*, our *butt* and *abut*.]

Bragia, iii. 109; 'a hot coal.' Fr. *braise*. Said to be from Norse *brasa*, 'to harden metal' or 'solder.' This word seems rather doubtful. No example of it is given by Vigfússon. Littré mentions O. G. *bras*, 'fire,' *brasen*, 'to burn' (mod. *braten*, 'to roast'). Eng. *brazier* is from the Fr. Skeat connects *brass*, but this seems doubtful.

Brago, viii. 50; 'mud.' O. Fr. *brai*, mod. Fr. = only 'tar' (in which sense *bray* is found in Eng. 16th cent.) Diez and Littré, regarding this as the original sense, derive from 'Scandinavian *bråk*'—unknown to Vigfússon.

Bronco, xiii. 26; 'a stump.' Sp. *bronco*, 'rough,' 'unpolished.' Probably from O. G. *brechan*, part. *gibrochan*, 'to break'; 'something broken off.' Hence too Fr. *broncher*. [Cf. Eng. *stumble* and *stump*.] For the inserted *n* see Diez i. 283. It is, of course, common enough.

Buca, xxxii. 125. See Gloss. Purg.

Buccia, xix. 29. See Gloss. Purg.

Buco, xxxii. 2. See Gloss. Purg.

Burchio, xvii. 19; 'a small boat.' From low Lat. *burclus*, the origin of which is unknown. Du Cange appears to connect it with low Lat. *bucia*, Fr. *buse*, Eng. *buss*.

Burella, xxxiv. 98; 'a hole in the earth,' 'cavern.' Fr. *bure*, 'a shaft' (e.g. in a mine). According to Diez connected with *buio* (q. v. in Gloss. Purg.) But is it not rather from Germ. *bohren*, our *bore*?

Burrato, xii. 10; xvi. 114; 1, 'a ravine,' 2, 'a precipice.' There is another form *burrone*, also *borro*; these last having, it would seem, always the sense of 'a hollow place.' Muratori refers them to Gr. βόθρος, and Diez appears to agree; though he does not account for the presence of the word in Italy.

Calare, xxvii. 81; 'to let down,' 'lower,' e.g. a sail; hence 'to fall.' From Lat. *chalare*, found in Vitruvius (x. 13); this from Gr. χαλᾶν.

Cennamella, xxii. 10; 'a shawm.' From O. Fr. *chalemel*, mod. *chalumeau*. Lat. *calamus*, 'a reed.' Bargigi has the form *cialamella*.

Cespuglio, xiii. 123, 131; 'a tuft of grass,' or (according to Bargigi) 'a shrub throwing up shoots from the ground.' Through *cespo*, from Lat. *caespes*, 'turf.' The termination is somewhat hard to account for; but cf. *miscuglio*.

Chiappa, xxiv. 33; 'a rocky ledge.' Benv. gives us a clue to the derivation. '*Chiappa*,' he says, 'est pars tegulae culmae [? culminis] qua teguntur tecta domorum.' He is, however, probably wrong in thinking that Dante means to say that he was like a man going on a roof. *Chiappa* evidently = 'a shingle,' and the slabs of rock, by the edges of which they climb down, are compared to inverted shingles on a roof. The word will be the same as *clap* in '*clap*board' or '*clap*bolt.' Germ. '*klapp*holz,' 'split oak.' 'From stem of *klappen* = *clap* in some one of its various senses,' Murray (probably that of 'fold' or 'lay together'). But may it not rather be corrupted from some form of O. G. *chlioban*, '*cleave*'?

Cima, viii. 3, etc.; 'a summit,' properly of a tree, in which sense it appears as early as 12th cent. in Fr. *cime*. From Lat. *cyma* (Pliny), in the sense of 'the first shoot of a plant,' especially a cabbage. This from Gr. κῦμα, which, however, does not seem to be found in this sense in literature, though its derivation from κύω makes it certain that the meaning of 'wave' must have originally been metaphorical.

Ciocca, xxxii. 104; 'a tuft of hair.' From the same root as *ciocco*, 'a log,' in Par. xviii. 100. Also Eng. *chock*, 'a lump,' *shock* (of corn or of hair), *shock* ('a concussion'), Germ. *schock*, 'a heap' or 'bundle' (usually of sixty), Icel. *skokkr*, 'a trunk, chest,' Fr. *choc*, and probably *souche*, 'trunk of a tree.' The original meaning seems to be 'stump' or 'bundle,' whence the idea, common in Rom. languages (cf. *bronco* and *intoppo*, Gloss. Purg.) of knocking against such an object.

Cionco, ix. 18; 'cut off,' for *cioncato*. Probably a variant of the same root as in the last word (cf. Eng. *chock* and *chunk*), modified by *troncare*. For the meaning, cf. 'truncus' and 'truncare,' 'stump,' and Germ. 'verstümmeln.' Bocc. says that in this sense the word is Lombard; *cioncare* in Tuscan meaning 'to drink copiously.'

Ciuffetto, xxviii. 33; 'forelock.' Dim. of *ciuffo*. This, according to Diez, from Germ. *schopf*; but O. G. *zoph*, mod. *zopf*, Eng. *top*, *tuft*, Fr. *touffe* seems more likely. *Schopf* looks more like a formation back from *ciuffo*. Cf. **zuffa**.

Cocca, xii. 77; 'the notch of an arrow'; hence, xvii. 136, 'the arrow itself.' Fr. *coche*. The connection with Eng. *cock* (of a gun) seems uncertain. May it not have originally denoted the catch of the crossbow? We find in Fr. 'mettre un quarrel en coche,' as the earliest (13th cent.) use of the word (Littré). Thence it would be transferred to the end of the arrow nearest the catch, or, in a longbow, nearest the string. If this was the earliest meaning, the word ought probably to be referred to low Lat. *cocha*, 'a block'; O. Fr. *choque*. V. s. **ciocca**.

It must be said, however, that the meaning 'notch' appears very early, e.g. Bocc. v. 2, where it can be nothing else.

Conciare, xxx. 33; 'to trim,' 'arrange.' See Gloss. Par. s. v. **acconciare**.

Coppa, xxv. 22; 'the head,' especially 'the back of the head.' Lit. 'a *cup*,' from Lat. *cupa*. [Hence Germ. *kopf*. Cf. Fr. 'tête,' from 'testa,' 'a potsherd'; the real words 'haupt' and 'chef' having acquired figurative meanings.]

Corata, xxviii. 26; 'intestines,' according to Buti, heart, lungs, and liver. O. Fr. *corée*, from *cor*, 'heart.' Prov. *coralha* means 'belly' as well as 'heart.' [Not to be confused with Fr. 'curée,' originally 'cuirée,' Eng. 'quarry'; the portion wrapped in the hide ('corium') and given to the hounds. See Littré, s. v. **curée**, and Skeat, **quarry** in Appendix.]

Cozzare, xxxii. 51; 'to butt'; and sb. **cozzo**, vii. 55; ix. 97. From *coictare*, freq. of *coicere* (Diez). Etymologically there seems no objection; cf. 'dirizzare,' from 'directus.' But is there any evidence for the existence of *coicere*?

Croio, xxx. 102; 'leathery' (perhaps 'stiff'). I think from *cuoio*, Lat. *corium*, with the *r* replaced in the wrong position. Diez takes it from *crudius*, a derivation of *crudus*; but apart from the doubt whether such a form could exist, it is hard to get the meaning from it. The 'sounding like a drum' makes it pretty clear what notion Dante connected with the word; though other uses of it would no doubt fit with *crudus*.

Crollare, xxii. 107, etc.; 'to shake.' From *corotulare*. O. Fr. *croller*, mod. *crouler*. Lit. 'to keep rolling.'

Crosciare, xxiv. 120: 'to let fall with a crash.' Usually intrans. Goth. *kriustan*, 'to gnash the teeth.' Sp. *cruxir*, 'to crackle,' Eng. *crush*, *crunch*, Gr. κρότος are doubtless akin.

Dilaccare, xxviii. 30; 'to split open.' From *lacca* in the sense of 'the hollow of the thigh,' hence 'to tear limb from limb.'—Dict. Crusc. But this seems hardly likely. *Lacca*, in the sense (e.g. Purg. vii. 71) of a hollow, may easily be transferred to the hollow of the body; and the meaning will be 'to open a hollow place'; possibly modified by *dilacero*. V. sub **lacca**.

Dogare, xxxi. 75; 'to enclose,' like the hoop of a cask, *doga*, q. v. Gloss. Purg.

Dotta, xxxi. 110; 'fear.' Lit. '*doubt*.' Sb. from ob. *dottare*, Lat. *dubitare* (cf. 'rotta,' from 'rupta'). For the meaning, cf. Fr. *redouter*.

Epa, xxv. 82, etc.; 'a paunch.' Said to be from Gr. ἧπαρ, 'the liver,' through Latin; but?

Fio, xxvii. 135; 'payment,' '*fee*.' Goth. *faihu*, O. G. *fihu*, mod. *vieh*, Lat. *pecus*, etc., 'cattle,' and hence 'chattels.' Goods (land and property) held by service to an over-lord; and ultimately the payment made in lieu of service, hence any repayment.

Gemere, xiii. 41; 'to drip.' See Gloss. Purg.

Ghermire, xxi. 36; xxii. 138; 'to seize with claws.' Tuscan form (?) of *gremire*. This from same stem as O. G. *krimman*, Icel. *kremja* ('to squeeze'), Eng. *crumb* from the same root ('anything torn to pieces,' Skeat); perhaps also *crimp*.

Gora, viii. 31; 'a channel,' properly 'a mill-leat.' From M. G. *wuore, wur*, in the same sense; probably connected with *wehren*, 'to guard'; the original meaning being 'the dam.' For the transfer from that which keeps in the water to the water itself, cf. 'pond' (='pound'). The form *wier* is found in Tyrol. Eng. *weir*, M. E. *wore* ('weary so water in wore') is no doubt akin.

Greppo, xxx. 95; 'a broken pot' (Ottimo Comento and Benvenuto). Others, 'rough' or 'craggy ground'; e.g. Fazio degli Uberti in Dittam. i. 2. Probably a dialectic equivalent of *crepato*, 'cracked,' 'split.' Cf. Romanisch *crap*, 'a rock.' In S. Tyrol *crep* means 'a narrow gorge.' (Schneller, Tirol. Namenforschungen.)

Gualdana, xxii. 5; 'a raid.' Probably from low Lat. *gualdus*, Germ. *wald*, 'a wood.' Hence originally 'beating for game.'—Du Cange.

Guercio, vii. 40; 'squinting,' or 'blear-eyed.' From Germ. *quer*, 'across' (Eng. *queer*). [This seems better than to derive it, with Diez, from M. G. *dwerch*, G. *zwerch*, 'thwart.'] The meaning may here be simply 'awry,' with no allusion to sight.

Lacca, vii. 16; xii. 11; 'a hollow' or 'ravine.' The word is generally derived from O. G. *lakha*; G. *lacke*, Eng. *lake, leak* (*leak* pron. *lake* = 'a drain' or 'gully' in the West of England), also probably *lack*, 'to want' and 'to pierce,' Lat. *lacus, lacuna*. The common idea in all these is evidently 'a breach' or 'opening.' Schneller (Tirolische Namenforschungen) mentions a narrow chasm called *la Slacca* near Lizzana, in Val d'Adige, and close to the 'Slavini di Marco,' to which Dante alludes in the same passage in Canto xii., where the word *lacca* occurs. The coincidence is curious, even if the existence of the compound *dilacco* (among other things) prevents us from agreeing with him that *slacca* (which, he says, means locally 'a rut,' and proposes to derive from O. G. *slac*, G. *schlag*) is the original word from which Dante formed his *lacca*.

Leppo, xxx. 99. According to Buti, the smoke arising from burning grease. The form of the word points to Lat. *lippus*, which in literature usually means nothing but 'blear-eyed.' It is, however, undoubtedly connected with Gr. λίπαρος, 'fat,' and may be explained as 'greasy,' 'sticky.' Martial (vii. 20) uses the word of an over-ripe fig, probably to denote its oily look and feel. No doubt in the spoken language the sense of 'grease' was preserved.

Lercio, xv. 108; 'foul.' There appears to be a longer form (if it be the same word), *gualercio*; which, apparently by a confusion with 'guercio,' also means 'squinting.' (Diez gives the latter meaning also to *lercio*; but Dict. Crusc. knows nothing of it. There is said, however, to be a Sardinian *lerzu*, 'distorted,' and there is a M. G. 'lerz' = 'lefthand'; but what is the connection between these and 'filthy'?) The verb, however, seems to occur earlier than the adj. Diefenbach gives, from a low Dutch glossary of 1420, *lerire*, 'ontreynen' ('to defile'). I am unable to trace the word any further back.

Logoro, xvii. 128; 'a *lure*' (for falcons). I do not feel quite sure that this word has been thoroughly made out. The forms are low Latin *lorra*, 'bait' (for fish); also, in a Spanish document of 1300-1350, *logres* (in the same sense). O. Fr. *loerre*, *loirre*, 'bait' and 'lure' (by 1250), mod. *leurre*. Prov. *loirar*, *lojar*, 'to attract' (12th cent.) Sp. *lura*, 'lure'; but apparently not the regular word, and probably introduced from French. Eng. *lure* (second half of 14th cent.) M. G. *luoder*, mod. *luder*, 'bait'; also 'carrion'; also 'dissoluteness.' The usual view is that the Germ. is the original of the others; but it must be noted that the word appears in Provençal, in Bertrand de Born, almost as early as in German. Then the form *logres* is singularly like Sp. 'logro' from 'lucrum,' while (unless it came directly from Italian) it is hard to see how it arose from *lorra*. Prov. *loirar* corresponds to *lucrare*, as 'oisor' to 'uxor.' From 'gain' to 'temptation' is an easy step. On the whole, I am inclined to think that we have two lines of words from different roots. ['Logoro,' adj. 'worn out,' 'decayed' (also 'dissolute'), is probably a different word = G. 'locker'; the resemblance of which to 'locken,' 'entice,' is curious.]

Lonza, i. 32; xvi. 108; 'a leopard,' 'ounce.' Fr. *once*, Sp. *onza*. The old derivation was from *lynx* (for *y* to *o*, cf. 'borsa,' from 'byrsa'). But it is far more probable that the article has adhered in the Italian form than that an initial has been dropped in all the others; and the word is now considered to be from the Persian *yuz*, 'a panther.' See Littré and Skeat.

Lordo, vi. 31, etc.; 'filthy.' From Lat. *luridus*; perhaps to some extent affected, especially in the sb. *lordura*, by *ordo*, Fr. *orde*, from *horridus*. The meaning, however, begins to appear in Hor. 4 Od. xiii. 10. Fr. *lourd*, Sp. *lerdo*, are from the same, but in a different direction. See Littré, s. v. *lourd*. The Epinal Glossary gives *lurdus*, 'laempehalt' (I presume the 'lemphealt,' which, according to Professor Skeat, s. v. **limp**, 'wants confirmation'); and *luridam*, 'luto pollutam.'

Mastino, xxi. 44; xxvii. 46; 'a *mastiff*.' For *masnadiro*, 'a house-dog,' from *masnada*, 'a household.' This from low Latin *mansionata*. See Gloss. Purg. s. v. **masnada**.

Menare, i. 18, etc.; 'to lead.' Fr. *mener*. From late Latin *minare* (Apuleius and Ausonius; perhaps much older in the colloquial language), 'to drive.' Cognate with *minari*, 'to threaten.' The original sense is perhaps 'to press' (Wharton, Etyma Latina). From *mener* come *demean*, *demeanour* (as 'conduct,' from 'ducere').

Meschino, ix. 43; 'a servant'; xxvii. 115, 'a wretch.' Found in all western Romance languages, having probably spread from Spain. From Arabic *meskin*, 'poor.' This is the original sense of the word, and the only one which it has in Spanish. 'Servant' is later.

Mezzo, vii. 128; 'moist,' 'soft.' With sharp *e* and hard *zz*. Not to be confused (as here by Benvenuto) with 'mezzo' from 'medius.' According to Diez, from Lat. *mitis*. But in order to obtain it, he has to assume a form *mitius*, of which there is no evidence; and also the passage, contrary to all rule, of Latin *i* into *e*. [In his Grammar (the French translation) mitis is written, perhaps by a printer's error.] On the other hand, tonic *a* does occasionally become *e*, so that it would seem better to take it from *madidus*. The original meaning would seem, as in this passage, to be 'wet'; and the other meanings are easily reached from this. Latin *madidus* actually occurs in the sense of 'soft,' and from this the sense of 'over-ripe' (especially of pears or medlars) follows directly.

Mucchio, xxvii. 44; 'a heap.' Perhaps from same root as Icel. *moka*, 'a shovel,' which again is connected with *myki*, our *muck*. The Gothic cognate seems to be *maihstus*, Germ. *mist*; but the root evidently contains a *k* sound.

Mucciare, xxiv. 127; 'to move away.' Earlier it seems to have been used transitively, 'fly from.' Benv. calls it 'vulgare lombardorum'; but it is used by Jacopone da Todi. [It also has the meaning 'to mock'; but is not this another word = Fr. 'moquer,' etc.?] The derivation is obscure; but it may be from some frequentative of *mutare* (itself probably a frequentative of *moveo*). *Mutitare* actually exists, but apparently only in the sense of 'to go out to dinner.'

Muda, xxxiii. 22; 'a cage,' '*mew*.' Lit. 'a place for hawks to *moult*.' Fr. *mue*. From Latin *mutare*, 'to change'; cf. *mutare* in this sense Purg. ii. 36.

Musare, xxviii. 43; 'to *muse*.' Lit. 'to stand with the *muzzle* (*muso*) open.' *Muso*, low Latin *musum*, from *morsum* (as 'giuso' from 'deorsum'), Diez. This derivation (given also in Dict. Crusc.) seems to hold water perfectly; and therefore, as Professor Skeat says, there is no need to look any further, whether to Germ. *musse*, 'leisure,' or elsewhere.

Nuca, xxxii. 129; 'the nape of the neck.' Low Latin *nucha*. Perhaps from *nux* (cf. 'duca' from 'dux'); but more probably connected with Germ. *knöchel*, Eng. *knuckle*; in the sense of the projecting bone at the base of the neck. In this case it will be akin to *neck*.

Otta, xxi. 112; 'an hour.' More frequent in the form *allotta* = 'allora.' Diez connects it with Goth. *uht-* (in comp.), 'early,' 'seasonable,' O. G. *uohta*, Icel. *ótta*, 'the hours before dawn.' If so, its meaning will stand to that of 'ora' much as Gr. καιρὸς to χρόνος. But it is curious to remark the tendency in Italian to substitute for certain words similar (though unconnected) words containing the sound *ot*. Thus 'piota' for 'pianta,' 'gota' for 'guancia.'

Peltro, i. 103; '*pewter*.' Fr. *peautre* (now only = a cosmetic). Original form probably *spelter* (Eng.), now used as a name for zinc in commerce. Skeat would connect this with *spall*, originally *speld*, 'a splinter'; akin to Germ. *spalt*, Eng. *split*.

Perso, v. 89; vii. 103; '*perse*,' 'of a dark colour.' The colour of a *peach*, '*persicum* malum.' See note, Purg. ix. 97.

Piaggiare, vi. 69; 'to coast.' *Piaggia*, Fr. *plage*, 'coast'; also, as in i. 29. etc., 'hillside.' (Cf. Fr. 'côte' in both senses.) From low Latin *plagia*, formed from *plaga*, 'a tract of country.' [An ingenious suggestion is that in this passage the word is from Gr. πλάγιος, 'crooked'; but as the phrase 'andar piaggia piaggia' is recognised, there seems no need to look further. Villani, viii. 69, uses 'piaggiare col' in the sense of 'to be in the same boat with.']

Piato, xxx. 147; 'a dispute,' 'quarrel.' From Latin *placitum*, originally 'a decision,' then 'legal proceedings.' Fr. *plaid*, Eng. *plea*. The sense of 'quarrel' or 'complaint' is found as early as the Strassburg Oath (842): 'et ab Ludher nul plaid nunquam prindrai.'

Piota, xix. 120; 'sole of the foot.' From old Latin (or Oscan) *plautus, plotus*, 'flat-footed.' Akin to Gr. πλατύς, Lat. *planta*. [Hence Germ. *pfote*, Eng. *paw*, etc.]

Pozza, vii. 127; 'a pond.' From *putea*, a bye-form of *puteus*, 'a well,' whence also O. G. *phuzza* ('well'), mod. *pfutze* (fem.), 'pool' or 'puddle.' Schneller (op. cit. p. 130) quotes from a Trentine document of 1214: omnes putee que ... aperte sunt in episcopatu. Perhaps the gender may have been affected by 'cavea.' An ingeniously suggested derivation from *putida* is barred by the fact that *u* hardly ever becomes *o*. Also the meaning, though appropriate here, would not suit other passages where the word occurs. Whether our 'puddle,' M. E. 'podel,' is connected seems doubtful.

Pruovo, xii. 93; 'near,' in phr. **a pruovo**. That the word is merely Latin *prope* is shown by the Prov. *a prop*, O. Fr. *a pruef* (Diez ii. 435). The change of *e* final into *o* need give no trouble. Cf. 'tristo.'

Raccapricciare, xiv. 78; v. sub **accapricciare**.

Ramarro, xxv. 79; 'a lizard.' According to Diez, from *rame* (*aeramen*), 'brass.' But it is said to be a green lizard. Also *-arro* is not a very common termination in Italian. The origin of the word must, I suspect, be sought abroad.

Randa, xiv. 12; 'an edge,' 'border.' Only in phrase *a randa*, which came to mean 'hardly,' 'barely.' Sp. *randa*, 'trimming of a dress.' From Germ. *rand* in the same sense, especially 'the rim of a shield.' Icel. *rönd*. See Skeat, s. v. *random*.

Rezzo, xvii. 87; xxxii. 75; 'shade,' 'coolness.' From a Latin *auritium*. See Gloss. Purg. s. v. *aura*. [Benv. in the former place reads *reggio*, and derives it from *rigidum* (sc. frigus).]

Ribadire, xxv. 8; 'to *rivet*,' 'clench.' Fr. *river*, Icel. *rifa* = 'to tack together.' Germ. *reif*, 'a hoop,' especially of a barrel, may contain the same root [? also *reef* (in a sail)]. This only accounts for the first three letters of the Italian word. It is almost impossible to doubt that its form has been affected by a supposed connection with *ribattere*; which occurs as a pretty frequent v. l. here. Nor does Diet. Crusc. give any other instance of its early use.

Ribrezzo, xvii. 85; xxxii. 71; 'a shiver.' From *brezza*, 'a breeze,' Fr. *brise*. There seems some doubt as to which language first shows the word. Diez is inclined to regard them all as starting from *rezzo* (q. v.), starting from *brezzo* as a strengthened form of that word. But this seems very doubtful.

Riddare, vii. 24; 'to dance in a ring.' From O. G. *ridan*, 'to turn.' Eng. *writhe*.

Ringavagnare, xxiv. 12; 'to recover,' 'store up again.' Cavagna est cista rusticana,' Benv. This seems quite satisfactory. Diez's proposal to derive it from O. Fr. *regaagner* (v. sub *guadagno*, Gloss. Purg.) is open to the objection that it does not account for *in*. *Cavagna* doubtless from *cavus*.

Risma, xxviii. 39; 'a pack.' Sp. *resma*, Fr. *rame*, Eng. *ream*, 'a bundle of paper' (480 sheets). From Arabic *rizmat*, 'a bundle.' Introduced by the Moors into Spain.

Rosta, xiii. 117; 'a switch' or 'twig'; hence 'a fan,' in vb. *arrostarsi*, xv. 39. Others take *rosta* as 'a fence' or 'railing.' Thus Benvenuto: 'rostae solent fieri ad defensionem, et iste non potest facere sibi rostam de manibus,' etc. But the early examples given in Dict. Crusc. make it impossible to reject the meaning 'fan.' Diez connects with Germ. *rost*, 'a gridiron' (whence our *roast*); and as the first gridirons were no doubt made of twigs, this brings both meanings together. [May not *roost* be the same, in the sense of a twig on which a bird perches?] *Rosta*, 'a twig,' may possibly be connected with Germ. *rauschen* and Eng. *rustle*.

Sbigottire, viii. 122, etc.; 'to frighten,' 'baffle'; also intr. Probably 'to frighten by fierce looks.' Sp. *bigote*, 'moustache,' *hombre de bigote*, 'man of warlike demeanour.' The derivation of this is obscure. Qy. connected with *bizzarro*, q. v. [*Bigot* is probably a different word: but even this is not certain.]

Scana, xxxiii. 35; 'tooth.' Apparently ἅπαξ λεγόμενον. Perhaps from Germ. *zahn*, in which case the insertion of the *c* would seem to be the converse of the process by which *zanca* (q. v.) has been formed. Another reading is *sana*, from Latin *sanna*.

Sciancato, xxv. 148; 'lame,' 'hip-shotten.' From *ex-ancatus*. V. sub **anca**.

Scimia, xxix. 139; 'an ape.' From *eximia*, a medieval corruption of *simia*. [For a similar attempt to give an obvious meaning, cf. 'lionfante,' from 'elephantem.']

Sciorinare, xxi. 116; 'to emerge.' From *ex-urinari*, lit. 'to dive out.' This from *urina*, 'water.'

Scoscio, xvii. 121; 'a shock,' 'jolt.' From *successus*, Fr. *secousse*; the *sci* being probably due to *successio*. (Seneca's definition of this, given by Forcellinus, s. v., suits the present passage well: successio est quum terra quatitur, et sursum et deorsum movetur.) *Scoscio* occurs in Bocc. Fiam. vi. in the sense of 'shock' figuratively.

Scuffare, xviii. 104; 'to grout' (like pigs). Doubtless from O. G. *skufan*, mod. *schieben*, 'to shove'; whence *schaufel*, 'shovel.'

Soga, xxxi. 73; 'a thong.' Sp. *soga*, 'a grass or hempen rope,' while the Italian word is said (on Buti's authority apparently) to mean one of leather. It is also used, like our 'chain,' to mean a 'measure of land.' *Soca* appears as early as Justinian; and there is a late Gr. σωκάριον. Probably of Celtic origin.

Sollo, xvi. 28; 'loose,' 'unbound.' From a Latin *solutulus* (Diez).

Sovente, ii. 74, etc.; 'now and then,' 'often.' Fr. *souvent*. From Latin *subinde*. (Hor. 2 Sat. v. 103, is a good instance of its use.)

Spiccare, xxx. 36; v. sub **appiccare**.

Squadrare, xxv. 3; 'to show.' Originally 'to measure with a *square*,' then 'to inspect'; and hence 'show for inspection.' Or perhaps merely 'shape.'

Strozza, vii. 125; xxviii. 101; '*throat*.' From O. G. *drozza*, mod. *drossel*. That there was originally an initial *s* is shown by Dutch *strot*. See Skeat, s. v. *throat*.

Stucco, xviii. 126; 'sated,' 'cloyed,' generally with a notion of 'disgust.' Perhaps only 'hardened'; cf. *stucco*, 'plaster'; from O. G. *stucchi*, 'a crust,' said to be modern *stück*. One is, however, tempted to ask if Gr. στυγεῖν ever got into Italian. Benv. explains 'idest . . . stuffam.'

Succhio, xxvii. 48; 'a boring instrument.' Lit. 'a *sucker*,' from the way in which the gimblet appears to suck out the shavings.—Diez. This seems satisfactory enough.

Terzeruolo, xxi. 15; 'the smallest sail in a ship' (Buti). Now it means 'the foresail'; but in Dante's time it must have been the mizzen. 'Mezzana' seems to have undergone the converse change. So 'artimone,' once the largest sail, is also now the mizzen. From *tertius*, being the third in size.

Tomare, xvi. 63; xxxii. 102; 'to fall.' From O. Fr. *tumer*, mod. *tomber*, Prov. *tombar*. These from O. G. *tûmon*, mod. *taŭmeln*, 'to reel.' Identical with Eng. *stumble*. [Sp. 'tomar,' 'to take,' is quite unconnected.]

Vincastro, xxiv. 14; 'a rod,' 'shepherd's crook.' Probably merely 'a large switch,' from *vinco*, 'a withy.' Diez regards this as from a supposed *vincum*, the parent of *vinculum*; but is it not rather formed in some way from *vimen*?

Zanca, xix. 45; xxxiv. 79; 'leg.' From an O. G. *scancho* (inferred from A. S. *scanca*), mod. *schenkel*. Eng. *shank*. The change of *sc* to *z* is unusual, but not unparalleled. *Shank* is akin to *shake* (Skeat).

Zeba, xxxii. 15; 'a goat.' Perhaps from Germ. *zibbe*, a local word for 'ewe' or 'lamb.' But why should it not be from *schöps*, the usual dialectic form in the Alps of *schaf*?

Zuffa, vii. 59, etc.; 'a quarrel.' From Germ. *zupfen*, 'to pull,' according to Diez; but this word does not appear to be old, and *pf* is always suspicious. It would seem better to connect it with the root that appears in Eng. '*scuffle*,' Icel. *skýfa*, 'to shove,' O. Dutch *schuffelan* In this case it will be a doublet of *scuffa*, q. v.

THE END

www.ingramcontent.com/pod-product-compliance
Lightning Source LLC
Chambersburg PA
CBHW022140300426
44115CB00006B/277